D0918878

PROMISES KEPT

PROMISES KEPT *A Memoir*

SIDNEY S. MCMATH

THE UNIVERSITY
OF ARKANSAS PRESS
Fayetteville ⟋ 2003

Copyright © 2003 by The University of Arkansas Press

All rights reserved
Manufactured in the United States of America

07   06   05   04   03   5   4   3   2   1

Text designed by Liz Lester

☻ The paper used in this publication meets the minimum requirements of the
American National Standard for Permanence of Paper for Printed Library
Materials Z39.48-1984.

LIBRARY OF CONGRESS CATALOGING-IN-PUBLICATION DATA

McMath, Sid. Promises kept : a memoir / Sidney S. McMath.
    p. cm.
Includes bibliographical references and index.
    ISBN 1-55728-754-6 (cloth : alk. paper)
    1. McMath, Sid. 2. Governors—Arkansas—Biography. 3. Arkansas
—Politics and government—20th century. 4. Lawyers—Arkansas—
Biography. 5. World War, 1939–1945—Personal narratives,
American. 6. World War, 1939–1945—Pacific Area. 7. Columbia
County (Ark.)—Biography. I. Title.
F411 .M14 2003
976.7'053—dc22

                                                    2003014841

The woods are lovely, dark and deep.

But I have promises to keep,

And miles to go before I sleep,

And miles to go before I sleep.

—ROBERT FROST

Dedicated to my beloved mother, Nettie Belle McMath

CONTENTS

PART 3. POLITICS AND AFTER

PART 4. CONCLUSION

APPENDIXES.
CASES THAT MADE A DIFFERENCE

ILLUSTRATIONS

DATELINE

I was born June 14, 1912, in Columbia County, Arkansas. My parents were Hal Pierce McMath and Nettie Belle Sanders McMath.

My sister, Edith Mae McMath, was born June 14, 1910.

We lived on the McMath Homeplace in Columbia County until I was five years old.

Entered the first grade in Bussey, Arkansas, September 1918.

Moved to Smackover, Arkansas, in the fall of 1921, then to Hot Springs, Arkansas, on my tenth birthday.

Graduated from Hot Springs High School in 1931.

Graduated law school, University of Arkansas, Fayetteville, June 1936.

Appointed 2nd lieutenant in the United States Marine Corps on July 1, 1936.

August 26, 1936, reported to duty, marine barracks, Quantico, Virginia. Served as a platoon leader, Company F, Second Battalion, Fifth Marine Fleet Brigade.

October 13, 1936, transferred to the Marine Corps Basic School in Philadelphia.

Resigned regular commission on March 15, 1937, and was commissioned as a 2nd lieutenant in the Marine Corps Reserve.

May 28, 1937, married Elaine Broughton.

1937–1940, practice law in Hot Springs, Arkansas.

August 17, 1940, returned to active duty, Quantico, Virginia, enrolled in the Third Reserve Officers Course.

January 28, 1941, appointed 1st lieutenant and was assigned as an instructor in the Officers Candidate School.

August 23, 1941, my son, Sidney Sandy McMath, was born at Quantico, Virginia.

February 2, 1942, appointed captain.

May 28, 1942, Elaine Broughton McMath died in Quantico, Virginia, United States Naval Hospital. Her death was on our fifth wedding anniversary.

August 12, 1942, transferred to New River, North Carolina, assigned to the Third Battalion, Third Marine Regiment.

September 1, 1942, embarked aboard the USS *Matsonia* with the Third Marine Regiment, arriving in American Samoa, the Third Marine Regiment becoming a part of the Second Marine Brigade.

November 1942, assigned officer in charge of the Second Marine Brigade Jungle Warfare School. Appointed major dating from August 11, 1942.

April 1943, assigned as operations and training officer for the Third Marine Regiment (reinforced).

June 1943, Third Marine Regiment became a part of the Third Marine Division and embarked for Auckland, New Zealand, then embarked with the division to Guadalcanal.

August 27–August 31, 1943, participated in operations on Arundel, New Georgia, assigned as observers with the Fourteenth Corps, United States Army, Forty-third Division.

November 1, 1943, Third Marine Regiment (reinforced) as part of the Third Marine Division landed at Empress Augusta Bay on Bougainville, the northernmost island in the Solomon Group.

December 21, 1943, received battlefield promotion to lieutenant colonel and awarded the Silver Star and Legion of Merit.

December 21, 1943, assigned as assistant training officer for the Third Marine Division.

December 25, 1943, returned with the regiment to Guadalcanal.

January 31, 1944, returned to States aboard the USS *George F. Elliott.* Hospitalized at navy hospital in San Diego, California.

March 20, 1944, reported for duty as training officer for the Marine Replacement Training Command at Camp Pendleton, California.

September 1944, assigned duty with the Marine Corps Headquarters, Washington, D.C., as officer in charge of the subsection of the Division of Plans and Policies as training officer, planning invasion of Japan.

October 6, 1944, married to Sarah Anne Phillips from Slate Spring, Mississippi. Marriage ceremony performed at Mt. Vernon Place Methodist Church, Washington, D.C.

December 1945, was granted a leave of absence. I joined Anne at the home of her parents, James Fair Phillips and Jimmie Vance Phillips, in Slate Spring, Mississippi. Son, Phillip, was born on Christmas morning, 1945, at the Baptist Hospital in Memphis, Tennessee.

January 1946, released from active duty and assigned to the Marine Corps Reserve, Eighth District at New Orleans, Louisiana.

January 1946, moved family to Hot Springs, Arkansas.

June 1946, elected prosecuting attorney, Eighteenth Judicial District, comprising Garland and Montgomery Counties, Arkansas.

July 1948, nominated (elected) governor of Arkansas.

December 1948, selected one of the ten outstanding young men in the United States by the Junior Chamber of Commerce.

October 25, 1949, our youngest son, James Bruce McMath, was born at the old St. Vincent's Infirmary in Little Rock, Arkansas.

June 1950, elected to a second term as governor of Arkansas. My opponent was former governor Ben Laney.

July 1951, promoted to colonel, United States Marine Corps Reserve.

August 1952, ran for a third term and was defeated by Francis Cherry, who in turn was defeated by Orval Faubus two years later, when Governor Cherry ran for a second term in 1954.

January 1953, opened a "people's" law firm with my partners Henry Woods and Leland Leatherman. Joined the National Association of Claimant's Attorneys that became the American Trial Lawyers Association.

August 15, 1953, our twin daughters, Melissa and Patricia, were born at the old St. Vincent's Infirmary in Little Rock, Arkansas.

June 1954, ran for the United States Senate against Sen. John L. McClelland. Lost the election by approximately ten thousand votes.

1962 ran again for governor of Arkansas against Orval Faubus—A voice in the wilderness.

July 1963, promoted to brigadier general, United States Marine Corps Reserve.

January 1966, promoted to major general, United States Marine Corps Reserve.

Summer 1966, two weeks active duty with the Marine Amphibious Force in Vietnam. Returned to Vietnam as a civilian observer in 1969.

In 1975, joined the International Academy of Trial Lawyers, was elected and served as president of the academy for the year 1977. Also was selected and remained a member of the Inner Circle of Trial Lawyers.

June 2, 1994, Anne Phillips McMath died. We had been married almost fifty years.

September 14, 1996, married Betty Dortch Russell.

Awarded Grand Cross by the Thirty-third Degree Masonic Order.

"Of Counsel" to McMath, Vehik, Drummond, Harrison & Ledbetter, P.A., Attorneys at Law, and to the law firm of Sandy S. McMath & Associates, P.A.

HONORARY DEGREES

1977—Distinguished Service Award, University of Arkansas for Medical Sciences

1987—Honorary Doctor of Science Degree, University of Arkansas for Medical Sciences

1989—Honorary Doctor of Law Degree, University of Arkansas at Fayetteville

1990—Honorary Doctor of Law Degree, Henderson State University

FOREWORD ⌇ DAVID PRYOR

The dominating spirit of public service has been the life force for Sidney Sanders McMath. Two decades ago, when Jim Lester wrote his insightful biography of this singular person, he aptly entitled it *A Man for Arkansas*.

Sid McMath has been a man for Arkansas—one whose enormous inner calling has challenged him to excel and inspire for his nine decades of life. If the description and much overused word "charisma" were to become attached to John F. Kennedy in the 1960s, it could have been employed two decades earlier to describe our state's thirty-fourth governor.

"Governor" McMath, in his ninety-second year, still exudes a magnetism afforded only a few individuals. His persona, even today, portrays resolve, confidence, humor, and a distinct sense of bearing. As one recent attendee was exiting the banquet hall after McMath spoke, he was heard to remark, "That man has class."

Promises Kept is his reflection, a story told in his words of a unique life's journey from the piney hills of South Arkansas to the epic battles he fought during World War II, coupled with the many other human encounters of the courtroom and marbled corridors of the State Capitol. It befell Sid McMath to face and overcome personal tragedies and defeats to reach into his deep reservoirs of courage and his sense of unfaltering purpose.

In this study of his life, one senses his total absence of bitterness or malice, although lesser men in the twilight of their lives might find room for each. Perhaps he was taught early a value system which rejected those character traits as too diminishing. For him, tomorrow is always to be another and better day.

Life's hard lessons tend to either weaken or strengthen us, and for McMath, it was the latter. For him, each day was a mission—whether as a Marine, prosecutor, politician, lawyer, or even now in his reflective years, imparting his knowledge to another generation.

Observers of Arkansas politics and history will be reminded by his book that only six years of Sid McMath's life were spent in public office—two years as prosecuting attorney for Garland and

Montgomery Counties and four years in the governor's office. His accomplishments in these short years became giant and legendary endeavors that sank deep footprints into our political, economic, and social landscape. Any one of these accomplishments would stand as great legacies, but considering the times and adversities of that period, they became even more remarkable.

At war's end, Lieutenant Colonel McMath was discharged from active duty in the Marine Corps and moved his young family to Hot Springs. His military service in the Pacific won him many commendations, including the Silver Star and Legion of Merit. For McMath, no part of his life is remembered with greater pride than his military service, in the course of which he rose to the rank of major general. Innumerable honors from various veterans groups hang on his wall today.

Within weeks of his return to civilian life in 1946, he organized and led another battle—taking on the entrenched and corrupt political machine of Mayor Leo McLaughlin of Hot Springs. The corruption was rampant, and the thirty-three-year-old war hero gathered like-minded veterans together to form a "Veterans Revolt" movement. McMath sought and was elected to the job of prosecuting attorney after taking on almost insurmountable odds.

The "audacity" of the young and forceful Sid McMath made him a leader and upcoming political star almost overnight. His ability to galvanize people to meet a common challenge was immediately recognized statewide by politicians and editorialists alike. The mystique of this dynamic young man from Garland County spread to every corner of Arkansas. McMath became synonymous with reform and the enormous vitality of the post-war period.

Sid McMath spearheaded a new movement in his home county and, only two years later, across his state. He became its undisputed leader as he rode the waves of excitement for the new battlegrounds ahead.

His well-publicized victories over the McLaughlin machine provided him the opportunity in 1948 to seek the Arkansas governorship. It is this particular political campaign that McMath developed and used his unique skills as a "campaigner." Many younger politicians after the '48 campaign attempted to emulate his style and techniques of connecting with voters. For that era, the artistry of his campaigning was legendary.

His victory in the Democratic primaries (then tantamount to election), catapulted him to national prominence. But during the summer and fall before his inauguration, then-governor Strom Thurmond of South Carolina bolted the National Democratic Party to form a splinter party known as the "Dixiecrats." Thurmond and several of his southern colleagues objected to President Harry Truman's civil rights positions and attempted to coalesce disgruntled voters against the National Democrats.

As a new and forceful voice of the New South, McMath worked with zeal and unabashed conviction to hold Arkansas in the National Democrats' column. In November, Truman frustrated all prognosticators by defeating Gov. Thomas Dewey of New York. Arkansas, on that same critical Election Day, provided only 17 percent of its vote for the Dixiecrats, in contrast to several other southern states which supported Thurmond. It should be noted that Gov. Ben Laney, who McMath was to succeed as governor, was deeply involved in and committed to the Dixiecrat movement.

President Truman never forgot how the young governor-elect had "saved Arkansas" for him, and a strong bond of friendship between the two was cemented and existed until Truman's death.

Soon, the young Arkansas governor would continue to follow his convictions on racial issues. He challenged the structure of the Arkansas Democratic Party's own "white only" stigma that had been practiced for generations. He had fought side by side with African Americans and was incensed that so many obstacles were placed in their way to the polling booth and access to equal education opportunities. The raw hypocrisy of the uneven and grossly unequal treatment accepted by our society and condoned by our governments became a passion with Sid McMath. He fought to eliminate the poll tax, supported anti-lynching legislation, and winced at the Southern Manifesto adopted by Congress in the early fifties, which carried with it the support of both U.S. Senators from Arkansas.

Later, as a private citizen, McMath testified against establishing the infamous Sovereignty Commission, patterned after Mississippi's state-supported "police force" to ferret out and harass members of the NAACP and other "groups" that supported integration. In 1957, he added his voice against the Central High School decisions of Gov. Orval Faubus.

Arkansas's young (thirty-six) governor was convinced that our state's cycle of poverty was directly attributable to an inferior educational system which comprised no less than 1600 separate school districts. He took on, once again, the "establishment" and through personal and persuasive cajoling, won legislative approval for major portions of his education plan. Many schools were consolidated, efficiencies mandated, and standards increased.

At the time of his swearing-in, there were relatively few paved roads in Arkansas. With an aggressive highway program backed up by the sale of highway bonds, the state's highway system began to emerge and flourish. Towns and rural communities were connected to their county seats, to major cities, and eventually tied into the Eisenhower Interstate Highway system. Commerce, agriculture, and especially rural Arkansas became a part of the Arkansas economic engine that lured trucking, poultry, and manufacturing interests to the state. It has been noted that Sid McMath paved more roads than all other previous governors combined.

The lack of quality healthcare consumed much of McMath's energies during his tenure as governor. After tedious consultation and aggressive campaigning, he convinced the General Assembly that with a two-cent tax on each package of cigarettes, Arkansas could build and maintain one of the South's premier medical science campuses. Today, the University of Arkansas for Medical Sciences stands as one of his proudest achievements and most enduring legacies.

No summation of the life of Sid McMath would be complete without his awesome battles in behalf of electrification for rural Arkansas. To wage this war, he knew he would be going up against Arkansas's most entrenched sources of political and economic power—the privately owned electric power companies, Arkansas Power and Light Company, Middle-South, and their fellow corporations.

Arkansas was predominately a rural state, but the opportunity for an enhanced quality of life would never be acquired without electricity. The companies had tentacles deeply embedded in towns and rural areas alike. Local banks had deposits from private power interests. Governors showed their appreciation by naming "friendly" members to the Public Service Commission.

McMath challenged the economic elite of Arkansas, seeking generating facilities to be owned by the Arkansas Electric "Co-ops" and licensing authority for operation in Arkansas. McMath supported the fledging co-op movement and demonstrated his support in a symbolic gesture of attending and speaking to a co-op barbeque in Berryville. He was the first governor to openly support the rural co-ops. Untold opportunities flowed from his undaunted and epic battles to obtain electricity for rural Arkansans.

Any retrospective of the McMath legacy will no doubt discover that his public versus private utility battles led to what many observe caused his political career to wane. Many of the private interests he challenged ultimately dominated the representation on the Highway Audit Commission of 1952, which attempted to associate McMath, and certainly his administration, with "scandal" in his highway department. In his memoirs, McMath paints a lucid picture of that period and the political and economic forces that combined to create his political Waterloo. A note: No member of the McMath Administration was found guilty of wrongdoing.

His bid for a third term as governor was unsuccessful.

From politics, he moved to another field which accommodated his magnetism and unique skills of persuasion—Sid McMath, attorney-at-law.

With his long-time and trusted friend, the late Judge Henry Woods, the firm of McMath-Woods and Leatherman came into being. His courtroom skills and fights for the "little guy" caused his reputation to soar in national and international legal circles.

At this writing, Sid McMath, in his ninety-second year, can still be seen and heard as he stands erect at a banquet podium before a hushed and reverent crowd. His hair is white, his voice is softer, his eyesight is gone.

But he is in his dark blue suit with a red tie with a crisp, white shirt. He extols patriotism and distant battles both at home and on foreign soil: the campaigns of yesterday, the courtroom clashes, the victories and defeats. And for this unique and genuine man, his most fervent and passionate moment comes when he admonishes all who listen that the cycle of poverty will surely prevail if we fail in our sacred duty to "educate our people."

Since statehood was granted to Arkansas in 1836, no public or private person has had a greater or a more positive impact on our state than Sidney Sanders McMath. *Promises Kept* is an intimate accounting of his meaningful and exciting adventure.

ACKNOWLEDGMENTS

This story of my life, covering a span of almost a century, was written over a period of seven years. Many people have encouraged and contributed to the writing of *Promises Kept*. Space permits me to mention only those most closely and constantly involved in assisting me in this project.

My son, Phillip McMath, an accomplished author, has published several books. He was a most dependable source for advice and counsel on this project. His wife, Carol McMath, diligently edited each chapter as it was written.

During the final stages of the book, my granddaughter, Sydney Bueter Blackmon, was a conscientious reader providing me the help I needed.

I am indebted to my secretary, Dillie Hudson, Larry Malley, and the staff of the University of Arkansas Press for their interest and effort in the publication of *Promises Kept*.

My wife, Betty, is an angel. She has been a constant source of support and encouragement in all phases of this book's writing and publication. She has been a wife, a secretary, a counsel, and a friend. She has walked with me all the way, and when needed, she has held my hand.

PROLOGUE

In 1948, I was honored by the good people of Arkansas by being chosen as their governor. I had specific goals and objectives fairly fixed in my mind. I needed no public opinion poll to unveil our public needs or to reveal to me our state's problems.

It was obvious that we had to get out of the mud and the dust, build and improve our primary highway system, and provide secondary roads to get children in the rural areas to school and to transport farm products to market.

I had experienced them, survived them.

Later, campaigning for governor, I had to ride a horse in order to travel over the road from Magnolia to Bussey and Taylor, Arkansas.

The economic blight and dislocation lingered like a black cloud that almost shut out the light to a better life and happier days.

I appreciated how the burden of labor, especially that of the women, could be alleviated with the boon of electrical service.

I picked cotton from prickly cotton bolls for one penny a pound, one dollar for one hundred pounds, which is what I could pick in a day when I was eight.

During cotton-picking season many schools were closed. One-room schoolhouses offering instruction in eight grades with one teacher would be closed so the children could join with the rest of their families in picking cotton.

Closing of schools for blacks presented no major problem—there were few, if any, black schools.

Even with all members of the family working, many Arkansans were hard put to earn enough to sustain them during the cotton-picking season and to save enough to provide food, shelter, and clothing during the winter months.

I saw farmers who received less for a bale of cotton than it cost them to plant, weed, pick, and have it ginned.

I remember hearing the refrain, "Ten-cent cotton, forty-cent meat, how in the world can a poor man eat?"

I saw how the prisoner leasing system worked. Come cotton-picking time the local law enforcement officials would be zealous about picking up black men in good physical condition, who might be involved in some petty crime or misdemeanor. They would be jailed, then often farmed out to a cotton grower for the season. If, for any reason, this indentured servant ran away, he would be brought back and punished.

There was much illness, particularly during the summertime, from malaria, typhoid fever, and the usual childhood diseases. Our country doctor was a saint. He made house calls at any time, day or night, often getting out of bed regardless of the weather, rain, sleet, or cold, hitch his horse and buggy, and respond to a call for help.

The country doctor was frequently called to make delivery of a baby. Often, the baby would arrive ahead of the doctor, as I did. My mother had an excellent midwife, Mother Mae, my grandmother.

So, another of my projects or goals, when I became governor, was to build an excellent medical school with a treating hospital, available for training and instruction, and hopefully, many of these graduating medical students would be encouraged to practice in the rural areas.

I was aware of the brutish horrors of the lynch mob. A popular sheriff in one county was killed and the man who killed the sheriff, or who was suspected of killing him, was seized and burned at a stake, a hitching post, on the west side of the county courthouse square.

As governor, I proposed an anti-lynching bill, but heated from the smoldering fire of the Dixiecrat rebellion in 1948, it failed to pass.

As a youth in Hot Springs, Arkansas, I observed the evils of the poll tax and how it could be a corrupting influence on the election process. It could be used as an instrument to perpetuate an illegal political empire based upon election frauds, intimidation, and the corruption of public officials.

As governor, I proposed a repeal of the poll tax. It, too, failed to pass. The custom of disenfranchising the black man and poor whites was too entrenched.

During my two terms as governor we built more roads than any prior administration.

When I became governor in 1948, 50 percent of the farms in Arkansas had no electricity. Today there are seventeen electric cooperatives supplying electricity at a reasonable cost to approximately 350,000 families in our rural areas—representing over one million people. In

1953, my lease on the Governor's Mansion was not renewed. My life-time friends and partners, Henry Woods and Leland Leatherman, and I formed a law firm, a people's law firm. That is, we were advocates for people in the courtroom.

Our policy was, after investigating a case thoroughly, to answer two questions:

1. Has this person been wronged?
2. Can we help him?

The cases that I reference in this book concern people, people whom we considered were wrongfully injured or had their property confiscated, destroyed, or depreciated. These people had no funds to hire a lawyer or to spend for costs in their pursuit of justice. We prepared and tried the cases, advanced the costs, in some cases amounting to substantial sums of money, with the understanding that, if successful, we would have our costs reimbursed. Generally, our fee was a third of the amount recovered. Many of these cases served as precedent, influencing the result of claims of other people similarly wronged.

After the facts in a case have been presented and put in evidence, and the jury instructed on the law, the judge will turn to the lawyer for the plaintiff, who has the burden of proof in the case, and address him thusly, "Counselor, you may go to the jury."

The lawyer moves center stage, in front of the jury box. All eyes are riveted upon him. Turning to the judge and then to the jury, he says, "May it please the Court and you, ladies and gentlemen of the jury." On the minds of the jurors will be these questions: Who is this lawyer? What is his background? Does he have credibility—Can we believe what he has to say?

He then proceeds to argue his client's cause.

This lawyer is the sum of all his life's experiences, up to the time he walks into the courtroom on this day of trial.

My life's experiences, as I will relate them to you in this book, the experiences of my youth, my education, my military service, my service as prosecuting attorney and governor, prepared and oriented me and, perhaps, destined me to become a trial lawyer, a "people's lawyer."

You, my fair and faithful readers, are the jury. Let the jury decide.

PART 1 ~

ROOTS

I was retired from the governor's office by the good people of Arkansas when I ran for a third term. When I left the governor's office in 1953, the governor's salary was ten thousand dollars per year before taxes. I was forty years old, with a wife and five children, and being encumbered by debt and broke, I turned to the law.

My roots were planted deep in the South, the Old South, the South that remembered. The South that could not forget memories of the Civil War and its aftermath, occupation by Union troops, carpetbag rule, economic depression, and hard times. These memories were handed down through three generations.

1 ⁕ THE OLD MCMATH HOMEPLACE

JOSEPH WASHINGTON MCMATH WAS BORN IN 1750, PLACE UNKNOWN, and died in 1825, in Warren County, Georgia. He was buried on his land near Briar Creek in Warren County. According to another great-grandson, William Thomas McMath, Joseph McMath was a private in the Continental army during the Revolutionary War and fought at the Battle of Kettle Creek, Georgia, in 1775; on October 7, 1780, at the Battle of King's Mountain, South Carolina; and on January 17, 1781, at the Battle of Cow Pen, South Carolina.

Joseph McMath was a Scotsman, a member of a famous Scottish clan with no love for the English. If he had a musket and was strong enough to carry it, and if he had a horse and could ride it, he would not have passed up an opportunity to fight the "Red Coats."

William Thomas McMath also reported that on May 18, 1791, his great-grandfather and a party of horsemen, ex-soldiers of the Revolutionary War, met Gen. George Washington, then president of the United States, at Fulcher's Pond, four miles from Augusta, Georgia. They greeted the president and welcomed him on his visit to the Deep South. It also is documented that before, during, and after the Revolution, Joseph McMath owned his land, farmed it, and paid taxes on it. The records also show that he served as land appraiser, sat on grand juries, and, of course, raised a large family.

It was well known in the family that Joseph McMath admired Washington above all men. His son, Elisha McMath, named his son Joseph Washington McMath after him. Joseph Washington McMath was the father of Sidney Smith McMath, who married Lula Mae Rudd, who was the daughter of James B. and Molly Rudd. Their children and grandchildren called James Rudd, "Papa," and Molly Rudd, "Mama." The Rudds lived only a quarter of a mile north of the McMath homeplace that was located about four and a half miles west of Magnolia, Arkansas. The two homes were connected by a one-lane dirt road, and on a still evening, with the wind just right, standing on the front porch of the McMath homeplace, you could hear Papa Rudd calling his hogs.

Lula Mae McMath (Mother Mae), grandmother of Sid McMath

My paternal grandfather, Sidney Smith McMath, was named after my great-uncle, Sidney Smith, who gained distinction during the war for Texas independence against Mexico. He was killed at the Battle of Goliad when he and his detachment made an ill-fated attempt to go to the aid of troops besieged at the Alamo.

Sidney Smith McMath's parents were Joseph Washington McMath and Glovina Henderson McDaniel. They left Georgia and settled in the Hillsboro community in Union County, Arkansas. Sidney Smith was the youngest of eight children, and he was the great-grandson of Joseph McMath.

Sidney Smith McMath, who served as sheriff of Columbia County, was killed in 1911 in a gunfight with outlaws for whom he had warrants to arrest. Following his death his widow, Lula Mae McMath, "Mother Mae," farmed the land and supported her large family. Much of this responsibility was assumed by Hal Pierce McMath, the oldest son.

In 1908, Hal Pierce McMath married Nettie Belle Sanders, the daughter of Edgar and "Jenny" Camp Sanders, who lived on a farm in the southern part of Columbia County. Hal and Nettie Belle were my parents.

Thus, being descended from a long line of Southern frontiersmen, I was born June 14, 1912, in a dogtrot log cabin on the McMath homeplace, at a time that reflected the old frontier atmosphere. I had a sister, Edyth Mae McMath, two years older than I. We shared the same birthday; she was born June 14, 1910.

The cabin had been refurbished so that we were comfortable according to the amenities of the time. It was located at the north end of a cotton field next to a grove of trees, mostly oak and pine. There was a large sycamore tree in the yard behind the cabin; in the front, weeds and cotton stalks had been cleared, the ground swept smooth and planted with flowers, making a yard without a fence.

Under one shingle roof, the cabin consisted of two rooms: a bedroom and a kitchen, separated by an open-air passageway. All members of my family slept in one room—my parents in one bed, my sister and I in another.

A large fireplace with a brick hearth and chimney made of mud and straw was on the east side of the bedroom. Although the fireplace was used only in cold weather, pieces of firewood—one large green piece and several smaller pieces of dry wood and kindling—were kept in a neat stack nearby. Well designed and constructed, the fireplace drew the smoke up through the chimney, and billowing out, it was clearly visible from the back field behind our house.

There were two doors in the bedroom. One led to the outside, the other to the open passageway to the kitchen. Over the transom of the outside door were a gun rack and a place for my dad, Pap, to hang his fox horn, used to call the dogs. Across the hall in the kitchen there was a large firewood cookstove with a stovewood box by its side. A large black skillet hung on the wall behind the stove.

A table covered with oilcloth was in the center of the kitchen, surrounded by four straight-backed chairs with cane bottoms that fit comfortably around the table. There was a pantry in the kitchen where Mother kept sugar, salt, coffee, cornmeal, and jars of preserves. Most of the time there would be biscuits, pieces of cornbread, and a small pitcher of molasses on the table, available for snacks. A large biscuit with a hole punched in the top with the forefinger and filled with molasses was "good eatin'—shut my mouf."

In cold weather, waking and smelling the aroma of freshly ground and brewed coffee, Sister and I would go into the kitchen and warm ourselves beside the cookstove while Mother prepared breakfast.

The open-air passageway between the two rooms ran north and south, allowing cooling breezes to flow in the summertime. It also provided passage for the dogs, hence the name, dogtrot cabin.

In the springtime bobwhites would come cautiously close to the yard. Crows would hold a conclave in the field, and a hoot owl in the grove of trees across the way would serve notice to the world that he ruled the night. The hoot of the horned owl was a tranquil and soothing sound to a small boy and little girl listening in the night.

My sister and I were always frightened by the piercing scream of the screech owl, perhaps because we were told that something bad was going to happen. Happily, this bird of ill omen seldom disturbed our sense of security.

I am sure the reader has endeavored to go back as far as memory would take him in his life to try and determine his earliest recall. We sometimes remember what we were told, and we may remember that as a personal experience. However, I have distinct memories of several dramatic events in my early life, living with my parents and my sister in that dogtrot cabin.

Sister and I had a white puppy. We had seen the picture of a white puppy that had spots, so we decided we would like to have a spotted puppy. We made dye from pokeberries and painted spots on our pet, who, upon being released from our tender care, ran away into the woods. When he returned he somehow had obliterated our artwork and was spotless.

One night, while Pap, my father, was away, there came a terrible thunderstorm. The wind blew and the lightning flashed. We had a large sycamore tree in our back yard, the only tree near the house. There was a tremendous flash and a roar of thunder as a bolt of lightning struck our tree, splitting it right down the middle. My mother used that incident many times to remind my sister and me that if we were out in a field or pasture and we heard thunder and saw lightning in the sky, we must not seek shelter under a tree for fear that the lightning might strike, the same as it had struck our sycamore.

We lived in this cabin until I was about five. We also returned to the old McMath homeplace from time to time until I was nine. During the intervals we lived at Bussey, Foreman, and Taylor, Arkansas.

This was a time in my life when I also frequently visited and spent time with my mother's father, Edgar Sanders, who lived on his prosperous, well-cultivated farm in the south of the county near Macedonia, Arkansas. It was during this period with Dad Sanders that many of my fondest memories as a boy were formed. This was before the time of television, radios, instant mass communication, before electricity, indoor plumbing, and fast-food service.

At day's end at Dad Sanders's house, after supper, when the table was cleared, dishes washed, kitchen cleaned, and chores completed, the family would gather. If it were summer, we would sit on the front porch. The children sat on the steps or in wicker-backed, cane-bottomed chairs, but the large rockers were reserved for Dad and Grandmother Sanders.

After a full meal and a hard day's work, Dad would settle in his chair and begin the conversation, and each one would relate the events of the day. When all were present and everyone had had their say, Dad would ceremoniously stuff his pipe with tobacco, and slowly, gingerly, and with anticipation, take in a couple of drafts clearing the stem. This done, he, with a dramatic flourish, would strike a kitchen match and light up.

Slowly, he would begin to speak; perhaps he would talk about something in the newspaper or a letter he had written to its editor; or he might tell stories about the war—the Civil War: Sherman's march through Georgia, the occupation of the South by federal troops, and carpetbag rule during Reconstruction. He would frequently reminisce about how his dad, John Ray Sanders, was wounded and left for dead, but survived and was taken prisoner by the "Yankees," and how after the war, having been released from prison, he made his way home. He would tell us about the family's long trek to this rich, fertile, and promising land when he, his parents, and his brothers and sisters left Georgia and came to Arkansas.

When the weather was cold at Dad Sanders's, the family would meet in the living room close to the warmth and the glow of the fireplace. The ritual would be the same, the grandchildren sitting on the floor, but there Dad would never strike a match to light his pipe. Instead, he would use a scissors-like poker to pick up a hot coal from the fireplace and light up. I still remember the aroma of the tobacco, the warmth of the fire, the sounds of the night, the call of a whippoorwill, the hoot of an owl. I still remember the stories Dad told and the stories that were told to him.

II 🙠 JOHN RAY SANDERS

JOHN RAY SANDERS WAS MY MATERNAL GREAT-GRANDFATHER, THE FATHER of Edgar Sanders, my mother's father.

He was born May 6, 1830, in Alabama. He was next to the youngest of eight children. His mother died when he was four, and all of the children were placed in different homes. A couple by the name of Worthy, who lived across the state line in Georgia, took John Ray and raised him as their own. Some of his memories became part of our family lore, such as riding horseback behind Mrs. Worthy to church, or entertaining her grandchildren with a song taught to him by her entitled, "Premeditate—Before It Is Too Late."

When he was old enough, he worked in the Pike County, Georgia, community, and at twenty he became a clerk in a general merchandise store. While in this employment on a beautiful spring evening, shortly before closing time, he met Sarah Frances "Frank" Allen. On this eventful day John Ray's employer had given him instructions to sell the coal oil that had accumulated in oil cans in the back of the store, even at a reduced price, because he wanted it moved out.

Miss Allen had been nicknamed "Frank" by her father because she was a tomboy, preferring animals, horses, and the people on the plantation to "socializing." Though she was small, she could bridle, saddle, and mount her horse herself, and was an excellent rider. Her body in the saddle, coordinated with the rhythm and the movement of her horse, was a sight to see. She was naturally cheerful and outgoing, with a happy smile for everyone. It was her belief that "a smile was not worth anything until it was given away." Workers, cotton pickers in the fields, even strangers, would return her wave.

Frank was helping her mother plan a birthday party for her sister, and she decided that some colored candies would be an artistic touch to the decorations. Saddling up, she rode to the store not far from the plantation. On arriving, she dismounted, hitched her horse to the hitching rail, and strode in, finding John Ray working behind the counter. He saw this vivacious dream walking toward him and was immediately struck.

Frank stated her mission: "We are having a birthday party for my sister this evening. Do you have any colored candies?"

"No, but we have lots of coal oil," John Ray responded.

Both paused, flustered, then broke into laughter.

John Ray escorted Frank home and was invited to the party that evening. Mrs. Worthy's tune came to mind, "Premeditate—Before It Is Too Late."

He meditated, worked double duty until he had saved five hundred dollars, then proposed to "Frank." She accepted, and they were married, embarking on one of life's great adventures, rearing a family, going to war, moving west, surviving, and providing a good life for themselves, their children, and their grandchildren. Their oldest child, born in Pike County, Georgia, was Edgar, my grandfather.

Edgar was eight when his father went off to war on March 12, 1862, joining the Forty-fourth Georgia Regiment in Gen. D. H. Hill's Division of the Army of Northern Virginia. (General Hill later became the president of the University of Arkansas, the same university from which I graduated. There at a men's dormitory, Hill Hall, which was named after the general, I waited tables and washed dishes for my room and board for the first two years of my university life. I did not know then that the dormitory was named after General Hill and that my great-grandfather had served under his command.)

John Ray Sanders fought until 1864. He was wounded at the Battle of Spotslyvania Courthouse, left for dead, and ultimately taken prisoner. His life was saved because a bullet struck a metal buckle on his uniform before entering his body. He was imprisoned at Fort Delaware until the end of the war.

While he was gone, Frank and her children lived on the Allen plantation with her sisters, who also had husbands in the Confederate army, all struggling to survive with their men gone to war. But the war came to them, arriving at Pike County in the form of General Sherman's army marching through Georgia. The fighting came so close to the plantation they could hear the guns.

Years later, when asked about the war, Edgar, my grandad, didn't like to talk about the part that was such a horrible experience for the women and children: the burning of houses and barns, confiscation of the livestock, dispersion of the workers, and the plunder of smokehouses and spring houses. When the slaves scattered, the women who had always had their work done for them now had to labor. While they did the washing in the spring water behind the plantation home, eight-year-old Edgar, "the only man in the house," would stand watch for the approach of any soldiers or strangers, straggling and scavenging behind Sherman's army.

At the time John Ray was released from prison he was weak and emaciated, and he found traveling difficult, but he was able to ride a train part of the way home. Wondering if he could make it, he walked until he came upon a detachment of Union soldiers, who generously gave him food and a horse and sent him on his way. This kind gesture from a former foe would always be remembered. It was a kind of balm to his mind and spirit and it softened the harsher memories. Arriving home, he was a long time recovering from his wounds, malnutrition, and exposure. He became reacquainted with his family and began his struggle to dig out from the war's wreckage.

John Allen, the brother of Frank, had come to Columbia County, Arkansas, when the war was over and had written to John Ray and Frank, who were still in Georgia, about the land and the people and the opportunities for building a new life. The conditions in Pike County, Georgia, had not improved after the war. The land had grown up in weeds, and labor to work the land was no longer available. John Ray and Frank made the decision to pack up and come to Arkansas. Their son, Edgar, was sixteen years old, and, of course, came with them.

In December of 1872, the Sanders, joined by several other families, taking with them only the barest essentials, set out for this land of promise. They were able to make connections by train to Monroe, Louisiana, where they were met by John Allen, who took them by wagon to their home in Arkansas. They were on the road for three weeks, but two weeks into the journey they ran out of money and provisions. Edgar and several other young men went hunting for game, and with this meat and other provisions from a friendly farmer's wife, they completed their trip.

Dad Sanders remembered that they had spent Christmas on the road. On Christmas Eve they built a large bonfire and sang songs, and the parents hung Christmas stockings for the children on the wagon wheels.

Dad described his father as being a quiet, peaceful man, a strong believer in getting an education and following the ancient and accepted principles of the Masonic Order of which he was an avid member.

He remembered his mother, Frank, as a beautiful girl and later as an attractive woman who had strength of will and "spoke her mind." And, she always had a say in things. She kept a diary and wrote letters to her family remaining in Georgia.

Frances (Frank) writes to her sister from the trading post, state line, Arkansas, January 15, 1873:

> We are in Arkansas, settled near state line. John was in Monroe to meet us with wagons. We suffered many hardships because of the snow and sleet, but made it in three weeks.
>
> John thought we had enough food to last 'til we got here, but we were out of both food and funds by the second week out. Fortunately, we stopped when one wagon broke down and a smithy's wife gave us collards and jowl. The men hunted bringing in squirrel, rabbits and birds. We made hunter's stew and baked bread to last a week.
>
> Edgar had been reading a book all the way here and is now reading it the second time. Sunday we stopped and attended church.
>
> Love,
> Frank

Frank writes again from Magnolia, Arkansas, November 20, 1876:

> We moved to a new house southwest of Magnolia. Big, solid oak trees shade the yard where acorns fall into deep sand. Plum and peach trees line the fields and there is plenty of sagebrush for brooms. Mr. Sanders' [John Ray] sorghum patch made 38 gallons of syrup and we canned a lot of berries.
>
> We went to camp meeting near state line last summer. Edgar is sparking Jenny Camp. I am piecing them a quilt using the "Star of Life" pattern. Must do some crocheting now.
>
> Love,
> Frank

Frank writes her sister from Magnolia, Arkansas, November 30, 1878:

We have had good crop years and are now in a new settlement. The Macedonia Community where there is a Masonic Lodge, school and church. The land is rich and fertile and there is enough for Edgar to farm. He and Jenny were married in the spring and he spent the past summer teaching subscription school. Had 15 pupils.

The house is log with two big rooms, shed and porch. I want you all to come. Keep planning your trip.

Love,
Frank

Frank writes from Magnolia, Arkansas, December 1, 1879, to her sister and family:

We had a good cotton crop. Mr. Sanders was able to remodel our place. We moved the house out to the public road. It is frame, five rooms, with front central hall, front and back porch. The kitchen is at the end of the L hall and smoke house is where the old kitchen stood. Our place is typical of all the modern homes in Arkansas. Guess there will never be the fine homes as we had back in Georgia before the Civil War. Wars have a way of changing the history of many families. Both John Ray and I might have reared our family in Pike County where we were married had the Civil War never happened.

Love,
Frank

P.S. Fall is beautiful here this year. From the front porch I can see across white cotton fields. The sweet gums running scarlet in the crisp autumn air. Stock feed on fodder all turned golden. Darkies in the fields are singing and the tinkle of the bell comes from over the hill where our cows pasture.

When John Ray Sanders arrived in this promised land on January 15, 1873, he lost no time in acquiring a modest acreage, building a house and a barn, and began farming. The soil was soft, sandy, and fertile, the climate temperate; the cotton and corn crops, melon patches, and gardens flourished when well attended. All that was needed was the will and the work, which was diligently provided.

My granddad, Edgar, worked with his father and learned to farm.

Gradually, he obtained his own land and married Virginia "Jenny" Camp. Granddad was an excellent farmer, studied all the farm journals, kept up with advances in horticulture, and raised his family.

Dad Sanders was an important part of my life, but when I was at the University of Arkansas, he died. I was deeply grieved and reflected upon our time together. I remembered when he dammed up a branch of water going across his land so that I could have a place to swim; when he took me fishing and to town with a wagonload of cotton to be ginned; and when he let me hold the reins to the mules when we were on a straightaway.

By the time I was five, Dad Sanders and I had formed a strong bond. We were very close. He called me "Horsefly."

III PAPA RUDD

MY PATERNAL GREAT-GRANDFATHER, JAMES B. RUDD, MY GRANDMOTHER Mae's father, was born in Georgia in 1833, three years before Arkansas was admitted to the Union. He died in 1915 when I was only three years of age.

I really shouldn't say that I knew him, but I have a clear memory of living with him and my great-grandmother, Mama Rudd, while my mother was sick with typhoid fever and had to stay in bed. Both Mama and Papa Rudd were pretty old, so I had the run of the place. Several things I remember vividly.

One of my memories was that I chased Mama Rudd's big Rhode Island hens. They were slow and couldn't run fast, and since I was fascinated with chickens, I spent lots of time chasing them.

Another remembrance was when I ventured down to the barn with my small dog. He jumped a big "wharf rat" that was in one of the stalls feeding on grain which had dropped from a horse trough. The rat easily escaped, retreating through a handy rat hole (no doubt used many times by this wise old rat for a hasty retreat).

At another time my dog and I went wading in the stock pond that was filled with water lilies. The water was shallow and cool to my feet and legs. All of a sudden, what appeared to be a water lily rose up and grabbed my dog. It was a half-grown alligator. He didn't get a good hold, and my dog pulled loose and survived. Frightened, we ran to the house crying for help. I never went into that pond again.

My next adventure was to wade barefooted through some hot ashes, remnants of a pile of leaves that had been burned. The soles of my feet were blistered and I had to stay in bed with my mother for sometime until I could walk.

One other thing I remember about Papa Rudd. He had a long white beard and looked like one of the patriarchs from the Bible. I later learned that he had the reputation of being the only man in the county who could swim the Mississippi River without getting his beard wet.

When Papa was twenty-one years of age, he had bought land in

James B. Rudd (Papa), Mother Mae's father

Columbia County for $1.25 per acre. In 1855, he married Martha Garrard, who had come with her parents to Arkansas from Georgia.

At the time of Papa's marriage, there was lots of talk about slavery, but Papa didn't have any slaves. There was talk about secession, about leaving the Union that Arkansas had so recently joined. The local newspaper in Magnolia, Arkansas, carried foreboding stories about the possibility of war. An ominous cloud could be seen over the horizon, and a sensitive soul, with an attentive ear, could hear rolls of thunder and see flashes of lightning in the sky.

Arkansas had called a secession convention in early 1861. The motion to secede failed, as the delegates from the mountain counties were opposed. But many Arkansawyers had come from Georgia, Alabama, Mississippi, Louisiana, and South Carolina and were reluctant to fight against their own kin.

On March 1, 1861, a second secession convention was held. During this second meeting word came to the delegates that Fort Sumter had been fired on and that President Lincoln had sent a call to states for troops to put down the rebellion in the Deep South. The president's call to arms included the upper Southern states, North Carolina, Tennessee, Virginia, and Arkansas. In Arkansas a motion to secede was passed, but there were still nay votes from delegates from the mountain counties. Then a motion was made to make the secession vote unanimous. The motion carried except for one strong, obstinate nay vote by Isaac Murphy from Madison County. This stubborn refusal by Murphy to make the secession unanimous infuriated the secession delegates, particularly those from eastern and southern Arkansas, who were about to assault Murphy. At this crucial moment, a distinguished lady, who had been observing from the gallery, tossed a bouquet of roses to Isaac Murphy's feet.

This gesture from Martha Trapnell, whose husband was a distinguished citizen of Little Rock and a Unionist, calmed the delegates. Martha Trapnell may well have saved Isaac Murphy's life. Ironically, three years later, Murphy would become governor of Arkansas and take the oath of office in the legislative chamber where he had voted against secession.

The motion to secede having passed, less the one dissenting vote, the delegates moved from the house chambers, through the halls, down the stairway of the statehouse, onto the capitol grounds, and into the streets, carrying their state into a war, a civil war, brother against brother, father against son, neighbor against neighbor, until at last it was done.

In the ten-year period preceding the Civil War, Arkansas had enjoyed its greatest prosperity. As the state was predominantly an agricultural society, this prosperity was enjoyed down on the farm.

But Arkansas was devastated by the war. Many families had their homes, property, and lives ravaged by both sides, but more cruelly by roving bands of guerrillas and bushwhackers, whose only loyalty was to their own avarice. Young farmers joined the army and left prosperous farms—their barns bulging with hay; their silos filled with corn; their smokehouses well provisioned; their lots and pastures well stocked with cattle, mules, sheep, and hogs. They returned home to ruins.

Back from the war, ill and suffering from old wounds and poor nutrition, they found nothing except the land. This is what happened to Papa Rudd. He had joined up with the Twenty-sixth Arkansas Infantry, Company G. His unit was engaged in the Battles of Prairie Grove, Fort Smith, Pleasant Hill, and Jenkins's Ferry.

Maj. Gen. Frederick Steele, commander of the federal forces in Little Rock, had moved south in an effort to join another federal army under Gen. Nathaniel P. Banks in Louisiana with the mission of taking Texas. But Banks was defeated at the Battles of Mansfield and Pleasant Hill by Gen. Richard Taylor. Then Steele became stranded with approximately fifteen thousand men in Camden, Arkansas, his supplies cut off by Confederate forces under the command of Gen. Kirby Smith. In an effort to supply his army, Steele sent out a caravan of one hundred wagons escorted by approximately thirty-eight hundred troops to scour the countryside for supplies. As the wagon train was returning to Camden, it was intercepted by a Confederate force at Poison Springs. The federal escort was defeated, the wagons that were loaded with provisions were captured, and Steele, marooned in Camden, was beginning to starve.

Papa Rudd's farm, in Columbia County and a day's ride by wagon from Camden, was apparently sacked by another of General Steele's raiding parties. But such raids didn't hold Steele's army for long, and they retreated to Little Rock, just managing to escape destruction at

Jenkins's Ferry at the hands of Papa Rudd and his Confederate comrades.

The Goodspeed Biographical and Historical Memoirs of Southern Arkansas, originally published in 1890, records:

> At the opening of the war Mr. Rudd espoused the cause of the Confederacy, becoming a member of Company G, 20-6 Arkansas Infantry, and served on the west side of the Mississippi River taking part in the battles of Prairie Grove, Fort Smith, Pleasant Hill, and Saline River [Jenkins's Ferry]. He surrendered with his command in Marshall, Texas, but having a leave of absence was not present at that time. [He was a lieutenant, commanding a platoon.] He came home, his stock had all been driven off and nothing was left him but his land—

Papa's first wife had died while he was in the war in 1863, so starting again, he married Mama Rudd ("Molly") in 1865. After the war, Papa again became prosperous, promoted education, was a Master Mason, and served through the chairs of Columbia Masonic Lodge No. 82.

In reviewing the short but eventful visit I had with my grandparents during my mother's illness and remembering the stories I heard about Papa Rudd, I have often wondered what would have happened if Papa Rudd had been killed in the war or had the alligator gone for me instead of my dog. No doubt, the 'gator viewed the mutt as a better meal, just as the Yankees decided that sitting out the war in prosperous Little Rock was better than trying to live off Papa Rudd's farm.

IV⁓ THE CONFEDERACY AND RECONSTRUCTION

IN 1995, I HAD THE PRIVILEGE OF BEING THE SPEAKER AT A VETERANS OF Foreign Wars (VFW) meeting. It was ladies' night. A fulsome meal was served, and afterward we gathered in small groups telling war stories as old veterans are prone to do. One lady was present who knew something about the Civil War or at least something about who was the second most famous Confederate general. She asked, "General, which war did you fight in?" I immediately responded, "The Civil War." The lady reflected a moment, then she asked, "Did you know General Stonewall Jackson?" I replied, "Why, he was a classmate of mine at VMI [Virginia Military Institute]." The lady moved away from our group, shaking her head in wonder.

Sometimes I have a feeling that I was in the Civil War, perhaps because I heard so much about it from people who were there. When I was a boy, it was always yesterday.

I remember stories of the war told by old Confederates who fought, endured, and survived. The last encampment of these veterans was held in Little Rock, Arkansas, at what is now War Memorial Park. As I recall it was in 1925. The Confederate veterans had held a previous meeting in Little Rock in 1911, which was the largest Confederate convention ever held. Their headquarters was at the Old State Capitol and the reviewing stand where these veterans had proudly marched by to the tune of "Dixie" was in front of the Old State Capitol building. It was fitting that the last convention for the Confederate soldiers be held in Little Rock. These soldiers, in their final encampment, burdened with years and suffering from old wounds and disabilities, retained their remarkable Rebel spirit.

I have a memory of meeting, visiting, and talking with these valiant survivors who had followed the star of Robert E. Lee. They followed him then; they would follow him still. To the people of the South, Robert E. Lee was an icon, the personification of nobility and gentlemanly conduct—the epitome of character. For three generations after the war, mothers in the South held him up to their sons as a model. Many a Southern mother admonished her son: "Son, I want you to grow up and be like Robert E. Lee"—as had my mother. Robert E. Lee, as president of Washington University, subsequently named Washington and Lee, was a healer of wounds, teaching, preparing, and showing the way to the future and national reconciliation.

While attending this convention, the veterans lived in tents. Boy Scouts were assigned to attend them, and I was there as a Tenderfoot Scout from Troop #3, Hot Springs, with our scoutmaster, Capt. Richard L. Gaffney, a captain in the national park police.

Central in the encampment was a large mess hall where the veterans ate and where the Scouts waited the table. The meals were the high point, not that their appetite was so craving, but their hunger for companionship and visitation with their comrades was insatiable. The meals would be extended in the discussion and the retelling of battles of long ago. Frequently, the conversations would be continued in a tent where small groups would gather. Veterans would repeat twice-told tales and would conclude with "what if" conversations speculated on by Southerners:

> "What if" Stonewall Jackson had not been killed at the Battle of Chancellorsville?
>
> "What if" Lee had not been denied his eyes and ears, the intelligence information as to the position and movements of the Federal army for five days prior to Gettysburg, by Stuart's absence from the impending battle?

These "what ifs" would be carried on when, in the hearts of these gallant survivors, they had come to understand it was not fated for the South to win. Destiny had ordained a historical role for America in the divine scheme of nations—"A nation divided cannot stand."

In the Confederate states, one-fourth of the men of military age were killed, wounded, or fell victim to disease or malnutrition. The long, lingering memories of the Southern people was the war's aftermath—defeat, military occupation, dislocation, economic ruin, the disenfranchisement of veterans, and the imposition of corrupt carpetbag rule.

I had the opportunity to see the Civil War through the eyes of these veterans. My people experienced the social and cultural backlash of the war, the economic dislocation and oppression that smothered the South for three-quarters of a century afterward.

Relocation, economic blight, and social disruption visited on the Southern people produced at least one blessing. "Sweet are the uses of adversity which, like a toad, ugly and venomous, wears yet a jewel in its crown."

Of course, the South was a rural and largely agricultural region. Families on small- and medium-sized farms and plantations worked and produced most of their own needs, lived together, survived together, frequently two or three generations living at the same place. Children, when they left the farm, would thereafter, as we did, refer to the ground where they had lived as the "old homeplace." This life-shared experience produced a bonded family unity and loyalty, similar to that of the clans in Scotland and Ireland from whence many came, with a pride in family, affection, and mutual support enriching the lives of those with Southern roots.

After the war, with the slaves freed, a landowner had no labor, the laborer had no land. Thus arose the sharecropper system which blighted the South and afflicted both blacks and poor whites alike. This system of semi-servitude continued until relieved by mechanization —the tractor and the cotton picker—and the social revolution of the Second World War.

Reconstruction and the human deprivations following the Civil War impacted not only the blacks and poor whites. A poor standard of life affected the small- and medium-sized farmer and their families in the South, including south Arkansas and Columbia County, up to and through the Great Depression of the 1930s.

During this period cotton was still "King." Large landowners relied upon the sharecropper system to cultivate the land, plant the seeds, hoe out the weeds, and pick the cotton.

As evil as slavery was, in some ways the sharecropper system was worse. A slave was a valuable piece of property, his health and well-being cared for and preserved. The sharecropper, with his ever-pregnant wife and hungry children, often was a transient, here for the season, then he would load up his bare belongings and was gone. Others staying would become indentured to the system, with no hope of relief.

Tragically, because of the pressing need for labor, our prison system also inflicted a form of slavery, a harsh, involuntary servitude on many prisoners who had served their sentence and had no outside family or friends to intercede on their behalf. Sheriffs in cotton counties could be helpful to cotton farmers by "impressing workers" who were vagrants or charged with petty crimes. Many were arrested, placed in jail, and leased out to farmers during the cotton-picking season. Gov. George Donaghey characterized the system as one in which the prisoners were kept in a "burning, seething hell." He attended a Southern Governors' Conference in 1912 where he heard the governor of South Carolina, Cole Blease, describe how he had used mass pardoning to attack this blackest of evils in his home state.

Governor Donaghey returned home and requested from the superintendent of prisons a list of all convicts, their crimes, their sentences, and the time that they had served. The governor found that many prisoners were serving long sentences for petty crimes such as vagrancy or disorderly conduct and were being held in prison after their terms had expired.

In 1912, Donaghey pardoned three hundred and sixty prisoners, representing half of the prison population. The governor's actions brought to the full public view this brutal practice of enslavement of the state's prisoners. However, the practice of leasing prisoners by county sheriffs in cotton-growing counties continued for a time.

Seared into my childhood memory is witnessing the return of a young black man to the cotton fields where he had been put to work. The young man had been "leased" to the farmer, but at the first opportunity he had run away. Upon being returned he was hobbled with leg chains. Before putting him back to work, his arms were placed around a tree, his wrists handcuffed, his back bared, and he was horsewhipped. The young man did not cry; he moaned. This I could never forget; I can still hear the crack of the whip followed by the deep, mournful sounds coming from the depths of his being.

From what I saw, from what I knew, came a deep resolve, a promise—someday, some way, I would help these people.

Gov. George Washington Donaghey, without a doubt, was one of the great governors of Arkansas and served as an inspiration to my administration and to others, particularly in the continuing struggle for human rights, and I decided to continue what he had begun.

V ⌇ "MOTHER MAE"

MY BEAUTIFUL AND EVER-PATIENT AND LOVING MOTHER, NETTIE BELLE Sanders, and Pap, Hal McMath, my father, ran away from home when they were sixteen years old, crossed over the Arkansas/Louisiana line to Spring Hill, Louisiana, where they were married by a justice of the peace in 1908.

Following the wedding, the bride and groom returned to their respective homes, Mother to her parents, and Pap to his, but the separation soon became unendurable. They informed their families as to what they had done, that they loved one another, and that they were devoted to finding a place to make their own home.

The couple, Hal and Nettie Belle, lived with Hal's family while a cabin on the McMath place was refurbished and repaired for them. Mother Mae had her own four girls, so Nettie Belle, being only sixteen, became her fifth daughter. When the cabin was completed, the young married couple set up housekeeping.

Mother Mae would often walk the mile from the McMath homeplace, down the trail to the cabin and visit. She was the matriarch of the family, my mother's mentor, and really came down to check on how they were doing and see if Mother needed any help, especially after Sister and I came along.

When I was about five years old, one day Mother Mae came down, and she was out of snuff, which she called her "consolation." Many ladies used snuff discreetly in the privacy of their own room. There was a country store about a mile from the cabin, so Mother Mae gave me some money and sent me to the store to get four cans of Garrett's snuff. I made this long pilgrimage alone, and as I was walking, I heard the bushes shake, followed by a wildcat's long scream. I hastened my pace to the store, made the purchase, and started on my return home. When I had traveled about halfway, my fears having subsided, I loitered and watched a toad hop across the trail. I thought he would make a great pet and wanted to take him home, but I couldn't carry the toad and four cans of Garrett's. I was holding the snuff, two cans in each hand, and I had a decision to make; so I placed two cans in a hollow tree, and picking up the toad with my free hand, I proceeded home.

Mother Mae with Sid and his sister, Edyth

For some reason, Mother Mae was not interested in the toad; she wanted to know about the two cans of missing snuff. She took me in hand, and as we retraced my route toward the store, "lo and behold," we had not gone very far when I discovered the cans in the hollow tree.

As I have mentioned earlier, when Grandpappy, Sid McMath, was killed, he left Mother Mae with eight children. My dad, Pap, was the eldest son, but on Mother Mae fell the responsibility of operating the farm, holding the family together, and seeing that her children got the education available at the time. Mother Mae soon became a good farmer, and she had to make tough decisions. As kind, loving, and wonderful as she was as a grandmother, with four sons and four daughters and being a lone parent, she had to be a firm mother and employer.

Supervising workers during cotton-picking season, she had to be strict during working hours, so no one came late or left early without a solid excuse. Cotton had to be picked clean with no leaves, cotton bolls, or dirt left in the cotton, and rocks in the cotton sack when a worker brought it in to be weighed was almost a capital offense—out of the field, out of the gate they would go.

Old hands would inform new workers that "Miss Mae" was mule-hide tough, "she had salt in her craw, iron in her belly, and ate barbed wire for breakfast." But then, they all knew that "Miss Mae" was also a softy. During the cotton-picking season she would keep pans of cornbread made by her with home-ground cornmeal. I heard many "darkies" come to the back door and call out, "Miss Mae, can I have a piece of cornbread? I's hongry." This wish would be instantly supplied with an admonition, "You get in a good day's work today, you hear? We got to get the cotton to the gin, so we can have a payday." The worker would respond with a thank you and a smile and, nursing a large slice of homemade cornbread with lifted spirits, go to the field for a hard day's work.

I would also get a slice of that cornbread or, perhaps, an oatmeal cookie kept in a jar on the pantry shelf.

Mother Mae kept a large orchard, where she grew pears, apples, peaches, and plums; and she had a vegetable garden and a watermelon patch. There was also a smokehouse not far from her kitchen, where there were smoked hams, sides of salt meat, and links of sausage.

She had chickens, geese, and turkeys. The turkeys had to be watched during nesting time, because they would wander off in the woods to find a secure brush pile, build their nests, and lay their eggs. She would keep watch on the turkey nests, so when the little ones appeared, she would bring them safely home by putting the freshly hatched turkey chicks in the folds of her apron to transfer them to her turkey pen, while the mother turkey would follow along, running in circles and protesting until she was united with her chicks.

She would let me help her look for the turkey nests so that we could save the little ones from old "Brer Fox" and would brag on me and tell my mother that I was a good turkey nest hunter.

Around 1920, Mother Mae and Maude, her youngest daughter, moved to Magnolia. Maude, who was paralyzed as a girl, lived in a wheelchair and was looked after by Mother Mae all of her life. It was said she was injured when she jumped from a fig tree, but the probabilities are that she was a victim of polio—an unrecognized disease at the time. Maude loved books, read widely, lectured, and for many years taught a Sunday School class at the Methodist Church, as well as being an accomplished artist, both drawing and painting.

In Magnolia, Mother Mae had a neighbor with whom she became a close friend. This good neighbor was a widow whose husband had also served as sheriff of Columbia County and who also had been tragically slain in the performance of his law enforcement duties.

Mother Mae, with all of her life's problems, labor, and responsibilities, maintained a keen sense of humor flowing with wisdom. At family gatherings, on holidays, and on birthdays, she would entertain her children and grandchildren, mostly her grandchildren, by playing the French harp and dancing an Irish jig. She entertained the younger ones by reciting poetry and jingles. For example:

> I had an old hat, and I had an old brim,
> I looked like a billy goat, a'straddle of a limb.

> I went up a sapling, I came down a pine,
> I tore my britches a mile behind.

Or she would sing tunes like "Old Dan Tucker":

> Old Dan Tucker was a fine old man,
> Washed his face in a frying pan,
> Combed his hair with a wagon wheel,
> Died with a tooth ache in his heel.

A quarter century later when I was sworn in as governor, there was a newspaper story about me having to greet so many people that my right hand was swollen. I immediately received a wire from Mother Mae:

"I read about your swollen hand. I will not worry so long as it is not your head."

VI⟿ "OLD JUDD"

EVERY BOY SHOULD HAVE A DOG, AT LEAST ONE DOG IN HIS LIFE, ESPECIALLY if he lives in the country. I always had one, but none like Old Judd, a dog Pap had when we lived in the cabin on the McMath homeplace.

Old Judd was a large dog Pap used for hunting, herding our sheep, and rounding up cattle. I do not know what breed he was; he might have been a cross between a redbone hound and a shepherd, as he had the trailing sense and tenacity of a hound and possessed the patience and intelligence of a shepherd. In addition to other duties, Old Judd was the self-appointed sentinel or watchdog, providing security for our family and livestock while we slept. He would often use the cabin passageway when making his nightly rounds.

In those days, hunting a wild hog, a timber wolf, or even a fox, following the hounds on horseback, fording streams, riding through sloughs and the underbrush was a yeoman's sport engaged in occasionally by the young men living on neighboring farms.

Judd's favorite hunt was for his old antagonist, the wild boar. A wild boar is a most ferocious beast with long, curved tusks that are rapier sharp—woe to dog or man who gets in range of a cornered boar.

The razorback is descended from the swine herd Hernando De Soto brought when he crossed the Mississippi River with his conquistadors in his search for gold or, as some believe, for the "Fountain of Youth" in the foothills of the Ozarks. These hogs, escaping from De Soto's band of adventurers, survived, multiplied, grew, and thrived in the lowlands and marshlands west of the Mississippi, along the Cache, White, and Arkansas Rivers, becoming the ancestors of the famous and ferocious razorbacks.

When dogs jumped a herd of these beasts, the boar would lead or entice the dogs away from the sows and piglets. This instinctive maneuver and the strong pungent odor of the animal would excite the hounds, leading them in pursuit of the boar.

The creature was strong, had great endurance, was crafty, and, once grown, tired of the chase or frustrated with the yapping of the dogs, could be expected to find a thick cane break—his natural retreat and refuge. The path leading in would be narrow through the cane break where the boar would make his stand, daring anyone to challenge him. As there was no maneuvering room, the dogs then were unable to circle or attack from the rear, to approach head-on was to die.

Old Judd had acquired scars and wisdom from such encounters, and these scars served as a check on any future rashness. He would satisfy himself that the monster was in the break, keep open a line of retreat, and signal Pap by the tone of his voice that he had done his duty. When a dog bays his quarry, he has a different tone, cadence, and depth to his bark. He, at first, picks up a trail with a slow, tentative bark, as if he is uncertain of what he has found; then when the scent gets hot, his bark becomes more rapid, closer together. As the game runs to ground, is treed, or holed up, the bay is slow, with tone-heavy sounds, as if he has his head up rather than his nose to the ground. A seasoned hunter, knowing his dog, would understand the dog's language. Pap understood Old Judd, would ride to the scene, and with his high-powered rifle, would end the hunt.

Of course, Judd was rewarded with juicy pieces of pork. The family would have two hams to smoke and cure and sides of meat to salt down and preserve as winter meat. Often the shoulder and other parts would be shared with another family on the farm or neighbors. Boar meat had a strong taste, but was nutritious and a welcome addition to our smokehouse.

The red wolf is another animal that survived for a long time in southwest Arkansas and east Texas. He thrived along the Red River, making an occasional foray into farm areas in search of a domestic meal such as a chicken, a kid, or a small calf. Or perhaps he would venture out for a frolic with the hounds, stirring up the neighborhood, serving notice that he was still around—howling, yapping, and generally raising sand.

The Red River was within a wolf's range of our community. The bottomlands through which it courses its way were a natural habitat for the wolf, one of the few places left in the country where these much maligned, cunning animals could survive. Sometimes, a wolf would come at night and make a wide survey of our place. If a lone hound, leisurely trailing a coon or a fox, would hit the hot scent, the woods would come alive. Then howls and baying could be heard for miles around. Other dogs, getting the message, would join the hunt.

Farmers concerned about their stock or looking for an adventure would take their rifles down from their gun racks, saddle their horses, and ride to the hounds.

Old Judd, responding to the call, would join up and soon overtake them. Pap, saddled, booted, and spurred, would follow the chase into the night. The next morning Pap would return, "plumb wore out," scratched by briars and thicket, wet from fording streams and splashing through the sloughs, tired and hungry. In no time, Mother would have a pot of coffee on our wood cookstove, perking, purring, and putting out the aroma of black Louisiana coffee laced with chicory. Soon this aroma would be followed by the smell of frying sausage or bacon and hot biscuits, mixed with scrambled eggs, grits, and sorghum molasses.

But Old Judd would not be there. He would limp home a day or two later, sore-footed, his eyelids and face scratched by briars, covered with wood ticks, and so tired. He would have stayed with the hunt until the wolf, deciding he'd had enough fun, would head for the security of his lair. The dogs would stay around, bay for a while, and then one by one respond to their master's horn calling them home. Judd, one of the last to leave the wolf's lair, having arrived home, would check for Pap's presence, take a long drink of fresh water from the horse trough, and moving slowly, walk gingerly to the barn where he would lie down on a bed of hay and sleep—"dog tired."

One spring the rains came heavier than usual. Our flock of sheep was not to be seen in their usual place; so Pap saddled up, placed his shotgun in his saddle scabbard, and he and Judd went in search of them. They were found marooned on a small island surrounded by the rising flood water. Pap sent Judd to drive the sheep off the island into the water toward the higher ground and home; yet the sheep were frightened, confused, and would not respond to Judd's urging. Picking out the belled ewe, Judd caught her by the wool on her neck and pulled her to the water. She resisted. Judd hung on and pulled harder, but the ewe pulled back. Pap hollered at Judd and commanded him to let her go, yet Judd refused. Pap was about thirty yards away with rising water up to his stirrups. He pulled out his shotgun loaded with birdshot, thinking that by firing in Judd's direction the bird pellets would cause him to release the sheep. Pap fired; Judd dropped. Quickly, Pap rode over to where wounded, his dog lay, picked him up, placed him across his saddle, and rode home, leaving the sheep to the flood. He laid Judd on a blanket in front of the fireplace where he died. Pap never recovered from his loss and never owned another dog.

Pap talked about Old Judd for years, bragging about him. He would tell people how smart Judd was. For example, if Pap and Judd went out on a hunt for a boar or a wolf, and they became separated for a length of time, Old Judd would come home and look over the mantle where Pap kept his rifle and shotgun. If either was not in place, Judd would return to the woods.

I owned several dogs during my lifetime, but my model for the greatest dog that ever lived was Old Judd.

VII ⁓ "PAP"

I LOVED MY DAD. HE COULD RIDE A HORSE, ROPE A STEER, OR SHOOT A rifle with the best. I called him Pap. This title for my father had a family history.

My dad, Hal Pierce McMath, was born in Texas. His mother was Lula Mae Rudd McMath. His father, Sidney Smith McMath, as a young man, had left Union County, Arkansas, to go to Texas where he became the foreman of a cattle ranch.

One day my grandfather, Sid McMath, was working with a horse wrangler in the corral. Hal, five years of age, was peering through the corral gate, watching his father and the wrangler work with the horses. Having finished, they came through the gate and walked to the saddle room. Noticing Hal, they began talking to him, and he responded and was referring to his father as Sid. The wrangler stopped, picked Hal up, held him at arms' length, and admonished him: "Don't call your dad 'Sid.' Call him Pap." So, from then on, Sidney Smith McMath was known by all of his children as Pap and by his grandchildren as Grandpappy. I also was taught to call my dad Pap, and so it was.

Grandpappy gave up ranching, returned to Columbia County, and farmed the McMath homeplace. He had an eighth-grade education, was smart, had an engaging personality, and was a natural leader. Everybody liked him. He was elected sheriff of Columbia County and served several terms before he was killed in a shootout with bootleggers in 1911, one year before I was born.

He had driven out in a buggy to arrest the bootleggers and bring them in. Finding their hideout in the abandoned sawmill, he ordered them to come out with their hands up. One suddenly appeared in the road armed with a rifle. Another stepped out behind him. It was an ambush. A gunfight ensued, and while Grandpappy killed the one in front, he, in turn, was shot in the back and died.

When Pap's dad died, he and my mother were living on the old McMath homeplace. But Pap was not really a good farmer. He simply was not interested; yet, in south Arkansas, there was little else. He and Mother Mae, with the help of the brothers and sisters, ran the farm and supported the family. Here on June 14, 1910, my sister Edyth Mae

McMath came into the world. Then I arrived, two years to the day, a birthday present to her—an intruder, competing for care and attention.

Though not a farmer, my dad loved horses, and like his father, he understood them. Neighbors, or sometimes even strangers, would bring a wild, unbroken horse over for Pap to break and train.

Pap had an appreciation for and a way with all animals. Trading and trafficking in horses and cattle was what he loved and excelled in doing. He also liked people and was a good judge of men, hence an excellent trader. With a reputation of being honest and straightforward in any business, he never traded a horse with a defect or blemish that he did not reveal. When Pap was trading, we were well provisioned according to the standards in the rural South at the time.

But Pap had a problem. We, his family and his friends, did not know or did not realize or appreciate the nature and extent of his addiction to alcohol. We did not know, as we later came to realize, that he had a disease, that his body, craving alcohol, was unable to metabolize the poison. Giving in to the demand, but not satisfying the craving, the disease leads to ever-growing personal and family grief. The victim must come to the realization that he cannot win this life-and-death struggle without receiving help beyond himself. Without this help he is lost.

We did not know about Alcoholics Anonymous and the required 12 Steps that can lead one back to a life of health and harmony. It simply wasn't around in those days.

When Pap, no longer resisting, would take a drink, one would lead to another. He then would be away from home for days on end. When drinking, he was aggressive and would become involved in fights, sometimes with more than one antagonist at the same time. Finally, he would return home, or we would go find him. Then, of course, he would be in desperate condition—physically and emotionally. He would be remorseful, apologetic, and contrite. Promising Mother that he would never take another drink, like most alcoholics, he meant it and was determined to keep that promise. But Mother, going about her work, was skeptical; recognizing the past, she was not too optimistic about the future. In truth, she didn't understand the disease, and, apparently, no one else did at the time.

There was always a tip-off. Pap loved to wear a white western

Hal McMath (Pap), Sid's father

Stetson hat; and with a brand-new white Stetson on his head, a new suit, and shined and polished boots, he was most handsome. The hat seemed to be designed for him—it was like Pap himself. With his size, good looks, and personality, he was the picture of success. But the new Stetson, the last one having been lost, was an ill omen. Up would go the hat and down would go the drinks, and he was on his way. "One is too many, and a thousand not enough," as the saying goes, and he would be gone. The pattern would be repeated and he would come home— the hat gone, the suit torn, and the boots scuffed and worn.

I continue to grieve that I could not help him, could not save him and the family from the dark tragedy that would unfold. But we did not find help. Had we known then what is known now, about the care and treatment, about the dynamics of this cancer, we might have been spared the darkest hours of our lives.

The only advice Pap ever gave me was: "Think twice; know you are right; and go your limit." I remembered.

VIII⁓ THE JACK PARHAM PLACE

WE MOVED A LOT. BY THE TIME WE BECAME STABILIZED IN THE COMMUNITY, enrolled in the school system, and acquainted with our neighbors, we would leave. When I was about five, we moved from the cabin where I was born to a small farm nearby, known as the Jack Parham Place. We lived there through at least one Christmas and one springtime.

I recall going to Mother Mae's on Christmas Day. I remember that the McMath girls had gotten a musical instrument. It was formed like a box with four legs on it and had a circular wheel that laid flat and was supported at the top of the box. The girls would place on the wheel a round, thin, disk-like object with a hole in the center, which was held in place by a projection coming up through the hole. They would turn a crank on the box, and then they would start the wheel turning by adjusting a lever on the side of the wheel. There was an arm on the side of the wheel that could be swung over the disk, which had at the end a nose-like projection holding a needle. The needle would be lowered on the disk, and the disk would make music. It was a miracle. I listened to it for half a day, sometimes with my ear pressed to the side of the box. After a period of feasting and wonder, we collected our presents and returned to our new home.

When springtime rolled around we were still on the Parham Place, as I remember. From the annual spring flood, which would probably have been May or early June, there were small sloughs or pools of water which were formed as the high water receded—pools filled with fish of all kinds and sizes. We caught the fish with seines made of tow sacks stitched together. A tall pole was woven or pinned to each end of the seine, and the bottom ends of the sacks would be weighted down. We would supply the neighbors, white families and black families, with fish, and we often had a fish fry, with all the trimmings. My favorite fish, then and now, is fried catfish with hushpuppies made from coarse ground cornmeal, salted and peppered.

It was at this time that I was introduced to an increasingly popular food, a cornflakes-type cereal. A neighbor had invited us to his house for Sunday dinner. He had recently gone to a dentist and had all of his teeth pulled but had not received his new ones, so he was eating soft food. He gave me some; it was good and crunchy. We did not have breakfast cereals at my house, because we ate bacon and eggs or sausage and eggs with hot biscuits or flapjacks covered with butter and honey or sorghum molasses. Cereal might be good for a starter, but not for a real breakfast or any other meal; unless, of course, it was all you were able to eat, as was the case with our neighbor.

He told us about his Rhode Island red hens, six of them, that had won the blue ribbon at the county fair. On this day at our neighbor's there were no children to play with, at least none my age. So, I went into the backyard in search of adventure. The yard was fenced and contained a mulberry tree, heavy with berries, and the large Rhode Island hens that had won the blue ribbon.

Suddenly, I had a craving for some of the berries, but they were beyond my reach until I selected a piece of stove wood with which I was able to knock down some berries. I would hit a limb of the tree and mulberries would shower down, but the chickens would flock around and gobble up the berries before I could get a single one. I patiently made about three tries with the same results. Determined not to be defeated, I made a quick decision. I am ashamed to say and embarrassed to tell, even after the passage of almost a century, I took the stick and killed the hens. Having satisfied my appetite, I went back into the house to find my parents preparing to leave—I was ready.

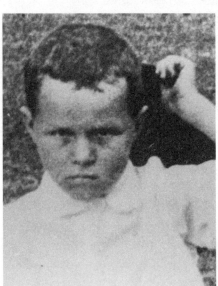

Several evenings later, at suppertime, Pap told Mother that something terrible had happened to our neighbor's Rhode Island red hens. A fox had gotten into the yard and killed his chickens.

But "Old B'rer Fox, he just lay low."

Sid McMath, age five

IX☙ "UNCLE SPOOKS"

WE NEXT MOVED BACK TO THE MCMATH HOMEPLACE WHERE WE LIVED with Mother Mae, her daughter Maude, and my great-grandmother Molly Rudd.

Mother Mae's second son next to Pap, Ray "Uncle Spooks" McMath, had been recruited for the First World War. He was training at Camp Beauregard, Louisiana. "Uncle Spooks" was the only member of our family in the service for the "Great War." Pap was not drafted because he had a family. Ray came home two or three times from camp. He looked good in his uniform, and we were all proud of him. He would tell us what he had heard about the war in France, about Kaiser Bill and how the Germans killed people—civilians, men, and women—and that the Huns would even bayonet children.

Our boys were going "over there" and fix all of that. We were going to help France because LaFayette had helped us defeat the "Redcoats" in our revolution against King George of England. Our boys were citizen soldiers, not professionals. They came from farms, ranches, and factories; and they were going to outfight and out-tough the regimented German soldiers.

Thus, with flags flying and bands playing, our boys marched off with high spirits to fight the "First Great War." "To make the world safe for Democracy," our soldiers marched off to memorable tunes:

> "Over There"—"The Yanks are coming, the Yanks are coming, and they won't come back until it's over, over there."

> "It's a Long Ways to Tipperary"—"It's a long ways to Tipperary, it's a long ways to go. It's a long ways to Tipperary to see the sweetest girl I know."

> "Pack Up Your Troubles in Your Old Kit Bag"—"Pack up your troubles in your old kit bag, smile boys, that's the style. While you've a Lucifer to light your fag, worrying is not worth while."

During Uncle Spooks's visits he became aware of my infatuation and preoccupation with monkeys and promised to bring me a big brass one. I was excited, talked about it constantly, and told everybody what Uncle Spooks was going to do.

But then Uncle Spooks never went "over there" or "fought the Huns" or "licked the Kaiser." His service was classified as indispensable at Camp Beauregard, Louisiana; there he served until the end of the war and received an honorable discharge.

After the war was over, Uncle Spooks joined the many veterans who marched on Washington, D.C., to demand a pension, in what was called the "Bonus March." There he saw a Maj. Douglas MacArthur and a Capt. "Ike" Eisenhower, the U.S. Army officers who were in charge of keeping order in the Capitol City.

Uncle Spooks fought the Great War in the trenches of Louisiana and received his pension, but I never got my monkey.

X~ BUSSEY

OUR NEXT MOVE WAS TO BUSSEY, ARKANSAS, A COMMUNITY OF ABOUT one hundred and twenty-five people. Bussey was the watering station for the Kansas City Southern Railroad going from Missouri to Dallas, Texas. We lived in a house next to the track, where a freight train passing through at night would almost come through our bedroom.

I entered the first grade at the school in Bussey. Since my sister was at home, recovering from the measles, Mother walked with me to school my first day on a dirt road, shaded over with trees whose limbs were reaching out and touching from each side of the pathway. The way seemed to me interminably long. My mother, sensing my apprehension and hesitation about the prospect of leaving home and meeting strange people, tried to cheer me up by singing and whistling a popular tune. One of her favorites was "Redwing:"

> "Oh, the moon shines tonight on pretty Redwing,
> as she lies sleeping the night away."

We arrived in time for the morning assembly at the one-room schoolhouse with its pot-bellied stove and rows of benches. The assembly was called by the ringing of a hand bell, and the children outside in the schoolyard came in and assembled in their assigned places.

This being the first day, and not having been assigned a place, my mother and I sat in the back. When the assembly was over, school took up, and since there were eight grades taught at the school, the class that was having their lesson moved to the front row. Mother left, and I moved to a window, where I could watch her disappear. When she was out of sight, I quietly eased out the front door and ran to the railroad tracks close by, which was a shortcut home.

I hotfooted it down the track, soft-pedaled over a long trestle that spanned a marsh infested by snakes and alligators, and raced homeward. When Mother arrived, I was sitting on the front steps.

Part of my excuse for my brief day at school was that while I was gone, my pets had been missing me. I had a half-grown wolf that I kept chained in the back yard. At night I would turn him loose so he could scout the area, sometimes racing the neighbors' dogs until he got tired, then ending the game by returning home to safety, and climbing through a hole he had dug under the back yard fence. I also had a turtle that I kept in a discarded washtub that still held water, along with a couple of frogs. I was concerned about these prized possessions; however, I did not get to spend any time with these objects of my affection this day. I was sent to my room where I stayed until suppertime. There was, in brief, a definite understanding that I would return to school, which I did the next morning—alone.

I was present when school assembled. The teacher led us in the Lord's Prayer. We then pledged allegiance to the flag of the United States:

> I pledge allegiance to the flag
>
> And to the republic for which it stands.
>
> One nation, indivisible
>
> With liberty and justice for all.

The terms "United States of America" and "Under God" had not been inserted into the pledge at that time. The phrase that caught my sensitive ear and taxed my imagination was "With liberty and justice for all."

The children then sang with great gusto the song "Arkansas":

> Arkansas, Arkansas, 'tis a name dear,
>
> 'Tis the place I call "home, sweet home."
>
> Arkansas, Arkansas, I salute thee,
>
> From thy shelter no more I'll roam.

This, of course, was my first introduction to the Pledge of Allegiance to the flag and to the song "Arkansas." We still pledge allegiance to the flag, but we don't customarily sing our state song. This is indeed sad, considering the rich and colorful history of our state. Arkansas is one of the great states in the Union, rich in resources, richer still in the character of its people, with a proud heritage and tradition.

By noon on each day at school, children would be famished for food. Everyone brought his or her lunch, which was kept on shelves inside the school, next to the door's entrance. Some brought their

Student body of Bussey School in 1918 with their teacher (Sid with gun pointed at him) *(Photo courtesy Southwest Arkansas Regional Archives/Dr. Robert Walz)*

lunch in a small tin pail, or if two or more were from the same family, a molasses bucket was most convenient. Others brought their lunch in paper sacks. The contents of the luncheon containers, whether sack, pail, or bucket, varied. Fried chicken, biscuits, sausage, boiled eggs, cookies, an occasional ripened banana, cornbread, ham, pickles, and slices of onion at about 12 o'clock noon would have mingled and merged their individual aromas, permeating the schoolroom, whetting the appetites of about twenty-five hungry children.

A lot of interesting things happened in Bussey. One day a man buzzed the town in his airplane. It was the first airplane I ever saw. Apparently, no one else in Bussey had ever seen one either.

After buzzing the town, the pilot landed in a nearby pasture and the whole town went out to look at the two-seater biplane. The pilot's plane was to take some passengers for a spin—at a price, of course—but the mob surged around and began whittling off pieces of the fuselage, and not being able to subdue the crowd's excitement or to control the souvenir hunters, the pilot cranked the engine, jumped back in his plane, scattered the crowd, and took off. He never came back.

Another exciting event occurred when a man came with a tent show. He had attracted a crowd with an organ that played loud music and a big muzzled black bear. The tent was big and contained a projector and a movie screen on which he showed a movie that was the talk of the town. I must have seen it three times, at least.

The movie was about a beautiful girl who had a pet white mule. Someone stole it, or at least the mule disappeared, so the girl promised to marry the man who would find and return her pet. Suddenly, there appeared a villain, dressed in black, wearing a long, curved mustache. He couldn't find her mule, so he painted one white, and with great "to do," he returned it to her. The girl, true to her word, agreed to marry him, but on the fatal day the beauty was saved by the hero, because he had found the real mule and was rewarded with her hand in marriage. Fittingly, they lived happily ever after. It made a great impression.

The First World War was still in progress when we moved to Bussey, where the troop trains stopped to take on water. Soldiers in uniform would get off to stretch, smoke their cigarettes, laugh, and joke, as if they were on a happy holiday.

Sometimes there would be other passengers on the trains: beautiful women. I saw my first women, of all things, wearing rouge and lipstick, bobbed hair, painted fingernails; and horror of horrors, they wore short skirts, high heels, and smoked cigarettes. The men thought these ladies most attractive, but the ladies in the Bussey community arched their eyebrows and lamented, "What was the world coming to?"

There was a German man who lived on the outskirts of Bussey. He drove a wagon, hauling logs. He spoke only broken English. He would come to town once a week to get supplies from the general merchandise store.

My buddy, Vance Alden, and I figured he might be a spy, providing secret information to the Kaiser as to what was going on in Bussey. We "shadowed" him on several evenings and followed him home.

After unhitching, watering, and feeding his mules, the German would go into his house. After a time, he would come and sit in the rocking chair on his porch and smoke his pipe.

We watched this from a concealed position behind a log. He was smart. We never caught him handing out information to the Kaiser's agents about what was going on in Bussey.

We celebrated the Armistice in Bussey twice. With our communications system, the old crank party-line telephone, we relied on our neighbors for news by listening to conversations on the party line. The first time we heard news of the Armistice on the telephone, we celebrated and only found out later that it was false information.

Needless to say, nights in fall, after the sunset, were quiet. We could occasionally hear the howl of a lone wolf coming from the direction of the Red River, the wailing of a dog on a cold trail, a whippoorwill, or the omnipresent hoot owl. But on the night of November 11, 1918, the sound of shotguns, pistols, and rifles being fired into the air could be heard everywhere. It was the real Armistice Day.

We had the excitement of celebrating Armistice a second time with even greater exhilaration. The men, shooting their shotguns, pistols, and hunting rifles in the air, used up all the local ammunition and consumed all the available "Southern Comfort."

Those so inclined could find a jug or jar of homemade moonshine whiskey, the distiller's pride, to elevate their spirits and enliven this historic celebration. Pap celebrated until it was confirmed to his satisfaction that the Armistice had been signed by all interested parties.

These were exciting times in Bussey. I recently returned to the place where we lived near the intersection of the road and railroad tracks. The house still stands.

XI ⟊ FOREMAN AND TAYLOR

WE MOVED FROM BUSSEY NORTH UP THE KANSAS CITY SOUTHERN railroad tracks and west to Foreman where we lived for a time. Pap bought a large house and called it the Foreman Hotel, where we lived upstairs, with the rooms downstairs available for hotel guests.

We didn't do too well with the hotel, but Pap did great with his real love—breaking, trading, and trafficking in horses. He bought a stockyard with a corral, pens, and a barn. Cattle were brought in for shipping, and horses were brought in for breaking and trading. Pap was in his element. I can still see him riding a bucking bronco, holding the reins in his left hand, his right hand free, in the air. He would never "pull leather"—hanging on by gripping the saddle—and as he rode with his feet in the stirrups, his knees locked tightly against the sides of the horse, his body would move in rhythm, synchronized with the bucking of the animal. I saw him thrown but once. He was immediately back on the horse to finish the ride. Always present was a flock of fence sitters, cheering him on—or sometimes rooting for the bronco. A horse would get a reputation for being untamed and unbreakable, and such a horse would gather a following who would cheer for him. This highly spirited animal would usually be bought by a circus wrangler and wind up performing in a circus or a rodeo.

Foreman, gate to the West, is on the border between Arkansas and Oklahoma. Once, Pap swapped for a horse based solely on the description given by the owner, with the understanding that Pap would go get it. The owner assured Pap that the horse would lead behind a slowly moving vehicle and that the horse would trot along without any difficulty. Pap's automobile was a touring car without a top. We piled in, taking along a rope and a head halter.

The horse was located over the Arkansas line in Oklahoma, and we found it pastured adjacent to the owner's barn. The horse was friendly; he gently came up to Pap and was haltered. Pap talked to the horse, rubbed his nose, and told him we were going to take a little trip, proceeding to tie the animal to the back of the automobile. We started toward home, and at first, the horse seemed to think it was a good idea and was in accord with the swap; however, before we had gotten off the farm and to the road, the horse began to have other ideas. He stopped, he balked, he sat on his haunches, he would not be led hitched to that machine. After much coaching, Pap gave up, inspired with a great idea: I would ride the horse home. Pap made an improvised bridle with both ends of a short rope secured to the halter, but there was no bit to be placed in the horse's mouth with which to stop the steed or firmly influence his direction. I was almost seven years old, and I could ride, so Pap put me on and headed me down the road, going east toward Foreman.

He followed behind in the car for a pace. Having satisfied himself that the horse and I were compatible, he drove home.

The distance was approximately fifteen miles, but it was a long bareback ride. The horse and I had several adventures and conflicts of will, but we eventually arrived home safely. Pap, after surviving the verbal scourging that my mother inflicted on him, thought this venture was a good idea. He told me he was proud of me, bragged on me, like he used to do about Old Judd. I was proud too—prouder even than he was.

Before leaving Foreman, two other memorable incidents occurred, which lingered in my memory. I was going to school in Foreman, but I don't recall whether it was the second half of the first grade or the first half of the second. There was to be a parade in which the school would participate, and my class would carry the flag and lead the march. I had not had any contact with Old Glory since the routine pledging of allegiance to the flag while in school at Bussey. However, I took that allegiance seriously and especially liked that part about "with liberty and justice for all." As it came time to form up for the parade, another classmate and I vied for the honor of carrying the Stars and Stripes. With the flagstaff in our hands, we tussled back and forth for the privilege of being the standard bearer. The flagstaff broke, but by quick action we spared the flag from hitting the ground. Frightened, I fled the scene, thus creating a presumption in the minds of those present that I was the aggressor, the offending party, and a bad boy.

After a period of negotiating between my mother and the teacher, I was permitted to return to class. I was kept after school for a period, a terribly long period, considering that I had important things to do. My classmate, fully a participant in the fracas, received no after-school confinement; thus, I was impressed with the meaning of "with liberty and justice for all."

I experienced my first stage appearance at Foreman. The school was putting on a play, and I was given a part. Although I do not recall the story or the theme, I remember well the character I portrayed. I was appropriately dressed, my mother had seen to that, with one exception. Wearing western boots, blue jeans, and a shirt with an emblazoned red bandana around my neck, I wore a western hat one size too large.

The play was widely advertised and was scheduled on Parents' Night, so on that evening the school auditorium was filled with students, parents, and neighbors. The show began and when the signal moment for my appearance arrived, on cue, like a seasoned trooper, I moved to center stage. With vigor I gave my much-rehearsed line, "I am an Oklahoma cowboy. You ought to hear my war whoop." Then, at the height of my voice, I gave it: "Wah Whoo, Yippity, Yippity, Yaa Whoo, Yippity-Yaa-Yea." I received a loud response from the crowd, clapping their hands, whistling, and some of the kids in my class gave my "war whoop." Me, my hat, and I stole the show, so my mother said.

I was now in good favor at the school with my teacher and my classmates, and my reputation must have been spread around town. Even the rail sitters at the horse corral all knew me. They called me "Cowboy."

We had not lived very long in Foreman, by the time that Pap ran through several white hats, and when he was offered a job as deputy sheriff in Columbia County, we moved again.

Our arrival in Taylor, Arkansas, about ten miles south of Bussey, was in time for the flu season. I remember my sister and me standing around a hot stove fired with wood, drinking what seemed to be gallons of hot lemonade—the accepted cure for the flu.

I have only a sparse recall of living in Taylor. I remember riding a horse bareback in the cold March wind, but this time it was supposed to be for fun.

I also remember an acquaintance with a girl in my class, who died of typhoid fever, a dreaded disease at the time. I only knew her in our classroom, but I was saddened—I grieved as if I had had a personal loss. She was beautiful, but I don't remember her name.

Public health was not a high priority. A butcher would come around each Saturday morning, peddling his beef that was laid out on the floor of his buckboard wagon, unprotected from heat, dust, and the insects that are drawn to fresh meat.

Taylor had the appearance of a western town. The stores were all on one side of the street, connected by a wooden planked sidewalk. Saturday was the big day for the merchants, as in most Southern towns. Farmers and their womenfolk would come to town to shop for the essentials of farm life. The women would visit and catch up on the news, like who was sparking whom and who was getting married. The men would horse trade, talk politics, or stroll leisurely to the wagon yard or stable and share a social drink from a private bottle of corn whiskey.

The people of Taylor were wonderful, hospitable, and caring, welcoming us as neighbors, but I was happy when Pap announced that we were going back to the homeplace. That was where I felt I belonged, where everything seemed in harmony—the woods, the streams, the animals, the smell of the barn filled with hay. That was where I was meant to be at that time in my life.

XII ⌒ HOME AGAIN

AFTER THE MOVE FROM TAYLOR, MY GRANDMOTHER, HER DAUGHTER Maude, my great-grandmother, my parents, my sister, and I lived together, for a time, at the old McMath homeplace. Since Papa Rudd's death in 1915, Mama Rudd had lived with Mother Mae. Mama Rudd received a pension from the State of Arkansas for Papa Rudd's service in the Confederacy. She had brought with her, in addition to her other sparse belongings, a large Bible and a grandfather clock. Mama Rudd had a small room, containing a bed, a closet, a small table, a homemade floor rug, the huge Bible, and this grandfather clock.

The big Bible sat on the little table in the middle of her room. It contained vivid pictures demonstrating what happened to people who were bad: devils holding people on their pitchforks over a pit of fiery coals. These pictures of Purgatory prompted my resolve to try to steer clear of that place; however, my firm resolve and determination to avoid the devil and his fiery furnace did not altogether release me from the fear that had been implanted in my mind. At intervals over the years of my childhood, I would have my sleep disturbed by dreams—bad dreams, nightmares—of being chased by that ole devil.

When I was twelve I woke up in a cold sweat after having been chased and barely escaping the grasp of that fiery fiend. At that moment, regaining my composure, I firmly determined to end this continuing dread of sleep. I made a solemn promise to myself that the next time I was being pursued by "Old Scratch," I would not run, I would turn on him.

In due course, I was again jumped by the devil. He looked just like he did in that big Bible with his horns, cloven hooves, a tail formed like a spear, fanged teeth, and eyes that burned like red-hot coals. What did I do? I remembered the promise I had made to myself, so throwing away all caution and fear, I stopped running, turned on "Old Scratch," and grabbed him by the horns. Surprise of surprises! He was not nearly as strong and fierce as I had been led to believe, because when I mustered all of my strength, I shoved his nose into the dirt. I thought I heard a slight whimper, and thus encouraged, my strength renewed and doubled; in triumph, I swung him around my head and shoulders and slung him away. He went sailing through the air, probably saved from serious injury by falling in a pile of brush.

The last time I saw the devil, he was skedaddling down the trail, his tail between his legs. I never saw him again—at least not in my dreams. Perhaps, if more of the devils, the fears that haunt us, were confronted and faced up to, they would be sent skedaddling out of our lives.

I remember more fondly Mama Rudd's grandfather clock. I only noticed it after everyone had gone to bed, when it would tick-tock, chime, and toll the passing hours. Bedded down in the folds of a featherbed, covered with freshly ironed, sun-dried sheets, the sounds of the clock were comforting, giving me a sense of security and a feeling that all was well in my world.

I don't know how old Mama Rudd was when she died, but she had been a young girl during the Civil War. To the last she had a strong voice and loved to sing spiritual songs as she went about her self-appointed tasks of dusting and straightening the furniture. By being real still, concentrating, and being attentive, I can still hear her singing, "When the Roll Is Called Up Yonder I'll Be There." I am sure she was.

All my life I remembered Mama Rudd's grandfather clock, and all my life I wanted one that would chime and toll the hour, just like Mama Rudd's. It wasn't until my eighty-fourth birthday that I went shopping and found at Brandon's Furniture Store a large, tall, grandfather clock, which was almost a duplicate of the clock of my memories. I bought it, brought it home, and placed it in a central and secure place in our home.

When my granddaughter, McKenzie McMath, then six, came to visit, she was interested in my giant clock. She wanted to know all about how I had gotten it. I related to her about Mama Rudd's clock, how I had always wanted one and how I had bought this one for my own birthday. "You got it for your own birthday?" she asked. When I answered affirmatively, McKenzie responded with exclamation, "Well, that certainly was no surprise!"

When my sister and I returned to school, it was another one-room schoolhouse near where we lived, typical of the time. On cold nights Mother and Pap would have us do our lessons in front of the fireplace, and I would do my multiplication tables and read out loud from the McGuffy's Reader. These were good days on the farm, and all seemed right with the world.

All the members of my family, like all farm families, had chores, varying only by the time of the year. My sister and I had chores to do, before and after school. Sister would feed the chickens and gather the eggs. We both gathered the vegetables from the garden, helped pick fruit from the orchard, and gathered wild berries to be canned. In addition, my regular tasks were to cut kindling, bring in wood for the cookstove and firewood for the open fireplace in cold weather, help feed the stock and put them up in the evening, and milk the cow.

This cow had a long tail, bushy on the end, and in the wintertime the end of her tail would be covered with cockleburs. I would sit on a stool and milk on her right side. On the coldest of mornings, when she was not in a good humor, she would switch her tail and hang it around my neck, the end with the cockleburs whipping across my cold right ear. When this would happen, despite the impending threats of Purgatory depicted in Mama Rudd's great Bible, I would have very bad thoughts about that old cow.

Pap got me a dog, an American pit bull named Bulga, and we immediately bonded as inseparable friends. The neighboring dogs that used to come sniffing around stayed away. Bulga had the ability to throw a cow, a yearling, or a steer. He would get them on the run, catch them by the nose, sit down, and set all four feet; then by pulling backward, he could throw the animal head over heels to the ground and hold on until someone ran up, put a rope on the animal, or tied up its legs for whatever needed to be done to be carried out.

In the summertime my friends and I would go down to Big Creek bottom, gather berries, and catch fish in small sloughs. I had my first experience with tobacco on a hot summer day when we were returning home from a swim in Big Creek. Passing a watermelon patch, which was in a field behind the log cabin where I had first lived, we picked the biggest and best melon in the patch, took it into the shade of the woods, burst it open, and began to eat. It was a good, juicy melon, but the meat was as hot as if it had been in an oven. Nevertheless, the juice quenched our thirst, with one complication. When leaving our swimming hole, each boy had taken a "chaw" of chewing tobacco, and as we "skylarked" along, each declined to be the first to spit out his cud of tobacco until we prepared to eat the watermelon. In the heat of the day, eating a hot watermelon, just after having "chawed" our first tobacco, I don't know

Sid and his dog, "Bulga"

who got sick first or who was the sickest; but for me, I never touched another plug of chewing tobacco—or ate another hot watermelon.

I remember a black couple who lived on our place. Her name was X, his name was XL, and that was the way they signed their names. X and XL lived in a one-room cabin that was spotlessly clean and had a table with an oilcloth covering sitting in the middle of the room. X would cook dodger bread made from cornmeal fried in a big iron skillet with bacon grease—that cornbread was good!

When the cotton crop was ready to pick, we would not go to school. I would pick cotton on our farm; then after it was gathered, I would pick for a neighbor. When I was eight I could pick one hundred pounds a day, for which I was paid one cent per pound. That is one silver dollar for one hundred pounds of cotton picked.

Silver dollars earned were hoarded until reluctantly spent. I kept my silver dollars in a sock. As the cotton season progressed and I had a sufficient number of dollars to make a stack, I would empty the sock, pour the dollars out on the floor, and count them one by one, carefully examining each, noting especially the date when it was made. I had been told that the older the dollar, the more it was worth. That may have been why I hung onto each dollar so tenaciously.

Eventually, I could no longer resist the pull of the general merchandise country store located at the fork of the road two miles from the homeplace. Even though Sears & Roebuck Company was the principal source for our family needs and the annual arrival of the Sears & Roebuck catalog was a red-letter day almost as exciting as Christmas, the country store was available for immediate needs. There items could be more closely inspected, and clothing could be tried on for a more comfortable fit. Going to the store with a few dollars in your pocket was an exciting event to be looked forward to, anticipated, thought about.

Buying at the country store in the early 1900s was a vivid childhood experience. The memory lingers forever: the layout of the store, the displays of the merchandise comprising the essential needs for a farm family, the aroma of coffee, the smells of hoop cheese, sardines, cottonseed meal, coal oil, ripe bananas, Florida oranges, new blue denim, pipe tobacco smoke from the cracker-barrel philosophers, all mixed and blended. This presence, if the wind was right, could be picked up a mile away.

This was one of my life's experiences in the year 1920, when I had a ration of silver dollars in my pocket and some pressing needs. Before making my purchases I looked at many things that caught my eye: saddles, bridles, dog collars, boots, britches, a .22 caliber rifle, a .20 gauge shotgun, and a large showcase with a glass front, containing a dream world of assorted penny candies.

Having completed my survey, I made my purchases. I wish I could remember the name of the kindly clerk who waited on me. He was most helpful, and he treated me as if I were grown up and his only customer. I didn't exactly buy out the store, nor spend all of my money, but what I did buy was a treasure. I don't remember everything I bought, but the following items stick in my mind:

A cap, snugly fit so it would not blow off my head in a high wind. This was a replacement for the dog-chewed, weather-beaten cap I was wearing at the time.

A pair of overalls and a blue shirt to match.

Two large golden yellow oranges, one for me and one for my sister.

Two long sticks of peppermint candy, one for me and another for my sister.

A pound of pyramid-shaped chocolate drops for my mother, who loved chocolate candy.

A collar for my dog.

Getting the candy for Mother was an effort to restore my pride and standing from my attempt to surprise her with her favorite sweet. At that earlier time, my sister and I had ridden a mule, "Old Mamie," to town on some errand or other. When we arrived in Magnolia, we hitched her and walked around the courthouse square, looking into the store windows. Having completed whatever mission we were on, we went into Hutchinson's Drug Store on the east side of the square. The store was a pharmacy and a confectionery, and we had a vanilla milkshake. Remembering my mother, I purchased some chocolate drops, pyramid-shaped, the kind she liked. I divided the chocolate drops, putting half of them in one pants pocket and half in the other pocket. We returned home, riding bareback four and a half miles, on that hot July day. Arriving home, I put "Old Mamie" in the pasture and hurried into the house. Mother was in the kitchen. I reached in my pockets for her surprise, but the chocolate drops had dissolved into chocolate mush. I was crushed. My mother's immediate response was to put her arm around me and say "I love you—and am proud of you." That's what she would always tell me when I hit a bump in the bristling road of my life.

My life on the farm, though brief in years, was a concentrated experience, leaving me with impressions and convictions that would form my life and would influence actions that I would subsequently take to improve the quality of life for families on the farm. It influenced my feelings and attitudes toward blacks who were struggling to free themselves from the final shackles of a kind of serfdom that denied them the opportunity of improving their lives and the right of an equal chance for education and employment—a right long withheld. We have made giant strides since the Second World War toward the goal of eliminating discrimination against blacks and women. America is the stronger for it.

I knew what it was like on a farm to pick cotton for one cent a pound, at the end of the day to have my fingers needled and bleeding from pricks by the cotton bolls. I saw families struggling to survive for a whole year on the low earnings they received during the cotton-picking season. I saw farmers having to sell their bales of cotton for prices less than it cost them to plant it, hoe it, pick it, and have it ginned. I remember the old refrain: "Ten-cent cotton and forty-cent meat, how in the world can a poor man eat?"

I knew what it was to ride a mule bareback over a muddy road or one washed out by high water.

I learned to swim—dog paddle—in a dammed-up creek that meandered across our back pasture. I hunted squirrels, rabbits, and raccoons and caught possums. I could call up a covey of quail.

I loved the sounds of the night—the katydids, the frogs calling for rain, the call of the whippoorwill, the hoot of the bird of the night, the distant lonesome baying of a hound dog.

I could find the Big Dipper and the North Star, to help find my way through the bottom lands. And I learned, at almost the cost of my life, not to catch a wild pig when its mama and a herd of wild hogs are close enough to hear its squeals.

My uncle Delma McMath was four years my senior. He had a Shetland pony named Woodrow, who had lost one eye and had a bad temper. One day I was in his stall watching him eat after I had served him a ration of corn, when all of a sudden, without any warning, he laid back his ears, and with eyes flashing, he caught me by the shoulder with his teeth. He bit me real good, and I learned never to stand at the trough in a stall with a horse when he is feeding.

Anyway, Delma would let me ride behind him on Woodrow, since I could stay on by putting my arms around Delma's waist. One spring day when I was about five years old, Delma decided to ride down into the Big Creek bottoms to see if any wild hogs were there, and he took me along, riding bareback on Woodrow.

It always seemed to me that when you got down into the bottoms, the world changed. It became darker as the trees blocked out some of the sunlight, and the air was cooler and had a swampy, musty, fishy smell. It gave you a kind of "spooky" feeling. Delma and I would not go down there on Sundays, nor should we have gone down there on this day, looking for wild hogs.

We found them. Seeing a small pig in the trail, wandering around as if he were lost, Delma told me to go catch him, so I slid off of Woodrow and proceeded to execute my uncle's command. The little pig seemed to be tame and was easy to catch. He came toward me as I approached, perhaps thinking I was his mother, but when I picked him up, he was anything but tame. He started squirming and squealing, and his squeals were so loud and piercing that they ran shivers up my spine. Immediately, out of the bush came the mama, charging like a wild bull, with a herd of hogs behind her. I dropped the pig and ran like a streak to Delma, still sitting on Woodrow, who pulled me up behind him. Woodrow needed no urging with a herd of hogs on his heels.

Delma told me not to tell Mother Mae. I didn't, at least not until suppertime. When she asked me her usual question about what had happened to me during the day, I related my close escape from a wild, infuriated mama hog. Her reaction, directed at Delma, would have led you to believe that she really did, according to her reputation with the workers, "eat barbed wire for breakfast."

My mother kept a scrapbook on my life. It included an anonymous poem that sums up the positive side of farm life for a boy:

Little he cares and the less he knows
Whither the road shall lead him,
Whither the life long journey goes
And if it shall bless or bleed him.

Sweet is the sun and the daisies cup,
Warm the south winds lagging.
Back of the house is a homely pup
That waits with his tail a'wagging.

Fat are the blue plums overhead,
Heavy the peach-bough's swaying,
And half a mile from the wagon shed
Are grey trout, lazy-straying.

The sky high climb to a linnet's nest
Waits where the pears are falling,
And after the evening's gift of rest,
A patch quilt bed is calling.

What matter the way the road must trend,
Whether it is smooth or bristling?
So long as he follows it to the end
And finishes up a'whistling.

—AUTHOR UNKNOWN

I saw my second moving picture when I was about eight at a local theater in Magnolia. A man came to town lecturing about famine and starvation in China, where the children did not have anything to eat but rice. This missionary for the Chinese had a movie that was shown at the local theater with the price of admission being a can or a jar of preserved food, but no rice. The movie was *Harold Lloyd and Grandma's Boy.* Harold Lloyd, as a boy about my age, lived with his grandmother and wore glasses. The other kids made fun of him, the big bully boys would beat him up, and he would always run home crying and tell his grandmother. His grandmother was wise, like all grandmothers, and she had the solution. She got him a magic rabbit's foot and instructed him that the next time he was picked on by one of the bullies, he should rub that rabbit's foot three times, and he would be able to defend himself. Sure enough, at the very next school recess, the bully boys with nothing better to do began picking on Harold. One of the bullies pushed him down and knocked his glasses off. As Harold was lying on the ground, slowly putting his glasses back on, he remembered his rabbit's foot. He pulled it out of his pocket, closed his eyes, and rubbed it three times. Then he got up and gave the bully a left to the nose and a right to the jaw. Grandma was right, and if the recess bell had not rung, I am sure he would have licked the whole gang.

Coupled with the joy of youth which was mine on the homeplace were the special times when I could go to visit Granddad Sanders. I once met a boy with a magic rabbit's foot the time I went to town with Dad Sanders to have a load of cotton ginned. On this day we left early, the cotton having been loaded on the wagon the night before. After a hot, hearty Southern breakfast, we hitched up the mules and were on our way.

Dad liked to get to the gin early to avoid the long line of wagons waiting with cotton to be ginned. However, on this occasion there was already a line of wagons with cotton in front of us. Our trip had been slowed down because we had to travel a good part of the way over a corduroy road. This was a road made of small trees or large poles laid parallel, over which wagonloads of sand were hauled, dumped, spread, and packed down. There had been heavy rains and sections of the road had flooded, hence our trip to town took longer than expected.

While waiting for his turn, Dad smoked his pipe and visited with other farmers. They talked about the weather, their crops, and the low price they were getting for their cotton. It seems they were not getting much more than the cost of growing it.

There were other boys on the wagons with their fathers, and after some reluctance, we began to get acquainted. We began to compare treasures. One boy had a flip gun that he had ordered from Sears & Roebuck, and one had a scout knife. Another older boy had a magic rabbit's foot. He said that if you went to the cemetery when there was a full moon, at midnight you could rub the rabbit's foot, make a wish, and the wish would come true. He hadn't tried it yet but was going to, when he could get somebody to go with him.

The object I had was in the seat of the wagon, so I shinnied up the wagon and retrieved it. It was a large fly swatter that was a useful tool I had mastered. I used it to swat horseflies that were buzzing in to land on the mules' haunches or had already landed and were settling down for a feast.

I had been unusually active in protecting our team from these bloodsuckers on this day when I was privileged to ride to town with my granddad Sanders in a wagon pulled by mules. He bragged on me, said I was a real fly swatter. That was when he began calling me "Horsefly." We were bonded then and there—I feel we still are.

I⤳ HOT SPRINGS

WE LEFT OUR FARM IN COLUMBIA COUNTY, THE OLD HOMEPLACE, IN THE fall of 1921. Loading all of our earthly possessions in a wagon covered with canvas, we headed for the oil boom in Smackover, where a burning oil well, ablaze and lighting the night sky, drew us like a moth to a lighted oil lamp. My playmate, Harper, a black youth my age who was living with us, came along, walking behind the wagon. The weather was cold, the ground was hard, and Harper had no shoes. My mother and Harper stood this as long as they could; then, on her signal, Harper shinnied aboard the wagon, and Mother tore strips from a bed sheet and made a bandage-like boot for his feet and legs. Rescued from the cold, Harper climbed on top of the mattresses with my sister and me, and, thus integrated, we moved at a wagon's pace into the future of the New South.

After living a short time in Smackover, where the oil boom was providing opportunities for farmers going bust on the land, yet missing out on the promised wealth of the oil fields, my parents moved in 1922 to Hot Springs. My sister and I were sent to Magnolia to stay with Mother Mae until Mother and Pap got settled. Pap still had his two fine horses, Cap and Dallas. They had worked faithfully, pulling a scoop used by the men digging oil pits. That had been Pap's job, and since he had used his own horses, he had received a higher wage. Pap was proud of his team, took good care of them, and fed them well. He had hitched up the horses to the wagon, loaded up their belongings, and traveled with Mother by stages to Hot Springs where they had friends, whom they had known in Foreman and with whom they were invited to stay until work and a place to settle could be found.

Once they had arrived in Hot Springs, there was no longer a need for a team of horses and a wagon. Pap drove to the stables located near the Garland County Courthouse, and he sold Cap and Dallas with the wagon. Whoever made that purchase got a bargain; there were no two finer draft horses anywhere. The sale of his team and wagon was a major step in Pap's life. He was moving from the country, as were millions of other people at that period in our history, to the city, severing his ties with an agrarian way of thinking and living.

He would now be required to adjust to a new environment that was a stranger to him. How would he cope?

Mother and Pap soon got jobs and rented a house on the same street and next door to their friends from Foreman. They were living on Woodfin, a side street almost at the end of Whittington Avenue.

Pap went to barber school, and after a short course, he went to work for Rasso's Barber Shop downtown on Central Avenue. Mother went to work at Rasso's as a manicurist.

Soon our parents were ready for us to join them, and Sister and I traveled along by train from Magnolia, changing at Butterfield, to Hot Springs. Since the railway station where we arrived was near the streetcar line, we then boarded a streetcar, which required a change at the Whittington-Park Avenue junction. My sister took great delight, in later years, relating what happened while waiting for the Whittington trolley. I walked out to the middle of Whittington Avenue, got down on my knees, and examined the pavement; then, with great surprise, I jumped up and shouted, "Suster, look'a heah. Heah is a sidewalk in the plumb middle of the street." That was my tenth birthday, and I had seen my first hard-surface road. Little did I know what an important role they would play in my life.

We found our new home that was located at the base of West Mountain, a part of Hot Springs National Park. Next to the house, I discovered to my great wonderment and pleasure, a baseball field for local and regional baseball games and a training field, used each spring by a major league baseball team.

Next to Rasso's Barber Shop, where my parents worked, was the Jack-O-Lantern Restaurant, a place that served more wonderful foods than I had ever dreamed of. My parents, when getting off from work in the evenings, would stop at the Jack-O-Lantern and bring home strange and delicious foods for our supper. They would come home on the streetcar, and oftentimes, when they had to work late, our supper would be delayed. The meals were usually sandwiches or cold cuts, fruit, cheese, and bread. One night I ate my first pimento cheese sandwich on rye bread, which is still my favorite.

But old ideas die hard, and for a small family, we used lots of fresh milk, so Pap bought a cow, a big, red milk cow. What would you do with a milk cow in the city? Well, we milked her, and you know whose job it was. Since we lived next to the national park lands, I would drive the cow, using a halter and a long rope, to the edge of the mountain to let her graze. This was my afternoon chore when I got home from school. I would then take her home, or, rather, she would take me home. Not having gotten enough grass in the time allowed and still being hungry and looking forward to her feed, she would head for home and drag me down the mountain behind her. It soon became apparent that the costs of the feed for the cow, plus tape and bandages for me, was not a profitable venture. Pap finally sold the red cow. I shed no tears at her going.

I came up with a business venture which would enable me to make some spending money. I bought a red wagon, one that I could pull, bought some cabbages from Mr. Womack's Mom and Pop store, located on Whittington Avenue not far from where we lived, and I peddled these cabbages from house to house on both sides of this long, wide street. I wasn't making my overhead, so I gave it up; however, I had made a contact with Mr. Womack, and he hired me on for afternoons and Saturdays. My job was to run errands, but mainly, to put displays out in front of the store when it opened on Saturday mornings and to bring back in all the items which had not sold at the end of the day.

Saturdays were the biggest days for sales. More items would be put on display in front of the store, facing the street, for people to see as they drove by. One day watermelons were the big item. Mr. Womack had gotten a load of melons from Hope, Arkansas, which we knew was the watermelon capital of the world (but, of course, did not know that it would become the home of a future president).

At the end of this particular Saturday, all the melons except the largest one had been sold. It was a big one, a prize melon, or was, until I, with great effort, was bringing it back into the store. The melon was so large that while holding it in my arms I could not see where I was stepping. I was moving in the right direction, and I thought the ground was clear, but I had only taken a few steps when I slid, and stumbled, and dropped that large, delicious, prize-winning watermelon.

Mr. Womack didn't exactly fire me. He was a man who had come from Galveston, Texas, after the flood, who spoke Spanish, or at least "cursed" in Spanish, and on that afternoon when he had finished the

Spanish part, he let me know in words that I could understand that he would endeavor to do without my services.

But I got a better job. I sold hot dogs and soda pop at the ball games. Also, I sold the *Hot Springs New Era* newspaper on the streets. When the *Hot Springs New Era* began rolling papers off the press about 4:30 in the afternoon, newsboys, who peddled papers on the streets, would be lined up waiting to purchase their papers, two for a nickel, which they in turn would sell for a nickel apiece, doubling their money. The larger and older boys would be first in line, but age and strength did not sell newspapers. Sales to the customers on the street went to the lads who were fastest—the fleet of foot. With my papers in a canvas bag, its strap fitted over my right shoulder and the bag resting comfortably on my left hip, I would make a dash for the spots where the most customers, hungry for the news, would be waiting for me to appear. Visitors, having the experience of a hot bath in the magic waters, plus a massage, would be leisurely sitting in chairs on the front porch of the bathhouses or on benches under the magnolia trees along Central Avenue or in the park across from the famous and luxurious Arlington Hotel. They might be visiting, contemplating, or even nodding, but they were always hungry for the news.

If I had not sold out by the time I cleared the Arlington Hotel, I would cross to the opposite side of the street on Central Avenue and work the bookies. They were usually good customers, eager to see the racing lineup for the next day. Many times, especially if they were winning, they would give you a tip. If they didn't have the correct change, they might give you a quarter, with a generous remark, "Kid, keep the change."

I would usually be sold out of papers by the time I reached the Princess Theater, about six blocks south of Bath House Row. That would be my stop. My wonderful, beautiful, loving mother would be there in the cashier's cage, selling tickets for the show. I would give her a report of my day at school and on the results of my sales. Then I would proceed home and have a romp with my friends.

When school started, I entered the Ramble School. My mother went with me, and we had a conference with the teacher. I had missed the fifth grade, so the teacher advised, and Mother agreed, that it might be best if I took the fifth grade before being promoted to the sixth. This put me a year behind. I never caught up.

During that year, we moved to the Oaklawn area near the race-track, and I entered the Oaklawn School. The principal, Leland Hull, was also one of our teachers. One day, during a recess, we were, as usual, playing sandlot baseball, and a classmate of mine and I got into an argument. We were about to exchange blows, which Professor Hull happened to observe. He stopped the fracas and told us he wanted to see us at the next recess out on the playing field. That afternoon recess slowly rolled around, and we assembled as instructed at the playing field. Professor Hull had a set of boxing gloves, and he assigned each of us a second, who helped us put our gloves on. Putting his arms around each of us, he thereupon pulled us together, gave us brief instructions, and said, "Now, come out fighting." I had never had or seen boxing gloves, and, apparently, neither had my opponent. Anyway, we slugged through three rounds, at the end of which Professor Hull instructed us to remove our gloves and to shake hands. This we did.

After leaving Oaklawn School, I never saw Professor Hull again. He was an excellent teacher and wonderful with children, a tall, strik-ing man, whose left arm, broken near the elbow and never properly set, hung down at an angle. I never saw my boxing opponent again either, but I remember him well. His name was Sidney Perkins, and we were the same age. It was my impression that he had joined the army early during the Second World War, was in the Normandy land-ing, and was wounded during the savage fighting through the hedgerows in France. I would like to have served with him. I know he was a good and courageous fighter.

We then moved to Hazel Street, and I entered Jones School in the sixth grade. We lived there for several years. Pap had rented a build-ing on Ouachita Avenue and opened his own business, known as Mac's Barber Shop.

Since Mother had gone to work as a cashier, first at the Royal and then the Princess Theater, I saw many movies, mostly westerns, but some that told stories about the First World War—*All Quiet on the Western Front* and *What Price Glory?* I would often see the good movies several times.

I saw one picture that told about the use of carrier pigeons dur-ing the First World War, how they would be used to send messages from the front of the battle area to the rear lines. This aroused my interest in pigeons, and I thought it would be great if I could train some to carry messages for the army.

I had trapped quail when I lived on the farm, catching them without hurting them, taking them home and feeding them for a while before turning them loose. Quail would, from time to time, come up to the edge of the woods of the homeplace and call. I never knew if they were the same birds I had trapped, but I would return their calls, as if they were my friends.

There were pigeons roosting on the roof of the Garland County Courthouse, about three blocks from where we lived. I built a trap and set it, using corn as bait, and caught several. They were easy to catch. I selected a half dozen, the ones appearing to be the youngest and strongest. We had a garage in the back of our house, and since we did not have a car, it was used for storage. I gathered some strips of lumber and built a loft, took the pigeons home, put them in the loft, and kept them well fed and watered. I fed them enough so that they would be attracted to home, but not enough to make them so fat that they could not fly for long distances or to slow them down so they could not escape the enemy.

Several months passed, and I concluded that time for training had come. I caught one of the pigeons, put an identifying ring on his leg, and put him in a box that I placed on the handlebars of my bicycle. Then I rode out to the Oaklawn racetrack. Inside the track was a nine-hole golf course—a wide-open area with no buildings or other obstructions—so the pigeon, when released, would be able to climb high, circle, get its bearings, and, hopefully, fly home.

I released one, tossing him up in the air. He circled as I had anticipated, and to my pleasure, he chose the right bearing. I watched him until he was out of sight. I followed this procedure with several others. Each passed the test and flew home, not to the pigeon loft where I was training them to go, but back to the Garland County Courthouse! I lost my interest in pigeons, and, besides, I heard that the army was using radios and was giving up pigeons as message carriers. I could understand why.

As the reader may have noticed, I usually had a dog. On Hazel Street we had a large back yard, which was fenced, so Pap got me an airedale that I named Rex. To keep her company, I got a billy goat, and I named him Billy. On school days I would have to keep Rex penned up, or she would follow me to school or be there when school let out.

But between the school and our house there was a lady who had a big yellow tomcat. If Rex was with me, the big cat, in the sanctuary of his yard, would bristle and bow his back and spit at Rex as we passed. It was all I could do to keep Rex in check, because Rex had a vendetta against cats. In her fights with this ancient enemy, there was no quarter, and Rex was death on all cats. One day when Rex had gotten out of her pen and met me at school, as we walked back home, the big cat was not in his yard. He was stalking a bird in a vacant lot across the street. Rex and the cat must have spotted each other at the same instance, because in a flash, they were at each other, dog and cat, cat and dog, tooth and claw, dog growls and cat screams, all mixed up in one rolling ball across that vacant lot.

Over the noise of the fight, I heard a door slam. I turned around and there was the lady of the house, the owner of the cat, waving a broom in her hand and charging toward me. She didn't appear to be in any mood to reason, so, I skedaddled.

I went home and sat on the porch, waiting apprehensively for my dog. It must not have been very long; it just seemed so. Finally, Rex came limping home—tail between her legs. She walked up to me on the steps, her face bloody and scratched, and she looked at me accusingly, as if to say, "You ran out on me, you bum." With that she turned, crawled under the house, and remained there for a couple of days, coming out only to get a drink of water.

On a Saturday afternoon, not long after the cat fight, Mother had gone to work. I decided not to go to a movie, but to remain home with my friends, Rex and Billy. At some point in the afternoon, I decided to make myself some hot chocolate. I went into the kitchen, leaving Rex and Billy in the backyard; and during the process of my culinary effort of making hot chocolate topped with marshmallows, Rex began scratching at the back door and Billy was bleating. In an effort to please my playmates, I let them both in the kitchen, proceeded to finish making my chocolate with the topping, and began to drink it. Then Rex, Billy, and I went out for some more adventure.

When I returned home, Mother was there. The minute that I

walked into the house, she fixed me with a piercing eye and an accusing question, "Did you let that dog and goat in my house?" I had no defense and no extenuating circumstance. Had I known about it, I probably would have taken the Fifth, but in my innocence, I confessed and took my punishment. Mothers are wise; they know about everything that's going on and have a sixth sense. I could understand my mother being upset, but the thing I wondered about was, how did she know?

It was exciting living in Hot Springs. I could go to a movie every Saturday afternoon and see it two or three times. Before moving there, I had only seen two movies that I could remember. But I missed the woods, the wildlife, the swimming hole, so Mother suggested I join the Boy Scouts. As cashier at the theater, she had seen Scouts from time to time coming in their Scout uniforms, had talked to them, and had gotten some idea as to what their activities were. She knew that they went camping, boating, and took compass marches through the woods. So I joined the Boy Scouts, Troop #3.

I immediately began preparing for the court of honor, where I would take the oath of a Boy Scout. To get ready, I swapped my bicycle for a Scout uniform, so I would be properly dressed for this ceremony. There were a number of boys joining up as Tenderfoot Scouts.

The evening arrived and we assembled in the Garland County circuit courtroom. After what seemed an interminable time, and the awarding of merit badges and promotions to the older Scouts, our names were called, and we moved down, stopping in front of the judge's bench inside the court rail. We were instructed to raise our right hands and take the Scout oath. With great pride and standing as straight as I possibly could, I raised my right hand with my first three fingers joined and extended, and I took the oath: "On my honor I will do my best to do my duty to God and country. To obey the Scouts' laws. To keep myself physically strong, mentally awake and morally straight—."

I never forgot those words, and I remembered them when, two decades later, I stood in the selfsame place within the railings of the court in front of the judge's bench, raised my right hand, and took the oath as prosecuting attorney for the Eighteenth Judicial District, Garland and Montgomery Counties.

In Hot Springs I came under the influence of two truly wonderful people who set my life's course. One was Richard L. Gaffney, captain of the national park police, a ramrod-straight, six-foot Kentuckian. An ardent advocate of physical fitness, the outdoor life, and "the manly art of self-defense," he enrolled me, with a platoon of other Hot Springs boys, in his youth program.

Captain and Mrs. Gaffney had no children. He corralled the boys within reach of his eagle eye—shoeshine boys, paperboys, bookie "gophers"—and placed them under his command as Scoutmaster of Troop #3, Boy Scouts of America. Captain Gaffney had prevailed upon the old Fordyce Bath House to lend its gym for a boys' club. The gym had punching bags, weights, mats, and all the accouterments for body building and instructions in boxing, wrestling, and gymnastics. Whenever any of the "off the street" youngsters would fight, he would make them "put on the gloves."

Famous athletes came to Hot Springs to train, and we could see some of the great fighters of the time—World Welterweight Champion Tommy Freeman and "Manasa Mauler" Jack Dempsey, who came to town with his bride, a famous movie star of the time, Estelle Taylor. Captain Gaffney would take us to see their workouts; seeing Dempsey made me feel like I was living in the capital of the world.

On occasion, after a scouting expedition over West Mountain, or after a vigorous workout in the gym, Captain Gaffney would take a hungry lad home with him to feast upon a specialty of Mrs. Gaffney—Hungarian goulash and fresh-baked sourdough bread.

In addition to being a park ranger and riding herd on Scouts and youthful gladiators of the ring, Captain Gaffney was also the unofficial, self-appointed recruiter for the United States Marine Corps. He supplied me with recruiting posters of marines chasing bandits in Nicaragua, which I used to paper my bedroom walls. These adventurous scenes stirred my youthful heart with a fervent ambition to wear the "Globe and Anchor," to become one of the "First to Fight." He encouraged me and suggested that I go to the Naval Academy. My appointment was to be arranged through Congressman D. D. Glover, a truly great man. All that was left to do to become a member of "the proud, the few" was to pass my written examination. I would, thereupon, be on my way to "the Halls of Montezuma." I could think of little else!

The other person who helped to form and fashion my future was

Miss Lois Alexander, the public speaking teacher at Hot Springs High School. I gravitated to her public speaking course because it appeared to be a lighter course than algebra! I found her to be the greatest—patient, understanding, recognizing and coaxing latent talents in her students, and a strict disciplinarian. She demanded attendance, maximum effort, practice, practice, and still more practice. Since she was in charge of the assembly program for the student body, she arranged programs to provide maximum opportunities for her students to perform before a live, and captive, audience.

One spring morning, Miss Lois informed me that I would participate as a member of a debate team, which would enter the district competition at Ouachita College in Arkadelphia. I allowed as to how I did not choose to participate; she allowed as to how I would "or else." Her "or else" settled the matter. I participated, and my partner was a girl. I don't remember the subject, but we had the affirmative. When we appeared in a large auditorium, filled with people mostly waiting for other events, wonder of wonders, we won second place! Our elation and relief were not marred or dampened by the fact that there were only two teams in the contest.

Thereafter, I was ordered by Miss Lois to enter a declamation contest. My subject was "An All-Embracing Americanism" by former congressman William D. Upshaw. To everyone's surprise, especially my own, I won the state competition.

I was then cast in a one-act play, "The Valiant." We won the state and southwest regional competition and were awarded a silver cup, which may still be found among the glories of Hot Springs High School. We practiced this play so frequently before the student body that, during a speech at a recent class reunion, when I asked how many remembered the final line of "The Valiant," those long-suffering classmates responded in chorus: "Cowards die many times before their death; the valiant ne'er taste of death but once."

But what of my plans to attend Annapolis? "Two roads diverged in a wood." I opted for public speaking and drama over science and mathematics with the inevitable outcome; I flunked my admission examination. And so, for a time, the United States Naval Service was spared my service. They seemed more interested in engineers than actors, for some reason.

After graduation from high school, I spent two terms at Henderson State Teachers College, "a school with a heart" and a great institution. Then I decided to go to law school, and I put on my Boy Scout uniform pack and hitchhiked to Fayetteville. Catching a ride was simple and safe during the depression. I entered pre-law and then law school, attending year-round, summer and winter, until June of 1936.

Still ambitious to be a marine, I signed up with the Reserve Officers' Training Corps at the university, was promoted to cadet captain, and commanded Company B, which won the streamers for excellence. But when I was offered a commission as a second lieutenant in the United States Marines, I faced a stone wall.

In order to obtain my law degree, I had to complete summer school; in order to get my commission in the marines, I had to complete ROTC camp. The law school was in Fayetteville; the training camp was in Fort Leavenworth, Kansas; they ran simultaneously for the first four weeks. What to do? It was decision time again, and I found a way to get through the wall. I signed up for law school, donned my ROTC uniform, hitchhiked to Fort Leavenworth, signed up for camp, and spent one week. I thereupon returned to Fayetteville and spent a week in class; thence, back to Fort Leavenworth for one week, then back to Fayetteville. Continuing this schedule, I completed both summer school and camp. They never missed me at either place.

II⁓ ELAINE BROUGHTON

MR. AND MRS. GARNET BROUGHTON LIVED ON RECTOR AVENUE IN HOT Springs, Arkansas. Back when I was carrying a paper route, I delivered their daily newspaper. Mr. Broughton was superintendent of the Garland County schools. Always eager for news of the day, he often would be sitting on the front porch in his swing, waiting for his newspaper. Being a school superintendent and, before that, a schoolteacher, he was interested in young people. We frequently would visit for a few minutes, and he wanted to know about what I was doing, where I was in school, and if I was passing my grades.

The Broughtons had a daughter with freckles and auburn hair whose nickname was "Speck." Once she was on the front porch with her dad, waiting for the paper, and we visited. It was then that I learned that Speck's name was Elaine.

For some reason, it seemed that Elaine would usually be out on the front porch when I came by, and our visits became longer. Some of my customers complained to the office that their paper was being delivered late; however, it continued to be difficult for me to pull away from a visit with my most favorite customer.

Elaine and I became better acquainted. We saw each other at school, and on Saturdays we would go to a movie, but I never called her "Speck." We both went to Hot Springs High School (I was a senior and she a junior), and we both performed in Miss Lois Alexander's drama and performing arts productions, so we saw each other frequently.

A bundle of energy, a ray of sunshine, Elaine had a bright and happy smile for everyone, her classmates, teachers, strangers. And since she left in her wake a feeling of goodwill as she moved through the halls, it was no surprise that she was elected the most popular girl in school. Although an excellent student, her talents and interests were for the performing arts, especially drama and dramatic reading. She was a born actress.

Elaine and I shared this interest in drama. So, we worked, we practiced, we each listened to the other say our pieces, and we performed before the student body during assembly. Miss Alexander, our teacher, built up our confidence and entered us both in the district meet held at Hendrix College in Conway, and we both won.

The winners in the district meets competed for state honors at the University of Arkansas at Fayetteville, and we each won the state competition. Though Mrs. Broughton (Willie) went to Fayetteville with us, she was a good sport, and Elaine and I had a good time and stored up warm memories that one day would be cherished and held on to.

When Elaine went to Christian College in Columbia, Missouri, I was at the University of Arkansas at Fayetteville. We, of course, wrote lots of letters, and although it was during the depression, and I was working my way through college, I would often splurge on a long-distance telephone call. During her two years there, I went to see her twice. The first time, I hitchhiked and I stayed at the S.A.E. House in Columbia, where I was provided with meals and a room. During her second year at Columbia, I went to see her, driving a Ford Model-T, an old car loaned to me by Uncle Spooks during one of his rare "pass-through" visits. This avuncular gesture made up for his reneging on his promise to me, as a child, to get me a "brass monkey."

In Elaine's junior year she transferred to the University of Arkansas. She was a Chi Omega, and I, an SAE. We went steady and attended all student functions, never missing a dance at the Union Hall on Saturday nights. The band music was great, and certain dances were designated as "tag" dances, so there would always be a line of guys eager to dance with Speck.

A band led by Rex Perkins provided the music for most of the student dances. In addition to directing, Rex was a master on the fiddle, and as the evening progressed, he would demonstrate it. When he judged the mood to be right and the spirits high, on a signal, the couples would stop dancing, gather around the band, and Rex would play his favorite number, "I Played Fiddle for the Czar."

Another activity on campus that I became interested in was student government. My first real venture into politics was when I ran for president of the student body. Campus elections were "big time," and the campaign, although a miniature one, was organized and fought with well-laid plans, vigorously executed. We ran a slate of candidates for the major student body and class offices. One of the candidates on my slate for president of the senior class was Francis Cherry.

McMATH'S STUDENT SENATORS – CAMPUS LAWMAKERS

SIDNEY McMATH
President

LOUIE IBISON
Treasurer

SIDNEY McMATH . . . . . President
FRANCES HOLT . . . . Vice-President
H. L. POOLE . . . . . . Secretary
LOUIE IBISON . . . . . Treasurer

● The Student Senate, representing all classes of the University, has gradually been granted more authority, and has been recognized by the school as a useful unit of the administrative organization.

● All student affairs, social functions, and elections are under the direct supervision of the senate. The president appoints the student members of the Publication Board, Social Committee, and the Vigilance Committee.

● This year McMath and Boatright attended a convention of College representatives from all parts of the nation held in Kansas City.

●

● MEMBERS ●

DAVE BOATRIGHT   JIMMIE ENGLISH
FLOYD OLIVE   IKE POOLE
BILLY RUTH JAMES   LOUIE IBISON
FRANCES HOLT   E. B. WARD
JIMMIE McDANIEL   COLEMAN NOLEN
ANDREW PONDER   BILL MAPES
SIDNEY McMATH

Olive . . . . Poole
. . . Ponder . . .
Mapes . . English
. . McDaniel . .
. . Boatright . .
Ward . . James
. . Holt . . Nolen

Page 36

Sid McMath, candidate for president of student body, with slate

My opponent was "Footsie" Benton, an outstanding Razorback football player, well liked and popular. We made speeches before student groups in the dormitories, fraternities, and boarding houses. We circulated literature and shook hands, probably several times, with all members of the student body, approximately seventeen hundred students, which was little more than an extended family, small compared to today's enrollment of approximately twenty-five thousand.

The election returns came in early. I was elected, and, as I remember, so was our entire slate of candidates. Elaine, who had been one of my most enthusiastic and tireless supporters, was elated over this exciting victory, this team effort, this victory with no runoff, no recount. I, too, was elated, but also exhausted. That is when one is most vulnerable, when one is most apt to let his guard down, lose his good sense, and surrender.

That evening, Helen Hays, the actress, was playing her final performance in Tulsa, Oklahoma. It was not a long drive from Fayetteville, and Russell Burnett, a friend and dramatic arts coach at the university, invited Elaine and me to go with him to see this queen of the dramatic stage. It was a privilege to see Helen Hays live on the stage, and it was a rare and meaningful experience for both Elaine and me. Yet, in going, I made a wrong decision, which I long regretted and which disappointed some of my most ardent supporters and friends.

When we returned to Fayetteville, rather late, waiting for me at Hill Hall was a disappointed and infuriated friend who had worked tirelessly for my election as student body president. Where had I been? Where was I when my devoted followers and friends came by to rehash the election, to relate incidents that had occurred, and to talk about how votes had been won—even from the most ardent of football fans and cheerleaders? Where was I when they came over to celebrate a hard-won victory? Where was my appreciation?

What is so significant about the failure of a candidate to join his fellows in celebrating the winning of a student election? It was most significant. I learned a lesson, one that I should not have had to learn and that should have been instinctive, intuitive. Waging a political campaign is a physical and emotional experience of people joining in a common enterprise to achieve a stated objective. One spends tireless days, restless nights, and the most ardent and faithful supporters do the same. They all become members of a team, a unit, becoming interdependent and bonded, even in a campaign for college office.

True, in the scheme of things, this was a small event, a minor incident in my life. Yet, it demonstrates a profound truth: Never is one more vulnerable to error than immediately following a personal triumph. It was a good lesson—hard to apply to oneself and easy to forget. At least, in all other elections in which I was a candidate, whether won or lost, I was available at our headquarters to celebrate or grieve with my loyal friends, ardent supporters, and members of the team.

My opponent in this election, Footsie Benton, and I became good friends. He was a great football player and an outstanding citizen, and I always had great admiration for him and his family.

In August 1936, when I received a regular commission in the United States Marine Corps as a second lieutenant, my happiness, my anticipation was not as I imagined it would be, because Elaine would not be going with me. A second lieutenant in the Marine Corps, at that time, could not marry until he had been in service for two years. The saying was, "If the Marine Corps wanted you to have a bride, they would issue you one."

Elaine decided to transfer to Ouachita Baptist College in Arkadelphia, Arkansas, which was near her home. Before I reported for duty at Quantico, Virginia, we had quality time together, and Elaine and I became engaged. Little did we know what the future would hold.

III "THE OLD BREED"

M⒴ career in the United States Marine Corps began when I accepted my appointment and took the oath of office August 22, 1936.

On August 28, I reported to the marine barracks, Quantico, Virginia, for duty, joining Company F, Second Battalion, Fifth Marine Brigade, Fleet Marine Force, where I was assigned as a platoon leader. Several other second lieutenants and I were stationed in Quantico, pending our assignment to the Basic School.

During this waiting period, we were placed under the watchful eye of marine gunner William Lee, a decorated veteran, famed in the Corps for his exploits in Nicaragua. In the evenings around the campfire in the combat training area where we were observing small unit maneuvers, Gunner Lee would regale us with past and future exploits of the Corps. He was confident that someday we would go to war against Japan. The gunner was looking forward to this "best of all wars." He had the battle plans all devised, and in a jocular vein, borrowing a line from Attila the Hun, he would conclude his dissertation by proclaiming, "We will make a surprise landing on Tokyo from the air, and 'we will kill all the males, rape the women, and steal the gold.'" Fortunately for the Japanese and unfortunately for this gung-ho marine, the gunner was with the marine detachment in Shanghai on December 7, 1941, was captured by the Japanese, and spent four years in a Japanese prison camp.

I saw Gunner Lee after his release from the Japanese prison. He had been a big man, tall, lean, muscular, possessing exceptional endurance and strength. Even though he appeared to have lost one hundred pounds, he had a gleam in his eye, his spirits were up, his head unbowed—he was still a marine of the "Old Breed."

Having been indoctrinated by the "Old Breed" at Quantico, I was transferred to the Basic School. There I would become acquainted with a Lewis "Chesty" Puller, who had already become a legend in the Marine Corps for his exploits with marine gunner William Lee and other "old-timers" in the "Banana Wars" fought in Haiti and Nicaragua.

Lewis Puller was born in West Point, Virginia, a town of fewer than a thousand people, a community steeped in the history of the Civil War,

Sid McMath, 2nd lieutenant, United States Marine Corps, August 1936

as was the state of Virginia. Puller's grandfather, John W. Puller, had ridden with Jeb Stuart, and both were killed at Kelly's Ford during the closing days of the war. All of Lewis Puller's relatives of military age had fought for the Confederacy, except for one great-uncle, who served with the federal forces at Gettysburg and was never forgiven by the Virginia side of the family for having worn the blue uniform.

Lewis's grandmother, the widow of John W. Puller, had kept the saber and spurs of her deceased husband and had hung them on her living room wall. A patrol of federal soldiers, foraging the countryside, stole the saber and spurs and burned down her house. She soon thereafter died of exposure—this, of course, was never forgotten.

Lewis's mother would talk to him and his friends about the war. A picture of Stonewall Jackson and Robert E. Lee hung in her house. She admonished Lewis and his friends that they should be proud of the Confederacy, the courage of the Confederate soldiers, and the leadership of the Confederate generals. But they should remember that it was a good thing that the United States won the war, because "we could not live as a divided people."

Lewis, when he was seventeen, entered and completed his first year at the Virginia Military Institute. But wanting to get to the First World War before it was over, he enlisted in the Marine Corps and was sent directly to boot camp at Parris Island in South Carolina. Puller was outstanding in every category of boot camp training, and he was selected for the Officers' Training School, where he obtained a commission as second lieutenant. But the war was ending, there was a tremendous cut in military forces, and he was discharged after serving as a marine officer for two weeks.

Hearing that there was a war in Haiti, that there was a demand for people with his training, and that he would get a commission there, Puller signed up with the Haitian Gendarme, saw plenty of action, and learned about jungle warfare, as did so many marine officers. Later, he served in Nicaragua fighting bandits and guerrillas. In Haiti and Nicaragua, Puller was known as "El Tigre"—he had become famous.

Reactivated and promoted as a marine captain in July 1935, Puller became recognized as a highly proficient and experienced combat leader and trainer of marines. In 1936, his services were requested by Col. Hal Turnage, commandant of the Basic School on League Island in Philadelphia, Pennsylvania. When Captain Puller reported for duty, Colonel Turnage's instructions were brief. There would be ninety-four second lieutenants in the 1936 class, all honor graduates from college and university ROTC or midshipmen from the Annapolis Naval Academy. They would get plenty of book work in the classrooms, but he wanted Puller to make field marines out of them. Captain Puller gladly accepted the assignment and the challenge.

I was in that class, which included several future general officers, including Lewis Walt, who became a four-star general, the commander of all marines during his tour duty in Vietnam, and later assistant commandant of the Marine Corps. The class also included Ben Robert Shaw, the Navy's All-American, and Gregory "Pappy" Boyington, the "Ace," who became famous for his flying Black Sheep Squadron, downing Japanese planes at Guadalcanal in the Solomon Islands campaign, after serving with Gen. Claire Chennault's Flying Tigers in China.

Getting us out every morning before daybreak, Puller drilled us with precision. Each student officer, taking his turn as platoon commander, practiced drill and command under the gimlet eye of Capt. "Chesty" Puller. I had completed four citizens' military training camps during the depression, and I had four years of ROTC, during which I had been cadet captain and commander of the honor drill company; hence, I was fairly proficient in the drill and command phase of military training, which Captain Puller noticed.

Puller gave us instructions in the art of jungle warfare with illustrations from his service in Haiti and Nicaragua. To all of us young officers, he emphasized the use of terrain for approach and attack and for maximum use in defense. Terrain was an ally to be used to the maximum extent. Three of these student officers and I would be together again at a future date, applying Captain Puller's instructions, and Colonel Turnage, our Basic School commandant, would be our command officer when these lessons and tactics would be applied for real on the battlefield.

However, planning to go back to practice law and marry my childhood sweetheart, on March 15, 1937, I resigned my regular commission in the Marine Corps. On the day I was packed up and ready to leave, I had a visitor, Capt. Lewis "Chesty" Puller. As we sat down and talked, he asked me about my plans. Then in a few minutes, he arose to leave, walked toward the door, turned, faced me, and erect as if at attention and looking me straight in the eye, he told me his purpose. "I can understand," he said, "your going home to take a bride and follow your trade, but you better take a reserve commission—we are going to wahh." There were no 'r's in war, as Captain Puller, the Virginian, uttered the word war, dragging it out, as if relishing a term that would play a major part in his life.

So with a reserve commission on the way, I returned to Hot Springs, made myself available for clients, and married my bride, Elaine Broughton, May 28, 1937. Puller, who had opposed young officers getting married, holding that they should be "married" to the Corps, proposed to the beautiful Virginia Evans of Virginia, who accepted and married him in 1937. As for me, I had been indoctrinated. I made a firm promise that should the war occur, as anticipated by marine gunner William Lee and foretold by Capt. "Chesty" Puller, I would return to the Corps.

IV⫷ MY HOMETOWN

HOT SPRINGS WAS A NATIONAL HEALTH RESORT WHERE PEOPLE CAME TO bathe in the magic waters. Elderly people came to seek rejuvenation in the "fountain of youth." But the spa city also offered a ninety-day divorce law that lured many "quickie" divorcees to Hot Springs to escape marital thralldom and taste the fruits of their newly found freedom.

In addition, Hot Springs was a sporting town, a wide-open gambling mecca. The elite of the underworld wintered in "Hot Town." They came with their entourage of gangsters and gals and "bag carriers." Rival gangs, like the Indian tribes of old, would "bury the hatchet" for an interlude. In this sanctuary, they would relax and, unmolested and undisturbed, divide hunting territories and plan future raids and forages against a tolerant society.

Law practice in Hot Springs consisted chiefly of divorces, wills, estates, and criminal cases. My office was not exactly running over with clients, but during this brief affair with the law, three cases—or almost three cases—impacted upon my memory.

My first criminal case (court appointed) was to defend a young man, nineteen years old, charged with burglary. He allegedly had broken into a home and stolen a ring valued at thirty dollars. We proved that, at the time of the alleged crime, the defendant was visiting his auntie at a location far removed from the scene of the crime. The verdict was "not guilty"; I had won my first case.

Thus encouraged, I thereafter frequented the circuit court on arraignment day, with a fond expectation of being assigned as defense counsel in a criminal case and becoming a great criminal lawyer. One morning, when the docket was moving at a leisurely pace at the convenience of the judge and the court entourage (which held office in perpetuity), an elderly gentleman was called to answer for a charge of murder in the first degree. My attention was immediately riveted. The accused approached the bench, and the judge explained the charge and asked him how he pled. He responded, "Not guilty, Your Honor. I ain't killed nobody."

The proceeding continued:

JUDGE: If you plead "not guilty" and have to stand trial, you could get life imprisonment or the chair. The prosecuting attorney has recommended that, if you plead guilty and save the county the expense of having to conduct a trial, the charge will be reduced to manslaughter and his recommendation will be five years.

DEFENDANT: Judge, I ain't killed nobody.

JUDGE: Do you have a lawyer?

DEFENDANT: No, suh, I ain't got no lawyer.

(Whereupon the judge signaled for me to approach the bench and announced to the defendant that I would be his lawyer.)

DEFENDANT: Judge, you say this is my lawyer?

JUDGE: Yes, Mr. McMath is a graduate of the University of Arkansas Law School at Fayetteville. He'll do a good job for you.

DEFENDANT: Judge . . . (pausing for a moment and looking from the judge to me and back to the judge and scratching his gray head) . . . I been studyin' 'bout dis. I think I jes' pleads guilty.

No doubt many other similar incidents have occurred in cases where the judge appointed a young lawyer, newly admitted to the bar, as defense counsel.

The third case that I remember, from this time, was the case of Cornelius Wren, whose days were ending at the army-navy hospital. He was a retired gunnery sergeant who came from Ireland at eighteen and joined the Marine Corps, saved his money, made wise investments, and accumulated a modest fortune. He had a terminal degenerative brain disease. Having heard that I was a fellow marine, he called me, as he wanted to make his last will and testament.

Sergeant Wren was unmarried, but he had nephews and nieces in Ireland. However, he wanted his estate to go to a friend, a lady living in Hot Springs, who was an immigrant from Eastern Europe with three girls. This family had taken Sergeant Wren into their home and became to him the family he had never had. He felt toward the young girls as if they were his own daughters. How could he reciprocate this family's loving care? It was a reasonable assumption that, due to the nature of the malady that was taking his life and since his friend and her children were not related by blood or marriage, there would be an immediate objection to his request. But as I talked further with

Sergeant Wren, I discovered that he was a Catholic and that he supported and was in good standing with the Catholic Church. When well, he attended Mass; when ill, the parish priest visited him. So it was my thought that Sergeant Wren could consider naming both the Catholic Church and his friend as beneficiaries. This was done, and a priest and a nurse were witnesses to his will.

As anticipated, upon his death and as soon as the word reached Ireland following the filing of the will for probate, the distant nieces and nephews contested it on the grounds that Cornelius Wren did not appreciate the nature and consequences of his benevolent disposition of his savings. However, the validity of his will was upheld by the court. The wish of this generous Irish heart was fulfilled, and this lady and her daughters, objects of Sergeant Wren's bounty, were most grateful for this unexpected inheritance.

One-half century later a lady came to my office and asked my secretary if she could see me, stating that it was important and would take only a few minutes. Of course, I would see her. She was alone, obviously dressed for traveling, and as I guided her to a chair, in a soft voice and with a genial smile, she thanked me for seeing her and apologized for not having made an appointment. She told me that she was living in California and driving across country and that she had selected Arkansas in mapping her route, with hope that she would have an opportunity to see me.

Then she promptly identified herself as the youngest daughter of the lady whom Sgt. Cornelius Wren had befriended some fifty years ago. The sergeant's kindness had provided for her mother, her sisters, and herself. Using the funds wisely, all three of the girls had received an education and were successfully and happily married. She also told me that she had a son who was in the service.

All she wanted to do that day was to thank me for helping them at a crucial time in the life of their family. To know that his adopted family had thrived and done well would have made Sergeant Wren a happy man indeed, as it had made me.

V⁓ THE PULL OF THE CORPS

IN AUGUST OF 1940, THE WAR ANTICIPATED BY GUNNER LEE AND foretold by Captain Puller was imminent. Keeping the promise that I had made, I left my law practice, my bride, and our new home we had built on Vermel Street in Hot Springs and returned to the marines. I was assigned to the Third Reserve Officers Training Corps, Marine Corps Schools, Quantico, Virginia.

Elaine, her brother, Dr. Cecil Broughton, and his wife, Verna, drove us to Quantico and dropped me off at the marine barracks. We had said our good-byes, and indelible in my memory is the scene of them driving away. Elaine was in the back seat, half-turned and looking through the car's rear window. She was crying—she did not wave.

After completing the course second in my class, I was retained at the schools as an instructor for officer candidates, serving also as platoon commander and, after being promoted to captain, as company commander.

The officer candidates being trained were college graduates, outstanding students, athletes, leaders, and volunteers who would become platoon leaders and company commanders. Several remained in the Marine Corps after the war and became generals; one became commandant of the Marine Corps. Some would go into politics and reach high office; others would enter the field of law and become justices.

My wife, Elaine, joined me in November 1940. No quarters were available on base, so we lived first in Fredericksburg, Virginia, where a gracious Southern lady rented us a room in her lovely antebellum home. However, soon we were able to obtain quarters closer to base at Dumphries—a bare apartment, sparsely furnished. Elaine scrubbed and decorated, sewed curtains for the windows, and made it our home.

We next obtained an upstairs apartment of one room with a stove and a bath, next to the railway station in the town of Quantico. Freight trains rolled and rocked the room all hours of the night, hauling the makings and machines and weapons of war. Soon we became so used to the trains that only the quiet would disturb us. We were happy. I had only to walk across the railroad track to the assembly area where the officer candidates fell out and formed up in the early, early dawn, "eager for the adventures of the day."

Sid and his wife, Elaine, in Hot Springs, Arkansas, 1940

Mrs. Betty Youngblood of Shreveport, Louisiana, was my mother's sister and the member of the Sanders family who kept everybody informed as to what was going on in the family. She wrote to us when we were in Quantico in a letter that was dated November 15, 1940.

Elaine responded immediately to Betty's letter:

Dear Betty:

Sid and I were so pleased to hear from you and I am answering immediately to prove it.

Yes, we like our new life very much. We have considerable time for leisure and Sid and I are taking advantage of it. He completed his course Friday, graduating at 11:00 A.M. Sid has made an excellent record and is being held over as an instructor. We will remain here for six months, perhaps nine.

We attended memorial services at Arlington. We got to see President Roosevelt. We expect to get home for Christmas. We are keeping our fingers crossed.

My parents are looking after our home on Vermel Street. They are doing a wonderful job and it is consoling to us to have them there looking after things.

Thanks again for your wonderful letter. Please give my love to all members of the family.

Love,
Elaine

Clyde and Rosalee Brown were dear friends of ours. Clyde and I were practicing law together, before I returned to the service in August 1940. On January 17, Elaine wrote to Rosalee, giving her the good news:

Dear Rosalee,

I can't begin to tell you how very much we both enjoyed your newsy letter. It pepped me up to no end and gave me that feeling I was really missed a little during the yuletide by at least one person.

The most exciting scoop which I can give for the year 1941 is this, on or about August the 28th the McMaths are expecting a junior partner in the Brown McMath Law Firm. Rosie, I am thrilled beyond words and so is Sid. You must prepare yourself to be called Aunt Rosie, and of course, Uncle Clyde will respond, I am sure.

Sid, in his way, is excited and what he lacks I make up for—of course, it wasn't planned and the surprise adds all the more to the excitement. Well, enough for the maternity department.

Clyde wrote to Sid telling him of his plans to be in Washington on or about February 1st. The January graduation is the 20th and Sid's men are to take part in the ceremony. Rosie, why don't you and Clyde come up in time for that and stay with us? We will have plenty of room. Studio couch and Uncle Sam's got lots of food. *Please think it over and do come*—We could have great fun. Answer me soon cause I love to hear from you.

Love to you both,
Elaine

The Browns were unable to visit, but our expectation of another arrival kept us occupied. Sandy was born August 22, 1941. When I received the word, I was on the firing range, shooting for record, and I became so excited that I failed to qualify as an expert, earning only the marksman's badge. That was the last time I had an opportunity to fire for record, so I never received my expert badge. I picked up my brass off the firing line, turned my rifle over to a friend to clean, and proceeded to the hospital posthaste to check on my wife and my son. He was six days early. He's been in a hurry ever since.

Our son was healthy and hardy. We named him Sidney Sandy, not Sidney Sanders, because we didn't want him to be called Junior. For the next nine months, Sandy and his mother bonded and had a warm relationship. Then on May 28, 1942, our fifth wedding anniversary, Elaine died of nephritis, a kidney infection, which at that time was apparently incurable. She, too, was a casualty of war; like so many, she gave up her home, her child, and her life for her country.

Elaine's funeral service was held at the Central Methodist Church in Hot Springs where she had taught Sunday School and that class had been named in her honor. Dr. Homer T. Fort, pastor of the First Methodist Church, in eulogizing Elaine, told a packed church, "Mrs. McMath is leaving upon this church an impression that can never be erased. Her anxiousness about others, her loyalty to her Christ stamps her as a true Christian. We marvel at the influence that she has had on this church."

Elaine had graduated from Christian College in Columbia,

Missouri, which was a two-year college. At the University of Arkansas at Fayetteville, she had been a member of the Chi Omega sorority and the Black Friars' Dramatic Club, and she had been elected regimental sponsor of the university's Reserve Officers' Training Corps. The B.A. degree she had received was from Ouachita Baptist University.

Before joining me in Quantico, Virginia, Elaine was president of the Hot Springs branch of the American Association of University Women and was on the board of directors of the YWCA. She taught a woman's bible class that was named Cress Math in her honor; the members of her class composed the choir for her funeral service. Elaine was teaching an eighth-grade English class before she joined me for active duty. She loved to teach; she related to young people, inspired them, motivated them. Her aspiration was to teach English literature and dramatic art. She would have been the greatest.

Our eighteen months at Quantico, despite the pressures and tensions of preparing for war, were good days, happy days, the best years of our married life, and are precious in my memory.

Sandy was left in the care of his grandparents. I returned to duty.

But I needed a change; I requested transfer overseas. After my third written request for transfer to a combat unit, Col. Lemuel Shepherd, school commander (a graduate of VMI, a future four-star general, and commandant of the Marine Corps), summoned me to his office. His orders were brief: "Pack your gear and get on the next available transportation for Camp Lejeune, New River, North Carolina. There you will join the Third Marine Regiment that is preparing for service in the Southwest Pacific." I was already packed and didn't miss the truck.

The Third Marine Regiment (called the Third Marines) was commanded by Col. Oscar R. Caldwell, who, the following year, was promoted to brigadier general and served as assistant division commander of the Third Marine Division. As the Third Marine Regiment was formed up, beginning in June 1942, it consisted of the First, Second, and Third Infantry Battalions, a Heavy Weapons Company, and a Headquarters Company. Recruits were fed into the regiment from the marine boot camp in Parris Island, South Carolina, while regular officers and noncommissioned officers were assigned from naval ships, posts, and stations.

Three of these officers assigned, I had known in Basic School where we, as I have indicated, had been "oriented" into the Corps by Capt. Lewis "Chesty" Puller. These officers were Lt. Col. Leonard "Spike" Mason, commander, First Battalion; Maj. Ed Hamilton, executive officer, Third Battalion; and Capt. Gordon Warner, company commander, First Battalion. Warner had an additional capability, a very rare advantage in this war, of speaking Japanese.

Reserve officers with excellent military backgrounds and high professional attainments joined up. One was Bert Simpson, an executive officer with Bell Telephone Company, and another John Monks, a graduate of the Virginia Military Institute, about which he had written a play and a novel titled *Brother Rat*. John Monks later wrote *A Ribbon and a Star*, a history about the Bougainville campaign; he was also a movie director.

There were also several officers, veterans of the First World War, who had served in France and had outfought and out-toughed the seasoned and bloodied German soldiers, "the Huns," at the Battles of the Argonne, Belleau Woods, and St. Mihiel. These "old-breed" marines could not resist another call to the colors.

The regiment did not reach full strength until after we were transferred to Samoa. However, from the beginning, we had a nucleus of people with the skills and backgrounds needed to build a fighting regiment, which we did. The base at New River, North Carolina, was ideal for the basic individual training of fire teams, squads, and platoons for the kind of war which we were expecting. The beaches there could be used for amphibious landings, and the terrain, partially swamps and marshes, was sufficiently formidable for our purpose.

Since I had been serving for approximately two years as instructor at the Marine Corps Schools, Quantico, training officer candidates, I had hoped that at Camp Lejeune, I would be given a company I could form up, train, and lead. However, my hopes were thwarted, and I was assigned as operations and training officer for the regiment—a staff position.

Training at Camp Lejeune began from scratch: physical conditioning; skill in the care, cleaning, and use of all infantry weapons;

Marine Corps Officer Candidate Class, Quantico, Virginia, 1941

map reading; compass marches; fire teams; squad and platoon tactics; health and hygiene; how to survive in a hostile environment; character and tactics of the Japanese soldier; the preparation of small unit defensive positions, the digging of foxholes and connecting trenches, and how to build and camouflage machine gun emplacements that were designed to provide mutually protective, supporting fire; terrain appreciation, how to use the ground for an attack and how to best organize the defense against a counterattack.

In August 1942, the regiment received orders to move by train to San Diego and ship out to an undisclosed destination. En route, the troop train was scheduled to take on water in North Little Rock, Arkansas. Colonel Caldwell graciously allowed me to wire my mother and Elaine's mother (who were jointly taking care of Sandy) to meet me at the watering station. The train was on time, and I experienced a memorable fifteen-minute reunion with my son. Then I was off to war, and not knowing when I would return, I could only trust that we would be together and he would know me as his dad.

Traveling across the country, the trip was uneventful, but the troop train was crowded and there was a continuous "chow line" in order to feed the troops. We were savoring the day, as we were told, when we would be aboard a ship and have sumptuous meals, prepared by navy cooks and served by white-jacketed mess men, and be eating on tables covered with white linen tablecloths—so they said.

We arrived in San Diego, our port of debarkation, went aboard ship, were assigned compartments and bunks, then showered and shaved. We lucky ones, having no logistical duties such as loading the ship, went ashore. Knowing that this would be our last liberty for a while, we pooled our resources and rented a suite atop the Grant Hotel. From that vantage point, with field glasses, we could observe our ship, and having informed the officer of the deck as to where we were, we surveyed our surroundings and made the best of the time available.

We saw two shows; one was memorable—*Porgy and Bess.* The music and lyrics lingered in my mind on nights when there was nothing to do but listen—and watch. And listening, I could hear:

"I got plenty of nothin'
And nothin' is plenty for me."

We embarked on our ship, the USS *Matsonia,* a converted cruise ship. As I recall, we were escorted out to sea by two destroyers. Soon our escort departed, and we watched them as they disappeared over the vast horizon of the sea, returning to the lights of San Diego.

I say we were unescorted. This was August 1942, and our navy was otherwise occupied. We did not know it then, but a young officer on Admiral Nimitz's staff had broken the Japanese code, so our navy had the advantage of knowing the general disposition of the Japanese fleet (as at the Battle of Midway). Sadly, we had not had such knowledge of the movement of the Japanese fleet on December 7, 1941.

Although a little uneasy about going it alone, we were assured that our converted passenger liner could travel faster than a Japanese submarine and that in the Pacific Ocean a lone ship was hard to find. So off we went on an extended cruise, at Uncle Sam's expense, to strategic islands in the Southwest Pacific.

VI⌒ AMERICAN SAMOA

AMERICAN SAMOA IS 2,200 MILES SOUTHWEST OF THE HAWAIIAN ISLANDS, 1,600 miles northeast of New Zealand, 2,770 miles east of Australia, and is not one island but six. Tutuila, the largest, is the site of the capital, Pago Pago, where there is a deepwater seaport.

American Samoa, an American possession and a strategic United States naval base, is tropical, and its beachheads are rugged, not conducive to amphibious operations or landing by boat as the land is rocky and of volcanic origin. There is little level land, except on Tutuila where there is a broad fertile plain with a number of coconut groves on the southwest part of the island. Tutuila also has high inland ridges, rising to peaks of six thousand feet, and from the coastline to the high ground is mostly jungle.

The people of Samoa are Polynesian, related to the natives of the Hawaiian Islands, and are very much like their cousins in their skill in navigating the vast Pacific Ocean. How they acquired this ability is one of humanity's great mysteries. Despite the influence of the United States, the Samoan people have retained their culture and their language, which is believed to be the oldest form of Polynesian speech.

Western Samoa, which consists of nine islands, during the Second World War was under a protectorate of New Zealand, with Apia, its capital. Since the beaches of Western Samoa are more suitable for landing operations, New Zealand permitted the marines to use these islands for our landing and training exercises.

Because of their strategic significance, the Samoan Islands were occupied and defended by American forces during the war. The islands' position in the south-central Pacific made them ideal for a staging area, and the jungle terrain was most suitable for preparing our marines for warfare against the Japanese.

When the Third Regiment shipped from San Diego, it was diverted to American Samoa to defend the islands against the Japanese southern advance, which seemed in those dark days to be inevitable. However, the only attack we experienced was from a submarine that surfaced in the Pago Pago harbor and shelled the town. Ironically, the

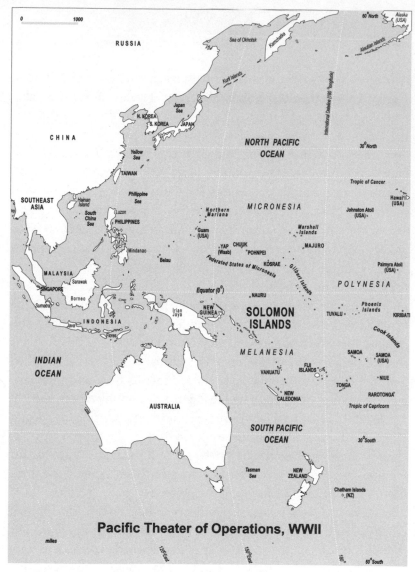

Map of the Western Pacific.

Major Sid McMath, commander of Jungle Warfare School, American Samoa

only damage was to a general merchandise store owned by a Mr. Shimaskake, a Japanese merchant!

On landing in Pago Pago, I had expected duty as a company commander, but during unloading, I was informed that I would command the Jungle Warfare School, Mormon Valley, to train junior and noncommissioned officers.

This school was vital to our mission, as warfare in any environment, on any type of terrain, is confusion, but jungle warfare is especially so. The lack of adequate communication and the absence of clear visibility through vines, trees, and jungle growth adds to this confusion. The smallest military units—the fire team, the squad, the platoon—often do not know what is happening in higher echelons of command and must be capable of operating independently. Hence, success is therefore dependent upon the training and condition of small unit commanders—junior officers and noncommissioned officers. We took full advantage of this time, the terrain, and the isolation to train our full-strength regiment for a jungle war against the veteran Japanese army.

I ran this school in Mormon Valley for eight months. Our first objective was to teach, or review, the use of all basic infantry weapons. The students had to fire, clean, and apply them appropriately according to the tactical use required.

The next phase of training was in communications: how to maintain contact within one's own and with adjacent units and how to maintain direction, read a map, stay on course, and arrive on time at a predetermined point. Timely arrival at an assembly area, or the line of departure for an assault on an enemy position, could be the difference between success and defeat—life or death. Communications and coordination are most difficult when moving through the jungle, and the struggle with it was as demanding as it was with the enemy. So the jungles of Samoa were ideal for training our squads, platoons, and companies. Scouting and patrolling was emphasized for the small units and reconnaissance in force for companies.

These tactics of small units, up to and including companies, were taught in the classroom and applied in the field. Many of our tactical exercises were conducted at night, moving to a predetermined line for launching a dawn attack. Our emphasis was placed upon the need of every marine to be informed of the overall mission and to understand that his job was essential. As long as everyone understands the combat mission, the loss of a leader need not be critical—the next in line can assume command.

It rained most of the time. Not only was the jungle growth thick, it was infested with carnivorous mosquitoes, ever present, and drawing blood. It seemed that whenever a patrol entered the jungle that word would be spread far and wide to mosquitoes of all species and genders, and they would swarm and form up for a feast on the tender Americans.

After the completion of an all-night problem, we would assemble in the mess hall for a hot meal, hot coffee, and a critique. On one such occasion, Lt. John Monks (the writer whom I mentioned earlier) gave me a report on another student, Lt. Johnny O'Neal. As their patrol had been moving most of the night, fighting mosquitoes, and being soaked by rain, Lieutenant O'Neal had lain down on his back, his face exposed to pouring rain, and asked the question on the minds of all the students, "What in the hell am I doing here?" I certainly understood. I had plenty of occasions to ask myself that question.

John Monks related this incident to me half seriously and half in jest and added with a twinkle in his eye, "Major, we really don't have to train to be miserable." He had a point, but the training and conditioning of these troop leaders—junior and noncommissioned officers—would prepare and motivate these men with the skill and know-how to instruct their people, their squads and platoons, so that in combat when the chips were down—as they would be shortly—every marine would do his job.

We received word that the Third Marine Regiment would soon be going to New Zealand to join the Third Marine Division. This news was welcome and exciting, and hopefully true. The marines could use some rest and recreation, and our regiment needed to marry up with the division.

I was moved from the school back to regimental headquarters as operations and training officer. The battalions had been training on their level, but we had not had a regimental problem. As operations officer, I, therefore, planned two regimental exercises. The first was in Western Samoa, where we made a simulated landing at Apia, two battalions abreast, the third battalion in reserve, each battalion having a tank platoon and a battery of artillery attached, until a beachhead could be secured.

Our mission was to seize the high ground on the island, and when we reached our objective, we had a view of both the island and its beaches—breathtaking scenery. We came upon the home of Robert Louis Stevenson, where he had found refuge during the last years of his life. From this vantage point, we could see ocean, beaches, and a view of the surrounding islands. The house was well preserved but appeared lonely and forlorn; adjacent to the house was a well-cared-for plot of ground, his grave. The tombstone bore an epitaph from one of Stevenson's greatest poems and my favorite:

> Under the wide and starry sky
>
> Dig the grave and let me lie
>
> Glad that I lived and gladly die
>
> And I laid me down with a will
>
> This be the verse you gave for me
>
> Here he lies where he longed to be
>
> Home is the sailor
>
> Home from the sea
>
> Home is the hunter home from the hill.

I was arrested by the place and stood alone for a few minutes, contemplating the life of this sensitive soul and musing on the circumstances that had brought me to this place. Here was I, halfway around the world, standing at the grave of one of the great writers of all time. He lifted the spirits, entertained, enlightened, and delighted millions of readers, young and old. I had read *Dr. Jekyll and Mr. Hyde,* about how evil in a man, given full rein and unchecked, consumes that life; *Treasure Island,* read and reread by the youth of my generation, reenacted on sandlot and stage, had incited my dreams of adventure yet also demonstrated where man's motives may lead.

Waking from my reverie, I turned, and in walking back down the mountainside to my duty post, I experienced a kind of elation—a splash of relief. This creative and imaginative writer who had brought happiness to so many generations, in search of health and relief from the world, had sailed the seas and found his place—a dot in the vast Pacific Ocean, an isolated and beautiful island inhabited by a beautiful people. There he lay "where he longed to be," in secure lodging, a holy place, where he found peace and rest at last.

But there was little time for contemplation—duty called. I returned to the work of the next regimental exercise to be carried out on American Samoa. The training objective was to attack an entrenched enemy position, consisting of small cannon and machine-gun emplacements in log bunkers, protected by bags of sand and camouflage. The machine guns were locked in, so as to provide mutually supporting fire, and enemy soldiers were dug in along the ridge line, likewise in mutually supporting foxholes. It was simulated that an enemy force, a two-day march away, was moving up to reinforce their position.

Our plan was to make a forced march at night, arriving at a pre-determined position for a coordinated dawn attack. We had two battalions in assault and one battalion in reserve. Moving through the jungle, there would be periodic halts at specified intervals in order to maintain contact and communications. At a time designated, the assault battalions and the heavy weapons company would lay down a barrage of fire. At a prescribed moment, the supporting fire would be lifted, and the reserve battalions, led by a platoon of tanks, would attack the enemy's left flank and rear.

The exercise started as planned. The movement of the regiment through the jungle to the position of attack demonstrated remarkable training and discipline. The preplanned barrage opened up and was lifted on time, except mortar fire from the heavy weapons platoon continued, threatening our tanks. We could see the tanks moving against the enemy flank, with mortar shells falling in their line of approach, alarmingly close and with near misses. The mortar platoon was on a reverse slope, about one hundred yards from our regimental command post, and we had no direct communications with them and no time to go through channels. I made a record dash, running and sliding down the hillside, yelling with every breath as loud as I could, "Cease fire! Cease fire!" Fortunately, the platoon leader saw and heard me coming, and the firing stopped. The tanks and the assault battalions completed their mission, and the objective was seized.

Then the assault battalions, Second and Third, began immediately preparing a defensive position, setting up an outpost line of resistance and sending out patrols. The First Battalion remained in reserve in supporting distance of the two forward battalions, and the regimental headquarters was set up forward and central to the three battalion headquarters. Once the machine guns were set up and heavy weapons zeroed in on the enemy's most likely avenue of advance, the problem was secure. Colonel Caldwell, regimental commander, was well pleased, which in turn, of course, pleased me.

For a time, I had nightmares about this close call. Nothing is so heartbreaking and devastating to morale than to injure or kill our own people. Sadly, tragically, it happens in the confusion and darkness of combat—what is known today as casualty by "friendly fire."

Mortar shells come in on a curved trajectory and are frequently used on infalated or area targets. However, in the jungle where lines or positions may not be clearly marked and troop positions are fluid or changing, there is an increased risk of mortar shells not hitting the target and falling on our own people. Artillery presents a similar hazard, as do all supporting arms.

The execution of this regimental exercise—moving the entire regiment of approximately twenty-five hundred marines through the jungle at night, maintaining contact, and launching a coordinated dawn attack—represented the culmination of the intensive training of all units, officers, and noncommissioned officers, during the previous eight months' occupation of American soil.

This training would enable our Third Marines to be decisive in the accomplishment of a marine mission at another, not too distant, time and place.

VII IN THE MOOD

THE TROOP SHIP THAT WOULD TRANSPORT US TO NEW ZEALAND WAS standing by. We would ship out the next morning, June 3, 1943, and we were all anticipating this adventure, at least a temporary release from the jungle, the rains, and the mosquitoes.

Steaks and potatoes, pork chops and rice, mutton with layers of freshly cooked vegetables, bacon and eggs and grits, bright lights and dance music—with these fantasies dancing in my head—I could not sleep. It was a beautiful, moonlit night. I dressed, strolled to my jeep, drove slowly down a shoreline road and pulled up on the beach, stopping next to one of nature's world wonders, a huge rock in the sand, washed by eons of incoming waves at high tide. Over a thousand centuries the waves had bored a hole through the center of this volcanic formation in the form of a chimney. This wonder would occur when high tide rolled these great waves ashore. At regular intervals the incoming tide, with the weight of eternity, would beat against this rock forcing water through the opening into the air, spouting like the geyser "Old Faithful" at Yellowstone National Park. The sea blowing through this outlet, spraying salt water into the air, would give forth a roar like a primeval beast in distress, serving notice to man that nature was still in control of this world.

Sitting there, wrapped in thought, reveling in the beauty of the night, I imagined I heard music. I listened attentively; it was music; it was a band. I dismounted from my jeep and walked toward this inviting sound. Presently, I came across a scene of revelry: the marines, sailors, and Seabees in Pago Pago were having a dance. They had built a recreation hut—I am sure with the help of the natives—with a thatched roof and a solid floor. There was a band recruited from the ranks, and the Samoan girls, beautifully attired in Western dress, looked and danced like debutantes. I observed but briefly, not wishing to intrude on this evening of gaiety. Most would be shipping out the next morning. This momentary release from war would be a memory these American boys could call up at a darker hour—some of whom would never see home again.

I returned to my jeep, and listening, sat for a few more minutes, while the band played Glenn Miller's "In the Mood," savoring the music as it mingled with the sound of the surf and the sea.

VIII⸏ NEW ZEALAND

In September 1943, the Third Marine Regiment joined the Third Division in New Zealand. The approach to New Zealand from the sea, along the coastline through the fjords, was one of the most spectacular views I have ever seen.

New Zealand had entered the Second World War in 1939, in support of the British—as they had in all the wars that the Empire had fought.

In the First World War the New Zealand soldiers had earned the nickname of "Diggers"—representatives of the strength, the endurance, the indomitable courage of their people.

In that war, the French and the British were bogged down in protracted trench warfare where a whole generation of young men was lost. In an effort to stop the annihilation, where everyone bled over a few acres of ground, Winston Churchill, First Lord of the Admiralty, conceived the idea of moving from this stalemate to a war of movement and maneuver. Churchill's strategy was to threaten the underbelly of the German army by opening up a second front in the Crimea.

The initial action of Churchill's strategic design would be a landing with an amphibious force at Gallipoli, Turkey. To get troops ashore, establish a beachhead, and carry the war to Turkey, Germany's ally, would compel the Germans to withdraw troops from the Western front. Churchill's strategy was accepted by the generals of the British army and the admirals of the Royal Navy.

The "Diggers" and the "Aussies" (Australians), under the command of British generals, were committed for this purpose.

In principle the concept was sound, in execution it was murder, and the Aussies and the Diggers were the ones who were slaughtered.

The British had not developed an amphibious capability that would enable them to land troops, establish and hold a beachhead, and use the beachhead as a base for further advance. As a result, when the British forces arrived, they were too long delayed in landing, giving the Turks ample time to discover their enemy's objective and to man, entrench, and fortify the heights of Gallipoli. Finally landing, the troops were ordered, using only rifles and bayonets, to take the high ground that was being defended by alerted and determined Turkish soldiers, laying down a barrage of cannon, machine-gun, and rifle fire with resulting carnage. This loss and usage of their young men threatened a cleavage between Great Britain and their most loyal and ardent cousins in New Zealand and Australia.

The one bright spot for the people of New Zealand during the First World War was their capture of Western Samoa, which they held until the people on the island gained their independence on January 1, 1962.

During the Second World War, the Diggers, with the Aussies, fought under the command of General Montgomery, saving Egypt and the Suez Canal from the Germans, but the Diggers were not returned home until after the war.

American sailors, soldiers, and marines were in New Zealand during the entire Second World War, and the people of New Zealand looked to the United States to defend them against what appeared to be an impending invasion by the Japanese. The victory of the American Fleet at the Battle of the Coral Sea and the securing of the Solomon Islands gave the New Zealand people their first confident feeling of security they had had since the beginning of the war. Like everyone in the Pacific, they were deathly afraid of the Japanese.

Likewise, following the Second World War, both Australia and New Zealand looked to and leaned upon the United States for security against another impending threat—world Communism. Australian and New Zealand soldiers fought alongside Americans in defending the Republic of South Korea against Communist invasion. A mutual defense agreement between Australia, New Zealand, and the United States, known as the ANZUS Pact, was signed on September 8, 1954, and further binding the tie among the three countries was the formation of the Southeast Asia Treaty Organization (SEATO), composed of nations in Southeast Asia whose independence was threatened by the Communist advance. The decision of the United States to defend South Vietnam against the Communists was influenced by the SEATO agreement, and both Australia and New Zealand, honoring their commitments, joined the United States in the support of that small country.

In 1943, during our short sojourn in New Zealand, although time was spent getting guns and gear in battle condition, emphasis was placed upon the morale and health of the troops. The colder weather and the change to our winter green uniforms were invigorating. In this most hospitable land, the marines were welcomed by the New Zealand people and invited into their homes. I found a home away from home in the Masonic Temple, or occasionally a cozy pub, or a USO reception where the "American Swing" was the vogue.

IX ◈ GUADALCANAL—
THE SOLOMON ISLANDS

IN THE MEANTIME, THE MARINES ON GUADALCANAL (WHERE WE HAD assumed the Third Regiment was being sent when we left the United States, until diverted to defend Samoa) were not faring so well. Guadalcanal was the first commitment of American ground troops to offensive combat in the Second World War. This island was a crucial link in Japan's advance toward Australia and New Zealand.

The First Marine Division landed there on August 7, 1942. The initial landing was unopposed, but the Japanese, recognizing the strategic significance of the American's assault, immediately committed all naval and ground forces in the area in an effort to throw the marines back into the sea.

For a time, survival of the marines on Guadalcanal was in grave doubt. On August 10, 1942, under cover of darkness, Japanese war ships and submarines launched a surprise attack on our naval forces. Devastating salvos struck five cruisers, sinking the *Astoria,* the *Quincy,* the *Canberra,* and the *Vincennes,* one destroyer and damaging the cruiser Chicago, with 1,024 seamen lost. This tragic defeat lasted only forty-six minutes.

Apparently, the Japanese admiral did not fully appreciate the extent of his victory. As the marine troop transports and cargo ships were in the process of unloading, they were sitting ducks, defenseless. At that defining moment, the Japanese could have eliminated this amphibious force and prolonged the war, but the Japanese admiral chose to withdraw. However, the navy transports and cargo ships were ordered to weigh anchor and pull out, and the United States naval force in the area was also withdrawn. The marines of the First Division were left without the supporting troops and the cargo that remained on the departing transport ships.

The Japanese now had control of the air and sea, and their land forces outnumbered the marines by 10 to 1. These marines had to reach down deep into the traditions of the Corps—courage, faith, and tenacity—in order to survive and to conquer. American fighting forces, historically, when confronted with an apparently hopeless

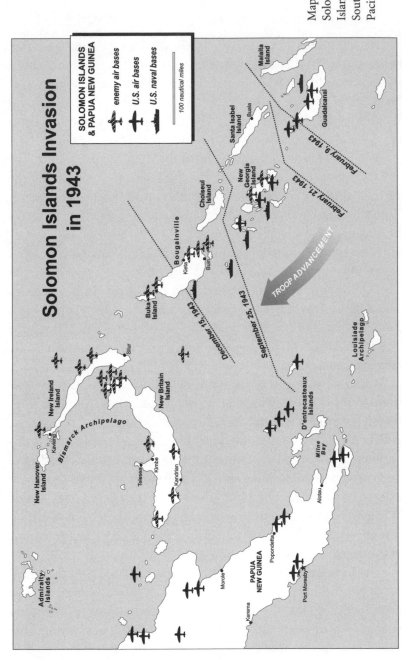

Map of Solomon Islands, Southwest Pacific

adversity, have maintained their optimism and found something in their situation ironically laughable.

The Americans on Guadalcanal never lost their confidence or composure. This was illustrated by the reaction of a marine private on receiving a letter from his hometown. Come what may, Uncle Sam somehow managed to deliver the mail, a critical morale factor with the troops. This private, hunkered down in a foxhole half full of water, received a letter from the owner of a music store in his hometown. The marine read the letter and began laughing. Nearby, his company commander, hearing this and thinking that this youngster might be cracking up, demanded to know what was so damn funny. The marine responded, "Well, sir, I bought a saxophone from a music store owner back home on the installment plan. Now, he tells me that if I don't make the installment payment due, I'm going to find myself in a serious situation." This story quickly made the rounds.

Since providing naval support to the marines on Guadalcanal would place our aircraft carriers in jeopardy, and their loss would seriously cripple our war against the Japanese in the Southwest Pacific, Admiral Nimitz, commander-in-chief of our naval forces in the Pacific (CINCPAC), called an urgent, high-level conference with General Vandergrift, commander of the First Marine Division on Guadalcanal, and high-level naval commanders, including Adm. William "Bull" Frederick Halsey Jr., in attendance. The compelling question was what could be done to support the marines with exposure of our three remaining effective carriers in the area a crucial consideration. After a lengthy discussion, it was Admiral Halsey, responding to a request from Admiral Nimitz for his opinion as to what action should be taken, who replied in the language of Admiral Farragut at the Battle of Manila, "Damn the torpedoes! Full speed ahead!"

The navy returned, and under the command of Adm. "Bull" Halsey, the marines were supplied and supported. After a long bloody, heroic struggle, Guadalcanal was secured, which made it possible for United States forces to capture or neutralize all the Solomon Islands. The land and sea victories in the Solomon Islands and the Coral Sea were a decisive turning point in the Pacific war.

The Third Marine Division was transported from New Zealand to Guadalcanal, arriving in September 1943. We were encamped in tents in a coconut grove, and we immediately began preparations for what lay ahead. At the first opportunity, Lt. Col. George Van Orden, commander of the First Battalion, Third Marines, and I walked over the ridge line (known as "Bloody Ridge") overlooking Henderson Field. There the Japanese army had made its all-out attack to seize Henderson Field and drive the marines into the sea, but it had failed as the Americans threw them back with very heavy losses to the attackers.

Remnants of the battle were everywhere: a perforated Japanese helmet, a Japanese two-pronged shoe made so that the big toe is separated from the smaller toes, the hilt of a Japanese samurai sword, shell casings, cartridge shells, and cast-off clothing and wearing apparel—all scattered, mildewed, rotting from constant exposure to the rains. The trees bore the scars of battle and the earth was marred from exploding shells. We carefully, gingerly, picked our way over this tragic scene, reviewing in our minds what had taken place and more fully appreciating the victory that had been won and those who had fought here—living and dead.

Following our view of the battlefield, we walked down the ridge line toward the beach to a cemetery where the fallen marines rested. Moving reverently among the grave sites, reading the markers, I came to a grave that riveted my attention, disturbed my mind, and grieved my heart—the marker bore the name of Maj. Kenneth D. Bailey, USMC. We stood silently by this brave marine officer's grave.

When I first reported for duty at Quantico in the summer of 1936, I had not only become acquainted with Lt. Kenneth Bailey, but we had become fast friends. Ken's lifelong dream to be a United States Marine had become a reality. He would have made a super recruiting poster for the marines, a first lieutenant who was athletic, six feet two inches and about two hundred pounds, wide of shoulder, slim of hips. He possessed a contagious, happy smile and was strikingly handsome.

When I met him, Ken had been in the Corps for over a year and was a crack platoon leader, and I looked upon him as an old hand. He helped me with my newly assigned duty as platoon leader in Company F, Second Battalion, Fifth Marines. We also spent time together riding horses, since the Marine Corps maintained a stable of excellent riding horses at the Quantico base. Why would the Marine Corps, a branch of the United States Navy, need riding horses? To that question, asked by an inquiring congressional committee, the response was that a marine officer should have the ability to handle, ride, or pack a horse or mule in jungle or mountainous terrain where a jeep or other motorized vehicles could not go. The congressional committee was convinced.

On Sunday mornings, Ken and I would saddle up and ride over the excellent riding trails provided at Quantico. Ken was an accomplished rider and had served in a reserve officers' training corps, training with one of the last army cavalry units. I had ridden bareback as a boy and later with a western saddle; however, Ken rode English style and was one of the best horsemen I ever saw. But Ken's first love was the Marine Corps. He was happiest in the field with his platoon of gung-ho marines. It was his life.

There were several antiquated buses on the base, which looked as if they were holdovers from the Great War, that were used for moving people to the training areas. Each bus had a step and a conveniently located handle for boarding, and after Ken Bailey would crowd his platoon on one of those vehicles, he sometimes, with the bus loaded, would ride standing on the step, gripping the handhold, facing the wind, happily going to the appointed place for the day's combat exercise. This is my memory of the last time I saw Ken in the summer of 1936.

When I was in New Zealand, I had read about the action Ken had taken against the enemy that claimed his life and for which he was awarded the Congressional Medal of Honor by the president of the United States, Franklin Delano Roosevelt.

We returned to our regiment with a keen appreciation of what lay ahead.

In this period of preparation, living in tents in a coconut grove, each marine had a foxhole, a slit trench, beside his bunk, because Japanese planes were coming down from Rabaul late at night to buzz, circle, harass, and drop their calling cards. Except for keeping one awake and having to listen to the grind of "Washing Machine Charlie's" ill-tuned plane engine, little damage was done.

These nocturnal visits from Japanese planes were interrupted when our pilots at Henderson Field obtained "Black Widow" night fighters. Our planes, equipped with radar, were able to fly out of the darkness and "zero in" on the unsuspecting Japanese bomber. The sound of our planes was smoother and more distinctive than "Charlie's." We would see a stream of tracer bullets piercing the night, followed by an enemy bomber bursting into flames, twisting, turning, and flaming like a meteor to the earth.

After repeated attacks, the Japanese suffered great losses and began to withdraw from Guadalcanal slowly. These enemy troops were harassed by our planes by day and our PT boats by night while they were in the southern part of the island, being embarked on barges and staged up the Solomons to Bougainville. The Islands of New Georgia and Vella Lavella were being used as staging areas by these troops.

The presence of Japanese stragglers on Guadalcanal made training more realistic, especially operating reconnaissance patrols which were pushed vigorously, well beyond our beachhead perimeter. This was a prudent and necessary precaution against a surprise suicide attack by remnants of the Japanese force.

As operations and training officer, I accompanied a reconnaissance patrol as we entered a native village that appeared vacated, since not even a dog or a chicken or a pig could be seen. As we moved through the village, we saw a large, tall, black man, distinctive in bearing and dignity, approaching us. He had the attire and the appearance of a Melanesian chief. The patrol halted. The chief stopped. I called out, "Americans!" and the chief responded in good English with an Australian accent, "Yes, I know; we have been watching you for several hours." We all relaxed and greeted each other with a handshake, and he invited the patrol leader and me into his hut.

Accepting the invitation and stationing our patrol on guard against any possible unfriendly interruption, we entered the chief's hut. It was large with a thatched roof and an earthen floor, level and packed down as if it had been trod down through time. In the center was an excavated, open fire pit, looking as if it had been used forever, and in the top of the hut was a hole for the escape of smoke from the fire. Apparently, this hut was used by the chief for receiving important visitors.

The chief had gone to school in Australia. He disliked and mistrusted the Japanese whose patrols had sacked his village, stealing chickens, pigs, and everything else of value. This pillaging had made him an even stronger ally, so he agreed to report to us any Japanese patrols that he might observe in the area.

Before we left, the chief informed us that missionaries had built the church in the village and said with great pride that the church had an organ and an organist. We thanked him for his courtesy and assured him that he would be most helpful if he would send us the reports on enemy activity. We formed up to move out of the village, leaving our friend well supplied with coffee and cigarettes. As we moved slowly away, we heard someone playing a familiar tune on the organ, no doubt taught to the organist by a missionary. One of the men in the patrol, being in good voice, softly picked up the tune, "You are my sunshine, my only sunshine. You make me happy when skies are gray. You'll never know, dear, how much I love you. Please don't take my sunshine away."

We moved back to camp, with appropriate caution, but in an expanded mood.

☞ ☜

The Solomon Islands were a key in MacArthur's plan to return to the Philippines. They consisted principally of Guadalcanal, New Georgia, Vella Lavella, Kolomvongara, and Bougainville.

In 1943, Henderson Field at Guadalcanal was in full operation, and New Georgia had been sufficiently secured by the army and the marines so as to permit air operations from the airfield at Munda, New Georgia. Since Bougainville was the northernmost island of the Solomons, an airfield there was needed to bring our planes within effective range of Rabaul, the center of the Japanese naval and air operations in New Britain. The Japanese move south through the Coral Sea toward Australia had been supported from Rabaul, and they would have gained their objective had they not been stopped by our air and naval forces.

Lt. Col. George Van Orden and I were ordered in August 1943 to New Georgia, a central group of the Solomon Islands, to serve as observers with the U.S. Army's Forty-third Division. Elements of this division were keeping pressure on the Japanese forces still on the island in the northern sector. We were airlifted on the twenty-seventh to Munda, New Georgia, and were jeeped to the forward line battalion near the enemy where we spent a day visiting with the officers, going over maps and intelligence reports. Spending the night in a battalion headquarters area, because of the mosquitoes, most of us slept in hammocks equipped with mosquito netting rather than in a foxhole, although Japanese planes from Rabaul were carrying out harassing raids. They would drop their bombs and hightail it back to Rabaul to escape our night fighters. As I have mentioned, the "Black Widow" night fighters, recently deployed at Henderson Field on Guadalcanal, were a complete surprise to the Japanese pilots who had been dropping bombs indiscriminately over our positions with little fear of opposition.

But the most dangerous bombers were the mosquitoes. They were a greater danger to the health and well-being of our people than any insect, reptile, or animal we encountered in Samoa and the Solomon Islands. Surprisingly, I saw no snakes, although there were large lizards that would occasionally stumble into a marine's foxhole at night, a startling wake-up event even though harmless. Also, not a problem to us were the many large bats, but the mosquito was a poisonous enemy—a real killer.

The bloodsucking habit of the female mosquito transmits yellow fever, malaria, and filariasis. The male mosquito of the filariasis species feeds on nectar and wild plant juices; however, the female requires a special protein in order to mature her eggs, and she gets this protein from blood. At the time she bites, she injects parasites which survive, flourish, and multiply in the bloodstream and tissues of the victim. The most effective treatment, at least at the time, was to remove the patient from the area to prevent further infection, giving the immune system a chance to respond.

Mosquitoes, buzzing and biting, were a constant annoyance, especially for those out on patrol or for a scout sniper waiting for a target. They lit on your face and buzzed in your ears, yet you were restrained from wiping them off, brushing them away, or smashing them with the palm of your hand for fear the sudden movement would reveal your position to the enemy.

Members of a patrol and scout snipers coated their hands and faces with black or brown mud, whichever was the most appropriate camouflage, both to escape detection by one enemy and for protection against another band of bloodthirsty enemies—the Japanese and the mosquitoes.

Approximately one-third of our marines became infected with filariasis while the Third Marine Regiment spent eight months in Samoa. Most of these infected marines were hospitalized and sent back to the States after Bougainville.

Mosquitoes, to an American reared in the city, are a new experience. Mosquitoes to a farm boy from Big Creek bottoms in south Arkansas, and the diseases they spread, are a condition of life. In Columbia County we had malaria and big mosquitoes. They would come at you in droves, increasing their buzzing by accelerating the beat of their wings. They would come looking for blood, so every summer on the farm I was doped with quinine and calomel for protection.

There was a story told in the Big Creek community that illustrates the size and ravenous appetite of our mosquitoes. A certain farmer needed to plow some acreage of new ground, and so he bought a big mule, a Missouri mule, to replace his cotton field mule which was too small for this work. The first morning of work went well. The big mule pulled the plow through the new ground with ease. At noontime, the time for the farmer to go to his house for dinner, the biggest meal of the day, he unhitched the mule from the plow, watered him from a fresh running branch of cold water, and tied him in the shade of a giant oak tree. The farmer went home for his meal knowing that the mule had been fed a gallon of oats and a quarter section of a bale of hay early that morning and that he would be fed the same ration of oats and hay again in the evening after the day's work.

The farmer, having eaten a fulsome meal, found his way to his favorite rocking chair and relaxed with a full pipe of Prince Albert smoking tobacco. He may have dozed for a few minutes. Refreshed and his hunger appeased, he returned to the big oak where he had tied his mule, but the mule was gone, vanished, and the only remaining trace was a bridle and harness. It was reported in the *Magnolia News*, our weekly newspaper, that a ravenous swarm of Big Creek bottom mosquitoes had carried the mule away. The local belief was that the little mosquitoes picked up the mule before the big ones could come in and carry it off.

While we were on New Georgia, army intelligence indicated that the Japanese were using Arundel, one of the nearby islands, as a staging area for barging troops at night to Bougainville. To check out this information, the army was sending a reconnaissance patrol to Arundel, and Lieutenant Colonel Van Orden and I were invited to join the patrol. Our mission was to observe army operations, we were told, so we accepted.

Australian coast watchers on the islands had withdrawn to the hills when the Japanese landed. Those surviving death or capture provided vital information about Japanese naval and army forces moving south toward Guadalcanal and the Coral Sea.

A coast watcher on Arundel was to meet our patrol at a selected landing place in the southernmost part of the island, since reports indicated the Japanese had moved to the north.

We boarded a PT boat and, accompanied by another PT boat as an escort, moved before dawn to the landing area, anchored a few hundred yards from the beach, and rowed ashore in rubber boats. My good friend, fellow marine, and senior officer was a big man, which made it a little crowded in the boat, but we reached shore without mishap.

It was a relief to see that the coast watcher was on station. With him were two natives, big Melanesians, black men with necklaces of teeth around their necks, earrings, and a tall pile of hair that in the daylight and under the sun appeared to be streaked with red. This, I was told, was caused by a chemical, perhaps a form of lime, that they used to kill insects that might be inclined to set up housekeeping on their heads.

It was reported by the coast watchers and verified by the two natives in his company that Japanese were on the island, but they had moved up to the other end. After a brief conference, the patrol moved out, through the bush and off the beach, but parallel to it. We saw signs of Japanese encampments, and though the signs were cold, the lingering smell was distinctive, so I was concerned.

Members of the patrol were good soldiers and had become seasoned to the jungle. They moved patiently, keenly alert to any sign of the enemy. The patrol had a limited mission: to determine if the Japanese were on the island and to examine the beaches for a possible diversionary landing.

In the course of things, we came to a stream, too small to be a river but about the size we might call a large creek. It was wide at the

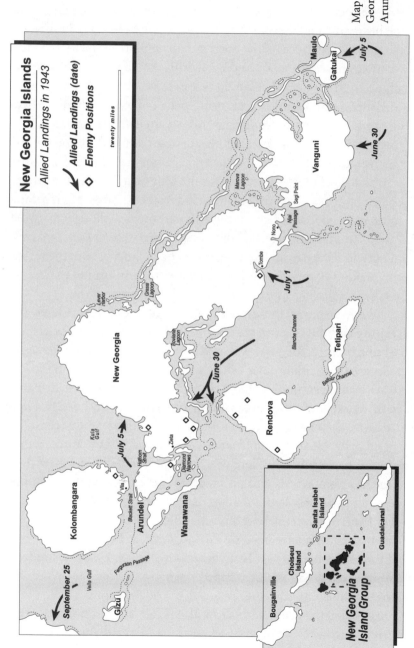

Map of New
Georgia and
Arundel Island

New Georgia Islands
Allied Landings in 1943

⤻ Allied Landings (date)
◇ Enemy Positions

twenty miles

mouth, as it emptied into the sea, but appeared to narrow upstream. The natives had paddled down this stream to the beach and had concealed their canoe in the bush.

We speculated as to the depth, width, and current of the stream further inland. In the event the beaches were used for a landing, would the stream be suitable for the operation of amphibian tractors or LCPs (landing craft personnel)? And would this be a source for an adequate supply of fresh water that would be essential?

After some discussion, the army patrol officer inquired whether one of us would like to paddle up this stream with the natives in their canoe and take a "look-see." His people were dispersed around the area at strategic points for local security. Lieutenant Colonel Van Orden wanted to go, but he was too big for the little boat. I was in the process of looking at a sketch of the beach, including the stream, when it became rather quiet, so I looked up, and all eyes were on me. I thought to myself, "Why should I volunteer for this canoe trip with two lean, lank, and hungry-looking natives I had never seen before today?" But then, I was supposed to be an observer, and this was an opportunity to observe, and I was a marine temporarily attached to an army outfit.

We loaded into the canoe. Both natives had large paddles, one steering and the other in the bow. As we moved inland, the current became more rapid, the stream narrowed, and it became darker as the foliage of the trees and vines joined hands over us, blocking out the sunlight. It wasn't very long before I began to get an eerie feeling, a tingling in the back of my neck. I became more interested in my hosts paddling the canoe than I was in the flow and conformation of the stream.

Shortly, I had seen all I wanted to see. I said, "Let's turn around, go back to the beach." There was no response. Using my forefinger, I made several circles and pointed back; even so, there was still no response. I became apprehensive, as it became increasingly apparent that I was "up a creek without a paddle." After several more futile attempts, I must have become excited, because I was facing the bow of the boat with my M-1 lying across my lap, and when I suddenly swung around, I must have tapped the native behind me on the chin with the rifle butt, since he fell out of the boat. Seeing that he was no longer using the paddle, I borrowed it. The native in the bow of the boat seemed to be as relieved as I was, so we rapidly turned around and headed full-speed back to the beach. Pulled by the current, we made a quick return. What an experience! And to think I volunteered!

I reported to the patrol leader and to the coast watcher, who both seemed more amused by my experience than concerned. From my pack, I pulled out a can of Chelsea cigarettes and presented it to the native who had returned with me to the beach. He seemed happy, spoke to the coast watcher in a language I did not understand, took the cigarettes, opened the can, pulled out a "Chelsea," tore off the paper, and chewed the tobacco—all, with great relish. Chelsea cigarettes, manufactured by Lucky Strike, came in watertight cans. The cans were a treasure, and I used one to hold a mixture of peanuts and raisins, an instant energizer and hunger appeaser between meals of C-rations.

Finally, our mission completed, we rendezvoused with our PT boat, climbed aboard, and returned to Munda, keeping a watchful eye for Japanese aircraft. PT boats ordinarily patrolled in pairs. This was indeed fortunate for us, because on our return trip the screws on our boat malfunctioned, setting us adrift. Transfer to our escort vessel necessitated our jumping from gunnel to gunnel, or deck to deck. The escort boat made several tentative passes as closely and slowly as the rolling sea permitted, as we, one by one, leapt across. Finally, the patrol had all jumped and were safely aboard our escort vessel, except Lieutenant Colonel Van Orden. As I mentioned, he was big man, in girth as well as in height. When he made the jump, his feet hit the gunnel of the passing boat, but he fell back into the sea. However, foreseeing this, a seaman had skillfully fastened a line around the colonel's waist, so that when he fell into the sea, the other end of the line was thrown over to the escort boat. The good colonel was hauled safely aboard, smiling and in good spirits. I think he rather enjoyed the adventure, a great story to relate to his friends over a beer in the comfort of a bar.

After help had arrived for the crippled boat, we got underway, and I went below to the head, which had a small mirror on the wall. Standing back from the mirror was a man, thin in the face, with a scrubby beard. It gradually dawned upon me that the man staring back from the mirror was me! I looked at him hard, borrowed the line from Lt. Johnny O'Neal and asked, "What in the hell are you doing here?" There was no response.

Returning to Guadalcanal safely and with great relief, we shaved, bathed, and changed clothes. Relaxing in the welcome tent that we shared, we leisurely drank a cold beer, treated ourselves to a big Havana cigar, and posed for our photograph.

⇒ ⇐

I never saw this picture of Lt. Col. George Van Orden and me until December 1999. It was taken by Sgt. Curtis E. Francis on our return from Arundel, New Georgia, in August of 1943. Sergeant Francis, a marine photographer with the Third Marine Regiment, sent it, along with others, to his mother. She placed all his war pictures in an album, which she later turned over to his daughter, Laura Pether. My daughter-in-law, Becky McMath, was scanning the Internet and ran across a request from Laura Pether for information as to a Lieutenant Colonel McMath, who served in Bougainville with the Third Marine Regiment. Becky called me, and I immediately contacted Ms. Pether, who was writing a biography of her father, who had a distinguished career as a photographer in the Pacific Theater. We have since corresponded and exchanged information, and she sent me this and several other photographs. It was a most happy coincidence, a tribute to our high-tech communications system and to the Marine Corps family—*Semper Fidelis.*

Lieutenant Colonel Van Orden, whose code name was the "Beast," would be awarded a Purple Heart and a Navy Cross for his heroic leadership in the Bougainville campaign. Then on our return to Guadalcanal from Bougainville, the colonel would write the official report on the Bougainville campaign.

His return home to the States happily would be in time to be a witness and to give his blessing to my marriage in Washington, D.C., to Anne Phillips in October 1944. I remember him clearly, promoted to full colonel, proudly wearing his dress blues with an eagle on each shoulder, smiling and giving me the "thumbs up" of approval, as Anne and I walked up the aisle as man and wife.

But in August of 1943, Lieutenant Colonel Van Orden and I, having completed our adventure, returned to our duties with the Third Marine Regiment at Guadalcanal. Electricity was in the air, excitement everywhere—the word was out that after months of preparation and training we were finally going to battle against the foe.

X BOUGAINVILLE

BOUGAINVILLE IS THE LARGEST OF THE SOLOMON ISLANDS AND THE northernmost of the island chain. My Third Marine Regiment was one of the assault forces. Our mission was to secure a beachhead and allow the engineer corps to construct a critically needed airfield. This airbase would hopefully enable marine, navy, and army pilots to gain control not only of the airspace over the Solomon Islands, but also Rabaul, New Britain, the Japanese base of operations for its thrust into the Southwest Pacific.

Our regiment had been reinforced and embarked from Guadalcanal on October 13, 1943. We traveled in four troop transport ships. The regimental headquarters, which included my operational and training section, was aboard the USS *President Jackson*. We moved first to New Hebrides and conducted a four-day (October 16–20) practice exercise that culminated in a landing maneuver similar to the one we planned for the beaches at Empress Augusta Bay, Bougainville. Resuming our expedition, we arrived at Empress Augusta Bay on November 1.

H-Hour, the time set for us to go ashore, was 0715. Our months of rigorous training were greatly tested. On signal, marines went over the sides of the troop ships and climbed down the landing nets into boats positioned alongside. There they met the navy coxswains who nervously waited to take them some five thousand yards and disgorge them on the sand beaches. As part of the Third Regimental Command Post, I remained aboard ship as the first assault got underway.

Unknown to us, on the beaches a disciplined, stubborn, well-trained, well-equipped enemy was waiting. This enemy, trained to not surrender, believed that surrender was cowardly and disgraceful. They had a creed encompassing a belief that to die for their emperor provided instant passage to heaven.

As I watched the men of my regiment descend into the landing craft and viewed the beaches looming in the distance, I could hear the ships' guns thundering and see high explosive shells bursting in the area of our immediate objective. As our men approached their assigned beaches, the naval gunfire lifted and a flight of marine torpedo planes

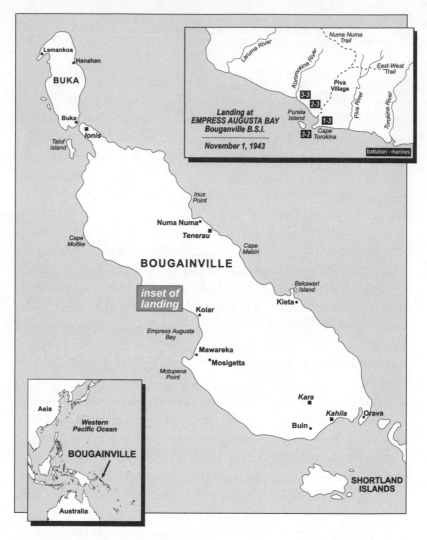

Map of Bougainville, Solomon Islands

and scout bombers, escorted by marine fighters appeared on the horizon. They came in high, but there were no enemy fighter aircraft—"Tojo must be asleep," I thought. The bombers worked over the landing area, then the fighters followed with strafing runs. Flying as low as possible, they subjected the jungle to a withering fire of machine-gun bullets.

It was strange—unreal. We were only two hundred miles from

Rabaul, the most formidable Japanese air and naval bases in the Southwest Pacific, but there were no signs of Japanese air and naval resistance. We were continually aware that we were sitting ducks as we unloaded men, weapons, ammunition, food, and supplies from transport and cargo ships just outside Empress Augusta Bay. We did not know whether we had obtained the critical ingredient necessary for a successful attack—the element of surprise. I wondered as I watched the drama unfold before me.

Whatever lay ahead, morale in the Third Regiment was high. Every marine had been trained, his skills honed to a sharp edge, informed of the mission, and educated on what was necessary to win the objective. After all the training, work, and waiting, it was a positive relief to be at war at last.

Within minutes after crossing the line of departure, the leading waves of the assault boats began receiving enfilade fire from Puruata Island, a small block of land on our left. Then heavier fire from a narrow stretch of beach called Cape Torokina was on the right flank. In addition to the machine guns, our men also began receiving deadly accurate fire from a 75mm gun. The boat group commander's craft, which gave direction and led the assault wave, took a direct hit. The boats following became disorganized, and in the confusion, companies began landing in the wrong places. Mortar and machine-gun fire from Cape Torokina was covering the beaches. A second shell struck the land commander's boat, and another penetrated the ramp and exploded in the boat's center.

Capt. John Monks, my assistant operations and training officer, described what happened in his book, *A Ribbon and a Star:*

> "After the first shell hit, the men in the forward part of the boat fell back toward the center as if a big wave had pushed them over," said Sergeant McAllister. "A shell fragment from the second hit me in the left thigh. The boat grounded, and I started over the side. It was an awful mess. Bloody men pulled themselves off the deck and forced themselves over the side. One man had part of his back blown off. Everyone kept hold of his rifle. Some of them only had a half a rifle. The water was up to my chin. As I hit the sand, I looked back and saw that Smith wasn't going to make it; he had a wound in his head. He was one of my boys. I went back, pulled him in, and dragged him behind a coconut log. Then a Jap

ran out from one of the slit trenches. He bent over and armed a grenade—hit it against his knee. As he threw it, I hit the deck behind a ridge of sand. Couldn't have been over three inches high, but it was enough. Then I threw a grenade. It seemed to go off in the right place, but I threw another to make sure. I didn't see it kill the Jap, but Hopkins, who was over on my left, said the first one blew the Jap all to hell. Then I got the rest of my squad who were wounded behind the coconut log. All the time snipers were popping away at us. My foot started to hurt, and I pulled off my shoe. There was a big hole where my ankle used to be. I figured it was broken—hadn't noticed it before.

"McNamara said he was going to get the boat off the shore. The ramp was jammed, but that was the only way we could get the wounded back to the ship. I saw him crawl over the side into the boat; he had a bad wound in his hand. A sailor crawled in after him. They got the boat off the beach and started back toward the ship. McNamara said he and D'Imperio, who was wounded, tried to plug up the big holes in the boat with some of the dead bodies. Then they put life jackets on all the other wounded. The boat sank. Four or five of the wounded were picked up. The rest of my squad who were injured and myself were sent back to the ship three hours later. I checked up. There were twelve killed and fourteen wounded out of the whole boatload. Lieutenant Kirk and Lieutenant Shelton were both killed when the second shell hit."[1]

The Japanese had constructed bunkers from seasoned coconut logs and bags of sand. They were camouflaged so as not to be visible. Each bunker was also hidden from the air by the native plants and foliage spread over them.

These emplacements housed machine guns, and one contained the 75mm Howitzer that had been playing such havoc on our landing boats. There were connecting trenches between the riflemen and the gun emplacements, and all were arranged so as to provide mutually defensive fire. Our pre-landing naval barrage, fired from some seven miles offshore, as well as the bombing and strafing runs by our planes, had failed to knock out the gun emplacements. They had escaped serious damage.

---

1. John Monks, *A Ribbon and a Star* (New York: Henry Holt and Company, 1945).

As we at the command post watched the desperate, heroic battle unfold, we received word that the commander of the First Battalion, Lt. Col. Spike Mason, had been seriously wounded. Spike was a classmate of mine in Basic School, but there was no time to grieve. My commander, Col. George McHenry, immediately ordered me ashore to assess the First Battalion's situation. As I reached the shore, I saw Maj. Steve Brody, battalion executive officer, and Maj. Chuck Bailey, battalion operations officer, engaged in collecting and organizing their platoons and companies to continue the attack. They were excellent officers and had assumed roles of responsibility when Lieutenant Colonel Mason was wounded. Being at the scene, I "lent a hand."

In spite of the confusion of battle, the intensive training of the Third Marines came into play. Each marine had been told and retold of the objective, as had the fire teams and squads. They had practiced many times, knocking out the type of bunkers, foxholes, and emplacements they now faced, with this difference: The enemy was laying down a withering fire from these emplacements and determined to die in their defense. When the First Battalion was reorganized and resumed the offensive, I returned to the ship and reported to Colonel McHenry. As a result of these events, I was later awarded the Silver Star.

The Japanese 75mm gun was the gun that had played havoc with our landing craft. Something had to be done. Sgt. Robert A. Owens collected a fire team of our marines and moved toward the target. One marine had a Browning automatic rifle (BAR), the other three had rifles—all had hand grenades. The marine with the BAR placed covering fire on the bunker, while the first team with Sergeant Owens crawled toward the target. Inching their way, Sergeant Owens got within a few feet of the bunker, then he tossed a hand grenade that landed outside the entrance of the gun emplacement and exploded. Three Japanese ran from the bunker, and Sergeant Owens threw another grenade that landed inside the gun emplacement and went off. The marine fire team was then on the receiving end of hand grenades, and Sergeant Owens was fatally wounded. But his last grenade had done its work—the 75mm gun was destroyed and the remaining occupants of the emplacement killed. Sgt. Robert A. Owens was posthumously awarded the Medal of Honor.

Individual marine fire teams repeated similar action against the remaining bunkers and connecting trenches on Cape Torokina. Thus, one by one, the Japanese resistance was destroyed, bunker by bunker, connecting trench by connecting trench, foxhole by foxhole, with their occupants all destroyed.

As our landings were gradually accelerated and the beaches clear, I thought how lucky we had been in not having Japanese naval or air opposition. But that soon changed as the enemy's air force began to react. The Japanese launched carrier-based planes to strike our transport and cargo ships as well as our land parties. Marine fighter squadrons out of Munda, New Georgia, rose up to meet them, and a series of dogfights ensued. I witnessed planes in flames crashing toward the sea, and watched for the white blossoming or fluffing parachutes opening. Sometimes they did, floating down with the pilot swinging into the sea. We made every effort to save all downed pilots, American or Japanese.

In the first day of attack our pilots shot down twenty-four enemy planes. However, several Japanese pilots penetrated our fighter screen. They dove at our ships, shooting and bombing, then pulling up by seconds to avoid crashing.

I was topside of the USS *President Jackson* when we first received warning of a Japanese air attack. I debated whether to stay there or to go below, knowing there were pros and cons to this option. But curiosity prevailed, and I remained topside to watch the action. A Japanese plane targeted our ship, closed in a long dive, and at the last possible moment, pulled up. We were sure that he had released a bomb with our name on it. An alarming and interminable moment passed, but no bomb landed on the ship, nor was there any explosion in the water. The Japanese pilot circled and came back down, flying around our ship so close I could see his face. It seemed as if our eyes met for an instant. Then we saw what he was searching for—his missing bomb was hanging from the bomb release section, on the belly, of his plane. I have often wondered what happened to that pilot when he attempted to land on his aircraft carrier.

When the air attack began, our ships went on red alert, abruptly stopped unloading, and pulled out to sea, to maneuver away from the enemy planes. We stayed out until the "all clear" was sounded, and the ships returned to land our division's remaining troops and cargo.

For the remainder of the day we moved to consolidate our positions on the beach.

We had little time to relax. Darkness brought news that the Japanese navy had launched a substantial task force from Rabaul. The fleet included six destroyers, two heavy cruisers, and two light cruisers. They arrived on November 2. Our naval officers, under the command of Rear Admiral Merrill, anticipated an attack and were standing by to block the enemy's approach. Merrill had four light cruisers and eight destroyers.

The task forces clashed at close quarters. We had the advantage of being able to locate Japanese ships with radar, but the Japanese partially compensated for their lack of electronic capability by expert use of star shells. These fireballs lighted up the area so that one could read the fine print of a newspaper. Capt. John C. Chapin, historian of the marine operation in the Northern Solomons, described the action:

> Merrill confused the Japanese ships with smoke screens, deceiving the Japanese as to the direction of his destroyers were moving. These "Little Beavers" under the command of Captain Arleigh Burke, who later became Chief of Naval Operations, closed with the enemy. First, the Japanese ship *Sendal* was sunk with 335 men. The *Hatsukaze* was sunk with all hands (240 men). The cruisers *Haguro* and *Myoko* were damaged. The American task force received damage to the USS *Foote* and light damage to the USS *Denver*, USS *Spence* and USS *Columbia*.[2]

The Japanese naval force was turned back, and over the next couple of days our marines gradually took control over a small section of the island. However, on the morning of November 7, a composite battalion of Japanese from the base at Rabaul, escorted by a fleet of destroyers, landed on the left flank of the beachhead occupied by my regiment.

Four Japanese destroyers put approximately five hundred Japanese soldiers ashore. They got ashore without receiving a single hostile shot. A weapons platoon with the Ninth Marines saw the land crafts coming ashore but held their fire because the boats looked like those in their regiment, with big white numbers on the prow.

---

2. John C. Chapin, *Top of the Ladder: Marine Operations in the Northern Solomons* (Washington, D.C.: Marine Corps Historical Center, 1997).

Having landed over a wide beach, the Japanese had the option of either taking advantage of the element of surprise, or waiting for a more coordinated and concerted attack. They chose to exploit their surprise landing and began an immediate, but piecemeal, attack.

These well-trained Japanese soldiers knew their mission, and they were all prepared to die for their emperor. In the closing hours of the battle we found a prayer in the knapsack of one of the dead, which voiced this fatalistic wish: "Whether I float a corpse under the waters, or sink beneath the grasses of the mountainside, I willingly die for the emperor." This seemed the spirit of the Japanese army.

I was at the Third Regimental Command Post, about two hundred yards inward off the beach when the first assault began. I heard the firing, and we were soon told that the Japanese had landed an amphibious force unopposed. Almost immediately, I received a call from Gen. "Speed" Caldwell, the assistant division commander. He asked me to meet him at the Third Battalion Command Post located on the beach near the mouth of the Koromokina River. He instructed me to bring the First Battalion's commander or the operations officer, whoever was available, with me as the First Battalion would probably have another job to do. Although the enemy's attack was aggressive, it had not broken through our defenses as yet.

General Caldwell assessed the situation and concluded that we could not give the Japanese time to dig in. We should immediately launch a counterattack. Gen. Hal Turnage, the division commander, approved his recommendation.

General Caldwell then asked me for a recommended plan of attack for the First Battalion. I consulted with the First Battalion commander, and we submitted a plan. Our strategy called for the First Battalion Third Marines, since it had been in regimental reserve, to go to the immediate support of the Third Battalion Ninth Marines. The latter had borne the brunt of the Japanese assault.

The First Battalion Third Marines executed a passage of lines through the Third Battalion Ninth Marines and carried out this attack order. As the battle progressed, Japanese commanders fed the remnants of the landing parties into the battle in an effort to restore the offensive. But they were literally destroyed. By nightfall, the Japanese offensive had been stopped.

During the night of November 7, we made plans for a coordinated infantry, tank, artillery, and air attack against the remaining Japanese on our left flank. We launched the attack at daylight on the eighth with a bombardment from five batteries of artillery and mortars. The First Battalion Third Marines, in conjunction with the First Battalion of the Twenty-first Marines, and supported with tanks and machine guns, advanced to a line approximately fifteen hundred yards west of the Koromokina River to engage the enemy. The firefight was intense, but by the end of the day the remaining Japanese troops were destroyed.[3]

The Battle of Koromokina River, as this engagement came to be called, on November 7 and 8 eliminated, for the time being, the Japanese threat from the west side (our left flank) of the island. However, there were still plenty of Japanese around, and the general command staff expected a counterattack. We turned our attention to gaining total control of the region. To do so meant gaining control of the terrain.

The Japanese had been utterly surprised, not that we attacked Bougainville, but at the site of the landing. They knew what we did not know.

The beaches at Empress Augusta Bay were natural places for an amphibious landing, but beyond the beaches was an almost impenetrable jungle, with swamps that contained only small islands of firm ground.

We had no choice but to build on what we had gained. On November 9 my Third Marine Regiment was ordered north into the swampy jungle terrain. The Second and Third Battalions (the First Battalion was returned to regimental reserve) were assigned a mission to expand the division's beachhead and search for firmer, higher ground where engineers could build an airfield—crucial to our long-term success. The Nineteenth marine engineers and navy Seabees, with their tractors, bulldozers, and the construction equipment needed to build the projected airstrip, followed us. Speed was of the essence. Our assault forces must secure a site for them to do their work.

---

3. For the situation on November 7–8 on the Koromokina River, see Col. George O. Van Orden, Combat Report, Third Marine Regiment, Bougainville Campaign. See also, Japanese counter-landing sketch, John C. Chapin, *Marine Operations in the Northern Solomons.*

Drawing by John Falter, Toromokina River, Maj. Sid McMath pointing to map
with Gen. Oscar Caldwell (*From John Monks Jr.,* A Ribbon and a Star)

During the move from the beach and our interminable struggle to penetrate, pass through, and emerge from the morass of swamps, I reflected on my job as regimental training and operations officer. What were my duties? I had been operations and *training* officer, with emphasis on training, from the day that the Third Regiment had formed up at New River, North Carolina. I believe it may be safely said that when we hit the beach, my duties as training officer stopped and my job as *operations* officer took over.

The overall mission of the landing force was to "find, fix, and destroy" the enemy, then secure sufficient solid ground to construct an airfield. Each member of the landing team had his part to play. As operations officer under the command and direction of our regimental commander, Col. George "Big Mac" McHenry, it was my duty to maintain contact with the battalion and division headquarters. I also had to maintain our direction of march, keep contact with the units on our right, look to the security of our left flank, and be prepared for a surprise attack.

Working with Capt. John Foley's Intelligence Section, I sent out patrols with specific instructions as to their mission and area of operations, and we debriefed them on their return, then passed on "need to know" information to headquarters. It was vitally important to make sure that each patrol was precisely informed of other friendly patrols that might conceivably be operating beyond our lines. This stark possibility could not be overlooked. We once had two patrols that made contact, neither being aware of the other's identity and in the subsequent short firefight, tragically, two of our brave young marines were killed.

By November 13, 1943, our regiment was emerging from its nightmare in the swamp—a living hell. We found ground firm enough to allow us to dig foxholes without striking water, and we had firm footing for a defensive perimeter at night. Of course, we were never dry; water was never absent for very long. Almost everyday it started raining in midafternoon and continued most of the night. Nights were always long, sleep always fitful, but our weapons were constantly tested and always ready. Many nights we slept sitting on the ground, in water, leaning against the trees, and often the marines used the buddy system: seated they would lean against each other, back-to-back, for a welcome snooze. Wet clothes, cold food, lukewarm coffee—sometimes, but at all times, we had to be constantly alert.

In short order after our forces broke out of the swamp, the Seabees and engineers completed a road from west to east across the top of our beachhead perimeter. On the higher ground we discovered two trails, one running east to west, the other from north to south. We learned that the native people called the east-west path the Numa Numa Trail. The north-south route they called the Piva Trail. There was a native settlement know as Piva Village where the two paths intersected.

General Turnage, our division commander, anticipated a Japanese counterattack. Since we had secured the beaches at Empress Augusta Bay, there was only one approach the enemy could take, at least with a substantial force, to attack our beachhead perimeter. Such an attacking force, using the east-west trail for an approach from the east, and the Numa Numa Trail for an approach from the west, could converge at the junction of these two trails near Piva Village. That was precisely the Japanese plan.

As we were to learn, the landing on November 7 and subsequent attack on our west flank was a diversion for the major offensive against our positions. While we were busy stopping the diversionary assault on our left flank, the Japanese Twenty-third Infantry assembled in the hills north of the trails' junction. According to the Japanese plan, their Twenty-third Regiment would hit our left flank first. Their additional forces would be brought in from the east (our right flank).

While anticipating a counterattack, we stepped up the size and frequency of our patrolling and expanded the search areas. Patrols to the north began making frequent contact with the enemy. When they shifted their search to the northeast, they met even heavier resistance from what appeared to be a Japanese company. Based on that action, we theorized that the Japanese were shifting their position to the east. Reports from other patrols confirmed that the Japanese were withdrawing from the northern sector and moving to a position east along the east-west trail. Reports further indicated that they were indeed moving up reinforcements from the east of the island.

To counter the Japanese buildup, General Turnage ordered a company of the Second Raider Battalion to clear the way and establish control of Piva Forks—the junction of the Piva and Numa Numa

Trails. Although the Raider Battalion was repeatedly engaged by Japanese patrols, they were successful in taking control of the trail junction by late afternoon on November 9. Over the next three days we consolidated our position around Piva Forks. On the thirteenth our Third Marine Battalion was directed to advance to the northeast and extend our patrol activities to one thousand yards to the front.

It didn't take long to get action. In midafternoon a scout patrol in Company L of the Third Battalion, under the command of Lt. John "Irish" O'Neal, reported that a column of Japanese soldiers was coming down the Numa Numa Trail. Quickly organizing an ambush, O'Neal and his unit waited for the enemy. It was not long until the enemy column came into view. O'Neal was astonished by what he saw: leading the column was a Japanese officer wearing white gloves and carrying a Samurai sword. He directed a scout sniper to take out this officer. When the sniper lined up his sights and slowly, deliberately, squeezed the trigger, the Japanese officer dropped. A volley of fire following from the ambush and a very hot firefight ensued before the Japanese were forced to withdraw.

Regrouping, the Japanese circled the roadblock and attacked O'Neal's patrol from the rear. O'Neal had anticipated such a maneuver, and the Japanese were again repulsed. This time they broke off and withdrew before nightfall. The next morning, O'Neal's patrol cautiously searched the battleground. They found a dispatch case on the body of the dead Japanese officer. Opening the dispatch case, O'Neal found a map and several sketches and notes written in Japanese. He immediately sent this map to Captain Foley, who, in turn, promptly sent it to Division Intelligence.

The map confirmed the Japanese were preparing a defensive position east of the Piva Forks along the east-west trail. This, with other "hot scoops" gathered from various sources, prompted General Turnage to order my regiment to alter our course and move due east. Over the next week, we repositioned our units and prepared to move forward.

While we were preparing to engage the enemy, the high command determined that our air force needed an airstrip for bombers in addition to the fighter strip the engineer unit was planning to build. The engineers determined that this would be feasible, but we would have to extend the beachhead and build a road to the airstrips that could withstand heavy equipment. We were ordered to clear the area of Japanese soldiers so the engineer unit could do its job.

As this mission began, I received constant reports from the battalion headquarters. The Third Battalion was directed to take two platoons, accompanied by a construction unit, to execute the plan. Even though we were facing dangerous conditions, I took time to observe the road construction. It was done with a bulldozer manned by a skilled and courageous Seabee. He plowed through the jungle underbrush a few yards at a time, digging drainage ditches and constructing a corduroy road through the swamp. This road was the same in design as the road that Granddad Sanders and I rode over when I was a child in Columbia County, Arkansas, with mules and a wagon, hauling cotton to the gin. Other Seabees cut narrow logs, piled them parallel to each other, then used dump trucks to haul and pour tons of sand over the logs. Bulldozers then completed the leveling process. Wooden sledges and amphibian tractors loaded with equipment would follow. Thus, a stretch of road that would be a crucial supply route was pushed through the swamp. It was solid enough for vehicles to deliver equipment and material to build the airfield.

On November 19, the Third Battalion moved out in an "attack imminent" formation along the Numa Numa Trail. The battalion picked up Lieutenant O'Neal and his platoon and moved forward another three hundred yards, set up an all-around defense, and spent the night. There was no contact with the enemy all day. The next two days passed in similar fashion. However, on the twenty-first, the Third Battalion encountered heavy mortar and artillery fire. The attack began about noon and in a matter of a few minutes, a major, a lieutenant, three noncommissioned officers, and eighteen corpsmen were seriously wounded.

After the initial volley, our men were able to take cover and avoid further casualties; however, our advance was stopped. We did not know that at the time, but this engagement was the preliminary action to a crucial battle that would determine the success of our mission. This battle would later become known as the Battle of Piva Forks.

We badly needed counter fire from our artillery and mortars, but without pinpointing the location of the enemy targets, counter fire could be extremely hazardous to our people. The situation was so fluid that I did not always know the precise location of our patrols. The artillery observer could ask for a barrage against an area target and walk the artillery fire back toward our general position, but the hazard of shells falling short presented a great risk to our own troops. We needed high ground from which the artillery observer could better see and direct artillery against the enemy.

On November 19, a reconnaissance patrol from the Second Battalion made a crucial discovery. They were scouting an area east of Piva River, to the north of the east-west trail, and several hundred yards east of the intersection with the Numa Numa Trail, when they spotted a ridge rising sharply to a height of four hundred feet out of the thick jungle and running in a general north to south direction. This was the high ground we had been looking for. Led by a seasoned leader, Lt. Steve Cipik, the patrol scaled the ridge. A brief reconnaissance revealed a number of foxholes and connecting trenches that had been recently occupied. Cipik surmised that the Japanese had occupied it during the day for observation. In addition to being the highest point overlooking the beachhead, the ridge provided a view of the approaches from the east along the east-west trail. Cipik also surmised that the Japanese withdrew each evening to escape the random artillery fire from the American position at night.

Cipik was correct. The next morning the Japanese returned to find "Cipik's surprise." He had diligently placed his platoon in an all-around defensive position, personally sighting the BARs and machine guns to cover the approaches. The result was that after a short fight, the Japanese survivors withdrew, regrouped, and attacked again with the same conclusion. They then broke off the engagement. Gaining this high ground was crucial in the upcoming Battle of Piva Forks, which in time, would lead to final victory on Bougainville.

At this point we had been in the jungle for three weeks. The men had been eating C-rations, were tired, had uniforms that had worn out and shoes that were rotting from exposure to mud and the swamp, and were suffering from a contagion of jungle diseases. Despite this, our morale was high. We anticipated that we were about to close with the main force of the Japanese army now committed against us—was the thing we had trained for—and we were ready.

Soldiers moving through jungle prior to Battle of Piva Forks

Our patrols further confirmed that the Japanese were preparing defensive positions east of the east branch of the Piva River and along the east-west trail. It was important that the attack be made before they could perfect their defensive position and receive reinforcements. That was my feeling, and I hoped and expected that an artillery barrage would neutralize the Japanese defense emplacements.

However, General Caldwell insisted "his" marines had to be fed a hot meal and be issued clean and dry clothing and replacements for their rotten shoes. He canceled an attack we had planned for November 23. The cooks and supply personnel went to work to comply with the general's order. We rescheduled the attack for early on the twenty-fourth, but someone realized that that day was Thanksgiving. President Roosevelt had ordered that all American troops be fed turkey—with trimmings—on this national holiday. I don't remember how it was accomplished, but it was. Someone moved turkeys to the battalion assembly areas and most of the Third Marines and their attached units had a "warm" turkey dinner—thanks to Uncle Sam, General Caldwell, and President Roosevelt. But the twenty-fourth was also D-Day for the Third Marine Regiment's attack against the Japanese army. It was not to be a typical Thanksgiving Day.

I was pretty busy on November 23. Colonel McHenry and I first conferred with the battalion commanders. We then talked with Bob Walker, our communications officer, responsible for keeping our communications lines open. Then we contacted our supply section, responsible for keeping the regiment supplied with "beans and bullets." Finally, we met with our regimental surgeon regarding the location of a first aid station and plans for evacuating the wounded to a hospital ship.

Also on November 23, we made plans to set up an advance regimental command post north of the east-west trail and south of the high ground taken by Steve Cipik and his patrol, now known as "Cipik's Ridge." The advance command post had to "be as close, centrally located, and accessible to the battalions as possible." I went out to examine the ground for a suitable spot. I was accompanied by a most loyal and competent assistant operations officer, Capt. John Monks, and Capt. John Foley, who was as good an intelligence officer, heading our R-2 (Intelligence) Section, as any regiment ever had. This was as it should be; both had been vitally concerned with the operation of the regimental command post since day one.

We were so busy scouting for a site to establish the regimental command post that I don't rightly remember what I had to eat for this Thanksgiving Day—but it wasn't turkey; I would have remembered that. As we always told our junior officers in our leadership lectures, "The troops eat first."

So, our troops had turkey. Some had to be on outpost duty on November 23, and others who came in late from patrols had a ration of turkey for breakfast. I saw several enjoying a turkey leg as they were moving on the morning of the twenty-fourth to their line of departure for what they hoped would prove to be a "turkey shoot."

H-Hour was set for 0830 on the morning of November 24. The Ninth and Twenty-first Marines and the Second Raider Battalion were assigned to support our regiment. The army's Thirty-seventh Infantry Division was directed to provide roadblocks against any Japanese troops coming down from the north along the Numa Numa Trail, while artillery was provided by the Twelfth Marines and the Thirty-seventh Army Infantry Division. In preparation for receiving casualties, C Company, Medical Field Hospital, was set near the rear of the regimental command post.

In search of our advance command post, we moved out north of and parallel to the east-west trail to the southernmost tip of Cipik's Ridge and selected a spot which we thought was suitable. Having come that far, and with Cipik's Ridge now being held by our people, we proceeded up the ridge to check the visibility from there. On the way up I saw the bodies of several Japanese soldiers killed in their attempt to retake this crucial piece of ground. I was struck by their size, because they were not small like the soldiers who had made the landing west of the Koromokina River on November 7 and 8. These men were big, appearing to be six feet tall and weighing over two hundred pounds. Later I learned that they were from an elite Japanese division, reinforcements from the eastern end of the island—veterans of China.

Seeing the dead elite Japanese soldiers added a new dimension to our upcoming Thanksgiving Day battle. Otherwise, the trek was like ascending the National Park Service tower on the East Mountain in Hot Springs. Doubly enjoyed after the confines of the jungle, it was an incredible view—a panorama—the sight of the beach with boats moving back and forth from the cargo ships, the sea, the sky, and our fleet on the horizon.

I was ordered to prepare a plan of attack. From my study of the Civil War battles, I had learned that maintaining control of attacking units, constant contact, and communications were essential to success. We had to maintain contact and communications between the regimental command post and the battalions and the battalions with each other, all particularly difficult in the jungle. Vital to coordination and control in the coming battle would be a readily identifiable and definable boundary between the assaulting battalions.

Our patrols reported that the Japanese were preparing defensive positions east of the east branch of the Piva River along the east-west trail. In fact, the east-west trail led directly to the core of the Japanese defensive position. Thus, I judged the east-west trail to be a natural dividing line between our assaulting battalions. The Second Battalion was assigned to the right and the Third Battalion was on the left of the trail. The First Battalion remained in its defensive position in reserve and provided supporting fire. From the top of Cipik's Ridge, artillery forward observers plotted their targets and adjusted their fire. The First Battalion sighted in forty-four machine guns and coordinated the action of twelve 80mm and nine 60mm mortars for a barrage across the front.

The line of departure was the position of defense being occupied by the First Battalion. As our units began to move out on the morning of November 24, the artillery opened up with the heaviest concentration ever delivered by marines up to that time. To the accompaniment of a continuing rattle and roar of machine guns, mortars, and artillery, the Second and Third Battalions advanced to the line of departure on schedule. As this fire was lifted, the battalions entered the Japanese lines and were met with momentary silence. The destruction of the enemy's positions within the battalions' zone of fire preparation had been complete. Gradually as the advance continued, the enemy rallied their survivors and began committing their reserves. The Second and Third assault battalions were moving in a column of companies, each company in a "contact imminent" formation with the east-west trail as their dividing line. They were advancing toward their first objective that was seven hundred fifty yards from the line of departure.

For the first one hundred yards "both Battalions advanced through a weird, stinking plowed-up jungle of shattered trees and Japanese dead. Some fell out of trees, some lay crumpled and twisted beside their shattered weapons. Some were covered by chunks of jagged logs and jungle earth, a blasted bunker."[4] The Second Battalion

---

4. Capt. John C. Chapin, United States Marine Corps, Retired, Historian for the History and Museum Division Headquarters, U.S. Marine Corps.

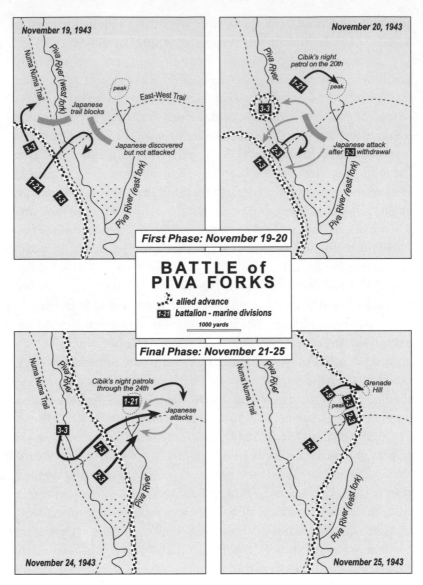

Maps, Battle of Piva Forks

was relatively unopposed and was able to reach the regimental phase line five hundred yards from the point of departure. After passing through the area ravaged by the artillery, the Third Battalion's left flank was struck hard by a Japanese counterattack.

Ironically, this attack came just as we were receiving some unexpected visitors. While our units were moving out, we set up an advance regimental command post at the spot on Cipik's Ridge selected the day before. The engineers dug for us and opened an emplacement just wide and deep enough for our communication equipment (to connect us to each of our battalions) and the few people who would be operating the advance command post. By sitting on the floor of the emplacement, one's head would be below the surface of the surrounding ground to avoid stray bullets or shell fragments, but there was no overhead cover.

We were in these quarters when I looked up to see Lt. Gen. Roy S. Geiger, commander of the Fleet Marine Amphibious Corps in the Southwest Pacific, now commanding the Bougainville invasion. He had set up his headquarters on Bougainville and was noted for his practice of going up front to the battlefield for first-hand observation. Now he, along with General Caldwell, assistant commander of the division, and Col. Al Bowser, division operations officer, paid a surprise visit to our forward regimental command post as the Battle of Piva Forks was in progress.

Hastily improvised with limited space and no overhead protection, the command post excavation was about ten feet long and eight feet wide. Our VIP visitors made their entrance into this already crowded space. We exchanged greetings, and since I, as operations officer, had been in constant contact with the assault battalions, I was asked to brief the general on the situation. I had hardly begun the briefing when a 90mm Japanese mortar shell exploded about one hundred yards west of us along the east-west trail. Since the 90mm mortar was the deadliest and most effective weapon the Japanese had been using, this got our attention. I was understandably concerned as to what would happen if the enemy lobbed a 90mm round into this command post. What a coup it would be for the Japanese to wipe out a lieutenant general, a brigadier, and a full colonel with one blast. When there was another explosion about one hundred yards east of our position, it became apparent the enemy was zeroing in on us.

Then all hell broke loose, and we hit the deck, clinging to the ground as close as it would receive us. Approximately fifty rounds of high explosives landed. The noise was deafening; the earth shook; we were covered with dirt and debris. There were cries from the wounded for corpsmen, and several of the communications crew in foxholes nearby were hit.

I stated incorrectly that we all hit the deck. General Geiger sat upright with his back against the wall of the excavation, appearing as calm and unperturbed as if we were sitting through a tropical midafternoon rainstorm—a remarkable display of a commanding general's calm and "grace under pressure." Also, our artillery observer on Cipik's Ridge had refused to take cover and stood gazing through his field glasses, searching for a flash of light or some other sign that would reveal the Japanese firing position. He finally sighted a flash and immediately called for counter-battery fire, which was instantly delivered. Thus, the enemy fire was silenced. Our communications system had been completely knocked out. It was now top priority to get it repaired, and Captain Walker and his crew were already at work getting the lines connected.

Meanwhile, as if having dropped by for a cup of tea, our visitors leisurely took their leave, thanking us for our hospitality and "warm reception," filing back down the east-west trail to resume their command of the war in our part of the world. They carried with them a tale of high risk and bold adventure, which when told to the attentive ears of junior officers at the general's mess should be impressive—it was to me when it happened!

I had to turn my attention to the battle at hand. Third Battalion's L Company had run into two Japanese machine-gun emplacements that had escaped the artillery barrage. Lt. Col. Ralph "Rex" King, commander of that battalion, called me to report that these guns were holding up L Company's advance. He requested artillery fire to eliminate the bunkers. This was a tough call for me. It was imperative that the regiment's advance not bog down. When Rex's call came in, there was now a gap of approximately two hundred yards between the Second Battalion, which had advanced to the first phase line, and the Third Battalion. Delay posed a real danger that the Japanese would rally and move around the Second Battalion and divide the regiment.

But as urgent as the need was, I couldn't order an artillery strike because we couldn't pinpoint the precise location of the machine-gun emplacements holding up L Company's advance. We could mark the area by smoke signals, but smoke drifts. To complicate matters, I couldn't tell the precise position of the other companies in the Third Battalion. They would have to be pulled back before the artillery could fire where the machine-gun emplacements were reported to be. In addition to a crucial delay, there was always a danger of some artillery shells falling short.

Nothing is more devastating to the morale of assaulting troops than to be struck by friendly fire. We were in a difficult position. Colonel McHenry was sitting nearby, attentive to my conversation with Rex. I asked Rex to hold and repeated his request to the colonel. McHenry thought for a moment, then asked what I suggested we do. I told him, that in my opinion, the Third Battalion had to continue to advance using its own weapons. The risk of hitting our own forces with artillery was too great. I also emphasized that delay could cause additional casualties and possibly jeopardize the mission. Colonel McHenry then took the phone and instructed Lieutenant Colonel King to destroy the enemy machine-gun emplacements with the weapons he had on hand, move forward, and restore contact with the Second Battalion.

Just as Lieutenant Colonel King was receiving his orders from Colonel McHenry, he also received word that Capt. "Bones" Turnbull, one of the two remaining officers in his company, had been killed while leading an assault against the two Japanese machine-gun bunkers that were keeping L Company pinned down.

He was left now with only two officers, Capt. Johnny Kovacs and Lt. Johnny "Irish" O'Neal. Kovacs was a tough Hungarian we called "Hunky." He was a formidable, aggressive troop leader in the field—a natural leader of men who inspired confidence and loyalty. The marines in L Company would follow him whenever he ordered the command, "Let's go." He was always up front, leading by example, as he was doing on this crucial day.

While Company L was getting the bad news about its officer casualties, Lt. Johnny O'Neal was standing by awaiting orders.

In the attack against the gun emplacement, both officers were hit by direct fire. However, the bunkers with their crews were destroyed. Using only their infantry weapons, the men of Company L applied their skilled training and courageous hearts and eliminated the obstacle to their advance. Kovacs took a machine-gun bullet through his stomach. He fell in the gun's zone of fire but was pulled clear by a heroic corpsman. He was put on a poncho and carried back to the first aid station. The surgeons cleaned his wound, applied antibiotics, and gave him a shot of morphine to ease his way to the hospital ship. Before he was loaded on the AmTrack for transportation to the beach, Lieutenant O'Neal arrived. Despite his wounds, he had leaned on a fellow marine and walked the distance to the rear. Irish and Hunky saw each other and talked for a few moments, then Hunky was placed aboard the AmTrack. Irish's head wound was beyond anything the surgeons could do, and this excellent officer, this brave young marine, died within a few minutes after visiting with his friend and brother officer. Capt. Hunky Kovacs survived his wounds, but they shortened his life.

I had worked with Johnny Kovacs since the regiment was formed at New River in North Carolina. There, in Samoa, and at Guadalcanal we were together. We had had an occasional beer. We were friends. Fortunately, I was to see Hunky five years later when he came to Arkansas, as did John Monks, to help me in my campaign for governor.

Having eliminated the Japanese strong point, the Third Battalion reorganized and resumed its advance. The Japanese survivors rallied and, after receiving reinforcements, launched another fierce, no-prisoner assault. Meeting this attack in full stride, the battalion continued its advance in hand-to-hand, man-to-man, no-quarter struggle that ended with the complete destruction of the enemy's assaulting force.

The Third Battalion (as the First Battalion had done on D-Day when naval gunfire had not destroyed the gun emplacements on Cape Torokina) used its infantry weapons—rifles, BARs, hand grenades, dynamite, explosives, and flame throwers to destroy the Japanese emplacements. But at what a cost!

During this mission, the Second Battalion encountered additional Japanese reinforcements, but they were also eliminated. They then connected with the Third Battalion. The two units reviewed their initial objectives, then advanced to a line 1,150 yards east of their line of departure. Late in the afternoon on November 24, Thanksgiving Day, the Second and Third assault battalions reached their final objective. They connected their flanks, "circled their wagons," and prepared an all-around defense. They were alert to any further challenge the enemy might present. The First Battalion remained in reserve.

With the situation stabilized, Colonel McHenry released me to make a trip to the regimental rear command post and the medical company stationed near the regimental headquarters. On my way back to the advance command post, I encountered some weary marines who had brought down casualties to the field hospital. I visited with them for a few minutes, inquiring as to what outfits they belonged. There was one big, tired, black-bearded marine who was from Captain Kovacs's L Company. I asked him what had happened. His response was reported in John Monk's book, *A Ribbon and a Star:* "He [the marine] was about to drop in his tracks, and when asked what had happened, he was almost too tired to speak, but he answered in weary, confused gasps: 'There were machine guns out in front of us, Rex say go forward, Bones gets up—Bones dead. The Hunky say we got to go forward—the Hunky go down. Irish get up—try to go forward—Irish dead. All officers gone. Whole company split up—I bring Hunky home.'" This was Thanksgiving Day.

There was an officer from the regimental Weapons Company standing by. I instructed this officer to get these men together, feed them, bed them down, and get them to their outfits in the morning. This young, compassionate marine officer promptly responded with an "Aye, aye, Sir," and with these tired and hungry marines under his wing, he moved them into his company area. I have no doubt that they were well fed, had a good night's sleep, and dutifully reported back to their units early the next morning. They were marines.

I proceeded down the east-west trail. I saw that every available officer, marine, and corpsman was on the job. They were directing traffic, moving stalled vehicles out of the mud, lifting wounded marines out of the amphibian tractors, getting them into the medical company for emergency treatment, then reloading the wounded on vehicles to be transported down the muddy and bumpy jungle road to the evacuation hospital. Everyone in the regimental supply station was busy responding to the requests from the battalions for ammunition, food, clothing, and medical supplies.

Capt. Jack Foley's Intelligence Section was assimilating and evaluating information that had accumulated during the day and transmitting it to the division headquarters. I visited with Captain Foley for a few minutes. He was keenly interested in the story of the distinguished visitors who had, without notice, appeared at our forward command post during the battle. He wished to know what would prompt a lieutenant general, commanding the First Marine Amphibious Corps in charge of Bougainville operations, to come up to an advance command post during a battle. I briefly related to Jack what had happened but had no explanation for why the general and his staff had "dropped in" on us.

(Moving to the present day, a short time ago I was reminiscing about this incident and called my friend, Gen. Al Bowser, who is now ninety years old and living in Hawaii, to ask about his memory of this event. Even though I had not seen him since the war, when I identified myself, he responded at once, "Oh, the governor." General Bowser was alert and young of voice and as we talked, I asked him what he remembered about his visit to the command post with the generals during the Battle of Piva Forks. He quickly responded, "What I remember most was thinking, 'How am I going to tell my boss, General Turnage, that I took the command general of the Marine Amphibious Force up to the front and got him killed?'" I could see that could have been a real problem.)

This Battle at Piva Forks was the engagement in our Bougainville campaign. It destroyed the Japanese opposition on the island and allowed the Seabees to build the fighter strip and the bomber field. They were both in operation by the time our regiment left the island. Bougainville then became a base to support the United States Navy. Henderson Field at Guadalcanal, along with the airfields at Munda and Bougainville, enabled our air and naval forces to command the skies and the sea lanes in the Southwest Pacific. This was essential for General MacArthur's return to the Philippines and the capture of other Pacific islands and atolls, leading to our ultimate objective— the Land of the Rising Sun.

Before shipping out of Bougainville, considering all that had happened to the Third Regiment in the fifty-five days there, General Caldwell arranged a memorial service at the beach cemetery for the marines—his marines, his people—who would not be going home. The service was brief, appropriate, and inspiring. It served as a closure, a release of the grief for those comrades who had fallen, as each one called up names and faces of their closest friends or others because of the manner in which they had died.

I called up the names and faces of Johnny "Irish" O'Neal, "Bones" Turnbull, and though he survived, "Hunky" Kovacs. I remembered the big, tired marine with the black beard who had told what had happened to the officers of L Company.

I still remember:

> Support us, Oh, Lord, all the day long, until the shadows lengthen and evening comes, and this busy world is hushed, and life's fitful fever is over, and our work is done. And then, Oh, Lord, in Thy infinite mercy, grant us a safe lodging, a holy place where we may find rest, and peace at last.

On November 27, the Third Marine Regiment was relieved by the Ninth Marines. We fell back to a defensive position of the division's right flank. On December 22, our regiment was relieved by the Second Raider Regiment. We were then reinforced with a parachute battalion and placed in corps reserve, preparatory to being shipped to Guadalcanal. On December 25, aboard the USS *George Climber,* we headed to Guadalcanal. There we received Christmas presents, letters from home, sleep, and three squares a day. Although we sailed with sadness, remembering friends who would not be present for the mail call, we were buoyed with pride in the knowledge that we had met the supreme test of battle and had won.

Capt. John C. Chapin, United States Marine Corps, Retired, historian for the History and Museum Division Headquarters, United States Marine Corps, writing about marine operations in the Northern Solomons recorded: "The Battle of Piva Forks (on Bougainville) had ended with a dramatic, hard-fought victory which had 'broken the back of organized enemy resistance.'"

Referring, again, to my reading of the history of the Civil War, I

Lt. Col. Sid McMath, Gen. Oscar Caldwell, and Capt. John Monks, home again U.S.A.

was impressed by the officers who received promotions on the battle-field. I was honored, following the Battle of Piva Forks, by receiving a battlefield promotion to lieutenant colonel. This award accompanied the Legion of Merit and the Silver Star for the D-Day landing at Empress Augusta Bay and Piva Forks.

XI﹥ COCONUT GROVE

THEN WE RETURNED TO GUADALCANAL, COCONUT GROVE, THE TENT camp that seemingly we had left years ago—showers, shaves, haircuts, underclothes, shoes, socks, service uniforms that fit, hot food, mail call, letters from home, Christmas packages, a ration of two beers in the evening—how could it get any better than this?

But then there always seems to be a down side. There was a gray cloud behind the silver lining. There was sick call with ulcers, athlete's foot, jungle rot, infections, malaria, and filariasis.

At full strength, the Third Regiment consisted of approximately 3,500 men. This did not include troops attached for landing operations, who after landing were returned to their parent organization. "The Regiment had sustained 485 combat casualties and 1,331 noncombat casualties. One-third of the total, or 417, noncombat casualties were victims of filariasis. Not less than 1,696 Japanese were killed in action in contact with the Third Marines, Reinforced."[1] There was no record of the number of Japanese wounded during the Bougainville campaign, but based upon experience, it would have been approximately three times the number of men killed.

Some of the 257 American combat fatigue cases (total exhaustion) subsequently displayed filariasis symptoms. I was no exception. The regimental medical officer found that I had filariasis, and I was ordered hospitalized. The treatment at the time was principally rest and removal from the endemic area, so I was ordered stateside to the United States Naval Hospital in San Diego.

Soon after receiving my diagnosis from the doctor, General Turnage, still in command of the division, sent for me. General Turnage was a great man, an outstanding field commander, a Southern gentleman to the core, in the most commendable sense. He had been director of the Marine Officers' Basic School when I was a student and had been commanding officer of the marine base at New River, North Carolina, when the Third Regiment was formed and had commanded

---

1. Col. George O. Van Orden, Combat Report, Third Marine Regiment, Bougainville Campaign, January 22, 1944

the Third Marine Division (reinforced) in the Bougainville campaign. I had the privilege of having a close association with General Caldwell, since he, as a colonel, was in command of the Third Regiment when it was formed up, and I was appointed as operations and training officer. I worked closely with him in training the regiment in New River, Samoa, and Guadalcanal. I was then moved to the division headquarters as the assistant division operations officer.

I had not the faintest notion of why the commanding general would be sending for me. I reported to the general's headquarters as instructed, was promptly escorted in to the general's desk, and stood at attention. He gave me "at ease," and informed me that he knew of the medical officer's diagnosis. He wondered if two weeks' leave in Australia would get me in sufficient shape to remain with the division.

General Caldwell had been ordered to return to the States and to take over command of the Marine Replacement Training Command at Camp Pendleton, California, and he had requested that, upon discharge from the naval hospital, I be assigned there as his operations and training officer. Requiring hospital care and having served under General Caldwell's command thus far in the war, I chose to go with him.

Leaving Guadalcanal, General Caldwell picked me up in his jeep, directed his driver to the Third Marine Regiment's tent camp area, where we drove slowly through the company streets, taking our leave from the marines in the regiment. With strong, conflicting feelings, and divided sentiments, I left the marines with whom I had lived, trained, and fought for what seemed to be a lifetime and boarded the ship that would carry me home.

At long last, after days at sea, we passed under the Golden Gate Bridge. There are few experiences equal that of sailing under this magnificent monument and into the beautiful and serene San Francisco Bay, returning home from war.

It is a feeling of celebration, firecrackers, Roman candles, flags, clusters of stars bursting in the sky, a bit of home, the girl next door, "a piece of Mom's apple pie."

I took a train from San Francisco to San Diego, checked into the hospital, remained there for approximately three months, receiving excellent care, and was then discharged. I was looking forward to returning to duty. I reported to General Caldwell as his training officer, but not before a visit home to see my family. My son, Sandy, was then almost three years old.

I received two weeks' leave. I was traveling on military, space-available transportation, hence, could not tell my mother the time of my arrival. I caught a ride on a military transport plane to Memphis, and from there took a bus to Little Rock where I changed buses for Hot Springs. The hour was late. I had been on the plane and on the bus a long time. I needed fresh air and exercise, so I walked home from the terminal.

I remembered the day that my mother had walked me to school my first day, in Bussey. I recalled how she had sung songs and whistled tunes popular at the time, her favorite being "Red Wing," which I had learned to whistle.

Three blocks from home I began whistling this memorable tune. My parents' home, 300 Cherokee Street in Hot Springs, sprang alive with lights. In no time my mother was out the front door and met me as I approached the front yard, greeting me as all mothers greet a son who may have been lost for a time and is found—she was crying as we embraced. This was a warm homecoming. The next morning, after two years' separation, I was reunited with my son.

XII⹆ ANNE PHILLIPS

I SERVED FOR A TIME AS TRAINING OFFICER FOR THE MARINE TRAINING Replacement Command at Camp Pendleton in California. In April of 1944, I was ordered to Marine Corps Headquarters in Washington, D.C., for temporary duty of two weeks, to work on a revision of infantry training, getting ready for what appeared to be the inevitable invasion of Japan.

We were entering a new phase of war and moving ever closer to the heart of Japan. It was time to alter our mindset from combat in the jungles and adapt to the tactics and training of a more conventional war. Since there were no indications that the Japanese would surrender, we had to presume that they would defend their home islands step by step, yard by yard, with no quarter asked or given. Based upon our experience on Tarawa, Saipan, Iwo Jima, and Okinawa, the Joint Chiefs of Staff had estimated, and so advised President Truman, that Americans would suffer a million casualties should we invade Japan. This was the reality the president would face when the burden fell on him to make the most horrendous decision any president had been called upon to make—to drop the atomic bomb.

Readying for the invasion, we had no knowledge, nor had we heard any "scuttlebutt," about a secret weapon; so we assumed that on that fateful day, victory or defeat would depend on the marine and the foot soldier, armed with infantry weapons and with supporting arms, as had historically been the case.

After I arrived in Washington, D.C., to join in the planning of this final challenge to the foot soldier, I called Nancy Nelson. She and Elaine had been roommates at Christian College in Missouri, and they had become warm friends over the years, staying in contact and corresponding. After Elaine's death, Nancy and I remained in touch. She was interested in Sandy and went to Hot Springs at least once during the war to visit him and his grandmothers.

During the war Nancy worked for Congressman Roger Slaughter from Missouri. Although she ran his Washington office, she would go to Missouri also to run the congressman's home office during election years.

The day that I called Nancy, she was going to a dinner party with a coworker in the congressman's office. I was invited and we met for the dinner. Nancy's friend and coworker was Sarah Anne Phillips of Slate Spring, Mississippi. Anne was tall, beautiful, twenty-three years old, and fascinated by politics. The hostess and her guests were all government employees, working mostly for senators and congressmen. Anne was most popular with the group and had just been elected Miss Capitol Hill. I fear I monopolized Anne's time. As we circulated among the guests, we found ourselves together and were dinner partners. Afterward, we found a relatively quiet corner where we spent the evening engrossed in conversation about ourselves and the subject of mutual interest—politics.

The two weeks passed rapidly—too fast. Anne and I both worked by day and then went out in the evenings, often to dance to the World War II popular tunes that we both loved. When I returned to Camp Pendleton, my thoughts remained in Washington—but not at the Marine Corps Headquarters. I would call Anne, frequently at night, disregarding the time difference between Washington, D.C., and California, many times, waking her up from a deep sleep. I courted her with poetry, quotes from *Romeo and Juliet* and *Omar Khayam*.

Around the first of September 1944, I was transferred to Washington, D.C., Marine Corps Headquarters, Infantry Section of Plans and Policies, for permanent duty. Upon arrival I checked in at the Old Washington Hotel, where I had stayed in April, unpacked, freshened up, and made an unannounced visit to the Capitol Hill office of Congressman Slaughter. Knowing that the congressman and Nancy were in Missouri campaigning, I walked into his office. No one was there except a beautiful, blond Southern belle named Anne. The office was silent except for the rhythmic purring of her typewriter and a radio that was playing "It Had to Be You." I knew then that I would ask her to be my bride.

During the next few days, in the evenings, we dated, dined, danced, and talked about my political plans—my aim to run for prosecuting attorney in Garland County, to change the political complexion of my hometown, and to run for governor—and some of the goals I hoped to reach for my state. We discussed the sacrifices that politics would require, and particularly, how savage the campaign would be against the "gang" in Hot Springs, who were backed by the mob.

We spoke about Sandy, talking in depth about the possible problems and rewards of newlyweds having a three-year-old as a wedding present. Sandy had had precious time with his mother before she died but had lived alternately with his grandmothers for two and a half years. How would he respond to us, virtually strangers in his life? After much meditation, Anne accepted the challenge. With all our discussions and probing of the future, there was no way we could foresee what would unfold, but we had no fears. We were young, in love, confident, and committed to our life's adventure.

As Anne's parents were at home in Mississippi, the only relative Anne had in Washington was her younger sister, Dorris Phillips. So I took my case to Dorris, presented my petition, and asked for her sister's hand. She gave us her approval with her blessing. On October 6, 1944, we were married at the Mount Vernon Methodist Church in Washington, D.C., with Dorris as maid of honor. The two friends who stood up for me were Chuck Bailey and A. B. Bonds.

Anne's parents were James Fair and Jimmie Vance Phillips. Her people had come to America during the colonial period, settling in Virginia and North Carolina. A relative, Zebulon Baird Vance, a governor and United States senator for North Carolina, is one of two people from North Carolina in the Statuary Hall in the United States Capitol.

Her family settled in Mississippi during territorial days and homesteaded large tracts of land. Due to the long-established family custom of parceling off a farm for a newly married son, the land was divided up and ownership eventually passed from the family. When the last parcel of land was sold, Anne and her sister, Dorris, kept a parcel of timberland for sentimental reasons; it is still in the family to be passed to the children.

Anne had graduated from high school at sixteen and was admitted as a freshman at Mississippi State College for Women. Her mother was an honor graduate of this college and had been a professor of mathematics there. During Anne's orientation week, all students were shown a glass case containing an annual opened to Jimmie Vance's picture, with a citation stating that "no student has ever equaled or surpassed her scholarship in higher mathematics." Her mother held master's degrees in both mathematics and Latin from the University of Chicago and was offered a scholarship in medicine by John Hopkins. This offer of a medical scholarship was an unusually high compliment for a woman before women's suffrage. However, she was unable to accept because she had to return to Mississippi to care for her dying father. After her father's death, she ran his business in the small town of Slate Spring until her daughter, Anne, was born. Thereafter, responding to the community's need, she became a schoolteacher and taught math and English for many years, instructing and endearing herself to scores of students who remembered her fondly and referred to her as "Miss Jimmie."

Anne's father, James Fair Phillips, also called "Jimmy," was a cotton farmer from Philadelphia, Neshoba County, Mississippi. He moved from there as a young man to the Delta at the end of the nineteenth century, where he hunted and farmed the rich bottomland near the river.

Restless and energetic, he also found a farm to his liking in north Mississippi, near Slate Spring. Here he met the other "Jimmie," Anne's mother, who, after a long courtship, he married.

Following his marriage, he sold the Delta farm and settled permanently in the so-called hills of Calhoun County, sinking his roots deep. Here, when not busy hunting and telling marvelous stories, he grew cotton, raised a family, built a house, a church, a Masonic Lodge, and a cotton gin. In a word, he was a successful and contented Southern gentleman of the old school.

After our marriage, Anne and I went first to Mississippi and then to Arkansas to visit our families and for Anne to meet Sandy. We brought him back to Washington with us, and my mother came also, remaining for several weeks to help Sandy and Anne to make the transition. When Mother went home, Sandy was happy to stay. Fortunately, we were able to obtain a first floor, spacious apartment within walking distance of Marine Corps Headquarters. This enabled me to be close by if needed. Anne was magnificent—being a new bride, taking over a little three-year-old boy, caring for and loving him as her own, which she did.

While in Washington, we celebrated the end of the war in both Europe and Japan. In the fall of 1945, Anne and I were expecting a blessed event. Since she wanted to have her baby at home, she and Sandy went to Slate Spring and stayed with her parents. I remained on duty until late in December and was able to join them on Christmas Eve. On the morning of December 25, 1945, our second son was on the way—earlier than scheduled. We drove to Memphis, and Anne was admitted to Baptist Hospital. I took a book, and since this appeared to be a good chance, I found a quiet place with a comfortable chair and settled down to read. But I had finished only the first chapter, engrossed in the story, when a nurse came in and excitedly announced that Phillip had arrived and both mother and son were doing well. I have yet to finish reading the book.

When Anne was released, we returned with our baby to Slate Spring. In January 1946, leaving Anne and the boys with her parents, I left Mississippi for Hot Springs, Arkansas, to find a place for our family to live.

Now released from active duty, immediately, with other GIs, I fought in another war—on the homefront—and, in a way, it was much more treacherous than the war against the Japanese.

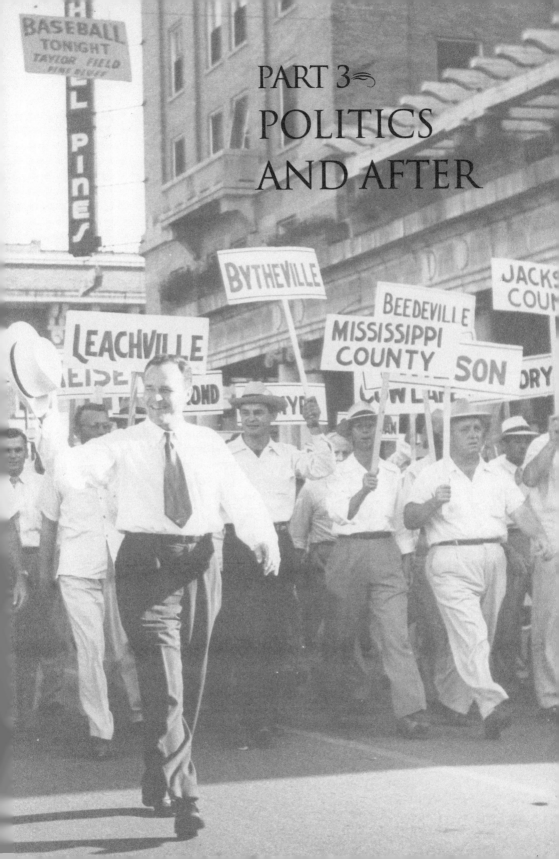

PART 3 —
POLITICS
AND AFTER

1 THE GI REVOLT

HOT SPRINGS WAS A NOTORIOUS, WIDE-OPEN TOWN. A MULTIMILLION-dollar gambling operation was its life, entertainment was its lure, civic corruption was its distinction. But unlike Las Vegas and other cities, gambling in Hot Springs was against the law.

Gambling itself is a lure to the unwary, a temptation to the weak, an addictive poison to the gullible. Innocent people are victimized, families are impoverished and children left to go hungry when the head of a family, drawn to the gaming table like a moth to a lighted lamp, throws away his paycheck or exhausts his savings on a throw of the dice, a turn of the wheel, or a deal of the cards. But the most sinister evil of illegal gambling is the very existence of those in authority, the elected officials, who further their own personal interests and private gain, rather than protect the rights of the citizens they are duty-bound to represent. Gambling powers have to control law enforcement, or the lack thereof, for their own security and the protection of their illegal operations.

This was the condition that existed in Hot Springs for a quarter of a century. The city machine was controlled by the mob, which in turn controlled the election commissions that selected the judges and clerks for the party primaries and the general elections. Election judges and clerks were recruited from casinos, bars, bookies, and allied businessmen. Thus, the outcome of any election in the city or county was "fixed," since a sufficient number of "magicians" in the polling places and "magic" in the ballot box ensured victory for the mob's slate of selected candidates.

The political bosses in Hot Springs picked the judges, the prosecuting attorney, the mayor, the chief of police, the sheriff, the constable, and grand juries—all those involved with law enforcement responsibilities.

Any citizen who dared to run for office, opposing a candidate anointed by the machine, was subjected to "reasoning and persuasion" as to the error of his ways. This, failing, the recalcitrant was subjected to certain sanctions. Perhaps, for example, this advocate of law and justice might have a mortgage, with payments due, that might be purchased and the mortgage foreclosed, or his business could be investigated and closed for some obsolete ordinance violation. If these "gentle" tactics were not productive, this "troublemaker" would be arrested, locked up, and subjected to a kangaroo court with punishment administered by policemen acting as "security guards" in the jail.

Not only did the machine control the elections and poll-tax registration, it also controlled the process of selecting petit jurors, supposedly the "twelve good men and true," who were judges of the facts in civil or criminal cases and serving on grand juries, were empowered to indict any "violators" of the law.

Reprisals were directed against those who did not "get along by going along," who cast an unfriendly vote in the ballot box, voted wrong in the jury verdict, or were "getting out of line." Even though reprisals were carried out quietly without any publicity the local press was "not nosy" about "such things." These punitive actions were known and spread around and about the city—in the bars, brothels, bathhouses, in the lobbies of the hotels, in the casinos, and the bookie organizations—all places where prosperity hung by the thread of approval by those in power.

In the winter season, Hot Springs could have in residence more gangland warlords than New York, Chicago, or Las Vegas. The "big boys" came and went, in and out of town: Al Capone, Lucky Luciano, Pretty Boy Floyd, the Barkers, and other underworld characters. As frequent visitors, they were big tippers, free spenders, high rollers. Oney Madden had become a permanent resident of Hot Springs, marrying the postmaster's daughter, after he was given the option by a rival mob in New York to either leave town or run the risk of being found in the Hudson River wearing "concrete shoes." Although I am unaware of any illegal activities in which he was involved on the local scene, he apparently maintained his connections and was a contact for visiting Dons of the criminal world and other displaced mobsters looking for a stake.

In 1946, the city bosses were more powerful, more deeply entrenched than before the war. The returning GIs were appalled that the people of Hot Springs and Garland County were denied "Free elections where the citizen could cast his ballot freely without fear and intimidation and have that vote counted as cast; and the Constitutional right of a fair and impartial trial by jury."

A 1942 federal grand jury reported that every provision required by the State's statutes for the preservation and protection of the bal-lot was wholly ignored and violated. A later grand jury report sum-marized the conditions in Hot Springs in the summer of 1946, the extent of graft and corruption in this city is unbelievable. It has touched our school system, our social, religious, and business lives.

The overthrow of the McLaughlin machine had been a long-resolved personal mission formulated during my early youth in Hot Springs. I had observed first hand the exercise of power by this admin-istration to control the life of the potentially rich national park city. In the pursuit of this objective, a promise I had made to myself, I began recruiting veterans, GIs, as they returned home from the war.

With a determination to confront these abuses, the GIs organized with military precision. We fielded a candidate for each office in Garland County (Hot Springs) in the Democratic primary of July 1946.

I filed for prosecuting attorney for the Eighteenth Judicial District. My longtime friend, Clyde Brown, filed for district judge. These two district offices included both Garland and Montgomery Counties.

The campaign was mean, tough, and hard fought. The political bosses tightened the screws, meeting with all city and county employ-ees, people working the gambling houses and hotels, and business-men who were dependent upon the tourist trade. Not only were they instructed to get their families and relatives of voting age to the polls and advise them to vote for the administration's candidates, they were told that the administration would know how they voted, so their jobs, dependent on the largess, were at stake.

Leo McLaughlin, the mayor of Hot Springs, was the leader, the head, the boss of the Garland County political machine. Flamboyant and colorful, he was a natty dresser, emulating the dress and bearing of Boss Crump of Memphis.

His Honor, the mayor, on fair sunny days, would entertain and favor his loyal subjects routinely. He would drive down Central Avenue, the main street in Hot Springs, in a carriage drawn by his prize prancing steeds, "Scotch" and "Soda."

Leo was an able lawyer, personable and persuasive before a jury, especially a jury of his people selected by his jury commissioners and presided over by his judge. Under those circumstances, he was unbeatable.

Mayor Leo T. McLaughlin and horses, "Scotch" and "Soda"

On election eve at the called meeting of his people at the city auditorium, the mayor, at the top of his form, was speaker and instructor and motivator. This rally was a must for all who were employed directly or indirectly in the business or service of catering to the appetites, the pleasures, the passions of the visitors who came for fun, with funds, to "The City without a Lid."

The faithful would be lavished with praise for their loyalty and contribution to the prosperity and reputation of the city. The mayor would point with pride and view with alarm, warning against any outsider that might threaten their beneficent system, or any insiders, troublemakers, that might seek to undermine the good order of things in his kingdom.

He sent them out thus motivated, to vote as many times as they had poll-tax receipts in hand on election day. Those with blocks of poll taxes would distribute them to drifters on the streets and to those in bars who would for a toddy or "ten-spot" be transported to the nearest polling place to "exercise their right of franchise."

Then there were the "magicians" in custody of the ballot boxes, who would, when the polls closed, wave a wand, so that magically the number of votes needed would appear, be counted, and certified as correct.

During the campaign the GIs had rallies in every precinct or ward, and everyone worked in pairs, no one worked alone, handing out literature urging people to go to the polls and vote for the GI ticket.

During the closing days of the election we used the radio extensively for talks, short announcements, and for messages urging the people to vote. This was summertime and few people had air-conditioning, so their windows were open. The night before the election I was greatly encouraged when walking through a neighborhood, passing houses along the street, I heard their radios—and they were listening to our program.

On election day we had camera crews set up at two of the largest wards where repeater voting was most notorious. With the knowledge of J. Edgar Hoover, director of the FBI, we circulated word that "G-men" were in town investigating the violation of election laws. In the two heavy-voting wards it was suggested that the cameramen themselves might be FBI agents.

In addition to cruising the wards and having watchers at the polling places, we held in reserve an emergency squad headquartered at the Clinton-Ricks Automobile Agency garage. They were provided with transportation and were in sufficient strength to be helpful in the event our supporters were muscled at the polls or an effort made to keep them from voting.

Our workers manned telephones and ran carpools to get people to the polls, but despite all of our efforts, the time and energy and money spent, the vote was unusually light. Many people stayed away from the polls, not sufficiently confident to go and vote for us for fear of reprisals.

But the machine got out its "vote," as their judges and clerks tallied the results. Every GI candidate was defeated in Garland County, despite the courage, sacrifice, and hard work, the "blood, sweat and tears."

However, Montgomery County was included with Garland County (Hot Springs) in the Eighteenth Judicial District where Clyde Brown and I were running. By coincidence or stroke of fate, telephone lines from Montgomery County to Hot Springs were temporarily out of order; hence, the Hot Springs "bosses," not being able to learn the number of votes I had gotten in Montgomery County, were denied knowledge of how many additional votes "to count" in Garland County to ensure my defeat. Therefore, their magicians in the polling places were unable to conjure up the votes required in the final tally to deny me the election.

When all the returns were in, I had carried Montgomery County with a sufficient majority to overcome the "count" in Garland County. Unfortunately, Clyde Brown was defeated. So, I was the only GI candidate nominated in the Democratic primary—tantamount to election.

Following the defeat of the GIs in the Democratic primary in Garland County, the mayor, his lieutenants, and all who formed the base of his organization celebrated. They had beaten back the only threat to their power and the goods and treasure that power supplied, and they were self-assured that I, the newly elected prosecuting attorney for the Eighteenth Judicial District, would not present a problem. The bosses still controlled all law enforcement officials, judges, jury commissioners, and the election machinery in the county. They also were certain that this young prosecutor could be convinced that to "get along would be to go along."

After the Democratic primary in July a meeting of all of the officials in the McLaughlin administration, plus key lieutenants, was held at the home of Judge Vern Ledgerwood at Lake Hamilton. Having won the nomination in the primary for prosecuting attorney, I was invited to attend.

When I went to this meeting, I knew everyone present and had known them most of my life—they had been perpetuated in office, being replaced only by death, which seldom occurred among those with a life tenure. I was warmly welcomed into the pack.

I sat quietly and said nothing, except to pass the time of day, but while listening, I studied each person closely and was impressed with their confidence, resulting from their pyrrhic victory. I knew something they did not know—but "Old B'rer Fox he just lay low."

The GI's failure in the Democratic primary to win a single office in Garland County was a blow. Not only to us, but also for the many citizens who were pulling for us, hoping we would win.

"Spider" Rowland, a gifted and popular political writer for the *Arkansas Gazette*, with a keen insight into Arkansas politics, prophesying on the GI Revolt against McLaughlin's empire, wrote, ". . . whether the GI's can shuffle up a majority of the votes is something else again, moreover McLaughlin is slicker than a bucket full of greased eels and . . . the GI's can expect a double injection of major league trouble, in fact, they're going to run into more difficulties than a guy trying to light a cigar in a revolving door."[1]

However, this disappointment was brief. Our hopes were restored, our energies revived and renewed, when it struck us that all was not lost: with no opposition, I had been elected prosecuting attorney, chief law enforcement officer in the Eighteenth Judicial District including Garland and Montgomery Counties. We had a camel's head in the tent, so to speak.

The general election was only three months away. We had another chance as every GI candidate, defeated in the Democratic primary, could run as an Independent and be on the ballot in the general election.

Having elected a prosecuting attorney, the GIs were sufficiently motivated and the people encouraged to wage a massive poll-tax drive for the general election. At that time, in order to vote in a political primary, the law required that a poll tax be paid a year in advance, but to vote in a general election, a poll tax could be purchased up to twenty days before the election.

It was also imperative that the fraudulent poll taxes issued by the machine, on which they relied, had to be challenged, declared void,

---

1. *Arkansas Gazette*, Little Rock, July 5, 1944.

and canceled. This required the filing of a petition in the court, presenting evidence to prove the fraud and pray for relief. Since such a relief could not possibly be obtained from a corrupt state court where the judge would be an accessory or at the least, a beneficiary, of the gambling syndicate's liberality, there had to be another way.

Nathan Shoenfeld, a longtime friend and associate, a courageous and brilliant lawyer, came up with the idea of obtaining federal jurisdiction, in which United States District Court judge John E. Miller of Fort Smith would preside.

In 1937, John Miller had taken exception to the fact that Gov. Carl Bailey had obtained for himself the Democratic nomination for senator, not by running in the primary, but by being named by the state Democratic committee. Believing that senators should be elected by the people, Miller had run as an Independent and been elected by a substantial majority. He had served with distinction, retiring from the Senate to accept an appointment as a United States District Court judge. He was an excellent judge, learned in the law and of sterling character, and he possessed the implicit trust of the Bar Association and the confidence of the people. Since he had run for the Senate as an Independent, he might, we felt, understand the GIs doing the same thing—in effect following the precedent which he had set.

In order to give the federal courts jurisdiction, the election had to involve the election of a federal officer, so Pat Mullis, a classmate in law school and a dear friend, whose residence was in Dumas, agreed to run for Congress. It was too late for him to file as a party candidate, but he announced as a write-in candidate. We immediately filed suit in the United States District Court in Hot Springs to have the fraudulent poll taxes voided, knowing that hard evidence was required to sustain the suit.

Having carefully laid our plans and mapped our course, we announced to the world our purpose. Each GI candidate, defeated in the Democratic primary, filed as an Independent in the coming general election.

We reactivated our telephone groups and our carpools. We divided up the wards and precincts and assigned teams to canvass the homes to get people registered to vote and revive the hopes of the people who wanted the old gang out.

Using the poll-tax directory, we began checking on people, especially in the Second and Third Wards, the machine's heavy-voting wards, to determine if the person listed in the poll-tax book had his poll-tax receipt. We remembered that a proxy could obtain a poll-tax receipt, but it had to be delivered within five days. We also knew that many of the votes which were illegally issued were being held by a few individuals to be given on election day to people who could be relied upon to vote the administration's ticket. We had to void these illegal poll-tax receipts, which otherwise would be used against us.

Two of our workers, Birdie Fulton and Otis Livingstone, gathering information on illegal voting, were "detained" by the opposition, the evidence confiscated, and they were threatened with bodily harm if they continued. Birdie and Otis, former football players, were not intimidated, but they had been deprived of the evidence they had so diligently gathered.

Clyde Brown, now an independent candidate for circuit judge, and I. G. Brown, a candidate for sheriff, who was strong and stout of heart, went with me to call on Mayor McLaughlin. In his office we diplomatically conveyed to him that if they wanted to play rough, we had some people on our side who had had recent experience in that kind of activity. We had no further problems of that nature, but we remained alert and kept our powder dry.

We went to court before Judge Miller on the issue of illegal poll taxes, and trial had been in progress for several days when the court indicated that we had to present more substantial evidence, or our case would be dismissed by the court.

My wife, Anne, and Rosalee Brown, wife of Clyde Brown, had been hard at work scanning the poll-tax books, searching for a key as to how the poll-tax receipts could be issued in blocks, held until distributed on election day, and voted. They were still working late into the evening, and with our court deadline looming, we were getting a little panicky. Then Anne let out an exclamation, "I think I have it!"

It had become apparent to her when she went over the names of the voters, one by one, in each of the wards, that blocks of poll-tax receipts had been issued in alphabetical order, six names, twelve names, or eighteen names. She realized it was inconceivable that citizens going into the clerk's office to pay their poll tax and get a poll-tax receipt would file up in alphabetical order, i.e., Adams, Brown, Casey, Davis, English, Fox, Garvelle, House, and so forth.

Taking this information to court, we were given a recess (extra time) to gather proof. We had alleged in our challenge of the illegal poll-tax receipts that some nineteen of McLaughlin's political followers held blocks of poll-tax receipts based on illegal or nonexistent authorization. We established, with witnesses now willing to come forward and willing to testify, that some authorizations were "signed" by dead people or by people who no longer lived in Garland County and had been absent for several years, and that the addresses on some receipts were nonexistent or the addresses were vacant lots.

We retained a handwriting expert from the Kansas Bureau of Investigation who examined many of the fraudulent authorizations and testified that they had been written in the same handwriting.

Several of our witnesses, at the moment of reckoning, became faint of heart and still could not maintain sufficient courage to oppose the "gang." However, one witness, a night-club operator, came forward with courage to defy his old masters and testified that he had two hundred receipts, poll-tax receipts, in alphabetical order that had been issued by the county collector which were to be voted on the day of election. The procedure would be to select a needy individual, one who needed a drink or was eager to make fast buck, to be given the poll-tax receipt with dollar bills attached with instructions to go forth and exercise his "right of franchise" at several polling places where it was known he would be welcome and warmly received.

We proved that 1,607 poll-tax receipts were invalid out of the 3,825 poll-tax receipts challenged. Also, we had information that one person had 2,100 poll-tax receipts, which had been obtained for use in the Democratic primary in July where all the GI candidates had been defeated, and although they could not be used in the general election, which was coming up in November, we believed this evidence would be relevant, in order to show a pattern of conduct or a standard procedure. This evidence was submitted to the judge, who was trying the case without a jury.

We knew that winning this case in federal court would have an impact far greater than the number of poll-tax receipts voided.

J. O. Campbell, a veteran and candidate for county assessor, who had worked with Anne and Rosalee when they discovered the unique method in which the unauthorized poll-tax receipts were being issued, testified about their finding. His testimony was so compelling that he was not even cross-examined by the defense lawyers.

On July 11, Judge Miller, United States district judge presiding, ruled on the case and canceled 1,607 poll-tax receipts, about 24 percent of the votes in Garland County. He directed the county election commissioners to revise the official poll-tax list and omit the names of everyone who held an invalidated receipt. The court voided 831 receipts obtained by eighteen of the nineteen friends and relatives of Mayor McLaughlin, who had been named as defendants in the case, and 776 of the 1,483 receipts obtained by one Will Page. Referring to the testimony of the GIs the handwriting expert from Kansas and the testimony of several witnesses that they wrote hundreds of names on "authorizations" to obtain receipts, Judge Miller held "that Mayor McLaughlin's organization had flagrantly violated Arkansas law." In his official ruling, Judge Miller went on to say, "The receipts were issued alphabetically, that did not happen accidently, but in accord with a plan devised by someone and without written authority from the individuals named on the receipts—receipts in the hands of individuals are *prima facie* evidence of the right to vote. Unless the plaintiffs are granted relief by this court, such receipts will be used as a means of casting illegal ballots which will dilute and diminish the effect of the legal voter."[2]

In response to Judge Miller's ruling, I issued the following statement, "The most important feature of this victory is that it proves that the McLaughlin machine is not all-powerful—we have just begun to fight. We will not quit until the government of Garland County is returned to the people and those individuals who hold positions of trust become responsive to the will of the people."[3]

We had established election fraud and had elected a prosecuting attorney. The morale of the GIs and their followers soared, and the hope of the people to remove the stranglehold of the McLaughlin machine was restored while fear was struck in the hearts of the opposition. Many

---

2. *Arkansas Gazette,* Little Rock, July 12, 1946.
3. *Arkansas Gazette,* Little Rock, July 12, 1946.

GI candidates were sworn in January 1947 in Garland County Courthouse, Hot Springs, Arkansas

began to abandon the sinking ship. Some came aboard to join the assault, which would take place on the first Tuesday in November, the day of the general election.

Our forces were reinvigorated and our poll-tax drive was accelerated. Telephone committee activities were doubled and carpools for getting out the vote were organized. Victory could be sensed in the air.

The vote on election day was the largest ever cast in Hot Springs, double the number of votes cast in the previous election. The GIs went "over the top," making a clean sweep. They captured every elective office in Garland County, plus the office of prosecuting attorney and circuit judge in the Eighteenth Judicial District.

Thus, the freedom of the ballot box was returned to the people of Garland County, so the rights of dissent and political participation were restored. Thereafter, they could vote for whom they chose without fear or intimidation and have their vote counted as cast.

The Seventh Amendment to the Constitution of the United States mandates that the right of trial by jury be preserved; this requires that a jury be fairly selected from a cross-section of the community, that they have no interest in the outcome of the case, and that they take an oath to, well and truly, try the case based upon the evidence. After the election, this inalienable right was restored.

The people of Hot Springs had been relieved of the conviction that only gambling was the source of a sound economy and the general well-being of the community. It was a bright new beginning for the city. Today, Hot Springs has moved into the twenty-first century, confident in the knowledge that their assets are unequaled, their environment for recreation unsurpassed. They are aware that their community can become a premier resort and recreational area in the United States.

The victory of the GIs in Hot Springs and Garland County and the benefits flowing from it was a fitting tribute to the young men who fought for freedom.

This GI movement was carried out in similar fashion in several other "machine" counties in Arkansas, securing improved and responsive local governments. But perhaps the most significant impact of the GI Revolt was that it paved the way for the political acceptance of more progressive ideas and candidates for state government.

II☙ PROSECUTING ATTORNEY

I ASSUMED THE RESPONSIBILITY OF PROSECUTING ATTORNEY FOR THE Eighteenth Judicial District, Garland and Montgomery Counties, in January 1947. I appointed two outstanding lawyers, who were war veterans and good friends, for my deputies.

Nathan Shoenfeld had been with me from the beginning of the campaign—part of all the planning and the execution of those plans. Not only had he conceived the idea of obtaining federal jurisdiction to expose the poll-tax fraud as I have mentioned, but he also was co-counsel with me in the trial of the case that won this crucial victory.

My other deputy was David Whittington, a brilliant lawyer, whose family was one of the oldest in Hot Springs. He had attended New Mexico Military Academy, serving in what I believe to be one of the last cavalry detachments in the United States Army.

David was an expert horseman and an adventuresome cadet. He believed that with guidance and persuasion, a horse could be ridden anywhere. To demonstrate this, on a dull day with boredom hovering in the air, he rode his prancing steed into the academy's mess hall during the lunch hour. The waiters were serving the main course. There followed a scurrying of waiters, a scrambling of cadets, broken dishes, and general bedlam. Cadet Whittington was punished by being unhorsed until his period of confinement to quarters had been served.

David had later served in the war with honor, and as my deputy prosecuting attorney, he served with distinction.

I left the running of the office and the trial of everyday cases to Nathan and David. I tried the major cases. One case I remember keenly and have thought about many times, recalling that, although today there is much debate about the death penalty, when I was prosecuting attorney, there was no debate at all.

In this case, a young man had followed his wife into a restaurant and bar on Central Avenue, proceeding without word or remonstrance to shoot her. She instantly died. He was arrested and tried for murder in the first degree. Even though the family of the deceased wife requested that I ask the jury for the death penalty, after putting on the facts of the case, which were overwhelming, I asked for life imprisonment.

This young man had followed his wife with the intent to kill and had deliberately executed her. But there was an extenuating factor which weighed heavily on my mind and rested on my heart. He had served heroically in the war and bore its emotional wounds, and his soul was obviously wrenched by what he had done. I asked the jury for life imprisonment, which was done by a unanimous vote of the jury. It is my earnest hope that the family, over the years, became reconciled to this verdict. I still feel that it was just.

In 1949, during my first term as governor, I was invited by Capt. Lee Hensley, the prison superintendent, to come to the prison at Cummins near Pine Bluff. He ran a tight ship with a firm hand, but underneath his exterior of firmness was a heart of compassion for the prisoners under his command and jurisdiction.

There was an Alcoholics Anonymous group for the prisoners, and Captain Hensley, being aware of my interest in this program, invited me to visit the prisoners who were struggling with this addiction. Because of my father's alcoholism, I was happy to do so.

Needless to say, the meeting was well attended and conducted in perfect order. I talked briefly; I could sense that a number of the prisoners wished to ask questions and make statements. So, we had a lively audience participation session where several inmates made moving confessions, attributing their imprisonment, their loss of family, jobs, and the respect of friends, to this demon that had made them captive—they were imprisoned before they came to prison, they said, "powerless." The meeting ended, each man with a new resolve to abstain from the first drink and to be mutually supportive in this "no quarter" struggle to regain their lives.

On the way out of the prison, when we had to stop at the main gate for identification and passage out of the compound, I recognized a prisoner on duty at the gate. He was the man who had killed his wife and had his life spared by the jury at my request.

As he approached our car, well armed with a pistol in his belt and a rifle on his shoulder, he walked to the side where I was sitting, removed his hat, and told me who he was. He then said to me, which I hope he intended as a compliment, "Governor, we want you to know how much we appreciate you coming down here to talk to us, and we want you to know that you couldn't come to a place where you had more friends." I assumed he meant it, because he was so well armed that in an instant he could have made me wish that, at his trial, I had asked the jury for the final punishment.

As I have said, Oney Madden came to Hot Springs following a gang war in which his opposition won. He frequented the Southern Club, making that his unofficial headquarters to visit, advise, and direct friends who might be visiting or passing through or friends of his friends who might have a problem.

We had moved to our house a little outside of town, over the Cedar Hill Road at the time, when I received the only call and made the only contact that I ever had with Madden. It was almost 10:30 in the evening, and he said he wanted to see me, so I suggested that we visit the following day. No, he said, it was urgent, and if at all possible he would like to see me then. I thought he might have information regarding some mob or syndicate operation in Hot Springs, so I agreed to meet with him.

But I did not want to invite him to my house and disturb my sleeping family, so I suggested meeting him at the top of Cedar Hill Road, which was about three hundred yards from our house. I took my time, put on a pair of walking shoes, got a flashlight, and slowly walked up the gravel road to the appointed place. As I reached the top of the hill, I saw the outline of a parked car in darkness. Shining my flashlight on it revealed a long, dark limousine. The only light coming from inside was a cigarette held by someone on the driver's side. As I walked up, the driver turned on the lights, and I had a good view of the occupants. Oney was in the front seat with the driver. We greeted each other, but he did not introduce me to "his friends." I made a quick appraisal. The driver, who wore a chauffeur's cap, was built like a Japanese sumo wrestler, and his features were definitely Oriental. Two men in the rear, wearing fedora hats, each looked like a movie version of gangsters you wouldn't want to meet on the back streets.

I asked Madden what was so urgent. He stated that it involved two men from New York who had robbed a downtown Hot Springs jewelry store and were coming up for trial. He indicated that they were friends of his and that if I would drop the charges, he would see they left town and never would return.

I made a quick estimate of the situation, and casting another appraising eye on the chauffeur and his back seat friends, I made the decision not to be provocative or highly indignant, such as, "Hell, no." I responded, in an even tone, that I would have to think about it. With this, we ended our meeting. I turned and walked slowly down the road toward my house. The motor of their car did not start, and I must admit to a little uneasy apprehension—the same tingling sensation in the back of my neck that I had experienced during the war canoeing up a dark river on an island in the Solomons. I sent both of the men to the penitentiary. They served time and were released for good behavior. Being discharged from the penitentiary, they called on Madden for a "loan" to get out of town. Madden obliged. They promised him they would not come back to Arkansas. I was informed that they kept their word to Madden—they were determined to steer clear of that cotton patch at the penitentiary!

In reviewing one's life, one must inevitably stumble over and uncover old memories long buried in the subconscious. This is one such memory—a similar danger to a wartime experience, enacted in a very different, and in some ways more treacherous, type of jungle.

Leo McLaughlin was indicted by a grand jury and brought to trial. He asked for and received a change of venue from Garland to Montgomery County. I prosecuted him on charges of graft and corruption and as an accessory to fraud, but a Montgomery County jury found Leo not guilty. Nevertheless, McLaughlin resigned as mayor of Hot Springs and was succeeded by Earl T. Ricks.

Flying was Earl Ricks's life. He had learned to fly before entering the U.S. Air Force. A big man and outgoing, he was known throughout the air force as "Pappy Ricks." During the war he had commanded the air base in Miami and had flown badly needed ammunition to General Montgomery in Egypt as that crusty old general defended Egypt against the famous and indomitable German general Rommel. Then flying in the Philippines, he flew members of General MacArthur's party to Tokyo, Japan, when General MacArthur signed the peace treaty with Japanese generals aboard the USS *Missouri*.

As governor, I appointed Earl Ricks commander of the Arkansas National Guard. Later he became commander of the Air National Guard at the Pentagon in Washington, D.C., and was ultimately promoted to major general.

The National Guard Armory in War Memorial Park, Little Rock,

Arkansas, is named in honor of Gen. Earl T. Ricks—a great Arkansawyer and American.

One case that I tried, as prosecuting attorney, against the city attorney of Hot Springs for bribery. He had, allegedly, received fifty thousand dollars from a bonding company for aid in securing a city bond issue supported by the credit of Hot Springs.

Judge Maupin Cummins of Fayetteville presided over the trial in which this city attorney was convicted and was sentenced to prison. A practicing lawyer, in addition to his duties as city attorney, he had a family of grown children, no previous criminal record, and significantly to me, he was but a small cog in a powerful and ruthless political machine. The grand jury that had investigated the gambling syndicate had indicted McLaughlin and had reported on the extent of graft and corruption in Hot Springs.

The city attorney served his time, but there were others who were more guilty than he who never served a day. Should I have recommended clemency at the time? This question I have never been able to answer with complete satisfaction.

There was another individual whom I had convicted. He was not an official but served as a strong arm for the establishment, reputedly having taken action or supervised others in disciplining the "incorrigibles" who still believed in a quaint system where the people had a voice in their government. I forget now the specific charge, but he was found guilty in a trial presided over by Judge Cummins. The culprit was put on probation and sentenced to go to church for the first time in his adult life, to attend the First Methodist Church in Hot Springs every Sunday until the probation period expired.

I was a member of this church, and I remember seeing him from time to time, dutifully and reverently attending church, complying with his sentence—ordered by the court to seek a revealing and guiding light.

When I returned to Hot Springs after the war, I sold the house where Elaine and I had lived. Anne, the two boys, and I lived in a rented house until after I was elected prosecuting attorney. We then began a house search, looking for a place with space that would accommodate our needs and permit the boys to have a horse and a dog.

Anne found what appeared to be an ideal house, an old, two-storied, colonial-type with approximately forty acres of clear-cut, uncultivated land. The house was vacant and in disrepair, presenting a challenge to Anne's talents for building additions to and redesigning old houses—a passion with her. It was conveniently located ten minutes from my office at the courthouse.

In addition, the place promised to be a challenge to Pap, who lived in Hot Springs, but was not employed at the time. The land needed to be fenced and the garden cultivated, demanding his time and attention. I hoped this would keep him sober.

We bought the place. Anne immediately drew up her plans, consulted with workmen, plumbers, electricians, and carpenters. She reconciled the costs of materials and labor against her budget and went to work.

Illustrative of Anne's close supervision of the workers was an incident regarding a "cowboy" roofer, who with his helper was putting on a new roof. Anne noticed that he was wearing a cowboy hat, but as work progressed she also noted that he was wearing sharp-toed, high-heeled cowboy boots. In her mind this presented two potential problems. One, that the roofer might lose his balance and fall off the building. Another, walking over the newly laid roof with high and narrow-heeled boots could cause a leak.

She had a visit with the "ranch hand" in which she pointed out her concern. He was not too receptive to her suggestion; however, she must have been persuasive, because the next morning he returned to work, precisely on time, wearing appropriate workman's shoes and cap. She continued to keep an attentive eye on his work; it turned out well, and he did a good job.

We spent Christmas 1946 in our new home. Phillip, one year old, got a live-wire puppy, white, equipped with a perpetually wagging tail. They became inseparable. Sandy, six years old, got a pony. The house was our Christmas present to each other and the family.

By the spring of 1947, we were settled down on our place. Pap had fenced the land and made a vegetable garden, in soil that though rocky was prolifically fertile. We had fresh corn, tomatoes, butter beans, string beans, squash, black-eyed peas, and cantaloupe.

I must qualify my statement that we had corn. We had to compete with the raccoons for the fresh, tender roasting ears. They got most of it—we seemed to be raising it for their exclusive benefit.

Anne and I liked to ride. We purchased two Tennessee walkers,

Colonel and Nell. They were excellent horses with a smooth gait and easy to ride. Uncharacteristic of Tennessee walkers, they were jumpers who would, without hesitation, jump obstacles like logs along the trail. We frequently would take a ride down the county road that passed our place to some nearby springs and the Boy Scout camp trails, which were excellent for riding in that area. Sandy would follow along behind on his pony. If the ride was a short distance, Phillip would ride with Anne in front of her saddle. In that event, Sandy might ride with me.

I was spending more and more time on the road, receiving increasing encouragement to run for governor. Leaving the routine administration of my office as prosecutor in capable hands, I began testing the troubled waters of state politics, accepting speaking invitations, responding to correspondence, making a list of the names of potential supporters, and formulating a program for my state in the event I should decide to run for governor in 1948. I was even getting behind in responding to letters from people pledging their support.

There was much to be done. We had won the war. The need now was to provide for the home front.

There was a pressing need for our free and democratic society to abolish the poll tax, which was an instrument for election fraud and which tended to deprive poor people and blacks of the right to vote.

These plans and my personal ambition to be governor took me more and more on the road and further away from my family.

Our victory in Hot Springs provided joy and exultation to many people. It also fomented a lust for vengeance by my enemies—a dark threat of danger to the lives and welfare of my family.

My opposition, being aware that I was away from home, would frequently make evil, threatening telephone calls to Anne late at night. She was reluctant not to answer the telephone for fear that it might be me or a member of her family in Mississippi calling. Her parents were elderly and in poor health, hence a cause for constant concern.

When Anne would go shopping, visiting friends or the children's grandparents, she would be followed. She would subsequently be called and informed of everything she had done that day, thus making her fully aware that she was being stalked, shadowed. She lived in a constant state of fear and at home she knew where my service

Sid and Anne McMath with sons, Sandy and Phillip, riding horses, "Nell" and "Colonel"

revolver was kept in my desk, the gun that had been my personal arm while I was an officer during the war.

Then there was Pap. He was not a weak man, but a strong man with a weakness. His addiction to whiskey and his unpredictable, hostile actions under its influence was common knowledge on the streets and in the bars of Hot Springs. This weakness was catered to and promoted by those who did not wish us well.

The last time I saw Pap alive he was in our pasture working with the horses.

I went off campaigning, leaving to attend a fish fry in Lake Village. On the afternoon of this hot, sultry summer day, I was told that I had a long-distance telephone call. I had a foreboding, a premonition that all was not well.

My dear friend Nathan Shoenfeld was on the line. He haltingly told me that Anne had shot Pap. The whole world fell in on me. I asked about Anne. He did not know, but she was in the care of Dr. Joe Boydston, a good doctor and a mutual friend.

I asked Nathan about my mother. She was with Anne, trying to console her.

In shock, I forgot to ask about my boys, but I told Nathan I would be there as quickly as possible.

On the way home from Lake Village I was stopped at Dumas by a state trooper, who told me that a plane had been arranged for me in Pine Bluff. When I boarded the plane for Hot Springs, I didn't know who furnished the plane nor the name of the pilot, and I still don't know, but they must know that I was grateful.

On the way home, I had to look again at the man "staring back from the mirror." Why was I not at home? Why was I not looking after my family, rather than pursuing this, what some referred to as a quixotic quest?

How could Anne, my mother, my boys, my family survive this Greek tragedy?

After spending a highly emotional period with Anne and my mother, I found out the essence of what had happened.

Reesie, the maid, who was devoted to Anne and Anne to her, had not seen anything and was not aware that anything was wrong until she heard the shots. She had been in the maid's house where she lived behind our house.

In the early afternoon, Pap had decided to go to town. He saddled Colonel, my Tennessee walker, a large, beautiful horse almost seventeen hands high. Anne knew I loved to ride Colonel and I was crazy about him.

Colonel had thrown a shoe on his right front foot, and Anne knew that cantering or pacing, which he would be doing, would be injurious to Colonel's unshod hoof, especially on the rocky road into town. She implored Pap not to ride the horse, but he was determined to ride down Central Avenue in style on a powerful, prancing steed.

This he did. He was gone for several hours. No one knew where he went, but he met some person or persons, who being clearly aware of his weakness, exploited it and supplied him with enough liquor that he had difficulty in riding Colonel home.

As Pap rode into our yard, stopping at the hitching post, and dismounting, Anne was there to meet him and to check the horse's condition. She had seen Colonel limping as he crossed the yard, and saw that his right foot was bleeding. She asked Pap to unsaddle the horse, water him, and turn him out in the pasture. This, drunkenly, he refused to do, threatening to kill the horse, and he became abusive toward her, using foul and threatening language.

They got into an argument. As he became even more abusive, she retreated to the house. He followed her. She retreated up the steps. He aggressively moved toward her in an uncontrolled frenzy; he cursed her and threatened her. As he started pushing her, in a moment of fear and panic, she reached for the gun, in the nearby desk, with the idea of frightening him away. She knew he was not himself and she became hysterical with fright and began firing. He died instantly.

A special prosecutor was appointed, a grand jury convened, and witnesses called. After a thorough investigation, the grand jury declined to return an indictment against Anne, acquitting her on a self-defense plea.

Friends and people we did not know rallied to our support, and we received hundreds of letters and telegrams of sympathy. The McMath family closed ranks behind Anne.

We survived.

III➔ MY RACE FOR GOVERNOR OF ARKANSAS

MY IMMEDIATE CONCERN WAS ANNE'S PHYSICAL AND EMOTIONAL HEALTH. The family's love, the support of friends, the encouragement of strangers was the best medicine.

We talked, prayed, and sought strength and guidance.

Seeking restoration and healing, we gathered up our boys, drove to Biloxi, Mississippi, and spent several days, perhaps a week. We fished, and the boys swam. Breathing the sea air and soaking up the sunshine was helpful to us all.

On the way home we stopped in Memphis and spent the night at the Peabody Hotel. The next morning a friend came over from Little Rock. I don't remember what time it was, but it was early because I watched the famous ducks march across the lobby of the hotel to their pool of water. My visitor and friend was Spider Rowland, who wrote for the *Arkansas Gazette*.

Spider had followed our campaign in Hot Springs. He had visited in our home several times, and we had become well acquainted.

We talked at length, while Spider chewed his perennial cigar—there were no interruptions. He wanted to know what I was going to do about the governor's race.

Before going to Biloxi, I had consulted, in person and by telephone, with key leaders over the state seeking advice.

Spider and I visited long enough to consume a pot of coffee. Getting up to leave, Spider put on his hat which he wore on the back of his head, shook my hand, looked me in the eye, and said, "You never asked me, 'Champ,' but I'm telling you this, and it only cost you a half a pot of coffee. '*Never call retreat.*'"

We drove home, arriving late in the evening. Reesie was there and had everything in order. Dinner was prepared, and the boys were hungry.

After dinner I reviewed the newspapers and read the mail. We had a good night's sleep, the best that we had had in sometime.

Anne and I spent the next few months rejuvenating our lives. We had to make a decision whether to withdraw from the course we had set and nurse our wounds, withdraw from the world, or to be involved in the world.

I had returned from the war with a mission, and Anne had courageously signed on. We made the decision to stay the course, wherever it might lead. In any event, we never looked back but went to work.

I contacted another graduate from Hot Springs High School and the University of Arkansas, but four years junior to me. I did not know him in school, but I knew his mother and sister, who were dear friends of my mother. He was Henry Woods, who was now practicing law in Texarkana. I asked Henry if we could get together, that I needed to talk to him about my prospects of running for governor. I had been president of the Young Democrats, and Henry had succeeded me. The Young Democrats, who were better organized and motivated than the parent party, had rejected the overtures of the Dixiecrats and their effort to deny to President Truman the Democratic Party's nomination. Henry was in an excellent position to be knowledgeable about the political mood in the state, not only as an active president of the Young Democrats but, having served with the FBI during the war, as an expert at gathering and evaluating information. I knew he would give me an honest opinion about what he thought my chances were.

When we met I asked Henry, if I ran, would he be my campaign manager. Before responding to my question, he had a pertinent question of his own, "How much money do you have?" I responded, "Fifteen hundred dollars in hand and fifteen hundred dollars pledged." With a twinkle in his eye and a smile on his face, he pressed my hand, saying, "I think we can win. I'll take the job."

I asked Henry to meet me in Little Rock, to join me for opening the campaign headquarters and for my announcement. We obtained the old Capital Hotel, in earlier days a magnificent structure, but now relatively vacant, and we took over the mezzanine floor. Henry met me, planning to spend the night, but it was a year and a half before he returned home—his wife, Kathleen, sent him his clothes. Thus began a lifetime friendship forged in political battles and later bonded in the courtroom.

I do not recall the date that I formally announced that I would run for governor. We organized a campaign comparable to our campaign in Garland and Montgomery Counties, magnified seventy-five times.

Sid McMath leading his supporters in Pine Bluff, Arkansas

Fortuitously, my campaign received an unexpected boost when it was revealed that the Junior Chamber of Commerce honored me by submitting my name to the National Junior Chamber to be considered for selection as one of the ten outstanding young men in the United States. Ultimately, I received this honor at the National Junior Chamber of Commerce convention held at St. Joseph, Missouri, historically famous, as it was the starting point for the Pony Express riders, delivering mail to California, and relay posts in between.

My campaign was manned by many veterans of the war, all of us relatively young, and despite the war's experience, or maybe because of it, idealistic in waging a campaign for freedom and justice on the home front. However, we were realistic enough to know that we had to have money to make a campaign.

To get campaign funds we had to create the impression, at least, that we had a good chance to win. We didn't have television, the direct means of reaching the voters, so what we initially lacked in funds, we made up for with energy, shoe leather, enthusiasm, and strength of purpose.

Our primary highways and our farm-to-market roads were rapidly deteriorating or nonexistent. We were literally in the mud or dust, depending upon the season of the year. We ranked forty-eighth in the United States in providing educational opportunities for our children. Only 50 percent of the farms in Arkansas had a quality of life and increased production afforded by modern electrical service. Our election system had to be reformed in order to truly affect the motto of our state, "The People Rule."

The poll-tax system, the instrument of fraud and for discouraging the poor, women, and blacks from voting, had to be repealed and replaced with a registration system for all citizens of voting age.

Black citizens were denied membership in the "all white" Democratic Party, the only viable party in Arkansas and the South—a one-party rule since the end of Reconstruction. The Democratic Party rules had to be changed in order to provide blacks the right, too long withheld, to a voice in the government.

The primary election at that time was in July, followed by the runoff between the two leading candidates for each office two weeks later in August. Since nomination in the Democratic primary was equivalent to election, the general election in November was a formality.

Nine candidates announced for governor and were on the ballot. The field soon narrowed to three serious candidates.

Jack Holt, former attorney general, circuit judge, prosecuting attorney, a forceful speaker and formidable candidate, was our principal opponent. Jack, as attorney general, had built a following all over the state. When he had run for attorney general, we had invited him to Hot Springs to speak to the Junior Chamber of Commerce and we were impressed. We gave him our support. Now this primary for the governor's race found us on opposite sides, especially on the issues raised by the Dixiecrats.

The other candidate was "Uncle Mac" MacKrell, a minister, a kind of roving preacher. He was available to conduct services on invitation and was present at most revival meetings in the rural areas of our state. Through his radio program, "Bible Lover's Revival," he opposed the initiated act to reduce the number of school districts on the ballot in the general election of 1948.

He had developed an appeal based upon what V. O. Key called "irrelevances, a fantastic ignorance of government problems, a spectacular platform manner, and a capacity to stir the rustic."[1] Uncle Mac had an orphanage for children which he supported through private contributions and alms received in his visitations to churches and congregations in the state.

At his rallies, Uncle Mac also had a quartet, who would sing with fervor the familiar, spiritually uplifting songs popular in brush arbor meetings, while free sacks of flour were distributed to the faithful.

I never received any indication that Reverend MacKrell had made common cause with the Dixiecrats in their efforts to defeat President Truman.

When President Roosevelt died, his vice president, Harry Truman, succeeded to the presidency and served President Roosevelt's unfinished term.

In 1948, President Truman was running for his first term as president. He had integrated the armed services and proposed to Congress on February 2, 1948, an enlightened civil rights program, designed to embrace all of our citizens, bringing them under the umbrella of our Bill of Rights, and establishing a fair employment standard. The opposition that this stirred up among Southern leaders was a severe obstacle to his nomination at the Democratic Convention to be held in July. These Southern leaders, the Dixiecrats, were threatening to bolt the party and thereby elect Thomas Dewey, a Republican candidate from New York, or throw the election into the House of Representatives.

Opposition to the Democratic Party had been rising since the 1930s. By 1948, the "Solid South" was no longer solidly in the Democratic fold.

In his civil rights message, President Truman had called for an

---

1. Joe Alex Morris, "He Wants to Make Something of Arkansas," *Saturday Evening Post,* February 18, 1950, p. 27.

end to discrimination in areas of American life in which blacks were cast in the role of second-class citizens. The president called for anti-lynching legislation, an end to segregation in state transportation, and the establishment of the Fair Employment Practices Commission (FEPC) to secure equality and job opportunity. He also made a strong appeal for the protection of voting rights. This civil rights speech accelerated the civil rights movement in America.

A number of Southern senators were irate at the president's message. Harry Byrd of Virginia stated that the president's civil rights proposals constituted a "devastating broadside at the dignity of Southern tradition and institutions"[2] and that its passage could lead to bloodshed. Senator Eastland of Mississippi accused the president of trying to "mongrelize the South."[3] Charles Collins wrote that an FEPC would "create a super gestapo in every corner of our land."[4] A more demonstrative rebellion against President Truman's civil rights address occurred at the Jefferson-Jackson Day dinner at Washington's Mayflower Hotel on February 19, 1948, when President Truman addressed the guests at the Democratic Party's annual fund-raising banquet. Senator and Mrs. Olin D. Johnson of South Carolina and Governor and Mrs. Strom Thurmond canceled their reservations to the dinner at the last minute, leaving their places empty near the head table. Mrs. Johnson was chairman of the dinner committee, her excuse for not attending was "because she might be seated next to a Negro" and that "Southerners want their seats left vacant as a silent protest."[5]

A similar demonstration occurred at the Arkansas Democratic convention at the Marion Hotel in Little Rock. United States attorney general Thomas C. Clark was the speaker, and after his address, toastmaster R. A. Lile announced that a radio broadcast of President Truman's address would follow, stating that "as head of the Democratic Party, the President deserves your respect."[6] Following Mr. Lile's

---

2. Monroe Billington, *The American South* (New York: Charles Scribner's Sons, 1971), 344.

3. C. Phillips, *The Truman Presidency* (New York: Macmillan, 1966;) p.206.

4. Robert Lemmon, "Ideology of the Dixiecrat Movement," *Social Forces* 15 (summer 1952): 171.

5. *Arkansas Gazette,* Little Rock, February 20, 1948.

6. *Arkansas Gazette,* Little Rock, February 20, 1948.

announcement, chairs were pushed back and over half of the nine hundred guests left the dining room.[7]

When the Democratic national committeeman from Arkansas was introduced, he presented to Governor Laney a petition signed by several thousand Arkansas residents. Laney had assumed leadership of the anti-Truman forces in the state and was at the same time making speeches against Truman throughout the South.

The petition submitted to Governor Laney read:

> We wish to commend you for your expression of dissatisfaction with the policies of the National Organization of the Democratic Party and to condone wholeheartedly the stand which you have taken with reference thereto. As titular head of the Party in this matter, it is your duty to speak for the Democrats of Arkansas in the National Council of the Party. We are convinced, more than ever, that the National leadership has manifested an increasingly indifferent and antagonistic attitude towards the interest of the South.[8]

I was present at this meeting. I remained very much in the background throughout the evening affair. However, while Governor Laney was leading an attack on the Truman administration, I was organizing for my governor's race. Immediately following the Jefferson-Jackson dinner, I met with political leaders from all over the state. There, at the Marion Hotel, we concluded that our best course of action was for me to obtain the Democratic nomination for governor. We would then be in a stronger position to meet the Dixiecrats' anti-Truman attacks.

Approximately a month following the president's civil rights message, Governor Laney was a member of a committee of Southern governors and senators who called on Sen. Howard McGrath, chairman of the Democratic Committee, to state their position opposing the president's civil rights proposals. In addition to Governor Laney, there was Gov. Strom Thurmond of South Carolina, Gov. Gregg Cherry of North Carolina, and Gov. Buford H. Jester of Texas.

This committee failed to convince Chairman McGrath to use his

---

7. *Arkansas Gazette*, Little Rock, February 20, 1948.
8. *Arkansas Gazette*, Little Rock, February 20, 1948.

influence to have Congress retreat from its consideration of civil rights legislation. Following the meeting, Governor Laney and the others issued a statement: "Southern states are aroused and the present leadership of the Democratic Party will soon realize that the South is no longer 'in the bag.'"[9]

Governor Laney continued his campaign against Truman and his civil rights proposals. At a radio address in Texas, he called upon the South to continue its fight until "exhausted" if need be.[10] In the Texas speech, Governor Laney gave a firm indication that if the Democrats nominated Truman that he and the Dixiecrats "would be better off without them."[11]

On May 10, 1948, the leaders of the Dixiecrat movement met in Jackson, Mississippi, to organize for the Democratic National Convention with the mission of denying the nomination of President Truman. Gov. Fielding Wright, of Mississippi, served as temporary chairman; Strom Thurmond gave the keynote address; and Ben Laney became permanent chairman.

The main streets of Jackson were decorated with hundreds of Confederate flags, high school bands marching to the tune of "Dixie," and delegates from seven Southern states were present, bearing their state banners.

Gov. Strom Thurmond, in his keynote speech, opposing Truman's civil rights proposals, proclaimed, "On the question of social intermingling of the races our people draw the line—and all the laws in Washington and all the bayonets of the Army cannot force the Negro into the white homes and schools, or the churches and their places of recreation and amusement."[12]

The Democratic National Convention met on July 12 in Philadelphia. The convention was in confusion as to who to nominate for president, with the party, for a time, appearing to be split between Henry Wallace on the left and the Dixiecrats on the right.

Seeking in vain for an alternative to Truman, for a brief period

---

9. Irwin Ross, *The Lonliest Campaign* (New York: New American, 1968), 66.

10. *Arkansas Democrat*, Little Rock, June 27, 1948.

11. *Arkansas Gazette*, Little Rock, May 27, 1948.

12. Hodding Carter, *Southern Legacy* (Baton Rouge: Louisiana State University Press, 1950), 143.

the Dixiecrats turned to Governor Laney. For twenty-four hours, he was a candidate, and Laney buttons were distributed; however, this boom died rather quickly when Laney refused to pledge himself to support whoever became the Democratic nominee. The South then turned to Sen. Richard Russell of Georgia. This too failed. With this, the Dixiecrats walked out of the convention and reconvened in Birmingham, Alabama, July 17, 1948. There they nominated Gov. J. Strom Thurmond for president and Gov. Fielding L. Wright for vice president.

These Dixiecrats, who opposed federal regulations they considered to interfere with states' rights, carried South Carolina, Mississippi, Louisiana, and Alabama, receiving thirty-nine electoral votes; their popular vote totaled over one million. If the Dixiecrats had carried Texas, Arkansas, and two other states, then the election for president would have been thrown into the House of Representatives.

In the meantime, the race for governor of Arkansas and the leadership of the state Democratic Party was being waged with the "tumult and shouting" of the Dixiecrat rebellion in the background. But now, as the election day approached, the race issue was injected into the Arkansas governor's race—big time! In the Democratic primary, I led the ticket; Jack Holt was second; and "Uncle Mac" McKrell was a close third. The runoff would be two weeks later in August.

Since Uncle Mac and his followers appeared to be the key in the election's outcome, Jack and I both endeavored to get Uncle Mac's support. Jack's forces were more "persuasive," and Uncle Mac joined Jack's campaign, with his quartet, collection plate, and sacks of flour.

During the runoff I was challenged by radio and newspaper ads and from the stump to answer these questions:

> Where do you stand on the race issue?
> What deals have you made with the Negroes for the Negro vote?
> How many Negroes have you promised to put on the state police force?
> How many Negroes have you promised to put on the state Department of Education?
> Did the *Arkansas State Press,* a Negro paper in Little Rock, write an editorial supporting you for governor?

How much money have the Negroes contributed to your campaign? Your silence on these issues is an indication of your true purpose.

With the race issue hot and spreading like a prairie wildfire and Uncle Mac's support of Jack Holt so crucial, had the election process lasted another two weeks, Jack may well have won. However, I won by ten thousand votes.

One dark hour occurred about three weeks before the preferential primary in July. We were broke—no funds to pay the help or for radio time. I went to see Guy Freeling, the father of Dick Freeling, one of my most ardent veteran supporters. Mr. Freeling took me to see W. R. "Witt" Stephens. Witt was helpful and encouraging. He arranged for me to borrow five thousand dollars on my personal note from a businessman in the oil industry in El Dorado. This, with some additional help, got us through the first primary. Being in the runoff, more financial support was forthcoming.

Following my election, I had approximately four months to organize my administration, appoint my department heads, and prepare for my first legislative session. I had promised the people I would get us out of the mud and dust, provide a quality education for all our children, provide electricity to the rural areas, repeal the poll tax, and establish a voter registration system. I did not wait until I was officially sworn in as governor to go to work.

We had an organization intact. It was buoyant with victory, optimistic about the future, and ready for the challenge. However, before going to work for the people, we had one more job to do for the party. Having failed to defeat the nomination of President Truman at the national Democratic convention, the Dixiecrats had devised a plan to capture sufficient electoral votes for Thurmond and Wright in the November election to shift the responsibility for naming the president to the House of Representatives. To accomplish this mission, the Southern states, including Arkansas, were targeted.

The front for the Dixiecrats in Arkansas was the Arkansas Free Enterprise Association, which maintained a state headquarters in Marianna, in the Delta. The Free Enterprise Association consisted of plantation owners, large farmers, and Little Rock corporate executives, representative of the conservative forces in the state. This

Comic strip created by George Fisher for Sid McMath's campaign for governor

SID, ANSWER THESE QUESTIONS

THE PEOPLE WHO VOTED FOR YOU ARE ENTITLED TO KNOW. THE PEOPLE WHO VOTED FOR MR. MAC KRELL, MR. THOMPSON, AND FOR ME ARE ENTITLED TO KNOW. THEY HAVE A RIGHT TO BE INFORMED OF YOUR STAND ON THESE VITAL QUESTIONS.

? No. 1 — SID, HOW MUCH INTEREST DO YOU PROPOSE TO CHARGE THE PEOPLE OF ARKANSAS ON THE BONDS YOU WANT TO SELL—BONDS THE PEOPLE WOULD BE PAYING FOR YEARS TO COME?

? No. 2 — WHO WILL HANDLE YOUR BOND DEAL AND GET THE CREAM WHILE THE PEOPLE PAY AND PAY?

? No. 3 — ISN'T IT TRUE THAT UNDER YOUR PLAN THE STATE HIGHWAY DEBT WILL BE LARGER FOUR YEARS FROM NOW INSTEAD OF SMALLER?

? No. 4 — SID, WHO WROTE YOUR BOND PROGRAM AND PINNED IT TO YOUR COAT TAIL?

? No. 5 — WHERE DO YOU STAND ON THE RACE ISSUE?

? No. 6 — WHAT DEALS HAVE YOU MADE WITH THE NEGROES FOR THE NEGRO VOTES?

? No. 7 — HOW MANY NEGROES HAVE YOU PROMISED TO PUT ON THE STATE POLICE FORCE?

? No. 8 — HOW MANY NEGROES HAVE YOU PROMISED TO PUT ON THE STATE DEPARTMENT OF EDUCATION?

? No. 9 — DID YOUR CAMPAIGN MANAGER, HENRY WOODS, RECEIVE A LETTER FROM A NEGRO KING-PIN IN TEXARKANA SAYING THAT YOU WOULD GET THE NEGRO VOTE IN MILLER COUNTY?

? No. 10 — DID THE ARKANSAS STATE PRESS, A NEGRO PAPER IN LITTLE ROCK, WRITE AN EDITORIAL SUPPORTING YOU FOR GOVERNOR?

? No. 11 — DID THAT SAME PAPER, ONLY LAST FRIDAY, CARRY A FRONT PAGE STATEMENT THAT YOU GOT THE NEGRO VOTE AND THAT THE NEGRO VOTE WAS RESPONSIBLE FOR YOU LEADING THE TICKET?

? No. 12 — HOW MUCH MONEY HAVE THE NEGROES CONTRIBUTED TO YOUR CAMPAIGN?

McMath anti-campaign literature used by opposition

dominant philosophy appeared to be anti-labor, consequently the Truman civil rights proposals were an anathema to their mission.

Governor Laney continued to serve as Dixiecrat chairman.

Representatives of the Free Enterprise Association in Arkansas had joined with others in Mississippi, Alabama and South Carolina in their support of a ticket of Thurmond and Wright. Their opposition to Truman was inflamed by his proposal for anti-lynch, anti-poll-tax laws, and the establishment of the Fair Employment Practice Commission.

In the pursuit of their strategy to capture the Arkansas electoral delegates for Thurmond and Wright, the Free Enterprise Association, supposedly acting on behalf of the Dixiecrats, arranged for a meeting for August 24, at the Bear Creek Hotel, a few miles from Marianna. Gov. Strom Thurmond would be present. I was invited to attend in order to serve as a host to Governor Thurmond. I extended my respects to Governor Thurmond, explaining to my friend, John Daggett, of Marianna, who had extended the invitation, that I would be unable to attend.

The Bear Creek Hotel meeting was significant. There Governor Thurmond met and talked to more than a hundred delegates and chairmen and secretaries of a number of Democratic county committees, mostly from the Delta and eastern Arkansas. It was an announcement that the Dixiecrats were going to make a fight for the presidential electors in Arkansas—the Democratic convention being scheduled for September 22.

With the encouragement and support of Governor Laney, the Free Enterprise Association and delegates from the Delta had high hopes of bringing Arkansas into the Dixiecrat fold.

The pressure was building up over the state for the Dixiecrat movement. Henry Woods, my campaign manager, and Joe Martin, my statewide organizer, who was from Craighead County in eastern Arkansas, were sorely concerned whether or not we, as loyal Democrats, would be able to stand firm and hold the line against this increasing pressure of the Dixiecrats.

Being the newly elected governor, and "no governor has as much power as he has before taking office," and with the assurance that I would serve at least one term (two years), I was able to reassure wavering delegates.

We began organizing the convention. Not leaving anything to chance, Joe Martin, an indefatigable worker with a keen insight into Arkansas politics, knowing who the key leaders were, arranged the nominating procedure so as to name loyal Democrats as presidential delegates.

Joe had detailed his plans to me in a letter written September 11, 1948, preceding the convention on the twenty-second. "I have asked Barney Smith to nominate Mr. Lewis Layer of Dierks, as one of the presidential electors at-large, at the convention—I have also asked Mr. Lawrence Honeycutt to second the nomination—and R. K. Rogers to move that the nominations be closed in connection with the nomination of Mr. Layer."

All nominees were party regulars. Supporting the plan laid out by Joe Martin, Henry and I had conferences with the delegates, including Dixiecrats. Again being the newly elected governor, I was persuasive with wavering delegates.

Governor Laney delivered a fiery anti-Truman speech at the Democratic convention, calling on all Southerners to "repudiate the shady, lousy actions of the Party's leadership of the last few months."[13] This speech threatened to derail our plan. Former congressman Charles Fuller, a loyal Democrat, arose on a point of personal privilege and, without recognition from the chair, shouted, "I have just been insulted by a Republican speech at a Democratic convention. I demand that someone be allowed to answer that man."[14] We had to put out the fire quickly to avoid the convention getting out of control. We convinced our regulars that the most effective response would be to proceed in an orderly manner and elect unwavering electors for President Truman.

This was done. The Dixiecrat effort to capture the state Democratic Party failed.

In the November election, Dixiecrats carried only the four states in which they had taken over the Democratic Party. In Alabama, South Carolina, Louisiana, and Mississippi, Thurmond and Wright won all thirty-eight electoral votes.

I had campaigned for President Truman in the general election,

---

13. *Arkansas Gazette*, September 22, 1948.
14. *Arkansas Gazette*, September 22, 1948.

urging the people of Arkansas to stay with the Democratic Party, the party of Roosevelt and Truman, and not to support a party with a history and philosophy of isolation and high tariffs or the Dixiecrats, who advocated exclusion of civil rights based upon race. The Dixiecrats ran well in the Delta counties, but Arkansas gave President Truman one of the largest percentage votes of any state in the union.

Having promised the people to support a program that would enhance the education of our children, I searched for a person with eminent qualifications who would also share our passion for making this promise a reality. I found the man, Dr. A. B. Bonds, an old friend whom I had known from Henderson State College days. I also had occasionally shared his mother's home cooking. He left the Department of Atomic Energy in Washington, D.C., and came home to become director of the Department of Education. His vision for the future education of the children of our state caught the imagination of the Arkansas Educational Association, our underpaid and unappreciated teachers.

Initited Act #1, put on the ballot in the general election in 1948 by petition of the people, called for the consolidation of school districts. The act passed with a vote of 135,606 for and 88,215 against.

As a result of the passage of Initiated Act #1, our school districts were reduced from 1589 to 426. Subsequently, these school districts were reduced to 395 in 1967 and 369 in 1983. Today. Arkansas has 313 school districts. However, in order to provide an adequate education for all our children, a further reduction in the number of school districts will be required.

An initiated act also provided for the removal of an eighteen-mill education property tax cap, which had, in effect, paralyzed local communities in providing the physical plants and educational needs for progressive education.

Dr. Bonds organized a caravan of buses and trucks, carrying school desks, projectors, training aids, blackboards, and all the accouterments of a modern classroom, acquainting the teachers with these aids and demonstrating their use. I joined Dr. Bonds and his caravan from time to time. We were successful in passing the controversial School Consolidation Act, and the eighteen-mill limit on property tax was also removed—a giant step in the right direction.

As the volatile issue of race was fanned by the Dixiecrats in 1948,

```
THE WHITE HOUSE
     WASHINGTON

                              November 12, 1948




     Dear Mr. McMath:

          I am deeply moved by the splendid

     message you sent me and I cannot tell you how

     much it means to me to have these assurances.

     It is a tremendous help to know that I can

     count on the cooperation of all of you.

          Kind regards and sincere good wishes

     to you on the occasion of your own election.

                         Very sincerely yours,



                         Harry Truman


Honorable Sidney S. McMath,
Governor-Elect of Arkansas,
Little Rock,
Arkansas.
```

Personal letter from President Truman, November 12, 1948

the year of President Truman's election, an event with symbolic significance occurred in Arkansas. Edith Mae Irby, a graduate of Langston High School in Hot Springs and Knoxville College in Tennessee, applied for admission to the medical schools of Northwestern University, Chicago University, and the University of Arkansas. She was accepted by both Northwestern and Chicago; however, it was her

THE WHITE HOUSE

WASHINGTON

November 13, 1948

Dear Governor:

I want to take this opportunity
to tell you of my sincere appreciation of
your efforts during the campaign.

It was a great victory and you
may be sure that I fully realize the part
you played in bringing it about.

Sincerely yours,

Harry Truman

Honorable Sid McMath
Governor of Arkansas
Little Rock, Arkansas

Congratulations on your election too.

Personal letter from President Truman, November 13, 1948

desire to go to medical school in her home state. There was nothing remarkable about this desire except for the time and the place—and her race. Edith Irby was black. Of 230 students applying for admission, the school's entrance requirements ranked her twenty-eighth in the field of applicants.

The problem of Edith Irby's admission was not her qualifications but politics. Ben Laney, governor of Arkansas at the time and a leader in the Dixiecrat Party, had been pressured to resist her admission.

Dr. Lewis Webster Jones, president of the University of Arkansas, and Dr. Chenal, director of the medical school, contacted me about Ms. Irby's application. They, of course, had been following the governor's race and were keenly aware of the candidates' positions on the race issue.

I suggested they wait to make their decision until after August when the race for governor would be over. On August 23, 1948, Vice President Chenal announced the names of the ninety-two applicants who had been admitted to the freshman class of the medical school. One of these students was Edith Irby. Of her admission Dr. Chenal said, "She'll be part of her class, just like any other member."

The decision to voluntarily admit a black female student to a Southern medical school was news carried in most major newspapers across the country. The *Washington Post* editorialized the Arkansas "example." Similar stories were published in *Life, Time,* and *Ebony* magazines. This publicity generated a file of letters to Vice President Chenal, 95 percent congratulatory. Representative of the letters was one from Houston, Texas:

> "Your action gives me the feeling that we do live in a true democracy—for Arkansas is truly a 'Land of Opportunity.'"

In order to comply with state law, Edith Irby had to have segregated bathroom and dining facilities. Segregated to her own small dining room for meals, Edith Irby received strong silent support from blacks employed at the medical center. Each day, going to her room for lunch, she would find a white tablecloth, napkin, a single rose in a small vase centered on her table, and a cold Coca-Cola by the side of her plate—no note or verbal message, just this magnificent gesture from those whose cause she also served. When other medical students began to come to her dining room for lunch, these barriers quickly vanished.

Arkansas was making progress on the race issue which had cost Arkansas, the South, and our country so dearly, all in a land where the handmaiden is Freedom, "dedicated to the proposition that all men are created equal and endowed by their Creator with certain unalienable rights. And among these are the right to life, liberty and the pursuit of happiness."

The people of Hot Springs raised funds to help Ms. Irby pay her tuition. Other donations from across the state enabled her to meet continuing expenses. Most of this money was collected by Daisy Bates, the black civil rights leader, who later received national prominence during the Little Rock Central High School integration crisis.

Would that this magnanimity, tolerance, humanity, yes, and wisdom, inherent in our people, been called forth by leaders when nine black children sought admission to Central High School in 1957.

I was sworn in as governor of my state on January 11, 1949. Anne, my wife, described the ceremony, the culmination of our efforts, in her book, *First Ladies of Arkansas: Women of Their Times:*

> Sid was inaugurated on January 10, 1949, before a joint session of the General Assembly. Sid's arrival in the house chambers was announced by a fanfare from the American Legion Drum and Bugle Corps stationed in the Capitol Rotunda. United States Secretary of the Treasury, John W. Snyder, President Truman's representative, preceded Sid down the aisle to the speaker's platform. A Marine Corps color guard, wearing dress blues and carrying the national and state flags, entered the chamber and took up stations flanking the rostrum. Sid proudly marched down the aisle in the glare of floodlights, winked at me as he passed by, mounted the platform, and was given the Oath of Office by Chief Justice Griffin Smith.
>
> After the ceremony, another fanfare by the Drum and Bugle corps and the Marine Hymn played by Tommy Scott provided background music while the color guard escorted the new governor out of the hall and across the building to the Capitol steps. He marched to the podium and in his speech outlined an ambitious program for the state.—Secretary Snyder read a personal message from President Truman. A huge flag, 40 feet by 60 feet, had been stretched across the front of the Capitol to form a background for the ceremony.—It was cold and windy and I shivered in my black wool suit. Eight year old Sandy was cold and totally bored with the whole thing and slumped down up to his ears in his coat. Approximately 2,500 people attended the ceremony.
>
> There was a reception that evening in the Governor's Reception Room at the Capitol. Sid's mother, Nettie McMath, and sister, Edyth Crane of Chicago, Secretary Snyder and his daughter, Drucie, Senator and Mrs. J. W. Fulbright, and the con-

Presentation of the model for the Iwo Jima statue at Sid McMath's inauguration
(by Felix deWeldon, sculptor, January 1949)

stitutional officers and their wives joined Sid and me in the
receiving line.

A sculpture of the flag-raising on Iwo Jima was the center of
attention on a table in the reception room. Felix de Weldon, the
artist and our personal friend, attended the inauguration and presented his statue to Sid. It is an exact replica of Mr. de Weldon's
magnificent Marine Corps war memorial in Arlington, Virginia.
Sid donated this model to Catholic High School in Little Rock,

Sid and supporters after winning 1950 primary. Left to right: Ed Williams, Dick Freeling, Julian James, Horace Cate, and Henry Woods. *(From Jim Lester,* A Man for Arkansas*)*

where it is on permanent display and serves as a inspiration to the members of the Marine Corps ROTC unit.[15]

I presented the Iwo Jima statue to Catholic High School because I was instrumental in establishing their ROTC unit—the students call themselves "Sid's Kids."

15.Anne McMath, *First Ladies of Arkansas: Women of Their Times* (Little Rock, Ark.: August House, 1989), 207–9.

Attending the inauguration and joining Felix de Weldon in presenting me the Iwo Jima model was Gen. Oscar (Speed) Caldwell, the former commander of the Third Marine Regiment; Capt. John Yancey, a true hero of the Guadalcanal campaign during the Second World War and later in Korea; and the marine recruiting sergeant in Little Rock.

It was a momentous year—I had been elected by the people of Arkansas to serve for two years as their governor.

Before I was sworn in as governor, the Arkansas State Society in Washington, D.C., invited Anne and me to attend a reception they were having in our honor, thus giving us an opportunity to get acquainted with the Arkansas team and other citizens of our state working in Washington.

This reception, held at the national Capital, was well attended with supporters and well wishers, all offering to help in any way they could for the success of my administration.

I was especially impressed and appreciative of the large attendance because of the weather. The most honored guest, who plowed through a snowstorm to be there, was the newly elected president of the United States, Harry S. Truman. The president came to give his blessing and best wishes to a friend and his first lady.

So little time and so much to do—I looked to the future with a will and hope in my heart.

IV⟡ THE GOVERNOR'S MANSION

WHEN I BECAME GOVERNOR IN 1949, THE GOVERNOR'S MANSION WAS under construction. We had to buy or rent a home adequate for our family and for receiving guests and visiting dignitaries.

Appropriation for the construction of a Governor's Mansion had been made during Governor Laney's administration. The Act providing for a Governor's Mansion went into effect July 1, 1947. It set up a Mansion commission and appropriated one hundred thousand dollars for "The acquisition of a site; of architect fees, for the cost of construction; for landscaping of a Governor's Mansion."

After the general election in November 1948, Anne began searching for a house in Little Rock suitable for our family, Sandy, Phillip, Anne, and me. The house had to be large enough to accommodate dinner guests, as we were planning to invite all members of the legislature, the house and the senate, for dinner. Anne, in addition to all her other activities, launched on her favorite hobby, remodeling and redecorating an older house. This, of course, all had to be completed before Christmas.

Anne was absorbed and involved, overseeing the work on the house, buying new furniture, moving, observing Christmas, and preparing for a house full of guests for the inauguration. Anne had excellent help—two maids, Marie Clayton and Queenie Esther Bohler, and a houseboy, Charlie Clemmons, who came with us from Hot Springs. Fortunately, the place we purchased was large enough for them to live on the lower floor.

Marie, Esther, and Charlie had worked with "Miss" Anne and knew exactly how she wanted meals prepared and served. She scheduled three dinners per week for the legislature, twenty to twenty-six members at each sitting.

Anne served as hostess in our house at 220 Ridgeway not only to members of the legislature but to other distinguished guests, one being Harry S. Truman, president of the United States.

These dinners gave us an excellent opportunity to get acquainted with the lawmakers and they with us. I worked with this legislature for my two terms in office. Many of them became longtime friends.

One of the senators with whom I wished to get acquainted was Sen. Doc Abbington from White County. He was not the most senior member of the state senate, but I believe he was substantially the oldest. He wore a vest, had an abundantly healthy waistline, and smoked Bull Durham cigarettes. He smoked these "roll your own" cigarettes all evening, spilling about half of the tobacco, being poured into the cigarette paper, on his stomach. He voted "No" so many times on legislative measures that his fellow senators referred to him as "Dr. No."

"Dr. No" had a great time. He had a hearty appetite. He smoked, drank his wine, told stories, and was the life of the party at his table. But despite our attempts to win his support, although friendly, he continued to vote NO.

The first official group to meet with Anne and me following my inauguration was the Mansion commission. They brought with them the plans for completing the governor's house. The committee had submitted a plea for an increase in the appropriation to complete the building, the original funds having been spent with the house only half finished. Anne studied the plans and immediately concluded that the house was too small, but it was too late to make any changes. However, she did request certain alterations. Since the second-floor bedrooms were needed for the governor's family, Anne recommended that the east wing be made into a guesthouse instead of a home office for the governor. The west wing had been planned as servants' quarters, but this one-bedroom/sitting-room cottage was inadequate for the staff, so it was agreed that both wings would be finished as guesthouses. The west wing eventually became housing for the state troopers. The original plans provided for a large, screened-in porch adjoining the drawing room on the east side of the Mansion. Since there were terraces on the back that would serve the same purpose as a porch, Anne asked that this porch be enclosed and made into a much-needed living room. The commission was in agreement, but there were no funds.

The maintenance appropriation for the Mansion began with the new fiscal year in July. This money was offered to Anne to pay the cost of running the Ridgeway house. She declined, letting it accrue, and used the money later to buy china, silver, and table linens for the Mansion and furnishings for one guesthouse, as well as to pay the seven hundred dollars needed to enclose the porch.

Only a few dollars of the appropriation had been earmarked for furnishings. Bill Heerwagen, the interior designer selected by the commission, an excellent choice, worked only for his expenses. Bill Heerwagen's grandfather had been the interior designer for the new State Capitol Building, which was completed in 1911 under Gov. George Donaghey, who had run for governor with the mission of completing this majestic building.

Anne did not feel that it was the function or the responsibility of any first lady to decorate the public rooms according to her own tastes. She felt that this part of the house belonged to the people and that decorating or designing the public rooms was the commission's responsibility.

Our personal furniture, china, silver, and linens were used to supplement the state furnishings, and we furnished all the kitchen utensils except for one set of chef's cutlery. By not installing hardwood floors under the carpet in the public rooms of the first floor, sufficient funds were saved from construction costs to buy a commercial range, a refrigerator, and a freezer.

A little colonial cottage on the west side of the Mansion grounds was converted into living space for the staff.

We moved into the Mansion on February 3, 1950, thirteen months after I took office.

Anne, twenty-eight years old, without a social secretary, guide book, or precedent, did a great job operating the Mansion and serving as first lady of our state.

Her greatest challenge was organizing an adequate staff to meet the Mansion's needs with funds available.

There was no way the appropriation committee and the commission knew the costs of operating the Mansion, not having any experience of operating a Mansion in the past. Hence, operating funds were inadequate to serve the Mansion's designed purpose. Anne, inexperienced at the job, had to come up with a plan of operation.

Attending governors' conferences, Anne took this opportunity to visit with other first ladies on how they operated their Mansions. She visited the Governors' Mansions of surrounding states in order to learn how best to do this job with funds available. A critical need was for a trained staff. Not being able to obtain the private help needed, she turned to the director of state prisons, Capt. Lee Hensley. He promptly offered to help. He made a survey of inmates and reported to Miss Anne. His prisoners, mostly serving time for robbery, burglary, drug trafficking, con games, and related crimes would not fit into the atmosphere and purpose of the Governor's Mansion. However, he had two young men, who, when well dressed, made a good appearance. They were intelligent and highly motivated, but both were in prison for murder.

Anne reflected on this, but being desperate, requested Captain Hensley to bring them to the Mansion for an interview. This was done. Captain Hensley's view of these young men had been correct. She decided to give them a chance. She put them through "Miss Anne's boot camp," which Anne describes this way:

> I trained them to be household servants. For weeks we had a practice session every morning until they learned how to set the table and serve different kinds of parties. They became quite good at serving, answering the phone, cleaning and polishing—in fact they did anything that needed to be done, including taking groups on tours of the house. They worked long hard hours without complaint and earned their freedom. My husband pardoned them at the end of his term in office. They both became good citizens and were never again afoul of the law.[1]

Anne's task as first lady was most helped by our chef, Johnnie Wright. Johnnie, as Anne described him, was irreplaceable. Anne related Johnnie's invaluable assistance:

> My chef was a godsend. I could not have run the Mansion with anyone less talented, even-tempered, capable, and willing than Johnnie Wright. He was a railroad chef who wanted to take a leave of absence in order to be home during his children's teenage years. If the truth were known, he probably would have had more time at home if he had stayed on the railroad. He was at the Mansion six days a week from breakfast until after the dinner hour, no matter how late that was. He never complained nor sought help and often turned down offers of assistance.[2]

---

1. Anne McMath, *First Ladies of Arkansas: Women of Their Times* (Little Rock, Ark.: August House, 1989), 189.

2. McMath, *First Ladies of Arkansas*, 189.

In addition to Johnnie Wright's other duties, he permitted Bruce, my youngest son, to come into the kitchen. This, of course, required that Johnnie keep an eye on him. He would place Bruce in the window above the dishwasher and feed him french fries. Bruce loved this delicacy and would sit and gorge himself. He became so roly-poly that coming down from the second floor of the Mansion he would alternately roll and slide down the stairway.

Johnnie Wright earned his retirement, spent quality time with his wife, Mattie, his children, and grandchildren. At the time of his death, I had the privilege of delivering the eulogy at the funeral of this good and faithful servant and friend.

In addition to her duties as first lady, Anne was the mother of three young boys, Sandy, Phillip, and Bruce. Bruce was born in 1949, during my first year in office. Anne also served as my consultant and best friend. She never hesitated to tell me when she thought I was making a wrong decision.

I was never, while governor, out of communications with the Mansion—my command post—for any length of time.

Once I was in Clinton, Arkansas, making a speech at the courthouse, when I received word that a tornado had struck nearby at Searcy and Bald Knob. I proceeded to Searcy and checked in at Truman Baker's Chevrolet Agency, where a temporary aid station had been set up. I had radio messages from the director of the state police, the director of prisons, and the commanding general of the Arkansas National Guard. They were standing by for orders. They had contacted the Mansion and were informed of where I was and that their help would be needed without delay. Anne had evaluated the situation and made the right decision, and acting on it, much valuable time was saved in the state's efforts to bring emergency relief to those citizens in distress.

We enjoyed living in the Mansion. The upstairs was adequate for our purposes and quite lively when we moved in with eight-year-old Sandy, four-year-old Phillip, and three-month-old Bruce, who was the first baby born to a governor's family since the birth of Ernestine Flora Rector in March 1861.

Before concluding this chapter on the Mansion, I feel compelled to relate an incident of an illegal nature that was being carried on during one of my absences from the state.

Anne McMath at Governor's Mansion with sons, Phillip, Bruce, and Sandy *(From Anne McMath,* First Ladies of Arkansas*)*

Apparently, an unlawful scheme had been devised and put in execution. Citizens, operating their own vehicles, rightfully coming onto the Mansion grounds, were being stopped at the entrance, and were, without any authorization, being charged an admission fee. The admitting charge was ten cents per person in the vehicle, including the driver. If they did not pay, a line which had been strung across the open gate to the Mansion would be raised so as to prevent passage.

A thorough investigation of this hold-up operation was made by the state police, and a report was on my desk when I returned. This imaginative, but illegal, enterprise was being carried out by my son, Phillip, and his friend and next door neighbor, Billy Koch, the son of Dr. Clarence Koch. Needless to say, the practice was stopped, and the funds collected went to the state treasury.

I am happy to report that both children, then six year olds, went on to become highly successful citizens, respectful of the law, with no further mark on their record. Young Bill Koch went on to graduate with honors from the University of Arkansas Medical School and became a prominent physician in Searcy. My son Phillip did equally well. He became a lawyer.

Security for the first family is a necessity. Two troopers lived on the Mansion grounds, and one was there at all times. Several troopers rotated duty, but Fred McKinley, Ben Kent, Carl Chambers, and Jack Murphy were with us the longest. They became members of our family and served "above and beyond the call of duty."

When we moved into the Governor's Mansion, neither the legislature, the Mansion Commission, nor Anne had any experience in managing it. There was no precedent for its operation or for what costs it would entail. Without a secretary, Anne had to recruit and train help, plan and hostess dinners, supervise three boys, and attend official functions with me. She was a great first lady.

The Mansion has always been a beautiful building, portraying dignity and warmth. We enjoyed our stay there, but, as previously mentioned, it was not large enough.

Now, in 2003, happily, the Mansion has been enlarged to accommodate the needs of the first family, the reception of visiting dignitaries, and appropriate public functions. During the construction, Governor and Mrs. Huckabee and their family were housed in temporary quarters on the Mansion grounds.

The governor and the first lady, with good humor, discussed the "transit abode," which provided them accommodations while the Mansion was expanded and renovated. In this humorous vein, it had been suggested that Governor and Mrs. Huckabee set a black washtub with scrubbing board on a table in the backyard, nail a raccoon skin on the front door, and get a hound dog to sleep under the porch, to stand guard and to bay at the approach of any strangers.

Sid McMath and Ol' Red

Now the Huckabees would not be the first to have a hound dog. I had a hound dog, a red-bone, named "Old Red." He was the best dog I ever saw next to Pap's "Old Judd."

At a road dedication in Scott County, the Scott County Coon Hunters Association gave me this mature, deep-voiced, trained dog, knowing that I was once an avid coon hunter. I brought Old Red home to the Mansion, kept him chained up for awhile, but when he got used to the place, I turned him loose. He stayed around as long as we fed him. I made the mistake of introducing him to canned dog food. Afterward, he wouldn't eat anything else.

A snooping reporter for a North Little Rock newspaper, reported that I was paying for dog food from the meager Mansion funds. This discovery set up quite a howl. After there was a feature story in the newspaper, how did I respond? I found that the best way to meet an accusation is to tell the truth. If you are guilty, confess. Tell the truth, and "the truth will make you free."

I confessed that the story was true. I related as how I had been given this prize canine by the good and loyal citizens of Scott County, but

McMATH, VEHIK, DRUMMOND, HARRISON & LEDBETTER, P.A.

711 WEST THIRD STREET
LITTLE ROCK, ARKANSAS 72201
501-396-5400
FAX: 501-374-5118

PHILLIP H. McMATH
JAMES (BRUCE) McMATH
MART VEHIK
WINSLOW DRUMMOND
PAUL HARRISON
SAMUEL E. LEDBETTER
SANDRA SANDERS
HANK BATES
EILEEN HARRISON

OF COUNSEL:
SIDNEY S. MCMATH
LELAND F. LEATHERMAN

October 27, 1998

TO: Editor   FAX: 372-3908
        Arkansas Democrat-Gazette

FROM: Sid McMath   RE: Miscellaneous use of
                                                Mansion Fund

It is a long established rule -- set 50 years ago -- the Governor cannot use the Mansion Fund to buy dog food.

I had a coon dog -- a Red Bone Hound -- called him Ol' Red. He was given to me by the Scott County Coon Hunters while I was Governor of Arkansas.

Ol' Red was placed on duty at the Mansion as a guard dog. He was fed dog biscuits bought from the Mansion fund. I considered this proper seeing as how he was on duty for the State.

However, this practice caused quite a ruckus. It was made a big issue by my opposition and frowned upon by a North Little Rock publication. Hence it was discontinued.

I do not know, at least until now, if this practice was resumed by a subsequent Governor, nor do I know if another Governor ever had a Red Bone Coon Hound working for the State.

Sincerely,

Sidney S. McMath

Ol' Red makes the news

Anne McMath with twins, Melissa and Patricia, August 1953

then in extenuation I added, "Old Red turned out to be a good watch-dog, especially at night. If any stranger came prowling around the Mansion grounds, he told the world about it. At least one of the neighbors told me how comforting it was that Old Red was standing guard."

This enabled me to release one of the officers on night security duty. Now, since Old Red was working for the state, free of charge, it was only fair that he be fed at state expense.

Now, fair is fair, and right is right and wrong is wrong. And so that reporter quit "kickin' my dawg" around. Old Red went on to "greener pastures" in Grant County, a paradise for boys with a good dog to hunt, to explore the deep woods and search out the wonders of nature.

Anne took great pride in operating the Mansion, leaving it ship-shape for the next residents, Francis and Margaret Cherry. Anne left a note on the living-room mantle, over the fireplace, "Welcome to your new home. We hope you enjoy it as much as we have. Everything is in order and firewood is laid in the fireplace."

Shortly after leaving the Mansion, Anne gave birth to twin girls, Patricia Anne and Melissa Anne—just what she wanted.

V⁓ MY FIRST TERM

PRODUCING A PROGRAM FOR THE COMMON GOOD IS A MIRACLE OF THE democratic process. The governor must work with members of the General Assembly, and also the various employees and commissioners in state government. But, bringing together the conflicting interests and varied personalities of one hundred representatives and thirty-six senators, servants of the people, assembled to do the people's business, is mind boggling. Each, in addition to having responsibility for looking after and contributing to the common good, has a constituency who look to him or her to be their leader and spokesperson.

In view of the diversity in the General Assembly, I was pleased, for the most part, with my first term in office. My team was substantially successful in reaching the goals we outlined in the campaign. My most immediate request to the General Assembly was for a bond issue to raise funds for a highway program.

Roads were the principal concerns of the people during my campaign. New highways were needed to be built and old roads needed to be repaired. There was a pressing need for an interstate highway system. There was even more of a compelling demand for farm-to-market roads on which the economy of the rural areas depended. The farmers had to have roads to get their produce to market and most essentially to get their children to school. There had been a long drought in road construction; farmers were desperate, and we were losing population from the rural areas. So, *roads* were what people had on their minds. Building these roads was what I was committed to do.

I was not an engineer; however, it was apparent to me that since our road construction had lain fallow for twenty years that our highway department was not equipped adequately and manned sufficiently with expert engineering personnel to meet the challenge.

Our program would require qualified personnel to receive bids and "let" contracts and to supervise the construction.

Therefore, I recommended that we obtain highly qualified engineering experts to make a study and to advise as to how we could, more efficiently and with less waste of time and money, carry out their "crash" road-building program.

I recommended that the question of a bond issue be referred to the people for their vote. The legislators agreed, and I scheduled a special election on February 15, 1949.

However, I was concerned due to the long drought in highway construction that our highway department would not be prepared to carry out efficiently my expanded road program.

In April 1949, I contacted the Highway Research Board of the National Research Council in St. Louis, Missouri, about surveying the Arkansas Highway Department to analyze and advise us as to how to carry out this road-building program. A representative was sent to Little Rock and appeared before the highway commission and was prepared to make an efficiency study for the highway department. The Arkansas Legislature refused to allow the study to be made, objecting on the grounds that it would take money from the road construction fund.

As we shall see, failure to make an efficiency study cost more in the long run than the cost of the original study. However, we proceeded with our highway program.

The demand for roads was so great that the people approved the bond issue to pay for the highway project by a 4-to-1 vote. This was less than six weeks after I had been sworn in as governor.

I then made a trip to New York to assist in the sale of our highway bonds. A cocktail party was given by one of the banks, which I think was Chase Manhattan.

Attending the party were several bank vice presidents from other financial institutions. I assumed that one of their duties was public relations. I had a good visit with several of them. In visiting with one group, one of the men asked me a question that riveted my attention and the attention of those who were standing by. The question was, "How close can one get to Little Rock by airplane?" Realizing that my questioner was serious, I responded, "We can get as far as Memphis by plane. We then take a paddle boat steamer down the Mississippi to the mouth of the Arkansas River, thence, up the Arkansas to Pine Bluff. There we transfer to a stagecoach and stage into Little Rock."

By this time the bystanders could hardly control their laughter. My questioner, seeing their expressions, also broke into a loud laugh, clapped his hands together, exclaiming, "I asked for that one." He was a good sport; we had a good visit and discussed that part of the country, west of the Hudson River, with which he was unfamiliar.

We sold the bonds at a good price, paying approximately 2.03 percent interest on the money borrowed.

We also made progress in education with respect to the public schools. The people's initiative to pass Initiated Act I, to consolidate small districts, and the General Assembly's referred constitutional amendment to raise the eighteen-mill limit on property taxes both passed in 1948. Those, along with an increased appropriation for education that I persuaded the legislature to pass, gave us a jump-start toward providing a better education to our children.

But even with those gains, we still remained behind—ranking forty-eighth among the states in the quality of education. We needed more help. While I firmly believed that the primary responsibility for providing quality education belongs to the states and the local communities, I also thought that the national interest would be better served if the federal government established minimum standards and provided supplemental funding. We had so much ground to make up in education that we needed outside help. Unfortunately, there was not enough time to deal with that in my first term. I did get a chance to discuss national standards with President Truman during my second term and will bring this issue up then.

One of the high points of my first term came outside the General Assembly. It developed when President Truman made a visit to the state early in my first term. The president believed in loyalty. He never forgot a friend. He never forgot Arkansas's overwhelming support in his bid for president and my refusal to join the Dixiecrats. The occasion was the U.S. Army's Thirty-fifth Division Reunion in Little Rock, in the summer of 1949. He had served with them as a captain of artillery in the First World War and had seen a lot of action. But he also came to see me and all his friends in Arkansas who had given him great support.

The reunion was highlighted by a parade down Main Street. The president led it, marching with the troops, and invited me to march with him. We were cheered by large and enthusiastic crowds as we proceeded north on Main Street, turned left on Markham, and peeled off at the old Marion Hotel.

President Truman and Gov. Sid McMath parade down Main Street, 1949—
Thirty-fifth Division Reunion

The president and I then went up to the presidential suite, just
the two of us. We were hot from marching in the summer heat, and
when we entered the suite, he asked, "Governor, how would you like
a drink?" I wasn't about to turn him down, so I agreed. He then
announced, "You are going to be waited on by the highest paid bar-
tender in the world." I looked around and there was no one else in
the room except the two of us. The president of the United States went
behind the bar, and using two low-ball glasses, made and poured us

each a drink of bourbon and water. We then sat down and talked, uninterrupted, for about an hour, or rather he talked and I listened.

The president apparently had some things on his mind and wanted a friendly, receptive ear, which I happily provided. However, I ventured a few questions. I remember one in particular.

Soon after I learned that the president was scheduled to visit Little Rock, I received a call from the commandant of the Marine Corps, Gen. Lemuel Shepherd. He had been a colonel and the commander of the Marine Corps Schools in Quantico in 1942, when I was serving there, training officer candidates. It was then Colonel Shepherd who, after I had put in three requests for a combat assignment, called me to his office, ordered me to pack my gear, and get on the next truck to Camp Lejeune, North Carolina. Now he, of course, was aware of the president's visit to Arkansas. His call was to "request" (order) me to obtain important information pertaining to the future of the Marine Corps—a recommendation which was in fact sitting on President Truman's desk.

From time to time there was a movement to eliminate the Marine Corps, or at least to limit their role. Predictably, at the end of the Second World War, there was such a concerted movement in Washington. Some contended that there was nothing the Marine Corps was required to do that could not be performed by the other branches. To counter this, Marine Corps friends in Congress had passed a bill supporting the Marine Corps's strength to be three divisions and three air wings.

As a former army officer, Truman had recently made a speech to the Army Reserve Officers Association in Washington. He had compared the Marine Corps's propaganda agency with that of the Kremlin, stating that the Marine Corps had a "public relations man in every squad."

The bill specifying the strength of the Marine Corps had been on the president's desk for some time. General Shepherd was apprehensive that he would either veto the bill or decline to sign it.

In keeping with the commandant's wish, I mentioned the general's concern.

The president, figuratively putting on his army captain's bar, had a good laugh, and replied, "I'm going to sign the bill. I just wanted the boys to sweat a little bit."

The commandant of the Marine Corps was able to "cool off" and was relieved and supremely gratified when I conveyed to him the president's response. Having received the good news, he appreciated the president's sense of humor and thanked me for the timely word. (The United States Marine Corps is the only branch of the services whose strength is set by an act of Congress.)

Having the privilege of this special visit with President Truman was one of the most memorable events of my life. It marked the beginning of a lasting friendship and is one of my most cherished memories.

In flight to Washington aboard the flying White House, President Truman wrote me the following letter dated June 11, 1949:

> Honorable Sid McMath
> The Governor of Arkansas
>
> Dear Governor:
>
> Thanks to you for a wonderful time in the Capital of the great State of Arkansas. Everything came out as I hoped it would.
>
> The airport reception yesterday, the march this morning, your excellent speech this afternoon to my mind left nothing to be desired. I am sorry I did not thank you publicly before I started to speak, but I told others why I did not. I was rattled as I always am before I make a serious talk. My best to your lovely family.
>
> Sincerely,
> Harry Truman

His humility and sincerity were obvious—his greatness has grown with time.

Not long after President Truman paid a special visit to the state, I had occasion to interact with him again. The issue involved a public water policy for the Delta region. Before I was elected, a feasibility study had been made and some public meetings were held to discuss the findings. But the project was slow to come to fruition. It was being held up primarily by a jurisdiction conflict between the Department of the Interior and the Corps of Engineers. The *Arkansas Gazette*, on May 26, 1949, carried an article on the project headlined, "Interior Department Will Oppose Project if It Can't Operate It."

The *Gazette* article stated:

> Interior Department spokesman said today that unless the Department can construct and operate the proposed $20 mil-

Governor McMath presents President Truman with key to city, 1949

lion irrigation project for the Grand Prairie rice region in Arkansas, it will oppose it.

The Grand Prairie project was designed to bring water from the White River to the rice and cotton farms in the Delta. Questions were raised as to how irrigation ditches to the farmlands would adversely affect the ecology of the rivers, particularly the White River.

President Truman had already recognized this need by the time I took office, and he was endeavoring to get action during his

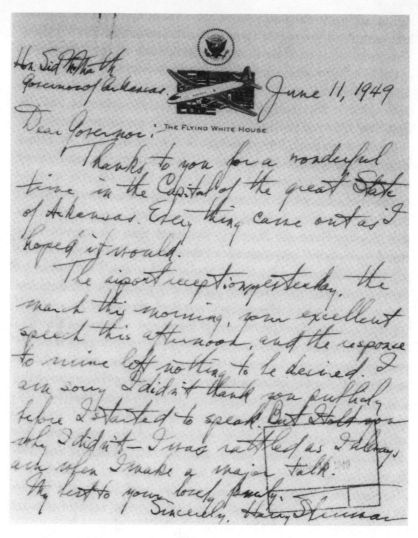

Letter from President Truman to McMath on the occasion of president's visit to Arkansas, June 1949

administration. I wrote to him about my interest in the issue and expressed confidence that this interagency dispute could be cleared up—for the good of the farmers. He responded with a letter written on June 21, 1949:

> Dear Governor:
>
>   I appreciate very much yours of the 17th in regard to the

Arkansas River Project and the Grand Prairie Irrigation Project.
I am familiar with both of them and I hope some means can be
found to work them out eventually.

Sincerely yours,
Harry S. Truman

But, despite the president's interest, and my commitment to rural
Arkansas, we could not make any headway. Repeatedly, the project
was held up. I couldn't get anything done, but then neither has any
other governor to date.

My keenest disappointment with the first legislative session was
the defeat for election reform. Having recently done battle against the
situation in my own hometown, Hot Springs, where the evils of election process, based upon the poll tax, were flagrantly perpetuated, I
wanted this one badly. I felt strongly that our election system had to
be changed. The poll tax was nothing more than a means of discrimination and a tool for enhancing and preserving the political power
used to protect and perpetuate special interests.

When the General Assembly failed to approve an election reform
bill, I decided to appeal to the state Democratic Party. The state convention was scheduled to meet September 22, 1950, in Little Rock. I
thought this was the proper forum for this boil to be lanced. Hence, I
requested the party leaders to openly confront this issue. Henry Woods,
my dear friend, former campaign manager, and now executive secretary, prepared a resolution eliminating the word "White" from
Democratic Party rules. The resolution was debated, heatedly opposed
by some, but courageously passed by a majority of the delegates. Thus,
this long denied right of citizenship was granted to our black citizens.

A half century later, on February 22, 1998, I received a note from
former United States senator Kaneaster Hodges of Newport, Arkansas.
In going through his files, Kaneaster had found a copy of the *Newport
Daily Independent* carrying the date of Friday, September 22, 1950, with
the headline: "State Demos Admit Negroes into Party."

In his note of transmittal Kaneaster stated:

It is very hard to believe that less than 50 years ago it took a
"stirring call for party unity" on your part to admit "Negroes"
into the Democratic Party.

THE WHITE HOUSE
WASHINGTON

June 21, 1949

321

Dear Governor:

    I appreciated very much yours of the seventeenth in regard to the Arkansas River project and the Grand Prairie irrigation project. I am familiar with both of them and I hope some means can be found to work them out eventually.

Sincerely yours,

Harry Truman

Honorable Sid McMath
Governor of Arkansas
Little Rock, Arkansas

JUN 23 1949

321-5

Letter from President Truman to McMath on the occasion of president's visit to Arkansas, June 1949

    This action by Arkansas Democrats was gradually followed by other Southern states. America, and the South, is the stronger for it, and the Democratic Party became the party of civil rights.

    In the first year of my first term I got the opportunity to help another group, organized labor, for whom I had a deep and abiding

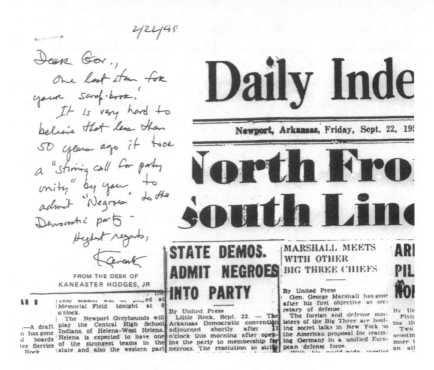

2/22/98

Dear Gov.,
One last item for your scrap-book!
It is very hard to believe that less than 50 years ago it took a "stirring call for party unity" by you, to admit "Negroes" to the Democratic party —
Highest regards,

Kaneaster

FROM THE DESK OF
KANEASTER HODGES, JR

Daily Inde

Newport, Arkansas, Friday, Sept. 22, 19

North Fro
South Line

STATE DEMOS. ADMIT NEGROES INTO PARTY

By United Press
Little Rock, Sept. 22. — The Arkansas Democratic convention adjourned shortly after 11 o'clock this morning after opening the party to membership for negroes. The resolution to strike

MARSHALL MEETS WITH OTHER BIG THREE CHIEFS

By United Press
Gen. George Marshall has gone after his first objective as secretary of defense.
The foreign and defense ministers of the Big Three are holding secret talks in New York on the American proposal for rearming Germany in a unified European defense force.

Note from Kaneaster Hodges attached to front page of newspaper with story about Governor McMath's call for admission of blacks to the Democratic Party, September 1950

interest. In October 1949, the Missouri-Pacific Railroad workers were on strike. MoPac was a big employer in our state but the disruption of railroad service quickly became national interest. Despite the national ramifications, I felt strongly that the states more immediately affected should make the first attempt to resolve the matter. I consulted with the governor of Missouri and told him of my feelings. He agreed and called a meeting in St. Louis for representatives of the workers and the Missouri-Pacific management. I asked my commissioner of labor, C. K. Call, to represent me at the meeting. He had empathy with labor and understanding of the problems in business. More important, he had the confidence of both. After a period of tough but good-faith negotiations, the strike was settled to the mutual advantage of labor and management.

Following the settlement of the strike, I received a letter from John Steelman, assistant to Pres. Harry Truman, on October 24, 1949, thanking me for my contribution in settling this dispute.

I also received a letter from the president of the Missouri-Pacific Railroad brotherhood expressing his appreciation for the fair and equitable manner in which the strike was settled.

I had an opportunity to further discuss with President Truman our pressing needs for quality education. I was in the midst of my campaign for a second term. Former governor Ben Laney was my opponent, and I was devoting my time and energy toward reelection. However, I had written a rather lengthy letter to the president outlining our need for more funds to help our children get a quality education. With the impending Korean War on his shoulders, this great president, this caring and compassionate man, took a moment to respond to my concerns.

> Dear Governor:
>
> Your letter of June 1st was highly appreciated.
>
> I am having a conference with Congressman Barden today on the Aid to Education bill, but the matter is so completely mixed in the House Committee on Education and Labor that I doubt seriously whether we will get it out only in small pieces.
>
> I am as anxious as you are to get some action. Sometime when I see you I'll tell you all the ramifications of the situation— or maybe you already know.
>
> Sincerely yours,
> Harry S. Truman

I did not know what the ramifications were in Washington. I did know about the ramifications in our own state. We have some of the most wonderful people in the world right here in Arkansas, but many of us are sometimes confused on our priorities. What was good enough for my grandfather, my father, and me, may not necessarily be good enough for my children and my grandchildren.

Perhaps the bottom line is a lack of appreciation for a student's need for a broad educational background in the sciences, the English language, literature, history, mathematics, and the arts, in order to provide every citizen with an opportunity for a better quality of life in this competitive world.

In addition to other duties, the governor is an ambassador of good will. I accepted invitations for speaking engagements around the nation. I appeared on radio and television programs. Among others, in

December of my first year in office, I was invited to appear on Arthur Godfrey's nationally syndicated radio program. His was the most popular show on the air. He had a young lady, Janet Davis, from Pine Bluff, who was his popular "man Friday" and chief lieutenant. I think it was Janet who prevailed upon Godfrey to invite me to appear on his program. I flew to New York for this purpose. Would the time and expense be worth the few minutes on the air? I thought I had gotten to be a pro, but I was nervous and a little apprehensive. On cue, I was introduced by Godfrey to his audience, referring to his helper, the young lady from Pine Bluff, Arkansas, he remarked: "Miss Davis, what you told me about the governor is true, except *that he does too wear shoes.*"

My response was that we not only wore shoes in Arkansas, but we manufactured them. With this, Arthur Godfrey turned his program over to me for a few minutes to tell his listeners over the country about Arkansas. You may be sure that I took full advantage of this free time on the air to inform the national audience about our resources, our climate, the industry of our people, our clean air and pure water, and our potential for the future.

I was pleased with the visit, and apparently so was Godfrey; he thereafter referred to me, from time to time, most commendably.

When I became governor in January 1949, the governor's term of office was two years. So, early in 1950, I began running for a second term. The Democratic Party primary was in July 1950—eighteen months after I had taken office. The political tradition had been that the governor would be given a second term without serious opposition.

My opposition came principally from the sources opposing my first election in 1948. However, this time I had a formidable opponent in former governor Ben Laney. Prior to my election in 1948, the condition of our roads was in shambles. Existing roads were not being repaired. Additional roads, especially farm-to-market roads, were not being constructed nor planned during the Ben Laney administration in 1945, 1946, 1947, and 1948. My road program was in full swing in the summer of 1950 when I was opposed by Laney for my second term. Governor Laney had no road construction program during his four years in office, and in his return to politics and his race against me in 1950, he still had not advanced a road construction plan.

Under my program, the counties in the state who had no hard-surface roads were getting those roads, either in the process of

Sid McMath, campaign for second term, July 1950

construction or on the planning board. Highway contractors were fully involved. Equipment companies were selling their machines; highway materialmen, owners of gravel pits, and truckers were actively engaged; workers were employed. Those having left the state were returning to find full employment. The whole economy of the state was being stimulated.

I had a highway construction program that was projected into the future to meet our pressing transportation needs. Included in the program was a 50 percent allocation of highway funds for farm-to-market roads. In this campaign against me for my second term, which of us would the road construction industry and the local communities, who at long last could see some relief from the mud and the dust, support for governor? They would support me.

Any housewife who had fought a continuing battle against dust penetrating her home, settling on all her household furnishings, or who had combated the red mud tracked into her house during the rainy season, would readily and vigorously announce her support for me.

Thus, I received votes and campaign contributions from the road construction industry and votes and campaign contributions from the communities whose interest and welfare had been long abandoned. I was reelected by a large majority. But Ben Laney was still deeply involved with the Dixiecrats. That group was very much alive, organized and pointing toward the next presidential election when President Truman was expected to come up for a second term.

Laney ran a business platform and was frequently referred to as "Business Ben." In the progress of the campaign either the governor, or his supporters, advanced the claim that during his administration he had cut taxes. In searching the records, the only information I found relating to tax cuts was on lightning rods, beehives, and buggy whips. So, inevitably, "lightning rods, beehives, and buggy whips" became the battle cry my supporters and I chanted at our enthusiastic rallies around the state. Otherwise, the campaign was not especially spectacular. It was, for the most part, a gentlemanly campaign with discussion limited to issues, what Governor Laney had done in the past, and what I was doing and hoped to do during the remainder of my tenure as governor.

Then in the midst of the campaign on June 15, the North Koreans invaded South Korea. In short order President Truman mobilized the Marine Corps Reserves, including the Sixth Rifle Company in Little Rock, for active duty. Many of the reserve marines, officers, and noncommissioned officers who had served in the Second World War had hardly had time to readjust their lives when they were called back for this new war in the Far East.

When the Sixth Rifle Company assembled in Little Rock at the War Memorial Stadium, I joined them there and made a short talk. My concluding remark was, "The only regret I have is that I am not

WESTERN UNION

JOSEPH L. EGAN, PRESIDENT   1207

Send the following message, subject to the terms on back hereof, which are hereby agreed to

HELENA, ARKANSAS   19 50
To_____ PRESIDENT OF UNITED STATES _____ 19___

Street and No._____
Care of or
Apt. No._____   Place_____ WASHDC

YOUR STAND AGAINST ANY FURTHUR ADVANCE BY THE COMMUNIST . YOUR RESOLUTE

ATTITUDE IN THE PRESENT WORLD CRISIS HAS WON ANEW THE FAITH AND

CONFIDENCE OF THE PEOPLE OF ARKANSAS. WE ARE READY TO FOLLOW YOUR

LEADERSHIP IN ASSUMING THE RESPONSIBILITIES REQUIRED BY THE

INTERNATIONAL SITUATION .

SID MCMATH GOVERNOR OF ARKANSAS

Sender's name and address (For reference)   Sender's telephone number

Sid's telegram supporting President Truman's decision to defend South Korea and
(*opposite*) Truman's personal letter responding to "Sid"

going with you." A chuckle could be heard moving through the
ranks—they didn't believe me, but I meant it.

I moved with them to the Missouri-Pacific Railroad station and
there, they boarded the train and were transported to Camp Pendleton,
California. They were shipped as rapidly as possible to Korea, to be fed
into the ranks of the beleaguered First Marine Division.

By fall, the war was bogged down and there was serious concern
that China might enter the war. The president was urged by many of
his advisors and allies to withdraw, that to do otherwise would be to
risk going to war with both China and the Soviet Union. President
Truman made the decision to stay the course and to save that small
country for the Free World.

This was a dark hour for the president. I greatly sympathized with
his position and was convinced that he had made the right decision.
I wired him such a message of support on December 4, 1950, immediately after he announced it. He responded the very next day on
December 5, 1950:

THE WHITE HOUSE
WASHINGTON

December 5, 1950

Dear Sid:

Far from regarding your message as an intrusion, I am more grateful than I can say for your telegram of December fourth. It warms my heart and soul to receive this assurance that I am in the thoughts and prayers of so faithful a friend.

You have a real grasp of the perils that are hanging over the free world in these tragic days. I shall ponder deeply all that you say and pray God daily to give me strength and wisdom in all the decisions that are part of the responsibility of office.

Very sincerely yours,

Harry Truman

Honorable Sid McMath,
Governor of Arkansas,
Little Rock, Arkansas.

Dear Sid,

Far from regarding your message as an intrusion, I am more grateful than I can say for your telegram of December 4th. It warms my heart and soul to receive this assurance that I am in the thoughts and prayers of so faithful a friend.

You have a real grasp of the perils that are hanging over the free world in these tragic days. I shall ponder deeply all that you say and pray God daily to give me strength and wisdom in all the decisions that are part of the responsibilities of office.

Very Sincerely Yours,
Harry Truman

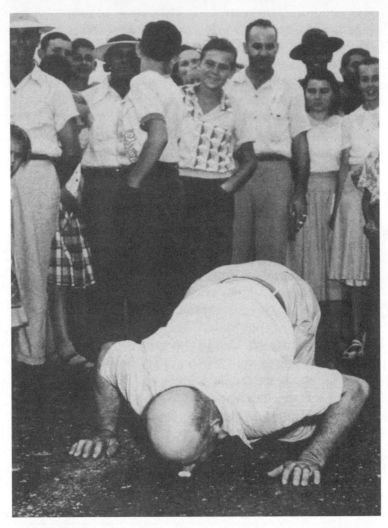

Man fulfilling his promise to push a peanut down the road if it was paved, which it was under Governor McMath's administration *(From Jim Lester,* A Man for Arkansas*)*

The Security Council of the United Nations passed a resolution supporting South Korea. President Truman's decision was in accord with his containment policy of the Soviet Union and Communism. The resolution of the U.N. Security Council was helpful but the burden of waging the war was borne by the American forces. However, we did receive support from the Aussies, New Zealand, and the Turks.

Notwithstanding the Korean War, I still had a campaign to wage for my second term. By this time, my road program was in full swing. The bond sales were good, and we had a steady stream of revenue. Highway officials were busy directing funds to repair and maintain existing roads and build new ones all over the state. We were careful to see that the funds were being equally divided between our primary highways and a farm-to-market system.

In the campaign for my second term, road building helped me more than anything else in the campaign. Throughout the state, county and local community leaders were having road openings and highway dedications. I tried to make as many of these dedications as my schedule would allow. I could feel the warmth of appreciation in the hearts of the people being served. They turned out and always gave me a warm welcome and an optimistic and cheerful send-off to my next rally.

At one such event, the crowd gathered around a local citizen on his knees on a newly built road. He had bet that if McMath built this road, he would push a peanut across the road with his nose.

He announced: "Every governor I can remember has promised us this road. Sid McMath is the only one who delivered."

I kept my promise, and he kept his, to the delight of the cheering crowd.

Some newspapers, like the *Hope Star,* opposed my road program. The editor had spoken out during the original bond election in my first term. He editorialized that the state had never recovered from the indebtedness incurred under the original Martineau plan in the 1920s. He stated that: "In relying on bond issues to solve Arkansas' highway crisis, we are merely turning back to the very method which helped cause today's trouble."[1] I disagreed with him then, and events of the

---

1. *Hope Star,* Hope, Arkansas, January 14, 1949.

previous eighteen months had proven me right. But, that didn't end his criticism, and he continued to oppose me in my second campaign.

My highway program provided the foundation for the state's economic development during the 1950s and 1960s. The 2,995 miles of primary and secondary roads constructed between 1949 and 1953 were more than any other administration in the state's history. That put us in good position to participate in the interstate highway program that came during the administration of Pres. Dwight Eisenhower. The developing tourist industry of northwest Arkansas, the expanding lumber business in the southern part of the state, the growth of the plantation economy of the delta area in the east, and the urbanization of central Arkansas, were all, to a large extent, assisted by the modern highway system built during my four years in office.

After I left the State House, northern automobile manufacturers, such as Pontiac, were forced to abandon the "Arkansas mud test" as the proving grounds of the durability of their cars. In the terms of a modern road system, Arkansas was genuinely on its way to becoming part of "the New South."[2]

Thanks to the road program, the progress we were making in education and race relations, as well as the hope that Arkansans were looking forward to a better tomorrow, I won reelection easily—much more easily than I initially expected. Rather than advancing any new proposals in my second campaign, I concentrated on completing the programs already underway. With a new, two-year cycle ahead of me, I felt confident in completing the tasks that we had started.

---

2. Jim Lester, *A Man for Arkansas*, 137.

VI⟶ MY SECOND TERM

WHEN I BECAME GOVERNOR IN JANUARY 1949, ONE OF THE CRITICAL problems facing the state was the possible loss of Class A rating for the University of Arkansas Medical School. Like other Southern states, we had a shortage of trained medical personnel. Loss of the medical school would aggravate the absence of trained medical personnel, particularly in the rural areas, which at the time contained about 80 percent of the population.

In my first term, January 1949, in my inaugural address to the legislature, I had proposed a long-range medical program to preserve our medical school's accreditation and to provide a teaching hospital in conjunction with the medical school and the state mental hospital. In my presentation, I said to the legislature that "the construction of a medical center is essential if we are to keep our medical school and provide doctors and nurses to meet the health needs of our people."

My proposal met with the statewide approval of the Arkansas Medical Association. The president of the medical association informed me that "a group of doctors heard your inaugural address over the radio Tuesday. We consider you our friend and pledge our support to the proposed Medical Center."[1] I received similar letters pledging support from other prominent members of the medical community. Confident of the General Assembly's support, I recruited Howard Eichenbaum, an architect with one of the state's most prestigious firms, to design the center. His design won national attention. For example, the senior engineer of the Division of Hospital Facilities of the United States Department of Public Health wrote Howard that "We consider it without a doubt, the most distinguished Medical Center design in the country." Unfortunately, the legislators in my first term did not share my vision for medical care in the state and failed to appropriate adequate funds in 1949 to complete the medical center.

Following my reelection, I came back to the medical center issue in the 1951 legislative session. I proposed a two-cent tax on each package of cigarettes to be earmarked for completing the hospital and a

---

1. P. W. Lutterloh, January 15, 1949.

Gov. Sid McMath, Dr. Lewis Webster Jones, and Hayden C. Nicholson breaking ground for the University of Arkansas Medical School, Hospital, and Medical Center

new building for the medical school. This time the legislators were more responsive and the tax passed. I considered a cigarette tax most appropriate because approximately 50 percent of the cost for operating a hospital was related to the treatment of nicotine-related victims, emphysema, lung cancer, and coronary disease.

My concern for the health of the people of our state also extended to the facilities for psychiatry treatment. In 1950, I outlined a program for improved neuro-psychiatric medical care at the Veterans' Administration Hospital. My proposal was carried in the *Bulletin of the Minninger Clinic*, which was most commendable to the program that I had outlined.

I also raised the question of adequate facilities for elderly citizens. In addressing the General Assembly I said: "We have failed to see this problem developing and failed to appreciate its true size and scope. We have sat idly by watching longevity being added into living and yet we have been doing nothing to add living to longevity."[2] I was gratified to see the legislators respond favorably and appropriate more funds to provide assistance to the elderly.

It so happened that in 1951, it was Arkansas's "turn to host" the Southern Governors' Conference. I was happy to do this, especially in view of the political schism that I had had with several of the Dixiecrat governors during the 1948 presidential election.

The conference was held at the Arlington Hotel in Hot Springs in November 1951. The governors of all the Southern states were in attendance. Gov. Fielding Wright of Mississippi, who had been the Dixiecrat nominee for vice president, attended the meeting, and as I recall, never missed a session. He was a personable gentleman. He never voiced any objection to the Democratic theme of our program. This was not true of one governor, who absented himself during our banquet speaker's address. He was a Republican and at the upcoming Republican Party Convention (1952) nominated General Eisenhower.

Gov. Earl Long of Louisiana registered for the conference but remained in his hotel suite without venturing forth to attend the meetings—he was otherwise engaged.

The Arkansas AM&N choir provided a beautiful chorus for our inspiration and entertainment. I invited Sam Rayburn, Speaker of the U.S. House of Representatives, to be our featured speaker. In my invitation to Speaker Rayburn, I pointed out the importance of having a staunch administration supporter, a speaker who was respected throughout the South, to make the principal address. I wrote to "Mr. Sam," "As you know, there will be a great deal of undercover anti-administration work going on at the conference. The pro-administration forces in the Southern states need all the help we can get."

Speaker Sam rose to the occasion. He gave his noted, "Stomp down depression," inspired Democratic speech—"ten-cent cotton, forty-cent meat. How in the world can a poor man eat?" and contrasted the prosperity of the early 1950s with the depression of the Hoover era. He also contended that if a Republican administration came to power in 1952, the Southern congressmen and senators would

---

2. Sid McMath, "Arkansas Mental Health Plan," *Bulletin of the Minninger Clinic* 14 (September 1950): 154.

lose important committee memberships in Congress. To the Truman critics in the audience, he said, "Whether you love or hate President Truman, he is our president and he will be our president until 1953. He is the voice of America or America has no voice."

The "ten-cent cotton, forty-cent meat" referred to by Speaker Rayburn was a refrain from a song that came from the troubled heart of the South during the depression. It summed up the despair of a people caught in an economic crisis not of their individual making. There are many in Arkansas and in the South who still remember.

Immediately following Mr. Rayburn's speech, there was a strong reaction from representatives of the Dixiecrat Party. Governor Talmadge issued a statement charging that the policies of the National Democratic Party were detrimental to the people of Georgia. The strongest reaction came from the former secretary of state, Gov. James Byrns of South Carolina.

I wrote President Truman giving him a report on the conference, the effectiveness of the Speaker's talk, and the reaction of the Dixiecrats. Jimmy Burns was a former justice of the Supreme Court of the United States, a United States senator, a secretary of state, and once a friend and supporter of President Truman, but he had "jumped ship" and embraced the Dixiecrats in the 1948 presidential election.

In response to my report to the president, he wrote me the following:

> November 27, 1951
>
> Dear Sid,
>
> I certainly did appreciate your good letter of the 21st very much. I am very certain that Sam Rayburn had made a good speech at the Governors' Conference because of the loud wails of the Dixiecrats. I was also highly pleased at your comments on my speech of the 20th. I hope it did some good.
>
> It certainly is a pity to see an able and distinguished senator and former justice of the Supreme Court of the United States go "completely haywire" as our friend Jimmy Burns has done.
>
> I hope everything is going well with you and that it will continue to go well. The first time you are in Washington be sure and come around so that we can talk the situation over.
>
> Sincerely,
> Harry Truman

Sam Rayburn ("Mr. Sam"), Speaker of the House of Representatives, and Governor McMath at Southern Governors' Conference, Hot Springs, Arkansas, 1951

Governor of South Carolina, Jimmy Byrnes, and Gov. Sid McMath at Southern Governors' Conference, 1951

THE WHITE HOUSE
WASHINGTON

3 ᵈ)

U. S. Naval Station
Key West, Florida
November 27, 1951

Dear Sid:

I certainly did appreciate your good letter of the twenty-first very much. I was very certain that Sam Rayburn had made a good speech at the Governors' Conference because of the loud wails of the Dixiecrats. I was also highly pleased at your comments on my speech of the twentieth. I hope it did some good.

It certainly is a pity to see an able and distinguished Senator and former Justice of the Supreme Court of the United States go "completely haywire" as our friend, Jimmie Byrnes, has done.

I hope everything is going well with you and that it will continue to go well. The first time you are in Washington be sure and come around so that we can talk the situation over.

Sincerely,

Harry Truman

Honorable Sid McMath
Governor of Arkansas
Little Rock, Arkansas

NOV 28 1951

Personal letter from President Truman to Sid McMath regarding Dixiecrats' reactions at Southern Governors' Conference, 1951

I wrote to Speaker Sam Rayburn, complimenting him on his straightforward Democratic speech and thanked him for accepting our invitation. "Mr. Sam" responded with a long letter and in referring to his critics stated: "It was funny to hear those people squawk about the speech when they had been doing all the politics they could think of and frankly trying to destroy the Democratic Party."

Southern Governors' Conference, 1951 (Gov. Earl Long from Louisiana was not present for the photo)

My friend Harry Ashmore, editor of the *Arkansas Gazette*, addressed the convention on Southern educational problems. He informed the governors: "The high cost of segregation has held back the overall development of our educational institutions." He also told this audience that "we were failing to provide the effective leadership that our own tradition demands."[3]

On a lighter, happier note, Marjorie Lawrence, a world-renowned

---

3. *Arkansas Gazette*, Little Rock, November 13, 1951.

singer from Australia, living in Hot Springs at the time, sang, and with her gifts and personality, enthralled our guests.

Engrossed and as involved as I was with the programs we had set in motion, I carried on a seemingly endless, running battle with the Arkansas Power and Light Company (AP&L) and its owner, Mid-South Utilities (Mid-South). The battle lines were drawn in my first administration and were fought out in my second term. In the eyes of the utilities' managers and director, I had committed the unpardonable political sin. I had opposed their desire to strengthen and perpetuate their monopoly and stranglehold on electrical service in Arkansas. In my second term, the struggle between the farm cooperatives to obtain electricity for the rural areas in Arkansas and the power companies became more intense. Mid-South, and thus, AP&L, continued their refusal to provide service to most rural areas and continued to block the electric cooperatives in their efforts to provide an adequate source of low-cost power for themselves. In 1950, the Arkansas Public Service Commission (PSC) appointed by me, had, by a 2-to-1 vote, granted cooperatives a certificate to build their own steam-generating plant in Ozark, Arkansas. The transmission lines would begin to serve the counties in northern and northwest Arkansas, who were without service.

Immediately upon this action by the PSC, the power companies filed a petition in the chancery court of Pulaski County to block this permit, which was a convenience and necessity granted to the cooperatives.

I took issue with the power monopoly, who having failed to supply this electrical service to meet the needs of our people in rural areas, now sought to obstruct the co-ops in obtaining this service financed by a loan from the government through the Rural Electric Association.

Mid-South and AP&L would not provide the services, but opposed the farmers providing it for themselves. Supplying electricity to the farms, with all the benefits that flowed from it to the farmers and their families, was with me a passionate commitment. I declined to be diverted from this most laudable goal and intense personal commitment and will discuss it in the next chapter.

Nine months into my second term, a local newspaper printed a story that got all of us involved in economic development very excited. Banner headlines in the *Arkansas Gazette* read:

"Tulsa Firm Seeks to Build a Hundred and Two Million
Dollar Metal Plant in Vicinity of Little Rock"

"Washington, September 12, 1951, Spartan Aircraft Corporation
of Tulsa Has Plans for a Hundred and Two Million Dollar
Integrated Aluminum Plant to Be Built near Little Rock. Final
Decision on the Project Now Rests with Jess Larson, New
Administrator of the Defense Materials Procurement Agency."[4]

The article went on to say, "The plant, which would employ about
one thousand persons, would reduce Arkansas bauxite to alumina,
transform it to aluminum and then roll it into sheet metal at the rate
of sixty thousand tons annually." This was confirmed by Wayne
Fletcher, my executive director of the Arkansas Resources and
Development Commission. The article went on to say that Fletcher
preferred not to discuss it until "it is in the bag . . . But it would be
the biggest single thing to come to Arkansas and I believe we are going
to get it."[5]

I had been working with Wayne Fletcher on this project and its
prospects for Arkansas.

I read the news story with great anticipation. The state was experi-
encing an extreme migration in population, and we desperately
needed every new factory we could get to offer our people jobs. This
new plant would process one of our own natural resources. The bauxite would be made into aluminum and then be processed by Spartan
Aircraft into finished aluminum products. This was where high wage
levels would be found. The bauxite industry had received a tremendous boost from the war, but we were now faced with massive cut-
backs if we could not develop some peace time uses. The Spartan
Aircraft plant seemed just the thing.

We were excited because processing aluminum into sheet aluminum products was where the higher-paying jobs were. Wayne
Fletcher had been in Washington several days working on the project. He conferred with Spartan Aircraft Company's representative,
R. H. Rush. He also met with Dr. John Steelman, a native Arkansan
on the White House staff, Jess Larson, newly appointed director of

---

4. *Arkansas Gazette*, September 12, 1951.
5. *Arkansas Gazette*, September 22, 1951.

December 20, 1948

Personal

Governor-Elect Sid McMath
Hot Springs, Arkansas

Dear Governor:

The Directors of the Arkansas State Electric Cooperative held a meeting in Little Rock on December 17, 1948. They had under discussion a proposal for construction of generating plants and transmission lines in Arkansas to serve themselves with power. The State Association represents the 18 rural electric cooperatives now operating in Arkansas. These cooperatives now serve 70,000 farm families in the State and will ultimately serve approximately 120,000. More than 50% of the area of Arkansas has been allotted to the electric cooperatives.

There was considerable discussion with reference to the attitude of the new Public Service Commission on the REA program.

You will recall the meeting you attended in my office on August 2 with representatives of the rural electric cooperatives. By unanimous vote at the meeting yesterday, I was requested to write you on behalf of the rural electric projects and let you know our vital interest in seeing the program go forward. As we told you at the August 2 meeting, we are vitally interested in expanding the rural electric program to serve every farm home in Arkansas at the earliest possible date. We are vitally interested in seeing the earliest possible development of the hydro-electric projects in Arkansas. We are vitally interested in generating electric steam power ourselves. We want to integrate this steam power with the hydro power now under development in the State. We sincerely appreciate your statements that this program, as discussed with you, will receive every encouragement under your administration.

The Arkansas Public Service Commission on many occasions has been hostile to the REA program. We know that any action that curtails expansion of generating capacity or extension of electric service in Arkansas is detrimental to the welfare of Arkansas.

Representatives of our State organization would be very glad to meet with you and the Public Service Commissioners to discuss in detail the steps that we think can and should be taken to insure the development of the resources of Arkansas through an abundance of low cost electric power.

We wish for you a most successful administration.

Cordially yours,

(Signed)   Thomas B. Fitzhugh

Thomas B. Fitzhugh

TBF/mh

Letter to Sid McMath from Thomas B. Fitzhugh, attorney for the electric co-ops, regarding their plans, which Sid McMath supported for building a steam-generating plant and (opposite) Governor McMath's response

January 3, 1949

Mr. Thomas B. Fitzhugh
Attorney at Law
Pyramid Building
Little Rock, Arkansas

Dear Tom:

I am in receipt of your letter of December
20. I had a very interesting discussion with Clyde
Ellis and some of the top people in the REA while in
Washington.

I am vitally interested in the success of
the REA program and I would be most happy to meet
with you and the representatives of your state organization just as soon as possible. I have checked my
calendar and find that my time is completely allotted
up to the inauguration date, but shortly after I take
office as Governor I hope that we can arrange the type
of meeting that you mention in your letter.

Very truly yours,

Sid McMath

SMcM/jah

Defense Materials Production Agency (DMPA), and with the under-secretary of the interior, Richard Searles.

Spartan Aircraft had a special interest in locating its plant in Arkansas, in close proximity to the bauxite mines. The company manufactured aluminum trailers in Tulsa and was eager to have its own supply of aluminum available rather than compete on the open market for it.

Spartan had another compelling incentive in that it planned to generate its own electrical power to produce aluminum. Reliable power sources could be supplied at a reasonable rate. This was possible because the company owned large quantities of natural gas, fuel that could be used to operate the power generators.

The Interior Department had been handling the aluminum expansion program until Jess Larson's new agency took it over. I should point out that in 1951, the World War II Defense Materials Act was still in effect. Among other things that law required that any new aluminum production be approved by the administrator of the DMPA.

Larson recommended that Spartan get an allocation of the sixty thousand tons of additional bauxite that the government had ready for assignment. The government would, of course, have top priority on all production. Spartan could use for itself all the allocated ore not required by the government.

Spartan's business plan presented a challenge to Arkansas Power and Light and its parent, Mid-South Utilities. The company had a monopoly on the generation and transmission of electricity in Arkansas.

Profits flowing to Mid-South's stockholders from its utilities services in Arkansas, Mississippi, and Tennessee were no doubt considered sufficient grounds for their policy for opposing any form of competition in their territory. They had opposed the construction of hydroelectric dams on the navigable rivers in Arkansas. In fact, representatives of Mid-South had testified before the Congressional Appropriation Committee, assuring the committee that electrical power from the Bull Shoals Dam was not needed in Arkansas.

Hamilton Moses, president of Arkansas Power and Light, had a model of a hydroelectric dam prepared, and he, with others representing the power company, used this model in their lectures to support their contention that hydroelectric dams on the Arkansas and

White Rivers were not compatible with flood control. For example, they testified before the Appropriations Committee of Congress that the power from Bull Shoals "was *not needed*."

The Spartan Aircraft Company was an example of a project over which the power company had no control, hence their all-out opposition to block it.

Wayne Fletcher had been working with officials in the Truman administration and Spartan Aircraft representatives to obtain approval for this project since my first year in office.

He gained the support of John Steelman, assistant to the president, and the undersecretary of the Department of the Interior, Richard Searles. We were encouraged to believe that Larson, the recently appointed administrator of DMPA, would act favorably on Spartan Aircraft's application since it had already been approved by the Department of the Interior and by the Anti-Trust Division of the United States Department of Justice. The Anti-Trust Division was interested in breaking up the monopolies in the aluminum production field and encouraging independents to become involved in aluminum production. H. Graham Morrison, head of the Anti-Trust Division, had taken the position that while quick production for the defense effort might justify the allocation to one of the big three, the long-range program should make provisions for production by other concerns.

Searles wrote a letter to Larson requesting approval of Spartan Aircraft's application. His letter recommending approval was published in the *Arkansas Gazette* on October 14, 1951.

The Spartan Aircraft's proposal to generate their own electrical power was strongly resisted by the power industry. Electrical power production was exceedingly profitable.

Notwithstanding its handsome return of 10 percent plus over the past three years, in June 1954, AP&L officials petitioned for a new rate increase from the PSC, appointed by Gov. Francis Cherry.

Arthur E. McLean, president of Little Rock's Commercial National Bank, opposed the power company's raid on the Arkansas ratepayers. Prior to the hearings, he wrote the following letter to the AP&L Board of Directors. He pointed out their most favored position as a monopoly and the rich returns the company was already receiving. He also stated that:

On the basis of 1953 operations, what will happen to the $3,900,000 increase for which you ask? Federal and state income taxes will take 54 percent, bondholders and preferred stock, representing 67 percent of the money in the business, get nothing, and 46 percent goes to the common stockholders (Middle South Utilities). Do you think that to keep faith with some 26,000 stockholders of Middle South Utilities Company (and for that statement I refer you to your application now on file with the Arkansas Public Service Commission) that you must have this increase from your 265,000 customers representing probably more than 1,000,000 people in Arkansas; that they shall be assessed this additional $3,900,000 so that Middle South's stockholders may get approximately $1,800,000 and have return increased from 10 percent to 13 percent? Will this help build Arkansas?

In writing this letter, I have no desire to do or say anything unfair to your company. The basis of my figures are those filed with S.E.C., and reported by Moody's Investment Service. I feel that you can check them and that you will find them reasonably correct. I believe in the private ownership of public utilities and wish the company only well, but if a monopoly is to be enjoyed, restraint must be exercised and public confidence must not be destroyed. Plausible statements but ones that cannot stand analysis and the light of day, as well as unfair rates in effect or proposed can wreck this industry. In this situation, the public has in no way been enlightened as to the real facts, they have no true picture of your real earning situation, and this is something to which they are entitled. A monopoly is in reality a privilege granted or permitted by the people. Abused, an enlightened public may become anything but reasonable.

If I were a director, I wouldn't risk killing the goose that lays the golden egg. I would want the application withdrawn.

McLean's opposition, notwithstanding the PSC, all members having been appointed by newly elected governor Francis Cherry, granted the request. The new rate increase allows AP&L to earn a 13 percent rate of return on its investment in 1954. It would be remembered that AP&L and Mid-South Utilities had been Cherry's principal supporters in his election for governor.

Arkansas, as I have previously stated, had 95 percent of the bauxite in North America. Bauxite was mined in Arkansas but shipped out of state for processing. It was my purpose as governor of Arkansas to induce the aluminum industries to establish integrated operations in our state. I could never see why the bauxite mined in Arkansas could not be processed, at least substantially, into aluminum to be fabricated into aluminum products in our state.

That was the reason I took such an active part in helping Spartan Aircraft Company obtain an allocation for aluminum production from the federal government. My position was fairly well summed up in a letter which I wrote to President Truman on October 8, 1951:

Honorable Harry S. Truman
President of the United States
The White House
Washington, D.C.

Dear Mr. President:

The people of the State of Arkansas are most anxious to have a greater opportunity to participate in the Defense Program.

Arkansas has been blessed with tremendous natural resources that should be used for the security and welfare of our country.

The aluminum industry is completely dependent upon Arkansas for domestic bauxite. More than 95 percent of the known bauxite reserves of the United States are located in Arkansas.

The expansion of the aluminum industry in Arkansas is in the public interest.

Electric power can be produced in abundant quantities at low rates from the coal, natural gas and lignite that is available in Arkansas. The rivers in this area can also supply large blocks of power.

The inland location in the Heart of America will provide greater national security.

Integrated aluminum production in Arkansas will reduce transportation costs and minimize dangers of sabotage.

Spartan Aircraft Company now has pending before Mr. Jess Larson, Administrator of DMPA, a formal application for an integrated aluminum plant to be located in Arkansas. This application has received the endorsement of responsible technicians in the Department of the Interior and DMPA.

Reynolds Metals Company and Aluminum Company of America also have plans under consideration for aluminum expansion in Arkansas.

We respectfully urge that in the interest of our national security the aluminum industry be expanded in Arkansas.

Cordially,
Sid McMath

But despite my best efforts, and notwithstanding the recommendations of the Department of the Interior and the Justice Department that Spartan be included in the allocation, Mid-South was successful in blocking any assignment of aluminum production to Spartan Aircraft. Significantly, President Truman did not respond to my letter. This was the first and only time that I failed to receive a response to my communication. I can only conclude that it was never called to his attention. When I learned of Mid-South's action I wrote to President Truman again on October 16, 1951:

Honorable Harry S. Truman
President of the United States
The White House
Washington, D.C.

Dear Mr. President:

With reference to our talk about aluminum production, the 60,000 tons of authorized expansion which I requested for Spartan Aircraft Company was given to Reynolds Metals Company. Mr. Larson made this allocation over the protest of the Department of Justice and without consideration of the unqualified recommendation of Spartan by the Department of the Interior.

Reynolds has indicated that it will place part of this additional production in Arkansas and we, of course, welcome such industrial expansion, but by comparison with Spartan's plan it will have relatively little economic significance to this region.

This decision aids the vested interests and thwarts competition. Necessarily, many of the key positions in O.D.M. are filled by men from giant corporations or men who are influenced by that segment of our society. Human nature and experiences of the past tell us that, if given a free hand, this group will improve its economic advantage at the expense of the future welfare of the country.

Mr. Wilson has said repeatedly that, in order to meet the demand, aluminum production must be increased about 100% beyond already authorized expansion. May I suggest a specific course of action designed to provide a purer atmosphere in this industry.

I would deeply appreciate your asking Mr. Wilson to get Mr. Fleischman to authorize a 60,000 ton expansion immediately, and simultaneously suggest to Mr. Larson that the allocation of this capacity is to be made to Spartan Aircraft Company, whose application is on file in his office bearing approval of all technical men whose business it is to examine such applications.

I am convinced that only your personal intervention in this matter will be effective. I would be most grateful if this could be done.

With kindest personal regards, I am

Sincerely yours,
Sid McMath

To add insult to injury the aluminum production allocation was granted to Reynolds Metals Company with the understanding that AP&L would supply the necessary electrical power to Reynolds. To supply this power, AP&L obtained the power production from Bull Shoals Reservoir, which was originally constructed for preferential customers, such as rural electric cooperatives and municipalities. Need I remind the reader that financial benefits of this huge dam, constructed with the people's money, was now going to AP&L (Mid-South).

This opposition of the power company to the construction of the Bull Shoals and Norfolk Dams was consistent with their long-established policy of opposing any power production facility which they did not control.

Remember that the same company had originally opposed the hydroelectric production at Bull Shoals, claiming that the power from the dam was *"not needed."* AP&L's initial profits amounted to approximately $1 million per year from the new contract.

The *Arkansas Times,* August 13, 1999, in its article, "The Top 100 Arkansas News Events of the 20th Century," by Bob Lancaster, reported: "Arkansas Power & Light Co. uses its influence with Sen. Joe T. Robinson to persuade the federal government to scrub plans for a federal hydroelectric project on the Arkansas River—a project that is ultimately implemented on the Tennessee River as the Tennessee Valley Authority, 1930s."

The story of the farmers' long struggle to obtain the benefits and the blessings of electricity down on the farm, and the story of Spartan Aircraft Company's efforts to establish an integrated aluminum production business in Arkansas are historical examples of what can happen when monopolies convert their private power into political power and employ it against the people's interest. The power companies were deregulated in California, and the result in 2001 was a massive blackout, resulting in an exorbitant cost of energy to the people.

During the later part of my second term, I became involved in another significant issue, known nationally as the "tidelands oil controversy." As I mentioned earlier, it is my general belief that problems are best settled locally—if they can be. As a general rule, states are better able to cope with problems peculiar to their own region than the federal government. I endeavored to carry out this policy while governor, insofar as possible. But there was one issue where I broke with that philosophy and argued for a national solution. The issue came up while I was serving as chairman of the Oil Compact Commission —late in my second term. This commission was composed of representatives from the states engaged in the production and distribution of oil and gas. My position with the commission got me involved in the dispute over the tidelands oil question.

The controversy had its origin in a 1947 decision by the U.S. Supreme Court concerning ownership of oil reserves off the coasts of Texas, Louisiana, and California. The question was whether the tidelands belonged to the respective states or to the United States. The issue of ownership arose after it was estimated that the oil reserve in the tidelands ranged up to 100 billion barrels.

The Supreme Court of the United States held that the United States had always had "paramount rights in and full dominion and power" over the tidelands and all their resources.

President Truman supported the Supreme Court's decision and directed the Justice Department to file suit against the states of Texas and Louisiana to confirm federal ownership to tidelands off their respective shores. Congress thereupon introduced legislation granting title of ownership to the states within their "historic boundaries." President Truman vetoed the bill.

I supported President Truman's action. I did not anticipate the storm of reaction I received from representatives of the petroleum industry, including those in my own state, even though Arkansas had no tidelands oil.

Arkansas and other states were in critical need for revenues to provide adequate education for all their children. It was my feeling that this rich resource, extending beyond the traditional three-mile limit, was a part of the public domain and belonged to all the states. In my opinion, those revenues could be used more advantageously for public education, in all of the states.

Continuing my policy as governor of accepting national speaking engagements, I received an invitation to talk to the National Convention of the American Federation of Labor in the fall of 1951. This was during the height of the Cold War and President Truman's attention was committed, in great part, to the containment of the Soviet Union.

Alexis de Tocqueville, a youthful French historian, visited America in 1831. As a result of his visit and observations, he wrote a book titled *Democracy in America*. In a comparison of Russia and America, he prophesied "their starting points are different and their courses are not the same; yet each of them seems marked by the will of Heaven to sway the destinies of half the globe."

A mutual friend sent President Truman a copy of my speech to the AFL convention. The president favored me with a letter on October 4, 1951:

Dear Governor:

One of our good citizens has sent me a copy of the speech you made at the Convention of the American Federation of Labor.

It was a fine speech. I liked the apt quotation you used from De Tocqueville contrasting Russia and the United States.

Very sincerely yours,
Harry S. Truman

THE WHITE HOUSE
WASHINGTON

October 4, 1951

Dear Governor:

One of our good citizens has sent me a copy of the speech you made at the Convention of the American Federation of Labor.

It was a fine speech. I liked the apt quotation you used from De Tocqueville contrasting Russia and the United States.

Very sincerely yours,

Harry Truman

Honorable Sidney S. McMath
Governor of Arkansas
Little Rock, Arkansas

OCT 8 1951

Letter from President Truman regarding Sid McMath's speech to the AFL-CIO in which Sid referred to De Tocqueville

Reflecting on my accomplishments during my four years as governor, I am particularly proud of my road construction program.

Being assured that our road program would be continued, within the limits of the projected revenue, an increased number of road committees from over the state would come to the governor's office at the state capitol to present their road needs, which was the custom over the year. Henry Woods and Orval Faubus would meet with these committees in the governor's conference room. It was my practice always to greet them, sit in the meetings briefly, and thank them for their support.

As pleasant as it was meeting with these friends and sharing their hopes, it was not an efficient administrative procedure.

It had been the custom in Arkansas as long as the state had been building highways and repairing roads for the road committees to visit with the governor and look to him for relief. This was the custom up through my administration.

However, it became apparent that these road committees should be meeting with their own highway commissioner and the chief highway engineer, who ultimately would have to determine the feasibility of their requests.

In my address to the legislature in January 1951, I reported on the progress of our highway construction plan. I recommended a change in the composition and tenure of the highway commission. "I recommend that the Legislature refer to the people a Constitutional Amendment reconstituting the Highway Commission so that one member will be appointed from each of the Congressional districts. The terms should be staggered so that there will at all times be experienced and informed men on the Commission capable of insuring a planned and continuous program."

My recommendation became the Forty-second Amendment to the Constitution of Arkansas, which was enacted in 1952. It provides for a highway commission of five members, each having a tenure of ten years with overlapping tenure. Each commissioner is appointed by the governor with advice and consent of the senate. There can be only one commissioner from each congressional district. This amendment is commonly referred to as the Mack-Blackwell Amendment #42.

Reflecting on my two terms, four years as governor, I am most grateful to those who played a key role in my administration. I wish to express my gratitude to the directors of my departments and to those board members and commissioners who loyally and faithfully served.

A chapter could be written on each. Space not permitting, I must at least mention several: Mrs. Henry Bethel, the first woman to head an Arkansas State Department, served as director of Department of Welfare; former governor Homer Adkins served as director of Employment Security; Dean Morley, former director of the FBI in Arkansas, was my revenue commissioner; Jack Stephens, a graduate of the United States Naval Academy, was my first appointment to the University of Arkansas Board of Trustees.

Jack Stephens was twenty-six years of age, an energetic and forward-looking member of the board. He supported our policy of admitting black students, like Edith Irby, to the university's graduate schools. He believed fervently that an opportunity for education was a basic right for every young person.

After half a century, we can look back with a feeling of pride for our accomplishments for the people of Arkansas.

VII ⟆ POWER VERSUS THE PEOPLE

TODAY THERE ARE SEVENTEEN ARKANSAS ELECTRIC COOPERATIVES serving electricity to their members. They have 350,000 customers representing approximately one-third of all electric consumers in Arkansas.

The electric cooperatives have a firm base of energy supply represented by three hydroelectric plants and seven steam-generating plants which they own or in which they have an interest. They have available transmission lines for delivery to their membership.

Their rates are generally lower than other providers of electric service. They have in fact reduced their rates several times during the past decade.

In the years that profits exceed the costs, a dividend distribution is made to the co-owners.

The cooperatives have not had a blackout. They planned and worked against it.

How did the cooperatives attain this position of strength of service and dependability?

Paraphrasing a wise old saying, "Their success did not come by sudden flight, but they while others slept were toiling upward toward the light."

In 1948, Arkansas was a rural state. Eighty percent of our people lived in the rural areas. Our people were farmers, mostly small farmers. They cleared the land, plowed the ground, sowed the seed, fought the weeds, and boll weevils, and harvested and marketed their crops. Cotton was the principal cash crop. There were times, too many times, when farmers would not receive on the market the cost of producing, picking, and ginning their cotton.

Our farmers labored, struggled, and most of them survived. The heaviest burden fell on the womenfolk. Their work was never done. They were not acquainted with air-conditioning. They had no refrigeration or washing machines or other appliances that were powered by electricity. The washing machine was a big black pot, half full of boiling water, flamed, and fueled by hand-chopped wood, a tub of soapy water with a scrub board for scrubbing, a tub of water for rinsing. The clothes dryer was a clothes line strung across the backyard. Electricity? Half of our farms in Arkansas had no electricity. This condition in rural Arkansas was representative of the rural condition in most of America. Yes, electricity was available, but not to these people.

The private power companies owned and operated the generation system and the transmission lines, and they had a monopoly in Arkansas. Sure, it would be, when settlements were built up in the rural area, but then they would not want any competition. It was not deemed profitable by the power companies to furnish this needed electricity, and they opposed any efforts on the part of the farmers to provide the electricity to themselves. The result was that President Roosevelt, under his New Deal, set up the Rural Electrification Program (REA), a program organized so as to assist the farmers in setting up cooperatives and government appropriated funds to loan to the farmers at a low rate of interest, in order that they could build generating plants and transmission lines to reach their farms and homes.

Originally the program was under the Department of Agriculture but then was transferred to the Department of the Interior. At the time, Claude Wickard was secretary of the interior. He fully understood the need and was aggressively carrying out the intent and purpose of a program that would transform the face of rural America and provide a stimulus to a sluggish economy. Who, with an ounce of compassion and an iota of common sense, would oppose it? Well, you figured it out—the power companies. They fought the program every step of the way in the legislature, in Congress, in the courts. The conduct of the power company was like that of the old story about the dog in the manger. The dog could not eat the hay and so he prevented the ox from eating it. The power company would not furnish electricity to the co-ops, but then they prevented them from supplying it to themselves. Additionally, it was rumored around and about that the REA was against the free enterprise system, that the farmers would be living off the government, that they were socialists, fellow travelers with the Communists. Some people luxuriating in the comfort that electricity provided gave credence to these rumors. Politicians for major office would not openly court the co-ops' political support and refrained from attending their meetings for fear that they would be tarred with the Socialist's brush.

I was the first Arkansas governor to attend a co-op meeting. I received an invitation from Russ Gates, a manager of the Berryville co-op, to attend their summer meeting. I readily accepted. I was committed to their program. I had lived and worked on a farm with my family, void of the blessings and benefits of electrical service. I flew up to Berryville in a two-seated aircraft. We had to land in a turkey pasture. My pilot made two passes to shoo the turkeys off the landing strip before we could safely land. I had anticipated being met by a committee and members of the press. I had prepared what we would call today "one liners" for the newspaper.

We landed, taxied up to the gate, the entrance to the turkey field, dismounted from the plane, and looked around. Nobody was in sight. Nobody, no committee, no press. Obviously, there had been a foul-up. Old Murphy's law—if there's anything that can go wrong it will. There was nothing to do but take off my coat and start walking down that dusty road—a road which incidently I subsequently paved. I had not walked and suffered the heat for very long before a farmer came along in a pickup truck. He stopped. "Where you goin'?" he asked. "To the co-op meeting," I responded. "Git in. That's where I'ma goin'." I did not introduce myself. I thought that since I had recently been elected governor and my name and pictures had been in the papers he knew who I was. We visited for a few minutes and quickly we came to the co-op meeting ground.

They were gathered in a large canvas tent, no air conditioning. The ladies went through the motion of cooling themselves with hand fans furnished by the local funeral home. Russ was apologetic about the "fowl-up" at the turkey pasture. He gave me a few minutes to shake hands and circulate around. The meeting took up; I was the speaker. The manager gave me a laudatory introduction, closing with great emphasis, "I give you, Sid McMath, the Governor of Arkansas." The farmer who had picked me up was seated on the front row. With this introduction, he turned to his neighbor and said in a loud voice, "He ain't no governor, he's a hitchhiker. I know 'cause I brung him to town."

Subsequently, I had an opportunity to again visit Berryville. It was a community civic program. C. Hamilton Moses, president of Arkansas Power and Light, was also there. We were both on the program. During the meeting, Mr. Moses came up to me and said he would like for me to ride with him as far as Harrison, Arkansas, on our return to Little Rock.

Mr. Moses was one of the most eloquent speakers I have ever heard, being most personable and persuasive. As I've mentioned, AP&L was one of the most powerful utility holding companies in the United States. Thus, Mr. Moses was the spokesman, not only for AP&L, but also for Mid-South.

I accepted the ride with Mr. Moses. We rode in his air-conditioned, chauffeur-driven limousine.

The trip was short, but it stands tall in my memory.

As a young man, Mr. Moses had served as secretary for three separate governors, and he knew Arkansas politics. He maintained an interest in elections, particularly the gubernatorial race because a governor could appoint the members of the Public Service Commission, which regulates the public utilities.

He was also attentive to the composition of the legislature, which might be called on to pass legislation affecting the power industry.

In the course of our short ride, Mr. Moses indicated that the best way for a young man in politics to *get along was to go along.*"

As we approached Harrison, Mr. Moses gave me the bottom line of his mission, "We don't mind your going around talking to these co-op people, but we would be strongly opposed to your helping them get that steam-generating plant—we don't need it."

I replied, "You have convinced me." Mr. Moses leaned back in his seat, tilted his head, half closed his eyes as if meditating, and said, "I don't believe I have convinced you—I don't believe I have." Of course, he was correct. He had not convinced me.

The steam-generating plant which he referred to as the "one we don't need" would be the first major step to get electricity to all the people in rural Arkansas. I exerted all energy and influence I had to get that steam-generating plant for the co-ops. The co-ops had petitioned the secretary of the interior, Mr. Claude Wickard, for a loan of $10 million to build a plant of this type on the Arkansas River near the town of Ozark. Wickard was sympathetic to their petition. They also had some great people crusading for the project. Members of the co-ops' board of directors gave time, money, and energy for the cause.

People like Congressman Jim Trimble, and former congressman Clyde Ellis, then president of the National Co-ops Organization, actively supported the project. Harry Oswald, manager of the REA system in the state, and Tom Fitzhugh, his legal counsel, took on the construction project as a crusade. There were other high-ranking friends from Arkansas in Washington, principally, John Steelman, assistant to the president, from Fordyce; Frank Pace, secretary of the army; and Les Biffle from Pocohantas, a card-playing buddy of the president, who also put in a good word for the co-ops.

You will recall that in the 1948 election, Arkansas gave President Truman an overwhelming vote. When the president returned to Arkansas in 1949 to attend the Thirty-fifth Division Reunion, Arkansas people again welcomed him warmly and enthusiastically.

I had been in contact with Secretary Wickard and had received an encouraging response. The co-ops had scheduled a meeting with the secretary for November 20, 1950. I had not called upon the president for help up to this time. He had been involved in the Korean War from the middle of June until the first week in November. The Korean War with all of its implications demanded his full attention.

I was confident that the effort to get electricity on the farms of rural America was one of the president's top priorities and that he would give our Arkansas farmers full consideration. On November 13, 1950, I presented our case to him. On November 20 the co-op committee met with the secretary of the interior as planned.

On November 25, 1950, I received a wire from Secretary Wickard announcing that he had approved the loan of $10,588,000 to the co-ops for the building of the steam-generating plant and some 548 miles of transmission lines. This loan was an essential and major step by the cooperatives to transform the face of rural Arkansas. The distance to this goal had been shortened. Celebrate? Not yet.

We were all aware of the determination and resources of our opposition. Before the loan could be finalized, the project had to receive the approval of the Arkansas Public Service Commission. The commission in the past, as Tom Fitzhugh had described it, had been "hostile to the cooperatives." However, now at least one thing had changed in the co-ops' favor, the PSC's composition had been changed. In my first term I appointed the commission's three members. One of my appointments was a lawyer, John Thompson, who formerly represented the Jacksonville cooperatives. My second appointment was a lawyer, Howard Gladden, who had served with the FBI during the war and also had supported me in my gubernatorial campaign. The third member, Judge Scott Wood, formerly represented the Arkansas Power and Light Company as an attorney.

The co-ops filed their request to have the loan approved with the commission. The Arkansas Power and Light Company immediately filed an objection. There was a long and extensive hearing. AP&L called experts and formidable political personalities, one a congressman, Boyd Tackett, who had described the co-ops as "fellow travelers" with the Communists. The co-ops responded by putting on a compelling case.

The commission granted the permit to the co-ops to move forward with their plan. John Thompson and Howard Gladden voted for the permit, and Judge Scott Wood voted against. AP&L and its parent company, Mid-South Utilities, immediately obtained a restraining order from a Little Rock chancery judge. The judge annulled the commission's finding and set aside the permit.

The co-ops appealed the case to the Arkansas Supreme Court. The Supreme Court upheld the chancellor's findings on the basis that Arkansas law did not authorize an electric cooperative to enter into an agreement with a federal agency. The "agency" the court referred to was the Southwestern Power Administration (SPA). This agency had been chartered—to market federal power from the hydroelectric dams, with preference being given to public bodies, nonprofit organizations, and municipalities. It was a division of the Department of the Interior and administered by the secretary.

The agreement with Arkansas Electric Cooperatives was necessary because co-ops in northwestern Arkansas had been unable to build transmission lines to reach all sections of that rugged, remote region. The agreement between the co-ops and the SPA was that the latter would buy power from the steam-generating plant and deliver it over its transmission lines, then resell it to the co-op members in northwest Arkansas.

Be mindful that the funds to be used had been appropriated by Congress for the purpose of helping co-ops get electricity to their members where none was being provided. In order to remove this technical defect, it required an act of the legislature.

The Supreme Court ruled that the co-op's plan to build the steam-generating plant and transmit electricity to their members was illegal. The Court must have been unaware of the ancient Greek philosopher and lawgiver's opinion that *"the people's good was the highest law."*

The Supreme Court supported the ruling of the chancellor, annulling the action of the PSC in granting the permit to the cooperatives to build the Ozarks steam-generating plant.

The Arkansas statutes authorizing the formation of the rural electric cooperatives for the purpose of extending electrical power to the rural areas were Arkansas Statutes Annotated Section 77–1135 (Acts 1937, No. 342s, 35, ACA 23-18-303). I must admit that I never fully understood the Supreme Court's ruling in this case.

The loan was from the government for the purpose of extending electrical service to the counties in the northern part of the state not being served and as a step to extending electrical service to all rural areas in the state not being supplied with electricity.

Funds would not be available immediately for the construction of transmission lines for this immediate purpose.

Southwestern Power Administration had transmission lines extending into the northern part of Arkansas. Under the arrangement between the cooperatives and the SPA, the power from the Ozarks steam-generating plant would be sold to the SPA and transmitted over its lines to the designated electrical cooperative. The purpose of the SPA was to transmit public power to preferred customers, such as municipalities. Supervision of the SPA and the rural electrification program was under the secretary of the interior, Claude Wickard. Secretary Wickard understood that the arrangement between the SPA and the cooperatives was to supply power to the people who needed it, which was the intent and purpose of the rural electrification program. In addition to the immediate benefit to the farmers being served, the execution of the design of the cooperatives would strengthen the general economy of the state.

Why would the Supreme Court declare this arrangement illegal? We have two federal agencies, the SPA and the rural electric cooperatives, both under the Interior Department, supervised by the interior secretary, Claude Wickard. The intent and purpose of both agencies was to get electricity to the people. The secretary of the interior, Southwestern Power Administration, and the rural electric cooperatives were in agreement and full accord with this arrangement. The only party opposing this transaction was the Arkansas Power and Light Company and its parent, Mid-South Utilities, whose mission, intent, and purpose was to prevent competition in an area where they had a virtual monopoly. In brief, the federal agencies involved were in accord and full agreement. It was approved by the secretary of the interior when he loaned ten million dollars to the rural electric cooperatives for this project. The intentions and the purpose of both agencies was to get electricity to the people, and the intent and the purpose of the power company, in opposition, was to maintain and protect their monopoly on service of electricity in Arkansas. Additionally, the legislature in passing the legislation authorizing the establishment of the rural electric cooperatives specified that the "Act should be liberally construed."

But did the co-ops give up? Capitulate? Throw in the towel? No way. They were crusaders. They could always take one more step and fire one more shot. By the time the Supreme Court made its ruling, I was out of office. However, the McMath Law Firm, which I had formed after leaving the governor's office, represented the co-ops, so I continued to be involved. The co-ops turned to the 1953 legislature— the first session for Gov. Francis Cherry. The co-ops introduced a bill to correct any alleged deficiency in the law, thereby allowing the co-ops to proceed with their efforts to get their steam-generating plant built. The bill failed to pass. There were members of the legislature from rural counties representing farmers without electricity who cast a vote against the interest of their own people. Some of the members of the legislature were lawyers and were retained by the Arkansas Power and Light Company. Some other members, not lawyers, also found work with AP&L. One state senator was employed by the power company as a lineman.The power company had a strong lobby.

Being rejected by the legislature was a tough blow for the co-ops, and their fight didn't get any easier. Governor Cherry replaced my appointees with three new members to the PSC; none was sympathetic to the co-ops.

Having defeated the co-ops and having returned the farmers to their farms without the prospects of electricity, AP&L officials now turned their attention to another longtime foe, the Tennessee Valley Authority (TVA), the symbol of public power which they had long opposed. AP&L, through its parent company, Mid-South Utilities, planned to undermine the services of the TVA in Tennessee, Mississippi, and Kentucky. They proposed to do so by joining with other private power companies in TVA's transmission zone and building a competing power plant commonly called Dixon-Yates.

The grand design was for Dixon-Yates generating plant to be built in Crittenden County, Arkansas. Mid-South would then take over the TVA's transmission lines in order to serve customers in Arkansas, Tennessee, and Kentucky. In due course the TVA would be limited to supplying power only to municipalities and atomic plants in Kentucky and Tennessee—not to farmers and domestic consumers.

To build this steam-generating plant and to carry out this plan, Dixon-Yates had to have a supporting bill passed by the Arkansas Legislature. Hamilton Moses, "Mr. Ham," called a meeting of selected legislators at the old Marion Hotel. He told the lawmakers about the benefits the state would derive from the Dixon-Yates project.

Harry Oswald, statewide manager of the rural electric cooperatives, the indefatigable, never-say-die crusader for the co-ops, not having been invited to "Mr. Ham's" meeting with the legislature, posted himself outside the door of the meeting room. He sat in a chair, listened, and took notes. Moses with his skills and means of persuasion received strong response from the legislators, particularly his promise that the Dixon-Yates projects would bring needed power to eastern Arkansas.

As the legislators left the room, fired up by Mr. Moses for his project, Harry Oswald shook hands with each and told them that electricity was needed not only in eastern Arkansas, but also in the northwest counties of our state as well. He informed each that he had a little bill that would accomplish exactly that.

The legislators were generally receptive to Harry's idea, but shied away from introducing his bill. He finally found a Republican, a representative from Newton County, who introduced the co-op bill. (Today, Newton County is the only county in the state that has its electricity totally supplied by the electric cooperatives.) Harry hitched his bill to the lobbyist momentum driving Dixon-Yates—both passed. It was some time before the legislature realized what had happened, but "Mr. Ham" knew immediately. They had been finessed. But AP&L and friends had one more shot. By now it was 1955. Orval Faubus had defeated Francis Cherry's efforts for a second term, in part because of the rate increases the PSC gave to AP&L. Undeterred, the power companies turned up the pressure on Orval. He was wobbly and reluctant to sign the bill. Harry and his committee called on him. Orval informed them that the co-ops did not have sufficient support. Moreover, they had a poor public relations program, and if they wanted his help they should build up their PR and then come back at a future time.

Harry was fully aware that the co-ops had plowed a long row. He had been there every step of the way, and he had experienced it. He informed the governor that there would not be another time and that the time was now. There was a danger that the loan of 1950 made by the government to the co-ops could be withdrawn. In this event, a large segment of rural Arkansas would be unhappy and Orval would lose their support. In other words Harry "shelled down the corn" and told Orval "how the cow ate the cabbage." The governor signed the bill. Five years had elapsed from the time the secretary of the interior notified me, approving the loan for building the generating plant, before it became a reality; five years of lost time that could never be recalled—five years of deprivation on the farms that could never be compensated.

Oh, yes, what happened to Dixon-Yates? The plan to undermine the TVA was killed by Tennessee senator Estes Kefauver and his friends in the U.S. Senate. I was subpoenaed by Sen. William Langer, chairman of the Senate Anti-Monopoly Subcommittee, on October 22, 1954, to testify concerning the power monopoly. Following my appearance before the committee, Senator Kefauver was provided a copy of my testimony and he sent me a wire that read as follows:

> Your testimony great and most useful. Terribly sorry due to illness of my father could not be present.
>
> Estes Kefauver

On February 4, 1955, when the bill passed authorizing the cooperatives to move forward with their generating plant, I informed

Senator Langer of this long-delayed victory for the people. I wrote the following to him:

> This victory was made possible to a great extent by the work of your committee in exposing the manner in which the power companies were exploiting the people and retarding the development of our power resources.

I received a most gracious response from Senator Langer, stating:

> Whenever I have become discouraged lately I have thought of your testifying before our committee and I was happy that I have had the opportunity to meet you, shake your hand, look you in the eyes and see a real fighter. It is so refreshing to find a man in public life who is not afraid of the consequences —good or bad.

This accolade from a great man, a dedicated and courageous public servant, was welcome compensation for a long and at times lonely struggle.

Some years later I received an even greater kudo from Harry Oswald, that longtime champion of the farm family. Although retired as a manager of the statewide electric cooperatives, he paid a visit to their statewide meeting in 1958. I had been a guest speaker at this meeting. Following his visit with the managers and board members, he wrote me this letter:

July 1, 1978

Dear Sid:

> I dropped by the Arkansas Electric Cooperative Annual meeting Tuesday and was told by several how much they enjoyed and benefited from your remarks.
>
> I was told that their affection and respect for you was expressed in their reception of you. I am sincerely glad of that. But my regrets are that they and their parents did not really understand what Sid McMath was to them and react as they did to your presence Monday. Now later they did, but we missed a golden opportunity to change Arkansas for the betterment of all of us, but we did finally get the Ozark steam plant which cost

you so dearly and things are better for those who live in 62% of the area served by the electric cooperatives. "Mr. Ham" before his end, knew of his mistake in opposing us and so did McClellan, if that is any consolation to either of us. Again, thanks. These are important days for both of us, enjoying grand-children—and both of us have good days.

Signed,
Harry
(Harry L. Oswald)

The farmers in rural Arkansas organized electric cooperatives, invested the money borrowed from the federal government, and moved promptly and with great energy toward the successful crusade to "turn the lights on down on the farm." Their crusade is a significant chapter in Arkansas history.

While I was governor back in 1951, battling the power interests on behalf of the Ozark steam-generating plant, I was introduced to another source of power exercised by the power monopoly.

In early January 1951, I had two personal visits from Hamilton Moses, president of AP&L, to persuade me to abandon my support of the co-ops' steam-generating plant at Ozark, Arkansas. This generating plant was a necessary first step in expanding electrical service to rural areas in Arkansas, where there was no electrical service and no prospects for getting any in the foreseeable future.

The Board of Directors of AP&L came as a group to the governor's office in their effort to persuade me to abandon my continuing support of the steam-generating plant. The power company had declined to serve this area on the grounds that it was not feasible—that is, *not profitable*. I told them that I could not understand why the power company would object to the farmers organizing and supplying electrical service for themselves if the power company was not going to supply the power. The farmers, organized into cooperatives, were a nonprofit organization. They could borrow money from the government at a low rate of interest and thereby make it feasible to supply this needed electrical service to the members.

So, I told the AP&L Board that I could not retreat from my commitment to help these people get this essential service.

ALEXANDER WILEY, WIS., CHAIRMAN
H. ALEXANDER SMITH, N. J.   WALTER F. GEORGE, GA.
BOURKE B. HICKENLOOPER, IOWA   THEODORE FRANCIS GREEN, R. I.
WILLIAM LANGER, N. DAK.   J. W. FULBRIGHT, ARK.
HOMER FERGUSON, MICH.   JOHN J. SPARKMAN, ALA.
WILLIAM F. KNOWLAND, CALIF.   GUY M. GILLETTE, IOWA
                                 HUBERT H. HUMPHREY, MINN.
                                 MIKE MANSFIELD, MONT.

FRANCIS O. WILCOX, CHIEF OF STAFF
JULIUS N. CAHN, COUNSEL

United States Senate

COMMITTEE ON FOREIGN RELATIONS

February 7, 1955

Hon. Sid McMath
412 Pyramid Building
Little Rock, Arkansas

My dear Governor:

         I cannot tell you how very much I appreciated your letter of February 4 and how happy I am that you have succeeded in winning a great battle in this war.

         Whenever I have become discouraged lately I have thought of your testifying before our Committee, and I was happy that I have had the opportunity to meet you, shake your hands, look into your eyes and see a real fighter. It is so refreshing to find a man in public life who is not afraid of the consequences--good or bad.

         Yesterday I was notified by Senator Kilgore the new Chairman of the Judiciary Committee, that I would no longer be Chairman of the Anti Monopoly Subcommittee, and that he had appointed himself to that position. Mr. Davis told me he has resigned as Counsel so I don't know what the future holds forth in connection with this power investigation, but in any event, I am going to give the main address at the National Convention of the Rural Electric Cooperatives, which Clyde Ellis tells me is going to have an attendance of about 6,000 from all over the United States, and I intend to put in a good word for you. What I regret is that I won't be in a position any longer to lead the fight.

         With every good wish to you and thanking you for your kindness in writing me, I am

                 Sincerely,

                 Bill

WL dfg

February 7, 1955, letter from Sen. William ("Bill") Langer regarding Sid McMath's testimony before his Senate Anti-Monopoly Subcommittee

Sid:

I dropped by the Arkansas Electric Cooperatives annual meeting Tuesday and was told by several

1. How much they enjoyed and benefitted from your remarks and

2. your references to me and my (our) role in the early and important early days of Electric Cooperatives. To tell you that I am grateful is gross under description of my feelings.

I was told that their affection and respect for you was expressed in their reception of you — I am sincerely glad of that but my regrets are that they and their parents did not really understand what Sid McMath was to them and react as these did to your presence monday. now later, they did but we missed a golden opportunity to change Arkansas for the betterment of all of us —

But we did finally get the "Ozark Steam Plant" which cost you so dearly and things are better for those who live in 62% of the area served by the electric cooperatives. And "mr Ham" before his end knew of his mistake in opposing us. And so did McClellan if that is any consolation to either of us — again thanks and these important days to both of us we enjoy our grandchildren and both of us have good dogs —

Harry

Letter from Harry Oswald, manager of the Arkansas Rural Cooperative

February 4, 1955

Honorable William Langer
Senate Office Building
Washington, D. C.

Dear Senator:

You will be happy to know that we have been successful in our fight to pass laws to permit REA to build steam generating plants in Arkansas. This, as you know, is a great defeat for the power interests in this state.

This victory was made possible, to a great extent, by the work of your committee in exposing the manner in which the power companies were exploiting the people and retarding the development of our power resources.

Certainly hope your committee will get the appropriation you deserve and that your anti-monopoly investigations will continue. It is most important, while the public is receptive, that all facts pertaining to the high-handed operations of the power interests be revealed.

I want you to know that as a private citizen I appreciate the vigorous manner in which you have pushed these investigations. I knew you would be happy to know that your efforts have already borne fruit in this state.

Yours sincerely,

Sid McMath

sm/fb

Letter from Sid McMath to Sen. William Langer reporting that the bill to build the steam-generating plant was passed

On January 13, 1951, I received a telephone call from an influential businessman in downtown Little Rock. He did substantial business with the Arkansas Power and Light Company. He told me he had a confidential communication which was very personal and which he was requested to relay to me. He asked me if it would be possible for me to come to his office at the noon hour, as his staff would be out to lunch. I went to see him. At the appointed time, he was alone, and he gave me the message. If I would back off from my support of the steam-generating plant, AP&L would support me financially and politically in my race for a third term as governor. I was curious as to what would be the alternative and was advised by the "messenger" that they would do all in their power to defeat me politically if I refused.

I left this meeting with a foreboding sense of an impending conflict. I didn't have to wait long to see the nature of the conflict that lay ahead.

On February 6, 1951, Sen. Ellis Fagan, senior member in the Arkansas State Senate, launched a radio attack on every phase of my administration. The senator was the leader of the utility forces in the legislature. He owned the Fagan Electric Company, and AP&L was his principal customer.

Soon after the radio attack, Senator Fagan had his Highway Audit Commission bill introduced. It passed the senate on February 12, 1951, after only two days of debate and also quickly passed through the house of representatives. The bill created a five-member audit commission to investigate activities of the state highway department. It was quite unusual in that it named the five commissioners who would conduct the investigation without participation by me as the governor, which would have been the normal procedure.

The audit commission chairman was R. H. Dickinhorst, president of the state banking commission and a member of the board of directors of Arkansas Power and Light Company.

Another commissioner, Vern Tindal, was a major AP&L stockholder. He also was campaign manager for Pratt Remmel, who was the son-in-law of Harvey Couch Sr., founder of AP&L.

The three other members of the audit commission were:

James H. Crane Jr.—eastern Arkansas planter;

Herbert L. Thomas—past chairman, University of Arkansas Board of Trustees; and

W. F. Fox—president of Arkansas Wood Products Association

James Crane was a Dixiecrat. Herbert Thomas had completed his term (of ten years) on the University of Arkansas Board of Trustees. I appointed Jack Stephens as his successor. Thomas was not happy.

The highway audit commission remained relatively dormant for almost a year. However, in early March 1952, when I was running for a third term for governor, the commission started conducting public hearings.

These hearings were conducted in a highly sensational and biased manner. R. H. Dickinhorst was the driving force. The attorney general, Ike Murry, served as prosecutor for the audit commission. (He also was a candidate for governor against me in the coming 1952 election.)

The witnesses were not permitted to have an attorney present and were compelled frequently to answer only *yes* or *no* to leading questions and not allowed any explanations. Neither was the highway department allowed to have an attorney to cross-examine the witnesses.

John K. Brown, purchasing agent for the highway department, was called a number of times regarding campaign contributions. Ike Murry would ask Brown questions, insinuating that the campaign contributions received were bribes. Brown was not permitted to explain the transactions and was allowed only *yes* or *no* answers. These traumatic experiences adversely affected his health.

Among other witnesses, Henry Woods was called four different times. Henry Woods had been my campaign manager in my campaigns for governor. He was my administrative assistant and my friend.

I was the audit commission's objective from the day that the audit bill was shepherded through the legislature by Sen. Ellis Fagan. The audit commissioners and the prosecutor sought to strike at me through Henry Woods.

Each time Henry Woods was called before the commission, he was forcibly questioned. One subject of the investigations was the checks that Henry had endorsed as my campaign manager and placed in the campaign fund. This was one of his duties. He would receive a check, delivered by a person or through the mail, endorse it, and put it in the campaign fund. If, perchance, he was not present, some other member of my staff would perform this duty.

Henry would be questioned about specific checks and the circumstances under which the check was given, what agreements were made between the contributor and the person receiving the check on behalf of the campaign fund. Henry, of course, had no way of knowing the details of those transactions.

Henry was questioned at length about our campaign records. After lengthy interrogation on what the records might contain, he was asked to produce them. Henry explained that these records contained confidential information privileged to the contributor. This related to his freedom of speech and expression under the First Amendment to the Constitution. To produce these records would, in his opinion, be a violation of a contributor's trust, and he could not do that.

The prosecutor, Ike Murry, thereupon made strong accusations for the benefit of the press and his campaign of "coverup and concealment of evidence."

This alleged coverup approach was used right down to the election day. The facts were that the audit commission could have received the *records* simply by having a subpoena issued. They had this power under the legislature's authorization. Ike Murry, of course, preferred to continue to charge "coverup" and bribery," rather than have the records produced. Much time and effort of the prosecutor was expended in trying to establish that Henry had been involved in accepting a bribe or in aiding and abetting bribery. This was impossible to do. Henry Woods had character. Accepting a bribe or being an accessory to bribery was in violation of his moral code. Honor and integrity were instilled in him by his mother and were an essential part of his training and career as an agent for the Federal Bureau of Investigation. He was a full-time FBI agent for the duration of World War II.

Henry's scalp would have been a great coup for Ike Murry and his campaign, but this would not happen. Any entertainment of bribery would be rejected by Henry's conscience and good judgment. If there had been any proof that Henry Woods had been guilty of bribery, he would have been indicted and tried.

As a matter of fact, when I left the governor's office at the end of my two terms, Henry was broke. He had to borrow money on his life insurance policy for him and his family to live. I was also broke, in debt, and it took many years before my campaign debts were paid off.

The findings of the audit commission were submitted to the grand jury, presided over by Judge Gus Fulk.

The grand jury was described by the newspapers as being a *"blue ribbon"* grand jury of sixteen members, carefully chosen from "higher echelons" of Little Rock's business community.

After considering all testimony, hearing all witnesses, examining all documents submitted, and after the expenditure of $125,000.00 on its investigation, they found "No Violation" of the law and so reported to the trial judge, Gus Fulk.

The grand jury precipitated an unusual outburst from four members of the grand jury, who resigned in open court, stating that they were opposed to the findings of the majority members of the jury. This, of course, was highly publicized by the press. The spokesmen for the protesters were:

> *S. J. Beauchamp*—a business partner of Hamilton Moses (president of AP&L, owned by Mid-South Utilities) and

> *Harold Young*—a member of the board of directors of AP&L, owned by Mid-South Utilities
> —campaign manager for Ike Murry, who was one of four candidates for governor against Sid McMath.

Extreme pressure was brought upon Judge Gus Fulk to convene a second grand jury to review again the highway audit commission's findings and return indictments against anyone violating the law.

Meanwhile, the Democratic primary election was in July 1952. I had four major opponents, each one carefully selected from different regions of the state.

> *Jack Holt*—former prosecuting attorney, and circuit judge and state attorney general
> —principal opponent in my election of 1948
> —from Harrison, in northern Arkansas

> *Boyd Tackett*—former congressman, former friend, and classmate at University of Arkansas
> —practicing law in Texarkana
> —from western Arkansas

Francis Cherry—former chancery judge in Jonesboro, eastern Arkansas

Ike Murry—attorney general, state of Arkansas
  —prosecutor, highway audit commission
  —from central Arkansas

Three of the candidates were forceful, vigorous campaigners and used the allegations and charges of the highway audit commission to attack me in the campaign.

In addition, Boyd Tackett accused me of being soft on Communism. This was during the Joe McCarthy era and was the vogue of some politicians to be searching for Communists in the government. Tackett accused the co-op as being Socialistic, bordering on Communism. He further accused me of harboring two Communist professors at the University of Arkansas— saying that "They had foreign sounding names." Tackett stated that Hamilton Moses had put him into the race for governor.

Judge Francis Cherry was more at home and most effective in an air-conditioned broadcasting studio. He adopted the talk-a-thon, suggested to him by Hamilton Moses, a radio campaigning technique successfully used by the governor-elect in Florida.

We did not have television at the time. Francis Cherry would sit in the radio studio and answer *pre-prepared questions that would be called in by his supporters,* and were directed against my administration, such as:

Will you quit feeding slop to the state mental hospital inmates?
Why is McMath using old folks' pension money to pay his
    campaign expenses?

Of course, most of the questions had to do with the flagrant charges of the highway audit commission. Francis Cherry, in the course of his radio program, would direct questions at me and invite me to respond. He would comment that he had an empty chair in the studio he was saving for me. One day, about noon, in West Helena, while Cherry was asking me questions over the air, I walked unannounced into the studio and occupied the chair which he had been so "thoughtfully" holding for my use—he was shocked! He immediately changed the tune of his program and cut it short.

No members of the highway department, who allegedly had taken bribes or supposedly violated the law, had been indicted or been tried before the primary elections in July and August of 1952.

Ike Murry and the other candidates for governor, running against me, used the allegations and rumors arising from the Highway Audit Report in their campaigns, continuing to election day—a web of suspicion clouded the minds of the people as they went to the polls to vote.

I survived the Democrat primary election in July. Francis Cherry ran second. The election runoff in August was between Cherry and me. My opponents, Ike Murry, Boyd Tackett, and Jack Holt, along with Sen. John McClellan and Hamilton Moses, joined together at Cherry's rally in Jonesboro. They combined their support for Cherry. That assured his election.

Governor Cherry, upon assuming office, immediately appointed a new Public Service Commission, which regulates utility rates. This commission rewarded AP&L a handsome *rate increase,* which gave the common stockholders of Mid-South Utilities, the parent company, a *13 percent return on their investment.* Normally, a *6 percent return was considered a fair and equitable return for a utility having a monopoly. This increase on the electric bills placed a heavy burden on the people of Arkansas.* (See letter from Arthur McLean to the board members of AP&L, page 258.) Governor Cherry served one term.

Judge Fulk, under continuing pressure to call another grand jury, and in failing health, resigned from the court. Before resigning, he issued an order for a second grand jury (January 1953).

I appointed Harry Robinson to fill the vacancy. This second grand jury, ordered by Judge Fulk and presided over by Judge Robinson, received the workings of the first grand jury and the report of the highway audit commission.

Unknown to the court, a fund was raised from private sources to hire a lawyer, to "advise" the second grand jury. This lawyer had served with Ike Murry on the highway audit commission. Among the contributors to this fund, which was $3,250, were:

> *Harold Young*—member of the board of directors of AP&L
> —member of the "blue ribbon" first grand jury
> —campaign manager for Ike Murry (who was attorney
>   general and prosecutor for the highway audit commission
>   and one of my opponents in the governor's race)
> —Mr. Young contributed $500 to the fund.

Alfred Kahn—chairman of the board of directors of Union National
Bank (president of Union National Bank was Harvey Couch Jr.,
member of the board of directors of AP&L)
—Mr. Kahn contributed $500 to the fund.

These people, raising this private fund, were not on the grand
jury, and they hired their own lawyer to advise the grand jury. When
this private arrangement came to the knowledge of Judge Robinson,
he dismissed the grand jury. He considered this an invasion of the
deliberations of the grand jury, the responsibility of the court, and
the duties of the prosecuting attorney.

The cruelest weapon upon the earth, when used with malice or
reckless indifference is that of the human tongue, resulting in ruined
reputations and wrecked lives.

The old Marion Hotel lobby was the capital of political rumors. In
the "Gar Hole," downstairs, the teller of "tall tales," floating with beer,
would rivet the attention of an inquisitive audience, with a "knowing
nod" and a "wink of the eye," he would impart to his listeners the lat-
est and most "secret" information. The rumor that caught the listening ears was that Henry Woods and Governor McMath had *bribed*
Judge Fulk to resign.

This was absurd and false on its face. Judge Fulk had served hon-
orably on the court for fifteen years. He had been presiding over the
first grand jury with fairness and judicial competence. We had no reason to seek his resignation. This grand jury, presided over by Judge Fulk,
and considering the records and findings, returned no indictments.

There was another rumor noised about that Orval Faubus had said
while riding in an automobile, "he heard McMath say that Judge Fulk's
secretary had received the money." Had there been any substance to
this rumor a grand jury or the prosecuting attorney would have subpoenaed at least these following witnesses to testify under oath:

1. *Judge Fulk's secretary:*
• Did you receive any money for Judge Fulk?
• If so, from whom was it received?
• If so, who delivered the money and what instructions did you receive?
• If you received the money, did you deliver it to Judge Fulk?

2. *Judge Gus Fulk:*
- Judge, what prompted you to resign from the court?
- Did you receive any money as an inducement for your resignation?
- If so, who was the person delivering the money and what was the agreement?

3. *Orval Faubus:*
- Did you make the statement, "I heard McMath say, while riding in an automobile, that Judge Fulk's secretary had received the money?"
- If so, when and where did this happen and who was present?
- To whom have you relayed this information?

4. Witness or witnesses to whom Faubus told his story:
- Did Faubus tell you that "he heard McMath say, while in an automobile, that Judge Fulk's secretary received the money?" or any words to that effect?

None of this happened. Had there been any credibility to these rumors, Henry Woods and I would have been indicted and the objective of my enemies would have been accomplished. These false and malicious rumors were also a great disservice to Judge Fulk, suggesting that he would be susceptible to taking a bribe.

I can't believe that Orval Faubus made this statement, but if in fact he did, there are many who still remember, when being pressed by an aggressive newspaper reporter, regarding a prior conflicting statement, Orval's response was, "Just because I said it, doesn't make it so."

A third grand jury was impaneled to receive and act on the Highway Audit Report. Judge Henry Smith of Pine Bluff was assigned to preside over this third grand jury and to try any cases that might arise out of the grand jury's deliberations.

The grand jury, at the conclusion of its deliberations, returned indictments against the following:

A. D. Mason—highway commissioner (for bribery)
John K. Brown—purchasing agent for highway department (for bribery)
M. C. "Fritz" Methvin—highway engineer (for bribery)

These three defendants were tried in Pulaski County Court.

A. D. Mason—October 13, 1953—tried by jury (found "Not Guilty")

John K. Brown—September 1, 1953—case dismissed by Judge Henry Smith (found "No Proof of Bribery")

M. C. "Fritz" Methvin—October 6, 1953—tried by jury (found "Not Guilty")

All three were tried and were acquitted.

The highway audit commission and one of the grand juries, in their final reports, also made charges of waste and inefficiency. During the initial stage, in 1949, of reorganizing the highway department, waste and inefficiency was predictable.

Our highway department had been relatively inactive for almost twenty years. During the Second World War and during Gov. Ben Laney's administration, there was no substantial road-building repairs and bridge construction of any significance. There had been a turnover of young engineers and key construction personnel because of relative inactivity and a low wage scale and salary compared to that available in private industries.

I had recommended to the legislature that we retain highway engineering experts to make a study of our highway department with recommendations as to how we could reorganize the highway department to carry out my proposed program.

I had an expert engineer come down from St. Louis, Missouri, to meet with our highway commission. He proposed making a study which the commissioners thought would be most helpful. However, his proposal was turned down by the legislature on the grounds that it would be paid for from highway construction funds. As it turned out, this proposal would have been a wise investment.

Our highway department team had been playing in the minor league, we were now thrust in the majors. We had to go with what we had. We continued our reorganization, employed key personnel and young engineers, obtained the equipment needed, and went to work. Although our wage and salary scale was still comparatively low, our employees got caught up in the movement. They had pride in their trade, their profession, and their state, and they met the challenge. We built more roads then any other state administration.

However, we still were accused of wasting highway funds. For example, one of the members of the highway audit commission in preparing the Highway Audit Report stated that $18 million of highway funds *had been wasted*. This statement had been echoed by one of the grand juries and naturally given prominence by the press. It had not been pointed out that this $18 million, which was supposed to *have been wasted* was spent on farm-to-market roads. Seven of these roads now serve seven county seats that previously did not have one hard-surfaced outlet. *I do not believe that the tax-paying citizens served by these roads consider that the money spent to get them out of the mud and dust was wasted.*

In addition, during the four years of my administration, we placed, under construction, on the primary system a total of 713 miles of roads and 22,862 linear feet of bridges, and on the secondary system a total of 1,582 miles of roads and 31,723 linear feet of bridges. This is a total of 2,295 miles of new roads.

This construction program cost $72,418,105, of which $38,298,048 was spent on the *primary system* and $34,120,057 for *secondary roads* to get our rural population out of the dust.

An important part of our construction program had been the completion of permanent bridges on several long sections of our highways.

We built sixteen paved connections to highways in adjoining states.

During the four years of my administration, we started the first tangible modernization of the Arkansas highway system by acquiring the necessary right-of-way for future four-lane arterial routes, by building bypasses to alleviate congestion in overcrowded areas, and by improving the efficiency for through travel at such places as Searcy, Hughes, Fayetteville, Beebe, Pocahontas, Alma, and West Memphis. We built four-lane routes between Alma and Van Buren, from Helena to West Helena, and built the first vehicular grade separation in the state at West Memphis.

At this time, the reader might be interested in reading an objective report by the National Advisory Board made in 1994. William H. Bowen became president of the First Commercial Bank, Little Rock, Arkansas, in 1971. He organized a National Advisory Board of state and national leaders. Their purpose was to promote the economic development of Arkansas. They convened once a year and focused on a subject of significant interest. Included among the members of the advisory board were the following: Charles Murphy, Murphy Oil Company; George

Stinson, president of National Steel, Pittsburg, Pennsylvania; Bill Dillard, Dillard Department Stores; Ernest G. Green, director, Lehman Brothers; Patricia P. Upton, president, Aromatique, Inc.; and Richard Weiss, director of finance and administration.

In its study, "Arkansas Highways: At a Crossroads, 1994," the National Advisory Board reported that "McMath built more miles of highway than any previous governor." The report continued:

> Road construction was stopped and maintenance was deferred on the highway system during the 1930s and materials and labor were unavailable for road work during World War II. The ancient highway system was deteriorating at the rate of $6 million a year by 1947 and the state was embarrassed nationally when the Chrysler Corporation advertised the durability of its vehicles by saying they had passed the "Arkansas mud test."[1]

The National Advisory Board concluded:

> Thus 20 years of neglect made roads the principal issue in the 1948 gubernatorial contest won by war hero Sid McMath. Under McMath's leadership the legislature in January 1949 authorized issuing general obligation bonds for highway construction and maintenance. Over the objections of fiscal conservatives, McMath campaigned vigorously for the bonds in a special election on February 15, 1949, and the voters approved the proposal by a four-to-one margin.
>
> In the next four years, the state spent more than $72 million, half on the primary system and the rest on secondary roads. During his tenure, *McMath built more miles of highway than any previous governor.* Dougan notes that seven county seats saw their first paved connections, and Newton County received its first paved road, a point also made at the NAB meeting in October 1994 by invited observer, Federal District Judge Henry Woods. (Emphasis added.)
>
> In addition, 12 weigh stations were built, roadside parks and picnic tables were set up and efforts were made to mark roads with proper lines and route markings. One administration bill also made it unlawful to run cattle, horses, mules, hogs, sheep or goats

---

1. "Arkansas Highways: At a Crossroads," 1994 Report of the National Advisory Board of First Commercial Bank, N.A., Little Rock, Arkansas, p. 9.

on the rights of way, and other laws raised the driving age from 14 to 16 (where it remains), required examination of drivers and established motor vehicle inspection.

The highway program also provided opportunities for partisan politics that ultimately helped end McMath's political career. . . .

Anti-McMath legislators formed the creation in January and February 1952 of the Highway Audit Commission. Several of the governor's enemies were placed on the Commission.

The Commission made numerous claims ranging from inefficient and politically motivated purchasing to embezzlement. No one was ever convicted of any wrongdoing concerning the Highway Department; in fact, they were cleared by both a court and a grand jury. *Then as now, however, the public often remembers the charges and not the acquittals.* (Emphasis added.)[2]

All of this could have been prevented, and the taxpayers' money saved. I would not renege on my promise to the rural electric cooperatives and the farm families they represented—nor would I surrender in the case of *Power vs. the People*—and *"gotten along by going along."*

The highway audit episode was a great disappointment to me—it overshadowed all the good we had done—the progress in race relations, the gains in education, the advancement in economic development, and despite the "investigation," the great gains we made in the highway department.

The statements by me in this chapter were made under oath before the United States Anti-Monopoly Committee on October 22, 1954. They were true and correct to the best of my knowledge and remain so to date.[3]

After half a century, I look back and see that all the rural areas in Arkansas are provided with a reliable source of electrical service. The old black wash pot and scrubbing board and all they represented, have disappeared, even from the memories of the womenfolk. The quality of the lives of our people has been enhanced and the economy of our state strengthened.

---

2. "Arkansas Highways at a Crossroads," 1994 Report of the National Advisory Board of First Commercial Bank, N.A., Little Rock, Arkansas, p. 9.

3. See Congressional Testimony at the web site mcmath.law.com.

I'm rewarded with the memory of the part I played, with others, in making this dream of so many become a reality.

In 1956, Henry Woods, Leland Leatherman, and I established our law practice and opened our firm in the National Old Line Building across the street and facing the state capitol.

Sen. Ellis Fagan had an apartment on top of this building. This was convenient for him and legislators, lobbyists, and friends. He had sponsored the highway audit bill and had been responsible for naming the five members of the commission who were my political opponents.

One morning, before noon, out of the blue, I had an unexpected call from the senator. I had not seen nor spoken to the senator since I left office three years before. He invited me to come up to his apartment to share a pot of coffee and a visit. This call was a shock, and I paused a moment, but then I accepted out of curiosity.

I took the elevator to his apartment. He was alone. After we exchanged pleasantries, we sat down, and he served me a cup of coffee.

The senator was running for reelection and as yet had no opponent. At the time, the McMath Law Firm was representing the Railroad Brotherhood and doing work for the teamsters and the steelworkers. I suspected he wanted to make an overture for their political support through me—but in the course of our general discussion, Senator Fagan abruptly stopped talking and, examining me closely, he remarked, *"You must hate me."* This remark was a surprise, however. I responded as forthrightly as he had made his statement, *"I do not hate you—I hate no man."*

I finished my coffee, thanked him for his hospitality, and returned to my office. I never saw the senator again.

VIII⹁ A RACE FOR THE SENATE

I HAD KNOWN SENATOR MCCLELLAN, OUR SENIOR SENATOR FROM Arkansas, since I was a student at Hot Springs High School when he ran for Congress. Judge C. T. Cotham, a former circuit judge, was McClellan's campaign manager in Hot Spring and Garland Counties.

Later, Artie Cotham, Judge Cotham's son, and I were, for a time, roommates in Hill Hall at the University of Arkansas.

In the summer of 1934, he was campaign manager for John L. McClellan, running against Congressman D. D. Glover, he gave me a job handing out literature and nailing up campaign signs for his candidate. This was during the depression and I needed a job.

Congressman Glover was a good congressman, a good man. He had a wonderful family. I became acquainted with the family later, especially Julian Glover, who was an outstanding lawyer in Hot Springs.

Congressman Glover got me an appointment to the United States Naval Academy so I could become an officer in the United States Marine Corps. I flunked the examination. I have no illusion that my juvenile efforts helped to defeat Congressman Glover, but I have always regretted working against him. I trust that his family has forgiven me.

I, again, supported McClellan in his unsuccessful race against Sen. Hattie Caraway for the United States Senate in 1938.

Hattie Caraway was appointed to succeed her husband Thaddeus Caraway's term in 1931. In 1932, she ran for election to the Senate in her own right with the help of Huey P. Long.

Sen. Huey Long of Louisiana was a rising national political power. It was in the midst of the depression. He was running against Wall Street—the utility moguls, the money changers—blaming them for the long lines of unemployment and the depression.

In 1932, Long was engaged in campaigning for the election of five senatorial candidates who shared, or purported to share, his views for emerging from our nation's moribund state—"Share the Wealth and Every Man a King." Senator Long came to Arkansas to campaign for Hattie Caraway. He, with his motorcade and the press covering this dramatic saga, stormed Arkansas for seven days before the election.

In addition to his eloquence and flare for hitting the front pages,

Long had an earthy quality that appealed to the average voter. He related to them.

He spent one night in the Arlington Hotel in Hot Springs. The next morning he had a load of wood with a chopping block and a double-bit ax delivered to the national park lawn across the street from the Arlington. Arising early in the morning, accompanied by the press and a gathering crowd, he put on a demonstration. Taking a stick of wood and using the chopping block and double-bit ax, he showed how to cut wood the right size to be used in an iron cookstove. This was impressive to 80 percent of the people in Arkansas who lived in the rural areas and used an iron cookstove, because, you see, they had no electricity.

Hattie Caraway won a resounding victory over seven opponents.

She ran for election to a second term in 1938. Her opponent was John McClellan.

I had supported McClellan when he was first elected to Congress in 1934. In 1937, I had come home from my first tour of duty with the Marine Corps to get married and to practice law.

My office was not exactly running over with cases so I had more time to spend in my support of McClellan versus Mrs. Caraway for the United States Senate.

The congressman had run against Mrs. Caraway with the argument "that a man could more effectively promote the state's interest." He was defeated.

McClellan was a vigorous campaigner. He had exhausted himself with his bid for the Senate. Following the campaign, he came to Hot Springs, enrolled in the army/navy hospital for rest and recuperation. I called on the senator to express my regrets. Later, McClellan became congressman and subsequently, United States senator in 1942.

Personally, McClellan and I had been friendly. During the war when I was stationed in Washington, I went by to see him. We visited about politics. On one occasion, I discussed with him the possibility of my running for prosecuting attorney in Garland County. He advised me that he could not become involved in local politics.

After I was elected prosecuting attorney, when he was in town once, he invited me to come by and visit. He was staying at the Arlington Hotel. I don't recall what we talked about or if there was any purpose in the visit, except that he thought it important enough to have me by for a chat.

While I was governor, and during President Truman's administration, we had some differences, principally over President Truman's actions and proposals on civil rights. At some point, being interviewed by a writer and questioned on McClellan's and my different views on this, a hot issue at the time, he responded succinctly, "McMath went North and I went South." McClellan was a dedicated segregationist and defender of the special interests. When McClellan stated that he went South, and I went North, he was substantially correct. He went South to join the old disappearing politicians who used race to frighten the "white folks." I went to the New South and joined in the hopes and aspirations of all our people.

Our philosophy on the issue of civil rights would be dramatized by his support of the Southern Manifesto in which the senators from the Southern states called upon the other states to resist the Supreme Court's decision requiring equal opportunity for blacks in the public schools.

We were also on opposite sides on the issue of electric power versus the people.

Senator McClellan and the president of AP&L were closely allied politically. They shared common interests. This alliance was effectively applied in my race for a third term in 1952.

The senator was coming up for his own reelection in 1954. I ran against him. In addition to the private power interest, he had a stalwart supporter and ally in the majority leader of the United States Senate, Sen. Lyndon B. Johnson, who had a long memory and owed McClellan his support as a "get along" member of "The Club."

Senator Johnson was still majority leader of the Senate and a conduit for campaign funds from the oil industry to favored candidates, especially incumbent senators up for reelection, on whose support he depended.

As I have related, the ownership—control—of the rich oil reserves lying outside the territorial waters of the coastal states was a burning issue during President Truman's administration. This was especially so in Texas.

The oil companies, interested in exploring and recovering oil reserves in the Tideland waters, were convinced that they could make more favorable leasing agreements with the state of Texas than with the federal government.

Hence, the Texas delegation in Congress gave top priority toward obtaining title to this land for the states, Texas having the greater interest.

In my opinion, consistent with the needs of the people, because of Johnson's position of influence, he was able to fund campaign contributions in substantial amounts to "deserving" incumbent senators. Senator McClellan fell in this classification and was appropriately rewarded.

I, in turn, supported President Truman's plan to use money obtained from the oil reserves for public schools in all the states.

President Truman's plan was defeated and President Eisenhower, at the beginning of his second term, deeded the Tideland oil reserves to the states, Texas being the greater beneficiary.

Senator McClellan, as has been indicated, was also an ally of the power companies, in their effort to deny to the electric cooperatives a reliable low-cost source of power with transmission lines which they owned and operated.

In my race for a third term, on election night, in the runoff primary when Francis Cherry was elected governor, Senator McClellan was present in his headquarters and proclaimed "victory."

My race against Senator McClellan was not entirely motivated by the issue of "Power vs. the People," or by the oil industry versus our public schools, but I had gradually become disillusioned with Senator McClellan's use of the race issue and political demagoguery to obtain and keep power and use it in the sport of special interest whose goals were not consistent with the needs of the people.

Sen. Lyndon Johnson's efforts to support McClellan in the Democratic primary in 1954 culminated in obtaining, from a number of Democratic United States senators, their endorsement of McClellan. An advertisement announcing their support was run in the *Arkansas Gazette* on the eve of the Democratic primary.

Two United States senators, so persuaded by the majority leader, were of special note: Sen. Hubert Humphrey from Minnesota, a friend of mine, and Sen. Paul Douglas from Illinois, a fellow marine. Not only did I consider them as my friends, but we also shared the same views on the rights of all citizens. We were friends and they agreed with me on civil rights and I found their support of my opponent particularly disappointing.

The Senate race was close, there were several counties in eastern Arkansas that I had reason to believe I would carry; however, I have no alibis. Had I not expended my assets in a race for a third term for governor, I may well have won. The election was very close, but we lost the battle.

I returned from my sabbatical to the pursuit of my third career—that of a trial lawyer.

IX LITTLE ROCK CENTRAL HIGH SCHOOL, 1957

AFTER MY SECOND DEFEAT IN TWO YEARS, I RETIRED TO THE PRACTICE OF law. For three years I worked to build a practice (more on that later). I didn't get involved in public affairs again until 1957 when the Little Rock school crisis brought an issue, near and dear to my heart, into the national interest. Because of my extensive work on race relations and my support for Pres. Harry Truman's civil rights bill, I felt that I had to speak out on the Little Rock situation.

Gov. Orval Faubus was a friend. We first met in Fayetteville, in the spring of 1948, during my first campaign for governor. Orval came to my hotel room at the Mountain Inn in Fayetteville, and we discussed the race for governor. He was considering who to support in the upcoming election.

Returning to Little Rock, I took Highway 23, better known as the "Pig Trail," stopping to drop Orval off at his home in Huntsville, Madison County.

Orval supported me for governor. Being from Madison County, he was helpful to me in northwest Arkansas. After the election, he told me that he would like to have a "paying job," so I put him on my staff with the primary job of visiting with county delegates concerned with road building and repair. It was obvious that Orval had a rapport with people, especially those from the mountain counties. He did an excellent job and built a base for his own campaign while serving my administration loyally.

Toward the end of my administration, I appointed him to the highway commission. Here, he also did a good job, worked hard and, of course, continued to build his political base.

Orval ran for governor against Gov. Francis Cherry in 1954. He was a natural heir to my organization. Orval won a historic victory. It was only the second time in the state's history that an incumbent governor was defeated for a second term.

I think the gubernatorial campaign had an impact on my race against John McClellan for the United States Senate. Although Faubus and I were running for different offices, it posed a problem to many of my stalwart county supporters. Despite my defeat for a third term, many had maintained their support of me. However, in a political campaign, time, energy, and money are limited and tend to be invested where the greater benefit can be the result. My supporters had to choose between Orval and me, and many worked for him because they and their counties or communities could be more directly and immediately served by a governor than a United States senator.

As I have said, I stayed out of public issues until the Little Rock school crisis moved to implement the *Brown vs. the Topeka Board of Education* decision. This came in 1957. *Brown* held that separate, but equal schools for black students, was unconstitutional. In September of that year, Little Rock's Central High School became a battleground for the ongoing struggle for civil rights in America, with the whole world's attention centered on Little Rock.

Governor Faubus's decision to deny the nine black students entrance to Central High, the subsequent court decisions, and the governor's meeting with Pres. Dwight Eisenhower have been well documented. At this critical moment in the history of America's slow, but steady movement to bring all of our citizens under the protective umbrella of America's Bill of Rights, President Eisenhower took action. He ordered the 101 First Airborne Division to Little Rock, Arkansas. The 101 First Airborne's mission was to escort and protect the nine students, ensuring their admission to Little Rock Central High School in compliance with the order of the United States Court.

When I learned that the 101 First Airborne would be used to enforce the law, I was so sufficiently concerned that I called Vice President Richard Nixon. I felt that the president could accomplish the same purpose without stirring memories of the South's invasion and occupation by federal troops during and after the Civil War. These hard memories ran deep in the minds of Southern people and had been handed down for three generations.

A few United States marshals, in civilian clothes, with their badge of authority representing the United States Government, upholding the Constitution of the United States, would have served the same purpose without the political backlash, in my opinion.

The invasion and occupation by the 101 First Airborne, equipped,

(This page and following page) Little Rock Central High School crisis, 1957, protests and soldiers of 101 First Airborne escorting and protecting nine black students *(Photos by Will Counts)*

trained, and dedicated to fighting a foreign foe was, in my opinion, an inappropriate use of the military. In my telephone call to Vice President Nixon, I expressed to him my feelings against using the 101 First Airborne. He expressed agreement. I have no way of knowing what counsel, if any, he provided to Eisenhower. But he had agreed that the use of United States marshals would accomplish the same purpose without the disturbances and disruptions, and I hung up with the hope that he could persuade the president on this course of action.

Arkansas had come a long way in providing to every child, to every student, an equal opportunity for an education. We had come a long way in removing discrimination against minorities. However, most of the progress was lost as people around the world watched United States soldiers escort a small group of black students through a hostile crowd.

Following this tragic, costly event, I ran against Orval for governor in 1962. I wanted to make a statement. Amid the shouting and hysterical tumult, even five years after the event, it was hard to get the people's attention. I was not heard. The mind of a majority of our people was set—for the time. I can still hear the refrains, "We had been invaded." "Our state's rights had been violated." "Orval had shown them!" "The federal government could not dictate to us how to run our business, how to run our schools."

Many thought Orval was politically invincible. However, I thought if I could put him into a runoff in the Democratic primary, this sense of invulnerability might be shaken. This was not to be. The 1962 race was my last for public office.

I conferred from time to time with different people who were actively involved on the front line with this struggle.

Congressman Brooks Hays endeavored to mediate this controversy between the state and federal government. He was concerned about the effect that his participation would have on his race for reelection as congressman. I tried to help him, but he was defeated.

Henry Woods, Ed Dunaway, Harry Ashmore, and I would have lunch periodically at the Old Brass Rail, a popular spot in downtown Little Rock for working newspaper reporters. From time to time we would have one or more of these reporters join us for lunch, in an effort to keep up with the news. One such reporter was a former correspondent with the Marine Corps during the war. His name was Johnny Popham from Chattanooga, Tennessee. He was a good marine, as well as a courageous war correspondent. He and I had an excellent rapport. We would exchange bits and pieces of information from our various sources. Popham and Harry Ashmore were both great storytellers, and we would be entertained by their efforts to compete with each other for front stage. Of course, the main subject was Central High School's integration crisis and the economic and political repercussions which would flow from it.

Several of us, from time to time, met at Henry Woods's home to compare notes and see what we could do to help alleviate the disaster.

It was at one of these meetings that the Little Rock mayor, Woodrow Mann, called President Eisenhower requesting the president's intervention. I was not present and was unaware of this request at the time I talked to Vice President Nixon. As I have indicated, I disagreed with the use of federal troops (101 First Airborne) to enforce a civil court decree, as the United States marshals, in my opinion, would be the appropriate agency for this duty. They would have been accepted by the people and the children admitted to the schools, without receiving the South's memory of another invasion of federal troops after the Civil War.

This whole incident proved to be a dark period which distressed Little Rock's economic progress for a quarter of a century.

On the day, and days following, when the National Guard barred the nine black children from Central High School, the Statue of Liberty was under a cloud and her torch of freedom was shrouded in darkness, but, lo, on the day and succeeding days when the black children freely passed to their classrooms, the Statue of Liberty could clearly be seen in the sun's light and holding her torch of freedom higher, it shown brighter than ever before.

X VIETNAM

FIFTY-TWO THOUSAND YOUNG MEN SLAUGHTERED, APPROXIMATELY THE same number severely injured and permanently disabled, all survivors with dark memories, no Main Street parades, no victory marches, no hero's welcome home, no "Yellow Ribbons around the Old Oak Tree"—that is Vietnam.

We have discussed the threat of invasion of Australia and New Zealand by the Japanese during the Second World War, while the "Aussies" and "Diggers" were busy for the British Empire in Africa, Italy, France, and Germany, and how the Australian and New Zealand people were spared the scourge of Japanese invasion and occupation by the skill and courage of American troops—soldiers, sailors, airmen, and marines.

Within five years following the end of the Second World War, there arose well-grounded fears in the minds of the Australian and New Zealand people about the advance of world Communism in Southeast Asia, supported by the might of the Soviet Union and Red China. Then there was Korea, the training and equipping of North Korean troops by the Russians, then the invasion of the Chinese army across the Yalu River into Korea, surprising and routing our United Nations forces and surrounding the First Division, United States Marines, who had reached the Chosin Reservoir in North Korea. As I have stated, this crisis was brought under control, a cease-fire obtained, and a line of demarcation between North and South Korea established through the political leadership of Presidents Truman and Eisenhower and the military skill of one of America's greatest soldiers, Gen. Matthew Ridgeway. Both Australia and New Zealand continued to work with the United States, who, as during and after the Second War, sent troops to fight the Communists in South Korea.

Although the Korean Conflict was a United Nations war, it was the United States of America's fight.

It became apparent that only international action could stay the further advance of Communism in Southeast Asia. America took the initiative in the creation of the Southeast Asia Treaty Organization (SEATO) to serve as an instrument of containment in Southeast Asia.

It was hoped that the NATO (North Atlantic Treaty Organization) would serve as a model. Unfortunately, several of the larger Southeast Asia countries were so passionately committed to neutrality between the Soviet Union and the West, they would not join this defensive coalition. These countries included India, Burma, Ceylon (Sri Lanka), and Indonesia.

Yet, the following nations joined the SEATO Pact: the Philippines, Thailand, Pakistan, the United States, Great Britain, Australia, and New Zealand. The Communists immediately branded this alliance as being "Imperialist."

The treaty was officially entitled the "Southeast Asia Collective Defense Treaty" and representatives met in Manila on September 8, 1954.

In the mutual defense agreement, it was not stated that an attack on one member would be considered an attack upon all. However, the treaty did provide for consultation and collective action if threats to any member developed in the form of subversion, rather than armed attack from without. It further provided for economic cooperation, including technical assistance, "to promote economic progress and social well-being." The treaty also provided in an attached protocol that Laos, Cambodia, and "the other free territory under the jurisdiction of the State of Vietnam" should be eligible for both the protective features and the economic benefits that the treaty provides.

The treaty established a council on which all parties were represented and organized so as to be able to meet at any time.

SEATO had annual council meetings and occasional joint military maneuvers, but any real deterrent to potential Communist aggression was clearly the power and dedication of the United States. The United States sent ambassadors to Cambodia, Laos, and South Vietnam and began providing economic and military aid as well. The United States also began the task of training and supplying the Royal Laotian Army and the South Vietnamese. The Soviet Union, in turn, began supplying military equipment to the Communists.

On August 1, 1964, North Vietnamese torpedo boats attacked an American destroyer, the USS *Maddox*, in the Gulf of Tonkin. The North Vietnamese apparently believed that the destroyer had supported South Vietnamese commando raids on nearby islands. Three days later, the

Maddox and another torpedo boat reported they were again under attack. The second attack appears to have been false, resulting from misleading sonar and radar equipment that was malfunctioning.

On the basis of these Gulf of Tonkin incidents, President Johnson requested Congress to pass the Gulf of Tonkin Resolution. The Resolution was passed by Congress after debate with two dissenting votes in the Senate.

The Tonkin Resolution was introduced and advocated by Sen. J. William Fulbright of Arkansas. It was delivered to the president intact, without any amendment or alteration. The Tonkin Resolution was approved by the House of Representatives, including all members of the Arkansas delegation. Senator Fulbright, acting for his friend, the president, was most successful and persuasive.

The week of August 5, 1964, the passage of the Tonkin Resolution and the actions of President Johnson, under the authority of Congress, embarked the United States on the Vietnam War.

President Johnson ordered the first direct attack by American air power against the North Vietnamese in response to what was described as an "unjustified" attack upon a United States destroyer in international waters of the Tonkin Gulf.

In addition to the Tonkin Resolution, President Johnson secured the passage of a congressional resolution authorizing the president to take "all necessary steps, including the use of the Armed Forces to deter further Communist aggression."

As the war expanded, the United States forces were increased from 16,000 to 500,000—soldiers, sailors, marines, and airmen. The United States of America, the most powerful nation in the world, opposed by a small Communist state in Southeast Asia, was stalemated in a war of attrition for ten years, until the growing impatience of the American people compelled a closure.

At the end of the Second World War, I retained my reserve commission. Except for my two terms as governor, I maintained my active reserve status, performing each year an active duty assignment.

In August 1966, with the rank of brigadier general, I was ordered to Vietnam for an active duty assignment with the Third Marine Amphibious Corps, with headquarters at D'Nang, South Vietnam.

The responsibility of the Third MAF (Marine Amphibious Force) was the northern sector of South Vietnam commanded by Lt. Gen. Lewis W. Walt.

The Third Marine Division was my old outfit, as I have related. I joined the Third Marine Regiment in the summer of 1942 in New River, North Carolina, and remained with the Third Marine Regiment and the Third Marine Division until after the Solomon campaign at Bougainville.

General Walt and I had been classmates as second lieutenants at the Marine Basic School Class of 1936. We had served together at the marine base in Quantico, Marine Corps School, at the beginning of the Second World War where we trained officer candidates. We were together again at Washington and Quantico when the war was winding down in 1945, kept in touch, and remained fast friends.

Lewis W. Walt was a truly great marine. As a mentor and an idol to enlisted marines, he was comparable to Lewis "Chesty" Puller. Lew had served with distinction during the Second World War and in Korea. He was now commanding general for the Marine Amphibious Force in South Vietnam.

I was transported to D'Nang by military aircraft, met by a staff officer, and transported to my quarters. There, I found an invitation from the commanding general to have dinner with him and his staff.

This first evening was a memorable one. Lew and I recalled "old times," caught up on news about old friends. It was only then that we turned to the subject of the war at hand. He gave me a brief summary of the current situation. He then warned me that he had arranged a tough schedule that would require rising early and staying up late. Transversing rough ground, I would have available a helicopter and a jeep as needed and a staff officer as a guide. If I wanted to see or do anything that was not on the schedule, just "give the word."

I have never experienced a fuller, tighter schedule, or seen so much, or had as much to absorb, think about, ponder. The intensity was comparable to the final days of a tightly contested political campaign.

I flew with General Walt on the first day. He wanted to show me the scenes of several recent battles and tell me about them, especially two villages that had changed hands several times, occupied by the marines in the day, then retaken by the Viet Cong during the night. The villages had trenches and caves where the remaining inhabitants could take cover, finding some security from the fighting. These emplacements, of course, were also used by the Viet Cong. The wounded, those ravaged by the war, was not limited to the military. Many of the Vietnamese people, especially old men, women, and children, were wounded or slain.

I was jeeped to an improvised field hospital for Vietnamese people wounded in the struggle for the villages. The building was covered, the occupants protected from the tropical rains, but otherwise it was improvised and primitive. One or more members of the injured villager would be present to help care for the wounded. One of the principal tasks, using a palm leaf or similar object, was to fan away the flies that were attracted by and then infested the wounds.

A medical corpsman, a nurse, a doctor, using all means and resources available, were hard put to bring relief to these innocent victims of the war.

The general gave me an overflight of the terrain, the jungle with which our people had to cope, similar in large measure to the jungles through which we had to fight in a little over two decades ago.

The Viet Cong, the native Communists, knew the jungle, the terrain, the streams, the valleys. This knowledge was used effectively by them in setting up ambushes, planting booby traps, anti-personnel mines, and land mines along roads and trails.

To our marines from the cities, the jungle was a strange, foreign land, forbidding and foreboding. The normal tour of duty was thirteen months, after which the marine was rotated home. It was, by then, that he too knew the jungle and how it could be best used to fight the foe. A few brave souls would stay over for another "extended" tour. They would become the corporals and the sergeants, leaders in this war waged by fire teams, squads, and platoons.

The land mines and the booby traps caused the more severe injuries to all the body parts. The general was making a tour of a field hospital, manned and operated by gallant, dedicated, and experienced doctors, nurses, and medical corpsmen. We made a tour of the hospital, the general first conferring with members of the hospital staff, and then he paid a visit to each wounded marine. The last in a long line of beds contained a young marine, eighteen years old, with blond hair, fair complexion. He was strapped to a life support system, his breathing was heavy and labored. He had been struck by an anti-personnel mine that had exploded on a jungle trail that he and other marines in his squad were following. His injuries had been to his lower body parts and extremities. His survival was in doubt, but he was aware that his general was there by his side.

Lew talked to him softly, pinned a Purple Heart on his pillow, patted him on the shoulder, and walked away. We had walked only a few steps when Lew turned to me and, with tears in his eyes, asked, "How would you feel if that young marine was your son?"

I already knew how I would feel. It was already clearly impacted on my mind. I had three sons, my first two, Sandy and Phillip, were already in the system and on their way—both would serve in Vietnam as marines. It was just a matter of time. My third son, Bruce, was not old enough to serve—not yet.

But all was not destruction. There were helpful signs of reconstruction, of help for the Vietnamese people who were in the path of this seemingly never-ending "no quarter" conflict.

There was a harbor, a combination school and orphanage, for children who had been lost or otherwise separated from their parents. I visited these children. I talked with them. They were already picking up a few words of the English language. There was no sign in their brave, smiling, happy faces, of their ordeal. War was a reality they seemed to accept.

There was an American doctor or teacher, I don't remember which, maybe both, for he served as such. In any event, he was a Mother Goose, an angel. He looked after the care, schooling, and feeding of many children. When he appeared on the scene, he was immediately surrounded with "chicks" like a mother hen. I regret I do not even have his name, but I have a picture taken at the time, showing him surrounded by his brood—I still have it.

There was a Civil Action Program, for example, where marine engineers dug and constructed sturdy, strong, concrete wells, free from flowing drainage, providing a fresh source of water for drinking and cooking.

There was, admittedly in its infancy, the program of establishing some animal husbandry in the blighted areas. Pigs were the favorite animal, but they did not last long. A fat pig was a rare catch for a hun-

Gen. Sid McMath with his two sons, Sandy and Phillip, at Marine Corps Schools, Quantico, Virginia, in preparation for their service in Vietnam *(U.S. Marine Corps Photo)*

gry neighbor who might come on an uninvited visit in the darkness before dawn and have roasted pig for his family supper.

I had a visit with my old outfit, the Third Marine Regiment, and the Third Marine Battalion. The battalion had one company assigned to a combined action program. They had several platoons that were combined with a similar unit from the South Vietnamese and assigned to a native village to maintain village security and to help the people. I had the privilege of inspecting one of these combined units. They were sharp, becoming well trained, and enthusiastic about their relatively independent mission. It was an inspiration to witness their spirit of mission.

The continuation of the war, scenes of the wounded, especially civilians, women, and children, was being noticed more and more by the American people. The media, especially television, was intensifying its coverage of the war, dramatizing its darkest side.

Congressmen and senators who had given near unanimous passage to the Tonkin Gulf Resolution, a virtual declaration of war, authorizing the president to take "such action as necessary, including the use of armed forces in order to halt the aggression of Communism," were having second thoughts. Had they acted precipitously, without due circumspection? Had they been duped or misled by the president? Had Senator Fulbright, known as the "intellectual senator," in sponsoring the Tonkin Resolution and delivering it to the president in the precise form requested, without amendment, been mislead by his friend, the president?

The National Guard had not been called up. A member of the Guard was deferred from the draft.

The Reserves had not been mobilized. A member of the Reserve was deferred from the draft.

Young men in college were deferred.

Who was fighting the war? Draftees and volunteers, commanded by professional officers.

Greek historians remembered ancient Athens's attempt to conquer Syracuse in Sicily. The line of supply was long for the sailing ships and oarsmen of the time. The war drug on, there was dissension in Athens, the project failed. The army lost.

Then there was England in its war against the Boers in South Africa. There, too, the line of supply was long, the conflict protracted; there was dissatisfaction in England; though the Boers won, the venture did not end happily.

But remember there was the South Eastern Asia Treaty Organization Pact which was initiated by John Foster Dulles, secretary of state under President Eisenhower, who envisioned an alliance in Southeast Asia comparable to the North Atlantic Treaty Organization putting in place a mutual defense against Communist aggression.

The wording of the SEATO Pact was not sufficient to compel the United States to take military action to deter the Communist aggression in Vietnam, but it created an expectation among the SEATO members, an implied agreement—it was a moral persuasion.

It was this containment policy that moved President Truman to react against the Communists in South Korea, and we were supported there by our English-speaking cousins, the New Zealanders and the Australians.

Marine private in Vietnam

But this was in 1966; the cloud over the horizon was only as large as a man's hand, so the war went on, micro-managed in great detail from the Oval Office by the president, who had in effect received a blank check from Congress with only two dissenting votes in the United States Senate.

I have a picture, which I wish to share with you, dear reader. You see the young marine slogging upstream; you see another marine, a buddy, in the background facing the same direction, both no doubt, members of a squad deployed in a skirmish line as they move through the jungle.

Who is this marine? He may not know about the SEATO Pact or about the Tonkin Resolution or Senator Fulbright or President Johnson, but one thing he does know—he is there in that jungle and he will be there until the end of his tour—thirteen months.

There was no cheering crowd at the dock when he and his buddies put out to sea, there will be no bands playing or marching down Main Street when he returns—there will be no "Yellow Ribbon Tied around the Old Oak Tree."

Who Am I?

Who am I?
What do I do—
A United States Marine,
One of the proud, one of the few.

I was never enrolled in college
There was no place for me in the Guard
I never went to Canada
Nor burned a draft card.

Who am I
What do I do?—
I'll carry this rifle for Uncle Sam—
We will see the whole thing through.

Who am I?
What do I do?
A United States Marine
One of the proud, one of the few.

—SIDNEY S. MCMATH

How will Vietnam be judged in the light of history?

How will this war be measured when weighed in the scales of freedom in the world?

In the Second War, America and Russia, the two giant protagonists, by necessity, fell into a truce in order to destroy a common enemy.

The war was won; Hitler was dead; the perennial struggle between freedom and tyranny was resumed.

"Their starting points were different, their courses are not the same, but each seems destined by high heaven to influence half the world." (By Alexis de Tocqueville).

Thus ensued a life-and-death struggle for survival; ultimately, by nature of the intensity and severity of the struggle, one would perish and the other survive to continue on its course.

Immediately following the end of the Second War, victory proclaimed and Hitler dead, the conflict between these two conflicting and incompatible systems was resumed.

From the signals that the Russians were sending out of their intent to spread Communism around the world, and the Kremlin's insatiable appetite for bringing more land, more people under its control, America's response under the leadership of Harry Truman was a far-ranging policy of containment.

Immediate steps in the prosecution of this policy was the formation of NATO to block any further Russian expanse in the Western European community. This was coupled with the Marshall Plan, designed to enable our allies, plus Germany, to dig out of the rubble of the war's devastation.

In the pursuit of this containment policy, there followed our defense of Greece against the Communists, the formation of an independent State of Israel, the Berlin airlift, aid to third world emerging people, the formation and support of the United Nations with the ultimate hope of a world community based upon law, free trade, and human rights. And finally, this policy of containment and protection, against Communist expansion, involved the United States in defense of South Korea and it's preservation in the free world.

In the meantime, United States had entered a mutually protective defense pact with Australia and New Zealand (ANZUS) and finally, the organization of SEATO which we have discussed.

And thus our course and policy led us to the defense of South Vietnam. Again, as in Korea, this was an American fight. However, we were loyally supported by our cousins in Australia and New Zealand. Their support was moved, not alone by the written pacts we had mutually agreed upon, but from the depths of our combined sacrifices and triumphs of the Second War.

What will historians tell the future generations about Vietnam? That it was a civil war that came under the policy of "self-determination" established by Pres. Woodrow Wilson? Or was South Vietnam a cat's paw used by Russia to further its expansion of its "Evil Empire" into Southeast Asia?

Will the historians find favor in the Communist argument pointing to the established fact that Imperialism is dead? That America was an imperialistic nation, replacing the cruel domination of the Japanese and the callous indifference to the needs of the Vietnamese by the French?

Wherever the arguments may fall, this fact is crystal clear, the American soldiers, sailors, airmen, and marines did their job. They fought with tenacity, skill, and courage in an intolerably cruel jungle environment, without the understanding and united support of the folks back home.

The American servicemen and women in Vietnam executed the limited mission determined by our national leadership in accord with the highest traditions of our military service and the other wars in which we have been engaged for human justice between nations and men.

Let it be remembered, and never be forgotten, that Korea and Vietnam were battles in a cold war that the free world dared not lose, and we won that war.

XI⌒ A PEOPLE'S LAW FIRM

I FOUGHT THE JAPANESE IN THE SOUTHWEST PACIFIC DURING THE SECOND World War with the United States Marines. I battled the gang and racketeers in Hot Springs, Arkansas, as prosecuting attorney. During my two terms as governor, I was engaged in a no-quarter conflict with the power monopoly and its political power, which it had structured and built for its purpose for two decades.

In 1953, I was forty years of age. My wife, Anne, and I had five children. I was broke and in debt—I faced another challenge. The challenge I faced was to build a law practice to become a trial lawyer, to represent people who I had fought for in the political arena and for those who have been led to believe that the idea of "justice for all" is reserved for those who have money to hire lawyers, to pay the costs, and to survive the "law's delay."

Henry Woods, Leland Leatherman, and I set up a law firm. They were from Hot Springs and had survived with me the political wars. We rented office space, installed a telephone, hired a secretary, and went to work.

One of the obstacles, which I immediately had to overcome was a question in the public mind: "Can an ex-politician, a former governor become a successful trial lawyer doing battle in the courtroom for the rights of his clients?" We became active in the Bar Associations: the Pulaski County Bar, the State Bar, and the American Bar. We joined the American Trial Lawyers Association, attending Bar seminars in order to brush up on the law and get reacquainted with members of the Bar. We each elected, in turn, to serve on the American Trial Lawyers Association's Board of Directors.

Henry, Leland, and I were selected for membership in the International Academy of Trial Lawyers, an association consisting of five hundred lawyers from countries all over the world. I was elected president of the International Academy of Trial Lawyers. During my term of office, we hosted a convention in Little Rock for the academy. Lawyers came from many other countries and were impressed with the reception, the hospitality, and the warm welcome they received. The visitors were amazed by the wonders of our state.

Henry and I were also selected for membership in the Inner Circle of Trial Lawyers, whose membership was limited to one hundred trial lawyers in the United States. This was a great honor.

In 1980, Henry Woods was nominated by Sen. Dale Bumpers to become a United States district judge. President Carter submitted Henry's name to the United States Senate Judiciary Committee for conformation. The subcommittee, chaired by Sen. Howell Heflin, conducted confirmation hearings. After the hearings were completed, Henry's appointment was confirmed by a unanimous vote of the subcommittee and by the judiciary committee as a whole.

Henry Woods was sworn in as United States judge on March 21, 1981. He served with distinction until his death on March 21, 2002. Though in failing health, he worked up to the end processing his cases. At the time of his death, all parties with cases pending in his court had had an opportunity to present their cause—his docket was clear.

United States district judge William "Bill" Wilson described Judge Woods as a "Giant." This he was, as a trial lawyer and as a judge, judging the law.

The only corporate client we had was the Arkansas electric cooperatives for whom we had fought "in the trenches of politics" for four years. Soon after the opening of our law offices, the manager of the Arkansas cooperatives, Harry Oswald, recommended that the board hire McMath, Leatherman and Woods. The member of the firm best suited by knowledge and experience to handle the cooperative's legal business was Leland Leatherman. I had appointed him, while I was governor, as chairman of the Public Service Commission in 1952. There he became thoroughly knowledgeable about utility law, rates, and territorial allocation.

The Arkansas Electric Cooperative publication, *Rural Arkansas,* in its January 2001 issue, in praise of Leland's legal service states:

> One lawyer who stands out in the group of stalwarts like Harry Oswald and some others, was Leland L. Leatherman. He served as legal counsel for the Rural Electric Cooperatives from 1955–1989.

Since the Rural Electric Cooperatives are authorized by the Arkansas Legislature, it should not be surprising that there was a need for an attorney to protect the co-ops interest in the Arkansas General Assembly.

Here again, during all of the battles for territorial integrity and the rights to generate their own power, the co-ops called on Leland Leatherman. He drafted the 1957 legislation that provided the first effective territorial protection for the Arkansas Electric Cooperatives. Though our only corporate client was the co-ops, our specialty was trial practice.

The McMath Law Firm continues to represent primarily individuals injured by the negligent or wrongful acts of others.

There are two McMath law firms. One consists of Phillip McMath, Bruce McMath, Mart Vehik, Winslow Drummond, Charles Harrison, Samuel Ledbetter, Sandra Sanders, Hank Bates, Eileen Harrison, and Paul Harrison. The other is Sandy McMath and Associates. I serve as of counsel with both law firms, which are located in the Sidney S. McMath Building in Little Rock, Arkansas. Sandy McMath and Phillip McMath frequently join together to prepare and try a client's case. They are a formidable team in the courtroom.[1]

Members of the law firm have been active in state and national Bar Associations and have been selected by their peers as outstanding lawyers.

In the eighties, after Henry Woods had gone on the bench, Leland and I began thinking about retirement. Bruce McMath, my son, began gradually taking over the management of the McMath Law Firm. Organizing a law firm is one thing, but operating a law firm of individualistic, independent trial lawyers with varying disciplines, and setting fees, expending costs, paying bills, taxes, and supervising personnel, meeting the payroll, and maintaining the ship on course, is indeed a formidable challenge. Bruce has met this challenge in addition to his trial practice.

Every dedicated plaintiffs' lawyer is a public interest advocate, committed to the pursuit of justice, both inside and outside of the courtroom.

---

1. For other precedent cases, see "Poisoning a Neighbor's Well," "Gee, Dad, That's a Lot of Tomatoes," "Insult and Outrage," and "Willful, Wanton, Reckless Disregard for Safety," on the Internet at www.mcmathlaw.com.

The firm does not bill its clients by the hour or for the time spent on the client's case. It charges on the basis of the result obtained, usually one-third of the amount recovered. The firm advances the costs, and, if the client wins, the costs are reimbursed.

When a new client or prospective client comes into the office, a preliminary investigation is conducted to evaluate the case and ask ourselves two questions—an approach borrowed from a great lawyer and teacher of the law, Jim Jeanes:

> Has this person been wronged?
> Can we help him?

Each of the lawyers in the firm has an excellent legal education in preparing for the law. Each has accumulated experience in the courtroom, applying the law in the pursuit of justice for those who need their help.

A number of young lawyers have been associated with us over the years, won their spurs, opened their own practice, and become outstanding advocates for their clients. Two of these young lawyers became judges. One, John Forrester, a United States magistrate, is doing an outstanding job. Another is William R. Wilson, an excellent and courageous United States district judge in Little Rock.

The young trial lawyers who were associated with the McMath Law Firm in the past, in addition to John Forrester and Bill Wilson, are Jack Lavey, Sy Brewer, Jim Youngdahl, Phil Kaplan, Ted Sizemore, and Bill Hodge.

The McMath family is a family of lawyers. In addition to Sandy, Phillip, and Bruce, I have twin daughters, Melissa Hatfield and Patricia Bueter.

Melissa is a trial psychologist. She assists lawyers in the preparation of their cases, interviewing and preparing witnesses, assisting the trial lawyer in determining the theme of the case, preparing the profile of the jury that would be most desirable in hearing the case, and assisting the attorney in the jury selection. Her sister, Patricia Bueter, works with Melissa in setting up focus groups in preparation for trials.

I have a granddaughter who is interested in following the law and who is currently enrolled in law school.

Melissa is married to Dick Hatfield, who has a successful law practice in Little Rock, specializing in wills, estates, and taxation.

Patricia is married to Randy Bueter, a lawyer, who has had extensive practice in banking and commercial law and is associated with Wilson and Associates in Little Rock.

The McMath Law Firm continues to represent individuals injured by the conduct of others. The members of the firm operate on the belief that the civil justice system, while a means of serving individual justice, is in a larger sense an essential tool for regulating private behavior for the benefit of all citizens.

XII⁀ BETTY DORTCH RUSSELL

My wife, Anne, had died June 2, 1994. My twin daughters, Melissa and Patricia, and I decided to have a portrait painted so that her family could remember her as she was.

I called my friend, George Fisher, a published cartoonist and artist, who once painted a portrait of me while I was governor. I asked him to paint the portrait of Anne. His response was that I was the only portrait he had ever done, but he would recommend an artist that specialized in portraiture, Betty Dortch Russell.

Betty was contacted and commissioned to do the portrait. She met with the twins and me to get pictures and information. The girls could wear Anne's clothes and jewelry so they could sit for the portrait to help. I sat in on the arrangements in my home. At one time, Betty noticed a grill on my balcony and asked if I cooked out there. I bragged about my ability and promised to cook her a steak when the portrait was finished.

All the children came to the unveiling; we could not believe how life-like it was. Anne was immortalized by the portrait on canvas.

I remembered my promise and invited Betty to dinner. In the course of dinner conversation, she asked if I liked to dance. I said, "Yes."

Several weeks later, Betty called to ask me to a dance that friends were having, featuring the Tommy Dorsey Orchestra. I was honored and I accepted.

We had a courtship of two years. I introduced her to the Marine Corps, Masonic Order of Scottish Rites, and Bar Association activities, while she included me in the art scene and civic interests in which she was involved.

Betty and I married on September 14, 1996, with Reverend Vic Nixon and Judge Henry Woods officiating at Pulaski Heights Methodist Church. Our families attended and gave us their blessings and support.

Betty's roots were also in the Deep South. Her maternal grandfather, Thomas William Steele, came from North Carolina in 1850, bringing workers and equipment to Scott, Arkansas. It took eight years to clear the land. His daughter, Nettie Pauline Steele, attended Salem

Academy and Washington University and then married William Pinkney Dortch. Her father gave them eighteen hundred acres as a wedding present. This acreage joined land her husband already owned. They named the plantation "Marlsgate." It took four years to build the home, and it is on the National Registry of Historic Places.

The couple had five sons. The eldest, Thomas Steele Dortch, married Mabel Ruth Wittenberg, and they made their home on Bearskin Lake in Scott. They had two daughters, Betty and Judy.

Betty attended Hendrix College and then St. Louis School of Fine Art at Washington University. She had spent much of her childhood drawing and painting the plantation environment, which included blacks—fishing, working in the cotton fields, and church activities.

Her lifetime interest in painting people expanded to painting portraits on commission.

During the Second World War, Betty met a Yankee from Boston, Henry Wellington Russell. Betty and "Rusty" were married at Marlsgate in 1942. He was sent overseas and later served at the Pentagon. They then moved to Boston where Rusty had grown up and attended Andover Academy and Harvard University. They moved to Little Rock in 1951.

They had five children, Diane, Judy, Mary, David, and Tom. In 1983, Rusty died after a long illness.

At no time had Betty given up her painting. Along with her painting career, Betty has been involved with numerous civic organizations. Among them are the Aesthetic Club, the Junior League of Little Rock, the Discovery Museum, and the "Committee of 100" that oversees support of the Ozark Folk Center. During the 1957 crisis when the schools were closed, Betty and her mother joined the Women's Emergency Committee to get the nine black students in school and the school reopened.

She has won many honors and awards. One of her main projects is Scott Connections—a nonprofit organization to promote and preserve the history of plantation life. The Scott Settlement is a window of history on Arkansas plantation life in the 1836–1945 period. Authentic artifacts and original buildings have been restored and preserved for educational purposes.

I have joined with her in advocating that visual and performing

Sid and Betty McMath

arts should be a requirement in every school. Art enables a child to reveal talents that may not have been previously observed. If encouraged and pursued, this can bring confidence and self-assurance to a child. Art requires discipline, creative thinking, appreciation, and wise use of time. It promotes a sense of responsibility. Betty has shared her talents as a teacher, a lecturer at symposiums, a juror of exhibitions and her own exhibits.

Betty and I stay busy. We share our family, our friends, and our many interests. We have something to do, someone to love, and we look to the future.

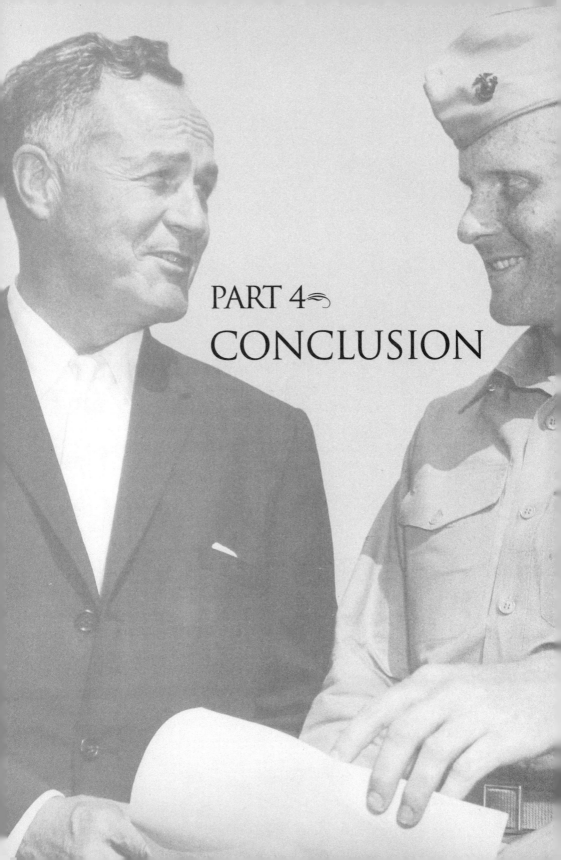

PART 4

CONCLUSION

We in America have been gratified by the advance of democracy around the world. Fires of freedom are burning, ignited by the precepts proclaimed in the American Declaration of Independence and the Bill of Rights to the Constitution of the United States.

Let it be remembered that the rights prescribed in these two documents were not automatically implemented and available to all citizens in the United States. The adoption of the first ten Amendments to the Constitution did not immediately secure the rights of women, children, and blacks.

Justice, liberty, and freedom are words lightly spoken, but they come at great cost. The rights of all citizens under the law to "life, liberty, and the pursuit of happiness" have been obtained by conflict on the battlefield, in the political arena, and in the courtrooms of America.

The concepts of freedom, equality of opportunity, and dignity for all people are the basis and bulwark of our national pride and our nation's strength. America's instinct for equal rights under the law for all citizens is the underlying force that binds us together. America's conscience dictates that justice is the moral essence of the law.

However, history and experience teach us that these rights are secure only if they are recognized by the people and preserved. We have to be on constant guard against the erosion of these rights which have been so costly won and constantly aware of unfair discrimination against anyone who by circumstance may be placed in a vulnerable condition for unjust treatment.

My concern for people who were unfairly treated has influenced my life and work. In retrospect, my awareness of justice began in a one-room school in Bussey, Arkansas, during the First World War, when each morning, we would pledge allegiance to the flag of the United States "with justice for all." The deep impression this made on my youthful mind heightened my awareness of injustice, as I became knowledgeable about the economic conditions under which we lived.

In contrast to our city cousins, we lacked electricity, passable roads, and schools beyond the eighth grade. I also observed that the blacks had no schools and that they struggled to survive, locked into their condition by longstanding customs of discrimination.

A tragic incident still weighs on my memory when we moved from the family farm to Smackover. I have related that my friend and playmate, Harper, went with us. Later in my life when called upon to take action or make a decision affecting blacks or other minorities, I could see in my mind's eye Harper, barefoot on a cold November morning, trailing behind the wagon, following the only family he had.

When we moved to Hot Springs on my tenth birthday, I became part of a metropolitan city with people of many national origins: Greeks, Italians, Syrians, Jewish, Irish, and Southerners, with names like Longinotti, Pappas, Mattar, Dowd, Page, Smith, and Brown. I became acquainted with many people by selling newspaper on the streets, carrying a paper route, shining shoes at Rasso's Barber Shop, clerking at the Kroger Store. I knew the children in grade school, junior high, high school, and on up through the University of Arkansas Law School, then as a young lawyer until 1940, when I responded to "the pull of the Corps."

Leaving Hot Springs for the war, I had a personal commitment, a mission, to remove the political gang that had ruled Hot Springs for a quarter of a century and return the city and county governments back to the people.

When the GIs from Hot Springs came "marching back from the war," as soon as they had time to take off their packs, I contacted them. We set up a plan of action, executed it with military precision, and in November 1947, in the general election, the GIs swept the field. We won all of the nine county and district offices, including prosecuting attorney, circuit judge, and constable. We returned to the people the freedom of the ballot and a fair and impartial law enforcement and judicial system.

I served a two-year term as prosecuting attorney, then ran for governor in 1948. I was opposed by the Dixiecrat Party that was against integration and equal rights for blacks and whose state chairman was our governor of Arkansas. Race was a big issue in my campaign used by my opposition. I concentrated upon my platform for the people of my state.

During this campaign in 1948, I was contacted by the president of the University of Arkansas, relative to the admission of Edith Irby, a black student, to the University of Arkansas Medical School. I assured him that I would support her admission, and one of my first acts after having been elected as governor was to fulfill that commitment. Miss Irby, an excellent student, was welcomed, and soon segregation barriers were removed by her fellow students.

Immediately after my election, I campaigned for Pres. Harry Truman, committing my energies and political resources toward his election. He carried Arkansas with a handsome majority.

The Dixiecrats, Strom Thurman and Fielding Wright, carried South Carolina, Georgia, Alabama, Mississippi, and Louisiana. Had they carried Arkansas, Texas, and one other Southern state, they would in all probability have been able to accomplish their goal of defeating President Truman's program of civil rights, including fair employment, educational opportunity, and voting rights for all people. Gov. Strom Thurman, Dixiecrat candidate for president, made firebrand speeches, charging that President Truman's civil rights proposal would "mongrelize" the South.

The long-established custom of segregation and discrimination still may be found lurking around in the minds of some people. In 2002, United States senator Trent Lott in a tribute to Sen. Strom Thurman stated that the country would have been better served had Strom Thurman been elected and Harry Truman defeated. However, in this instance, there was an immediate negative response, and members of the Republican Party, disassociating themselves from Senator Lott's assertion, immediately removed him as leader of the majority party of the United States Senate—"hope springs eternal."

With reference to voting rights, at my first opportunity as governor, September 1950, I recommended to the Democratic Party that it strike the "all-white" provision for membership. It was my feeling that by granting to the blacks a right, long withheld, to vote would put them in a bargaining position so that they could further advance their opportunities as citizens equal before the law.

Remembering past tragic racial events, I endeavored to have the legislature pass an anti-lynch bill. It failed. I also endeavored to repeal the poll tax, an instrument for election fraud and voting limitations. It did not succeed, as Dixiecrat sentiments remained strong in the legislature. However, the poll tax was repealed by a Constitutional Amendment in 1965.

There were other people who were also being discriminated against, unjustly treated. When I became governor in 1948, half the farm families in Arkansas were being denied a quality of life which electrical service would provide. A five-year fight ensued before the barriers erected by the power companies could be removed and these rural families were supplied with power from electrical cooperatives, which not only improved the quality of life on the farm, but made a substantial contribution to the economy of this state.

When I launched my highway construction and rebuilding program to get our state out of "the mud and the dust," there were seven counties in the northern part of the state with no hard surface outlet from the county seat to the rest of the world. These counties were discriminated against because they had small populations, and it was not considered "politically feasible" to build roads and expend limited construction funds where there was no commensurate return in votes. Yet we built roads for these counties. At the end of my term, each had a hard surface outlet for traffic and transportation. Since then, the population in each of these counties has been increased, their economies enhanced.

After leaving the governor's office in 1953, I established my law firm. I continued to represent people who had been discriminated against, unjustly treated, or denied their rights.

It has been a long, slow process for women to gain the rights of full citizenship, including the right to own property and to vote. Up until 1958, women in Arkansas and in forty-eight other states in the Union were denied a right, equal to that of their husbands in a court of law, involving the loss of the marriage relationship and companionship of a spouse. If the wife was wrongfully injured, the husband could recover for the loss of her services, the marriage relationship (conjugal rights). A woman was denied this right of recovery when her husband was wrongfully injured, because in the language of the court "conjugal rights were not important to a woman."

This right, long withheld, to women was restored by a case which Henry Woods and I tried and won. Upheld by the Supreme Court of Arkansas, this victory for women became a precedent in other states.

It is gratifying to me that women are advancing as first-class citizens. For example, a majority of the members of the Board of Directors of the City of Little Rock in 2003 are women. We have a woman U.S. senator, among other women senators in Congress, and many women are judges and CEOs.

Children of school age in the United States have been discriminated against, treated unjustly by pharmaceutical companies for profit. For a quarter of a century, these companies manufactured a toxic vaccine, which caused injuries to children, and in some cases permanent brain damage. For at least a ten-year period, the Federal Drug Administration and the pharmaceutical companies were aware of a safer vaccine, during which the policy of these companies was to defend any litigation arising out of injuries to children, rather than spend a few cents more on each shot of vaccine.

I filed suits with other plaintiffs' lawyers on behalf of children against these pharmaceutical companies, thereby prodding them into making a safer product. When I won the cases for twenty-five children in Arkansas who had been injured by this excessively toxic vaccine, they received compensation which was put in trust for their future care and welfare.

It happened that in 1956, the United States senators from the South passed a Southern Manifesto, calling upon the people in their states to resist integration in the schools. This resolution was signed by all the Southern senators, including Sen. J. William Fulbright and Sen. John McClellan from Arkansas.

Emboldened by this support, Gov. Orval Faubus played his racial card. He mobilized the Arkansas National Guard to block nine black students from admission to Little Rock Central High School, an admission which had been ordered by the United States District Court. Then by order of Governor Faubus, the school was closed. As students scattered to find a place to continue their high school education, some went to live with relatives in the state, but others left Arkansas. There is no telling how many never returned to school to graduate and receive their high school diploma.

As I have related, a group of courageous, caring, and civic-minded women formed an emergency committee. They took action and challenged the men in the community to join them. At this time, there were two pictures seen on television screens and in the eyes of people around the world. One was that of our Statue of Liberty, holding high the torch symbolizing freedom in America. The other image was soldiers of the 101 First Airborne escorting nine black children to class. From these two contrasting pictures, what conclusions about America would be drawn?

After two years, the struggle, for what is right and just, won. The school was reopened, the soldiers were withdrawn, and the black students were attending class. The Statue of Liberty could be clearly seen, holding high her torch of freedom, burning ever the brighter for the world to see.

Abraham Lincoln, in the throes and agony of our Civil War, proclaimed, "America is the last clear hope of mankind." History has confirmed the truth of Lincoln's pronouncement.

I am gratified by the ever-growing support for a democratic form of government by the people in emerging countries. Their hopes for freedom have been fused and fueled by the American Declaration of Independence and Bill of Rights and by what they have seen personally and observed on television as to the quality of life in America.

My conviction is that it is America's destiny to lead the way toward fulfilling man's hopes for a community of nations, living at peace, engaged in fair trade, and "WITH JUSTICE FOR ALL." So might it be.

A Nation's Prayer

Grant us, oh Lord, a Common Faith—

That man shall know both bread and peace—

That he shall know justice, and righteousness and freedom
and security—

That every man shall have an equal opportunity and an
equal chance to do his best—

Not just in this, our land, but throughout the world—

And in this faith, let us move toward the kind of world
our hands can build.

—STEPHEN VINCENT BENET

Written by Stephen Vincent Benét, and read by Pres. Franklin Delano Roosevelt
on June 14, 1936, in his Flag Day Address to the American people. Sid McMath's
birthday is June 14.

APPENDIXES

CASES THAT MADE A DIFFERENCE

APPENDIX I ❧ GET THE FACTS

More and more, we lawyers are awakening to a perception of the truth that what divides us and distracts us from the solution to a legal problem is not so much uncertainty about the law as uncertainty about the facts—The facts will generate the law. Let the facts be known as they are, and the law will spring from the seed and turn its branches towards the light.

—JUDGE BENJAMIN CARDOZO

One of my first cases was *John Short vs. Hogan Construction Co.* John W. Short, thirty-two years of age, with a wife and children, was injured in a two-car collision. As a result, he suffered for sixty-three days and died. One passenger in his vehicle was killed; another severely injured. The collision occurred when a pickup truck crossed the center line and collided with the John Short vehicle. Three lawyers declined to take the case on behalf of the surviving widow and children of John Short.

Many lay people are under the impression that, in a trial of a lawsuit, the truth will out—that justice will prevail. This perception, no doubt, is generated by Hollywood and television productions where a trial lawyer, by a brilliant extemporaneous cross-examination, destroys the opposing witness; falsehood is exposed; and truth and justice are triumphant. Unfortunately, this does not happen unless the truth is laboriously and meticulously presented to the jury, the triers of fact.

The pursuit of the facts begins in the lawyer's office in the first interview with the client. In obtaining the client's confidence, the lawyer in a small town has an advantage over the city lawyer in establishing this essential rapport with his client. The lawyer may know the client or his relatives or neighbors. He knows the community and its traditions, its customs. He does not leave his client cooling his heels in the reception room, as if he were in a doctor's office. A lawyer does not direct his secretary to escort the client to his office; instead he greets the client and ushers him to his office. He directs his secretary to hold his calls, so that he will not be disturbed. This is a reassuring message to the client that he is important and that his case is significant and the lawyer is receptive and wants to help him.

This confidence, having been obtained, the lawyer must never lose. It is a good practice, at the conclusion of the first conference with a client, to have the client go home and write out a narrative of everything that happened from the day of the event to the present date—every detail—whether or not he thinks it is significant. This has two purposes. It gives the client something to do—a participation. In addition, it is amazing how frequently, when the client is ask to go home and write down everything that happened, what he remembers. Facts he might consider insignificant may, in the eyes of an expert, be extremely important in formulating his opinion.

The first introduction to a case may come through a personal representative of the client—a relative or one having a power of attorney or an administrator. In this event, the representative should bring to the initial conference all documents, records, reports, and correspondence that have any possible bearing on the case. However, the experienced lawyer has learned never to make a final evaluation of a case, where substantial injuries are involved, based upon the documents and reports until they have been established to be credible. This is particularly true of police or other investigative reports. Before passing judgment, *get the facts.*

In the case of John Short, his father-in-law came to see me in Little Rock. He had been to see other lawyers in his hometown. He had with him the police report, which indicated:

1. John Short, prior to the collision, was driving 80 miles per hour in a 65 mph zone;
2. A strong odor of alcohol was present in the John Short vehicle; and
3. A bottle of Medley Brothers Whiskey was found near the right door of the John Short car.

In addition, the driver of the pickup truck, which had crossed the center line and collided with the John Short vehicle, had no liability insurance. Understandably, the lawyers who had been consulted had refused the case.

John Short's father-in-law, a longtime friend and supporter of mine, requested that I investigate the case as a personal favor to him. I personally investigated the case as requested.

The police officer who made the investigation still had the bottle of Medley Brothers Whiskey. The seal had not been broken. There was a crack in the shoulder of the glass bottle from which whiskey would leak when the bottle was tilted.

The nurse on duty in the emergency room of the local hospital, who had assisted the emergency room physician in caring for John Short and who accompanied Mr. Short in the ambulance to a Little Rock hospital, stated that there was no odor of alcohol on John Short and that the emergency room physician remarked that "this is one automobile accident where no alcohol was involved."

The witness who had told the police officer that John Short was traveling eighty miles an hour prior to the collision could not be located at his given address. However, since he was an over-the-road truck driver, it was a reasonable inference that he was a member of the Teamsters Union. I contacted the business manager of the Teamsters Union in our area and determined that this witness was, indeed, a member. He was found in Houston, Texas. In a personal interview, the driver stated that John Short passed him going west traveling approximately eighty miles an hour, but there was other traffic moving in the same direction, and when Short passed these vehicles, he reduced his speed and "flowed with the traffic."

Louis Melton, driver of the pickup truck, stated that the highway where the collision occurred, which ran east and west, was being resurfaced and that there was a drop off on the south shoulder of eight to twelve inches, and the right front wheel of his truck dropped off the pavement onto the shoulder. In an effort to regain control and get his truck back on the highway, he overcompensated and crossed over the center line, striking the John Short vehicle.

The state trooper stated that the shoulder of the highway on the south side had been excavated and packed with sand, but the rains had washed the sand and caused a drop-off of several inches. He stated further that the condition of the north shoulder was such that it would not carry traffic.

The resurfacing work had been done by Ben Hogan Construction

Company under a contract with the Arkansas Highway Department. The contract provided that "the contractor shall schedule his operations in widening existing pavement under traffic so that, in no case, shall trenches be open on both sides of the existing pavement at one time; the base course for widening on the side first opened shall be completed to the specified grade and shoulder material pulled back against the outside edge of the base course, and that side opened to traffic before the trench on the opposite side is opened."

My partner, Henry Woods, and I filed suit against Ben Hogan Construction Company on behalf of the John Short estate and the surviving widow and children. At the conclusion of the trial, the court instructed the jury that Hogan Construction Company had a duty to exercise reasonable care to comply with the provisions of the contract relating to the safety of the traveling public, and if such failure to exercise ordinary care contributed proximately to cause the injuries, they should find for the plaintiff.

In the complaint filed by the widow, as administrator, on behalf of herself, the children, and the estate of John Short, we asked for:

1. Compensation for the estate, for the pain and suffering experienced by John Short and all medical expenses and costs related to his death;

2. Loss of pecuniary support to the widow and children that John Short would reasonably have been expected to make over his life expectancy; and

3. Mental anguish of the widow and children arising out of the loss of their husband and father.

The pecuniary loss experienced by the widow and children could be established rather easily. John Short was employed by the Bell Telephone Company. His earning records were all available and his future with the company assured. It was a simple matter to establish the base of this pecuniary loss by multiplying his prospective earnings by his life expectancy and reducing it to present value. Mental anguish of the widow and children could be established by friends and relatives.

Proof of John Short's pain and suffering presented a greater challenge. The attorney for the insurance company frequently will take the medical records and, on examination of the physician, point out the schedule of drugs given the patient, in order to reduce pain and keep him comfortable. Physicians and nurses frequently, because of their constant contact with suffering, subconsciously, at least, may tend to become inured to the pain of the patient. Psychologically, this may be necessary in order to prevent the doctor or nurse from being overwhelmed to the human suffering to which they are exposed. Doctors and nurses, of necessity, have to be called in order to prove the nature and the extent of the injuries and treatment provided. Friends, relatives, and neighbors are called in order to establish pain and mental anguish of the injured person. However, there are occasions when the nurse and the doctor will adequately meet this burden.

In this case, the nurse on duty in the emergency room was called. She testified that she had helped load John Short in the ambulance and rode with him to Little Rock; they applied a Thomas splint to his left leg to completely immobilize it, packed him in sand bags, and gave him 200 cc. of blood in route because his blood pressure dropped about fifteen points; he was conscious all the time and endured great pain and suffering.

Dr. Henry Hollenberg, the treating physician, was called as a witness. Dr. Hollenberg was the dean of Arkansas surgeons. He was tall, slim, erect, with gray hair. His bearing personified integrity, and he had the compassion of a Christian missionary, which, in a way, he was.

Dr. Hollenberg testified to Short's extensive injuries and surgical procedures:

> It was necessary to operate a second time. He had another obstruction and terrible peritonitis. Three or four feet of bowel was removed and the ends reconnected. The wound became infected and he developed a suppression of urinal output. He survived five days after the second operation, but died from anuria, an adrenal failure.

The last question directed to Dr. Hollenberg and his response was:

Q. Dr. Hollenberg, did your patient suffer any pain as a result of his injuries?

A. The patient was conscious up until the last four or five days. He was very uncomfortable and in pain most of the time. He suffered so extensively and fought so valiantly for his life, I was grieved because I could not relieve his pain. One Sunday morning, to show my concern, I brought him an orchid.

Defense counsel: "Objection—prejudicial."

The defense attorney moved to strike the concluding remarks of the good doctor's testimony. How strike from the minds of the jury this moving gesture of concern and care by the treating physician, who had traveled across the state of Arkansas, over hazardous roads in hot weather to reveal to a jury the tragic injuries his patient had sustained?

The jury, having received the case under the instructions of the court, was out for an interminable period of time. The most trying period for lawyers is waiting for a verdict. One agonizes over what he did not do that he should have done or what he did that might be injurious to his client's cause. We could go outside the courthouse and see through the window into the jury room. Henry and I could not hear the deliberations, but we could see that two jurors had separated from the others. From time to time, the other jurors would approach and what appeared to be heavy arguments would ensue. At long last, the verdict was returned for the widow, the children, and the estate of John Short.

After the jury was discharged, we asked the foreman what had caused the delay. His prompt response was, "There were two mule-heads who wanted to give the widow more money than you sued for."

Harold Hill, one of the passengers in the John Short vehicle, joined as a plaintiff in the suit by the widow of John Short. Hill had sustained fracture to the vertebrae in his low back, sustained a wage loss, and medical expenses. The jury returned a verdict for Hill.

Hogan Construction Company paid off the judgment obtained by the widow and the children of John Short. However, Hogan appealed the Hill judgment, contending that the verdict was excessive, and that the court was in error in admitting into evidence the provision of the contract between Hogan and the highway department pertaining to public safety.

On appeal, the Arkansas Supreme Court held that the instructions of the trial court were correct—that the safety provisions in the contract were for the benefit of the traveling public. The Supreme

Court further held that the instructions given by the trial judge to the jury that they could take into consideration the contract between Hogan and the highway department inserted for the protection of the traveling public was not error and that the admission of the safety provision of the contract into evidence was proper.

The trial lawyer will get the facts: There is no eloquence like the eloquence of the *facts.* "Let the facts be known as they are, and the law will spring from the seed and turn its branches towards the light."

This case further illustrates that where there is a competent judge and good lawyers on both sides, the facts will be presented to the jury, truth will out, and justice will be done. In the John Short case, we got the facts. The widow, the children, and the estate were provided for— Justice was done and a grandfather consoled.

APPENDIX II ⟡ LET THE JURY DECIDE

The Right to Trial by Jury Shall Be Preserved

—SEVENTH AMENDMENT TO THE
UNITED STATES CONSTITUTION

Pat Brinegar was twenty-two years of age, paralyzed, totally disabled, and unable to work. He had no means of paying off mounting debts nor any way of supporting himself, his wife, and his two-year-old daughter.

Pat was injured when he was working as a crew member on a motor boat on the Arkansas River. Henry Woods, my law partner, and I met with Pat in our office. He was in a wheelchair. He told us his story. He was upbeat and optimistic. He was going to get well. He had a contagious Irish smile. We immediately wanted to help him. We thought a jury might feel the same way.

The jury system with its human frailties is the best ever devised to decide controversies between citizens or to stand between an individual citizen and the state. Jurors' votes are not dictated by financial interest in the case, career considerations, lobbying by special interests or campaign contributions. We have confidence in our judicial system. We have an abiding faith in the wisdom of "the twelve good men and true."

The vast majority of juries, by their verdict, approach justice. Justice, like happiness, is constantly pursued but never completely realized. Juries do substantial justice, and if in isolated cases they seem to fall short, fault may be found not with the jury or the system, but the manner in which the case was tried. This responsibility lies, principally, with the lawyer and the trial judge.

One of the rewards of being a trial lawyer is an intangible one—the human relationship, the bond formed between client and the lawyer during the days of painstaking preparation and the ordeal of trial. This relationship begins with the first visit and continues with the search for the facts, the discovery proceedings, the jury selection, and the trial. The lawyer has the duty to do for his client what the client would do for himself, were he able. To accomplish this, the lawyer must identify with his client—walk in his shoes, share his sorrow, understand his frustrations when harassed and hounded by collection agencies.

A lawyer cannot acquire the desired identification with his client merely by office visits. He has to go where the client lives—the home, the trailer park, the rehabilitation center. In the wrongful death case of a breadwinner, the lawyer must go into the home, get to know the family, the children, their plans, hopes, and aspirations.

When the lawyer achieves this kind of identification, has gotten the facts, and briefed the law, he will be eager to tell his client's story. When the moment comes for him to go to the jury, he will be able to speak for his client with conviction. He will be motivated by a passionate desire to help his client. This feeling for this client as he presents his case will hopefully be shared by the jury—and they, too, may wish to help.

Pat Brinegar was employed by San Ore Construction Company. San Ore was engaged in the construction of a dam across the Arkansas River. Seven of the fourteen gates had been completed, and the others were surrounded by a cofferdam. For the purpose of raising the upstream water level, the superintendent of San Ore ordered all the gates closed except one adjacent to the cofferdam. By 1:30 P.M., the water level was four or five feet above the dam. The flow of water through the gate was extremely turbulent, and there was a waterfall effect. The superintendent ordered a twenty-two-year-old operator of a boat, designated the "Hal-B," and its deckhand, Pat Brinegar, to take the boat through the open gate and return with an empty water barrel. On the return trip, the Hal-B capsized. Pat Brinegar was struck by the boat and his spinal cord severed.

Maritime law came into the courts of Arkansas with the opening of the Arkansas River for navigation. Maritime law was a new field to Arkansas lawyers and to the judges. Brinegar filed suit against San Ore Construction Company in the U.S. District Court, Eastern District, Pine Bluff Division. U.S. District Judge Oren Harris presided at the trial. The basic issue was whether Pat Brinegar was a member of a crew of a vessel. The defendant contended that this was a workers' compensation case. In fact, the attorney for the defendant who tried the initial stages of the case, in his opening statement, told the jury:

> If Pat Brinegar was a member of the crew of a vessel, you couldn't put enough money in the courtroom to compensate him.

Judge Harris ruled, as a matter of law, that Pat was a member of the crew of a vessel.

The issues of the defendant's negligence and whether or not the defendant had violated a Coast Guard regulation were ruled to be questions for the jury.[1]

Pat Brinegar was our last witness. He had not been in the courtroom. He was brought to the courthouse by ambulance and transferred from a stretcher to a wheelchair in the lobby of the courthouse.

Pat testified from his wheelchair as follows:

> Q. Pat, how are you doing?
>
> A. I'm doing fine.

He was then given the opportunity to tell his story—not one whimper or complaint or pitch for sympathy. The last question I asked Pat was:

> Q. Pat, if you could do anything you wanted to do in this world, what would you do?
>
> A. I would buy me a stock car and outfit it so I could drive it, and I would enter the stock car races all over the country.

Fantastic! Upbeat all the way. You could feel the jurors' hearts go out to that young man.

After Pat testified, we rested our case and the court excused the jury. We went into the court chambers for the defendant's motions. When the motions were denied, the insurance company made an offer. For the time and place, it was a substantial one. Expecting an offer, we had asked Pat to wait in the courtyard. We went downstairs

---

1. For a brilliant treatise on maritime law and its application in the *Brinegar* case, see Judge Oren Harris's opinion in *Brinegar vs. San Ore Construction Company,* 302 F.Supp. 630 (E.D. Ark. 1969); see also a comprehensive article by Henry Woods entitled "The Law's Concern with Those Who Go Down to the Sea in Ships: San Ore Construction Company," *Arkansas Law Review* 23 (1969).

and conferred with him in the ambulance. We told him the offer, pointed out that this amount of money would support him and his wife, pay off his debts, and give him independence. We explained that there is always a gamble in going to the jury, that all twelve jurors must agree on the verdict. Pat listened to our story and then, flashing that Irish smile, said: "Let the jury decide."

We let the jury decide. They returned a verdict for Pat in an amount double that offered by the insurance carrier for the defendant, San Ore Construction Company.

Predictably the defendant filed a motion for a judgment n.o.v. (notwithstanding the verdict) and for a new trial. The defendant's motion contained two serious charges: the jury verdict was excessive, and the jury was unduly influenced by Brinegar and the Brinegar family.

The following allegation was made:

> During a recess at the close of the plaintiff's case, the plaintiff, then on a hospital cart and with his three year old daughter and his young attractive wife standing by his side, were permitted to engage in displays of affection, embracing, emotion and hysteria in the presence of the jury.[2]

The court set a date for a hearing on the defendant's motion in order to give the parties an opportunity to present evidence. No witnesses were produced by the defendant to substantiate the above allegation. Attorneys for Brinegar submitted affidavits denying the defendant's contention. Notwithstanding the defendant's failure to submit evidence in support of its allegation, the court made a finding based upon its own observations during the trial and stated:

> The following facts, however, are known to the Court and bear on the allegations. Plaintiff was a patient in the Rehabilitation Center in Hot Springs and did not appear at the trial until the morning of the third and last day. He was brought to Pine Bluff by ambulance and taken by ambulance cot to the third floor of the Federal Building, where the courtroom is located. Outside the elevator Brinegar was transferred to a wheel chair and rolled into the courtroom to give his testimony. He testified between

---

2. *Brinegar vs. San Ore Construction Company, Inc.*, 302 F. Supp. 630 (E.D. Ark. P.B. Div. 1969), at 642.

twenty and thirty minutes. His testimony was given in a calm, unemotional manner. *There was not the slightest display of emotion by him or any member of his family.* (Emphasis supplied.)[3]

The defendant also made the following allegation:

The plaintiff's wife, on the closing day of the trial, and as the jury left the Courtroom, took a seat next to the aisle which the jury was required to use, where the plaintiff's wife took her child in her lap and again exchanged affections with the child and gazed soulfully into the eyes of each of the jurors as they passed single file by her seat.[4]

Commenting on this allegation, the court stated:

This Court is in an excellent position to dispose of this allegation. The Court at all times had the Brinegar family under close observation. Besides plaintiff's wife, his parents, mother-in-law and grandmother attended the trial. His daughter was in the courtroom only on the morning of the final day. His wife and grandmother testified. By the agreement of defense counsel, they were excused from the rule and could sit in the courtroom during the trial. The conduct of plaintiff's wife was at all times exemplary. She testified factually and unemotionally. She made no outburst or shed no tears either on the stand or in the courtroom. *Her presence in the courtroom as observed by the Court was completely unobtrusive.* (Emphasis supplied.)[5]

On the question of the excessiveness of the verdict, the court reviewed the evidence.

At the time of his injury, Brinegar was twenty-two years old with a life expectancy of forty-six more years. He was in good health, happily married, and the father of a two-year-old daughter. He was an excellent mechanic with a good work history.

It was calculated that Brinegar's future earning loss and his future

---

3. *Brinegar vs. San Ore Construction Company, Inc.,* 302 F. Supp. 630 (E.D. Ark. P.B. Div. 1969), at 642.

4. *Brinegar vs. San Ore Construction Company, Inc.,* 302 F. Supp. 630 (E.D. Ark. P.B. Div. 1969), at 642.

5. *Brinegar vs. San Ore Construction Company, Inc.,* 302 F. Supp. 630 (E.D. Ark. P.B. Div. 1969), at 642.

medical expenses would exceed the amount of the award returned by the jury. The doctors testifying agreed that all of his life Brinegar would be faced with recurring kidney, lung, and skin problems that would require frequent periods of hospitalization and specialized treatment.

Brinegar's future wage loss and medical care, in excess of the jury verdict, was determined without any consideration being given to the "intangible" elements of damages which must be accorded great weight. His pain, suffering, and mental anguish (particularly the latter) could justify a substantial portion of this verdict.

In addition, Brinegar could justifiably be awarded for the permanency of his injuries: the almost complete loss of bodily function and the loss of his ability to enjoy life's non-work connected activities are embraced within their element of damage—the loss of the ability to enjoy sports or to take his daughter for a walk or to the circus or to church. He can never again drive an automobile or engage in his principal hobby which was building racing cars. His wife, once a loving companion, must now become his lonely nurse.

Having reviewed the evidence, the judge concluded:

> Besides the intangibles of pain, suffering, mental anguish, and permanency of the injury, the jury was instructed that Brinegar was entitled to recover for the visible nature of his infirmities. *When all these intangibles are considered, the jury could justifiably give them equal or even greater weight than the economic losses sustained by this young man.* (Emphasis supplied.)[6]

Having reviewed the economic damages and the intangible losses sustained by Brinegar, the court made this finding with reference to the defendant's motion to set aside the verdict:

> A verdict will not be set aside in a case of tort [personal injury] for excessive damages, unless the court can clearly see that the jury have committed some very gross and palpable error, or have acted under some improper bias, influence, or prejudice, or have totally mistaken the rules of law, by which the damages are to be determined. . . . unless the verdict is so excessive or outrageous, . . . as to demonstrate, that the jury have acted against the rules

---

6. *Brinegar vs. San Ore Construction Company, Inc.,* 302 F. Supp. 630 (E.D. Ark. P.B. Div. 1969), at 642.

of law, or have suffered their passions, their prejudices, or their perverse disregard of justice, to mislead them.[7]

The Brinegar case is significant:

1. Pat was provided funds for his future care and to compensate him for the injuries wrongfully inflicted by the defendant;

2. The *Brinegar* case was the first admiralty case filed in Arkansas, the Arkansas River being a navigable stream falling under admiralty jurisdiction;

3. A verdict of $1 million, not impressive by current inflated standards, was the largest admiralty verdict returned at that time;

4. Allegations that a jury had returned an excessive verdict based upon sympathy and had been unduly influenced, a charge one frequently hears about jury verdicts, was overwhelmingly refuted by the evidence and the findings of the court; and

5. A jury verdict should not be disturbed or set aside if it is supported by the evidence, not influenced by improper conduct, and is not shocking to the conscience of the court.

When Pat Brinegar testified in the courtroom, he told his story, was not emotional, made no pitch for sympathy, and in the face of all the medical evidence to the contrary, he was optimistic about the future and demonstrated indomitable courage.

The jurors had an opportunity to see and hear Pat Brinegar. Pat had an opportunity to see the jurors as they were: as people, as people like his neighbors, as people like himself. Pat had confidence that the jury would do what was right when he told his lawyers to "let the jury decide."

During the course of Pat's trial, John Shephard from St. Louis assumed the role of lead counsel for the defense. John was a frequent and popular speaker at bar meetings and functions. One of his favorite stories, which he told with great humor, was how he lost a multimillion-dollar verdict to a former governor and his partner down in Arkansas. With poetic license and embellishment, he told how, when the judge was presented a problem, he would turn to Henry Woods and ask, "Mr.

---

7. *Brinegar vs. San Ore Construction Company, Inc.,* 302 F. Supp. 630 (E.D. Ark. P.B. Div. 1969), at 642.

Woods, what is the law on that?" Then John would add with glee the punch line of this story:

> During Mr. McMath's summation for the plaintiff, I had occasion to object on the grounds that his argument was not supported by the facts or was irrelevant or prejudicial. The third time I objected, Judge Harris, the trial judge, leaning forward in his chair, peering over his spectacles, admonished me, saying: "Mr. Shephard, don't interrupt the Governor while he is talkin'."

In order to raise the jury to heights of their opportunity to do justice, a trial lawyer may have a duty in his closing argument to fuse empathy and persuasion, shed a tear, quote a poem befitting the facts and the atmosphere in the courtroom. Pat Brinegar, in his brief courtroom appearance, displayed his indomitable courage and irrepressible hope for the future. Henry Woods rose to the occasion and, in a masterful and moving argument, closed with a quote from "Invictus:"

> Out of the night that covers me
> Black as the pit from pole to pole
> I thank whatever gods may be
> for my unconquerable soul.
>
> In the fell clutch of circumstance,
> I have not flinched nor cried aloud;
> Under the bludgeoning of chance,
> My head is bloody but unbowed.

And that is the way Pat Brinegar is. His "head is bloody but unbowed."

APPENDIX III   SAUCE FOR THE GOOSE

We hold these truths to be self-evident that all men are created equal and are endowed by their creator with certain unalienable rights, among these are life, liberty and the pursuit of happiness.

—DECLARATION OF INDEPENDENCE

D. W. Miller was thirty-two years of age, married, and had three children. He was steadily employed and provided well for his family. He had a bright future. He was diligent in his work, but also zealous of quality time with his family. He and Mrs. Miller were active in the PTA. They and the children attended Sunday School and church regularly, and they were supporters of the school's ball teams. They enjoyed picnics and fishing. Those were happy days.

Mrs. Miller's mother would sometimes stay with the children in order that the Millers could have time together or be with friends. The Millers had a good life, but their plans and hopes for the future ended abruptly and tragically on November 16, 1955.

D. W. Miller was a passenger in a Missouri Pacific Transportation Company bus. The driver of the bus was engaged in a conversation with a passenger. He was not keeping a lookout and not watching the direction he was driving. A vehicle swerving across the highway and zigzagging across the road was not seen by him. The vehicle was seen by some of the passengers on the bus. They started shouting, but it was too late. The bus and the vehicle collided head-on.

Miller was severely injured, transported to the hospital by ambulance, where he remained under intensive care for an extensive period. He was rendered a paraplegic.

He had no control of his bodily functions below the waist. He wore a catheter and his bowel movements had to be manually activated. He had to be fed, bathed, and frequently turned in his bed. He was a shadow of his original self.

All the chores now fell on Mrs. Miller. She loved her husband and unselfishly devoted her physical and emotional energies to caring for her paralyzed mate. The wrongful injury of her husband caused her to be converted into a full-time nurse, cook, housekeeper—a scullion. They had had a good life, shared mutual interests, planned and hoped for the future. All of this was destroyed. Their stream of life became stagnant.

Did Mrs. Miller have a remedy for the wrongful deprivation of her husband's services and marriage relationship? Up until this time, the Arkansas courts and the common law "notoriously enveloped the identity of the wife and all her possessions in the personality of her husband." It was a rule that, "the husband and wife are to be regarded as one person." The wife had no remedy under the law to pursue her claim for the loss of consortium—the services and companionship of her husband—against a wrongful offender.

The precepts proclaimed to the world by the American Declaration of Independence and by the Bill of Rights to the Constitution were not automatically implemented for all citizens. The rights of women to come under the protective umbrella of these inspired documents were granted slowly, reluctantly, begrudgingly by the courts. Archibald Yell, governor of Arkansas, in the first legislative session following the state's admission to the Union in 1833, vetoed a bill passed by the legislature granting to women the right to own property. His holding was that to give women the right to own property would undermine the relationship between husband and wife, the husband being the dominant member and head of the household.

Women were not even given the right to vote until 1920 by passage of the Nineteenth Amendment—a century and a half after our Declaration of Independence. The poll tax, as a requirement for voting, used as a means of disenfranchising blacks, women, and poor whites, was not repealed until 1964 by passage of the Twenty-fourth Amendment.

Many women and children were required to work in factories and textile mills twelve hours a day, six days a week, for less than a subsistence wage. In 1936, the Supreme Court of the Untied States held:

> New York minimum wage law for women and minors, forbidding wage which is less than fair and reasonable value of services and less than sufficient to meet minimum cost of living neces-

sary for health, was in violation of the due process clause of the Fourteenth Amendment protecting freedom of contract of the employer.[1]

It was 1943 before the Supreme Court of Missouri held:

> The statute prohibiting employment of females in manufacturing establishments for longer than 9 hours per day or 54 hours per week is unconstitutional as "discriminatory," and as denying employers "due process of law" and "equal protection of the law."[2]

So it was that in 1955 women in Arkansas were denied the same rights under the law accorded to their husbands. The husband had the right, under the law, to recover compensation for wrongful injuries inflicted on his wife that interfered with and damaged their marriage relationship. The wife was denied this crucial right of recovery. Before *Hitaffer vs. Argonne Company, Inc.,*[3] all the courts of this country and England had held that a wife had no standing in court to pursue the cause of action for loss of consortium resulting from negligent injury to her husband. In *Hitaffer,* the court forthrightly overruled this ancient and unjust provision of the common law. The court, quoting a New York case,[4] an enticement case (alienation of affection—right of wife to recover for loss of consortium), stated:

> The modern rule is thus well stated by the Court of Appeals of New York: "The actual injury to the wife from loss of consortium, which is the basis of the action, is the same as the actual injury to the husband from that cause. His right to the conjugal society of his wife is no greater than her right to the conjugal society of her husband. Marriage gives each the same rights in that regard. Each is entitled to the comfort, companionship, and affection of the other. The rights of the one and the obligations of the other spring from the marriage contract, are mutual in character, and attach to the husband as husband and to the wife as wife. Any interference with these rights, whether of the

---

1. *Morehead vs. People of the State of New York et al.,* 50 Supreme Court Reporter 918 (1936).
2. *State vs. Taylor,* 173 S.W.2d 902 (1943).
3. *Hitaffer vs. Argonne Company, Inc.,* 87 U.S.App. D.C. 57, 183 F.2d 811 (1950).
4. *Bennett vs. Bennett,* 116 N.Y. 584, 590, 23 N.E. 17, 6 L.R.A. 553.

husband or to his wife, is a violation, not only of natural right, but also of a legal right arising out of the marriage relation. . . . As the wrongs of the wife are the same in principle, and are caused by acts of the same nature, as those of the husband, the remedy should be the same."

Based upon the ruling of the U.S. Supreme Court in *Hitaffer vs. Argonne,* Mrs. Miller joined with her husband in filing a claim against Missouri Pacific Transportation Company for the wrongful injury he had sustained. Mrs. Miller sought damages for the loss of her husband's comfort, companionship, and services. Circuit judge Elmo Taylor tried the case. He was the same judge who had denied the widow's claim for loss of consortium in *Short vs. Hogan Construction Co.* (see Appendix II). However, in the *Miller* case, Judge Taylor was persuaded to change his opinion. He submitted the issue to the jury. The jury returned a favorable verdict for Mr. Miller for his injuries and for Mrs. Miller for the loss of consortium. At this time, only three other courts in the United States, plus the District of Columbia, had recognized the wife's right to make such a recovery. The Missouri Pacific appealed the judgment. The Supreme Court of Arkansas (Justice Holt dissenting) affirmed the award for Mrs. Miller for the loss of consortium. The court followed a Georgia decision, which had been cited persuasively by my partner, Henry Woods, in his brief and eloquent argument, which held:

It is as much the duty of this court to restore a right which has been erroneously withheld by judicial opinion as it is to recognize it properly in the first instance.

It is appropriate in this day, *when human rights are on the tongues and in the hearts and minds of men, women, and children everywhere, and where the very existence of civilization depends on whether fundamental human rights shall survive, for this court to recognize and enforce this right of a wife, a right based on the sacred relationship of marriage and home. Answering the defendant in error's argument, we do indeed have a "charge to keep," but that* charge is not to perpetuate error or to allow our reasoning or conscience to decay or to turn deaf ears to new light and new life. (Emphasis supplied.)[5]

---

5. *Brown vs. Tennessee Coaches,* 77 S.W. 2d 24).

Thus justice was done. Another advance was made in the courts to achieve for women, under the law, first-class citizenship in our free society.

Other courts have followed *Miller vs. Missouri Pacific*. The Court of Appeals in New York, in the case of *Millington vs. Southeastern Elevator Co.*, stated:

> [T]he concept of consortium includes not only loss of support or services, [but] it also embraces such elements as love, companionship, affection, society, sexual relations, solace and more ... Consequently, the interest sought to be protected is personal to the wife. It is the interest which may have turned a happily married woman into a life-long nurse and deprived her of the opportunity of bearing children ... Disparagingly described as "sentimental" or "parasitic" damages, the mental and emotional anguish caused by seeing a healthy, loving, companionable mate turned into a shell of a person is real enough. To describe the loss as "indirect" is only to evade the issue. The loss of companionship, emotional support, love, felicity and sexual relations are real injuries. The trauma of having to care for a permanent invalid is known to have caused mental illness.[6]

Described in the past as a "parasitic" claim and still regarded today by many plaintiff's attorneys as a "throwaway" element of damage, judges and juries are beginning to recognize the wife's claim as being on an equal basis with the husband's. The plaintiff's lawyer who treats it as a minor element of the damages or as a "throwaway" claim, not to be dwelt upon or emphasized to the jury, is derelict in the representation of his client.

Incidents sometimes occur during a trial that, though having no bearing on the issues involved, are fixed in one's memory. D. W. Miller, following his injury on the Missouri Pacific coach, had an onset of multiple sclerosis. The defendant, Missouri Pacific Transportation Company, contended that multiple sclerosis was a disease and could not be caused by trauma. The treating physician, an eminent neurologist from Memphis, Tennessee, came to Helena, Arkansas, to testify. He stated that based upon his own experience and his research of the

---

6. *Millington vs. Southeastern Elevator Co.*, 22 N.Y.2d 498 (1968).

literature, 15 percent of the cases of multiple sclerosis were caused by injury and, in his opinion, the most probable cause of Mr. Miller's paralysis was the trauma he sustained in the accident. The doctor was excused following his testimony.

I had just completed direct examination of another witness when the bailiff approached the counsel table, where Henry Woods and I were seated. He had an urgent message from the doctor, who was in the hall outside the courtroom and wanted to see me. Henry went out to see the doctor and to appease his anxiety. Henry soon returned and announced to me that the doctor wanted his fee of five hundred dollars for his time and expense and he wanted it now. In 1956, when our law practice was just getting underway, five hundred dollars was a lot of money and we didn't have it. Nevertheless, to oblige the doctor and to be able to continue our case without a disturbance, we wrote him a check. At the first recess, we called our partner, Leland Leatherman, and asked him to cover the check. The check was honored when presented.

Mrs. Miller won a victory for women's rights in Arkansas and set a precedent for other states to follow. She proved that an ancient right, long withheld, can be made viable by a trial lawyer in a court of law.

Mrs. Miller's victory further illustrates that a jury, given the facts and correctly instructed on the law, will do justice—and justice for all citizens, including women and children, of all races, is the hallmark of an enduring, civilized country.

APPENDIX IV ⌒ A SUBSEQUENT SHOCK SHOWS HOW: ADMISSIBILITY

Richard Lee Johnson, age thirty, in 1976 was found dead on the job. No apparent cause of his death could be found. The death of this young man, who left a surviving wife and young child, was a complete mystery. Mrs. Johnson, following the death of her husband, could not bring herself to dispose of his clothes he was wearing when he died. This clothing, along with a pair of shoes, was stored in the family garage. In the course of the investigation, the existence of the deceased's clothing was discovered. In an intensive interview with Mrs. Johnson, the clothing was obtained, examined, and the pair of socks and shoes which Mr. Johnson had been wearing told a tragic story.

Richard Lee Johnson, a painter by trade, was found dead on the flat roof of a building where he had been working. His body lay under a high-voltage power line. A twenty-two-foot aluminum ladder that he had been using was lying nearby. There were no burns on the ladder, power line, or Johnson's body to indicate contact with electric current. He was survived by a widow and one small child.

Mr. Johnson and other members of a crew had painted a building with one coat of paint and had begun the second coat, with Johnson repeating the work he had done in applying the first coat. They were working on a flat roof of the building. The wall of the building ran north and south. Parallel to the wall and twenty feet above the flat roof was an Arkansas Power and Light Company primary conductor carrying high-voltage electricity. There were no trees or anything in the vicinity to obscure a view of the wires. The weather was clear on the day of the accident.

Mr. Johnson was using an aluminum ladder extended to twenty-two feet and an electric spray painting machine. Working with him was Robert Cochran, another painter. The two had painted along the west side of the building, going from north to south. While Mr. Cochran went down to the ground to get more paint, Mr. Johnson picked up the ladder, holding it vertically, and proceeded south with the ladder to go around the corner of the second level of the building.

While on the ground, Mr. Cochran heard Mr. Johnson make a groaning noise. He ran around the building and up a ladder to the flat roof. When he arrived, Mr. Johnson was lying on the roof on his back at the south side of the building. The aluminum ladder had fallen and was hanging from the side of the building, tangled in telephone lines. There were no burn marks on the ladder or on any of the high-voltage power line wires. There were no burns on Mr. Johnson's hands nor any indication that Mr. Johnson had come into contact with the power line.

When Mr. Cochran arrived, Mr. Johnson was breathing irregularly. Artificial respiration was given, but he died shortly thereafter. An autopsy was performed. Blood alcohol examination indicated a .06 percent weight volume. The autopsy finding was myocardial ischemia with early myocardial necrosis. The secondary diagnosis was fatty degeneration of the liver, severe, associated with early cirrhosis of the liver; the third, pulmonary congestion, acute; and the fourth, status postoperative fracture of the skull and craniotomy: (a) plastic cranial plate left frontal bone, and (b) focal cordical encephalomalacia.

The medical examiner testified that he had examined the body for markings and found a pale, brownish-yellow unbiligated lesion on the right foot at the base of the little toe. The examiner considered this lesion a wart. He testified:

> For a period of a couple of years, I did have a good deal of doubt in my mind as to what had actually happened to Mr. Johnson and as to what might have caused his death. I did think initially that this was a wart on his toe. On the initial slide that I examined, I did not see features that I would associate with an electrical mark.

Two years after Mr. Johnson's death, evidence was discovered which caused the medical examiner to recheck his findings.

In the process of investigating the case, we discovered that approximately two months after the death of Richard Johnson, Earl Looper, a roofer, working with a twenty-two-foot aluminum ladder and moving around the southern corner of the roof of the same building (the identical spot where Mr. Johnson had been working) received a severe electrical shock that rendered him unconscious. Fortunately, Looper survived. There were no electrical marks on the power line or on the aluminum ladder. Nor were there electrical burns on Looper's hands. Having discovered this subsequent shock incident, we reviewed the autopsy findings with the state medical examiner. He had kept the slides he had made of the lesion on Johnson's right little toe. Upon our request, he went back to the lab and made a minute microscopic examination of the slides. The state medical examiner testified as to his findings:

> It was only in the last few months that I did what is known as step section. That is take a section and cut it deeper all the way through the entire lesion and then we have about ten or fifteen slides to look at. It was only on the fourth or fifth slide of this step section that I began to see what I associate with an electrical burn. I am convinced that what was on the right toe was evidence of some kind of electrical burn.

When we first learned of the medical examiner's "step section" tests and his conclusion that the lesion was, in fact, an electrical burn, we began a search for Richard Johnson's shoes and socks. The medical examiner no longer had them. Perhaps they had been thrown away. However, there was a possibility that they had been returned to the family. We contacted Mrs. Johnson. Her husband's personal effects, including the clothing he was wearing at the time of his death, had been returned to her. She would search for them. As fortune would have it, she could not bear to discard the bag containing her husband's clothing, so she placed it in a closet, where it had remained. She retrieved the shoes and socks. We submitted them to the medical examiner. The right shoe had small perforated holes in the area of the little toe. One of the socks had a burned hole which corresponded to the hole in the shoe. These facts, plus the minute examination of the lesion section slides and the subsequent injury of Earl Looper, persuaded the medical examiner to reach the conclusion that Richard Johnson's death was due to electrocution.

We also called Dr. J. T. Francisco, a noted pathologist in Memphis, Tennessee, as a witness. He testified that in his opinion Richard

Johnson's death was caused by contact with a high-powered electrical current. His conclusion was based upon two main factors:

> No. 1, no recognizable or identifiable cause of death is present in the autopsy examination, such as stroke, heart attack or things of that nature. Secondly, the finding of the very characteristic burn that is present on the skin. This type of burn is different from the ordinary thermal burn, such as one you get from a hot coal or stove or something of that nature, primarily because the electrical current as it passes into or out of a body produces very rapidly and very quickly an extreme degree of heat at the point at which it either enters or leaves the body. Now this extreme degree of heat literally cooks the tissue; cooks the point of the skin in a very characteristic manner.

Dr. Francisco blew up the slides and used those to demonstrate his findings to the jury:

> The bottom of the slide is in fact the top of the skin, the keratin layer. The clear areas that are present are actually bubbles of fluid in which the high heat produced by the electrical current has boiled away the water from inside the cells and deposited it between the cells and the keratin layers, so that each one of these lakes is in fact a form of blister on the surface of the skin produced by the passage of this very high heat-producing current through the skin.[1]

To show that Richard Johnson's death was caused by a high-voltage current of electricity, we also offered in evidence the testimony of Earl Looper, relating how at the same place where Richard Johnson's body had been found, in an effort to maneuver a twenty-two-foot aluminum ladder around the corner of the building in close proximity to the power lines, as Richard Johnson had done, he received a severe shock which rendered him unconscious. Looper's testimony was offered to show causation and the existence of a hazardous condition. The trial court, Circuit Judge Tom Digby, overruled the power company's objection to this evidence.

The jury returned a substantial verdict for the widow and children of Richard Johnson.

---

1. For the direct examination of Dr. Francisco, see Scott Baldwin, *Art of Advocacy* (New York: M. Bender, 1981).

The power company appealed the verdict on two grounds:

1. that the admissibility of Earl Looper's testimony was an error; and

2. that the power company, having established that it had complied with the National Electrical Code regarding the installation and maintenance of the power lines, was, as a matter of law, entitled to a directed verdict.

The Supreme Court of Arkansas held that since the power company had stipulated that the conditions at the accident scene were the same at the time of trial as at the time of Richard Johnson's death, the trial court did not abuse its discretion in admitting the subsequent accident as proof of what had happened to Richard Johnson.

The court further held that even though the power company had complied with the standards set forth by the National Electrical Code, these were minimum standards, and there were circumstances and conditions under which a higher standard in construction and maintenance of the power lines should be observed. The court held that the jury could have found that in this case, the power company's failure to meet higher standards than those required by the National Electrical Code was a violation of the standard of care to which power companies are held in the transmission of high-powered electrical currents.[2]

This case had to be tried twice. The jury in both trials returned substantially the same amount of money. In the first trial, the jury had returned an award solely for the benefit of the estate. Richard Johnson had been killed instantly and experienced no pain and suffering, and the expenses related to his death were nominal. The jury had clearly intended that this sum of money go to the widow and children. The verdict in the first trial was set aside by the trial judge, and a new trial granted, resulting in an award for the widow and children of Richard Johnson.

A lesson to be learned by trial lawyers: when discussing with the jury the various elements of damages which are being claimed and in discussing answers to interrogatories[3] with jurors, we need to be care-

---

2. *Arkansas Power & Light Co. vs. Johnson*, 260 Ark. 237, 538 S.W.2d 541, 546 (1976) (Special Judge Walter Niblock).

3. Questions submitted to the jury by the court to determine the jury's finding of facts in the case.

ful, thorough, and explicit, in order that the jury may not be confused about what they are required to do. In the first trial, we clearly had failed to explain to the jury how the damages, should they find for the plaintiff, should be allocated.

An example of how interrogatories may confuse a jury is a case which we tried in Dardanelle, Arkansas. The case had been submitted to the jury on interrogatories. The jury, after a long time, knocked on the door and had the bailiff deliver a message to the court that they had a question. The judge thereupon had the jury brought in and lined up in front of the jury box. He demanded to know what the problem was. The foreman responded: "Your Honor, we are confused over these interrogatories. We know a lawyer across the river in Russellville. Could we have him come over here and explain them to us?" We had failed to explain to the jury the meaning of the interrogatories they would be required to answer. In self-defense, nobody understood these interrogatories, not even the judge.

APPENDIX V⧁ GUNS DON'T KILL: FLEEING FUGITIVES DO

Daniel Lon Graham, on June 1, 1971, escaped from the state penitentiary where he was serving a life sentence for kidnaping and murder. On June 18th, Graham robbed a grocery store in Springdale, Arkansas. He kidnaped three young men who were clerking in the store, two of them college students working part-time. He drove them to a remote area, explaining that he was taking them out in the country so they would have to walk to a telephone, giving him an opportunity to escape. Upon reaching an isolated wooded area, he required each of the young men to leave the car and lie face down on the ground under the headlights of the vehicle. He then proceeded to shoot each of the victims in the back of the head. Only one survived.

The Code of Federal Regulations requires:

> A licensed dealer shall not sell any firearm or ammunition to any person, knowing or having reasonable cause to believe that such person; (1) is under indictment or has been convicted in any court of a crime punishable by imprisonment for a term exceeding one year; or (2) is a fugitive from justice.
>
> Prior to making an over-the-counter transfer of a firearm, the licensed dealer shall obtain a form 4473 from the transferee, showing name, address, date and place of birth, height, weight and race of the transferee, and the certification by the transferee that he has not been convicted of a felony and is not a fugitive from justice.
>
> Before transferring a firearm, the licensee shall cause the transferee to identify himself in any manner customarily used in commercial transactions, e.g., a driver's license, and shall note on the form the method used and, if satisfied that the transferee is lawfully entitled to receive the firearm, the transferee shall sign and date the form.[1]

---

1. Code Federal Regulations, ch. 27, sec. 178.99(c) and 178.23(c).

The day before, Daniel Lon Graham had gone into the Western Auto Supply store in Rogers, Arkansas, owned and operated by Marion Bunyard, late on the afternoon of June 17 near closing time. He informed the clerk on duty that he wanted to buy a washer and dryer. After making this purchase, he asked if the store had an old pistol he could use to shoot coyotes that were catching his chickens. He was shown a used pistol, which he purchased along with a box of ammunition. The clerk began filling out the required gun transfer form and asked Graham for his driver's license. Graham said he didn't have his driver's license with him; it was in his billfold at home. He said he had been bush-hogging that day and had just gotten off the tractor. He said he came to town to buy the washer and dryer as a surprise for his wife who was returning from California. He informed the clerk that he would give him the driver's license when the washer and dryer were delivered. Graham told the clerk where to deliver the merchandise, gave him a check for four hundred dollars on a local bank, and left the store with the gun and ammunition. He first gave his name to the clerk who was filling out the transfer form as Jim Shaw, and later on in the course of the conversation, he told him his name was Bill Shaw. The clerk noted that Graham had a hard time explaining where to deliver the washer and dryer.

On June 18, Western Auto Supply made an attempt to deliver the washer and dryer, but there was no such address. They called the bank on which the check had been drawn and were told there was no such account. Thereupon, one of the employees of Western Auto proceeded to fill out the firearms transaction record, forging the name "Bill Shaw." Marion Bunyard, president and majority shareholder of Bunyard Supply Company, d/b/a Western Auto, certified the transaction to be lawful and executed the transfer document as required.

Jo Anne Franco, widow of Gene A. Franco, deceased, one of Graham's victims, filed a lawsuit on behalf of herself, their children, and her husband's estate against Bunyard Supply Company, Inc., and Western Auto Supply Company. The defendants filed a motion with the court asking that the widow's claim be dismissed on the grounds that they were not responsible for her husband's death.

The circuit judge in whose jurisdiction the case had been filed granted the defendants' motion to dismiss the widow's case. The judge ruled that Graham's criminal use of the gun was an "intervening efficient cause" of Gene Franco's death, not foreseeable by the seller.

We appealed the summary judgment entered by the trial judge to the Arkansas Supreme Court on behalf of Jo Anne Franco. We contended that the violation of the federal gun control law was evidence of negligence and that the criminal act of Graham, a convicted felon and a fugitive from justice, was foreseeable. We further contended that when Congress passed the Federal Gun Control Act, it was concerned with the widespread traffic in firearms and the ease with which they could be obtained by criminals and others not legally entitled to possess them. The principal agent in the scheme of federal enforcement of the law is the licensed dealer, who is required to keep records and is criminally liable for negligently placing lethal weapons in the hands of criminals.

The Supreme Court of Arkansas found that the regulations issued under the Gun Control Act required the dealer, before making an over-the-counter delivery of a firearm, to complete the firearm transaction record, providing the essential information which the form required. Justice George Rose Smith, writing for the court, commented that Graham, when he purchased the gun, had no wallet, no money, no driver's license, no identification of any kind, gave a worthless check for the washer, dryer, and gun in the sum of four hundred dollars, was allowed to leave the store with the pistol without even signing the required form, and that the form was filled out the next day after it was learned that the store had been duped. There were, of course, omissions in the form as filled out, such as Graham's driver's license number. Again, according to McDaniel (the store clerk), he forged the name that Graham had given (Bill Shaw). Marion Bunyard signed the required certification that "it is my belief that it is not unlawful for me to sell . . . the firearm" to the purchaser.

Passing on the defendants' contention that the criminal act of Graham was an independent intervening cause of Jo Anne Franco's loss, the court held:

> . . . [I]t is enough to point out that the tragedies could not have occurred as they did if the federal rules had been obeyed. That is, Graham had no means of identification—an essential prerequisite to the purchase of a gun. This is not, as the appellees argue, a mere matter of record keeping. Form 4473 required the

seller to obtain and record Graham's identification before handing over the gun. Graham had no identification. Thus, had the law been obeyed, he could not have obtained possession of the gun and could not have used it to shoot innocent men the next day. On the issue of foreseeability, we need say only that the very purpose of the law is to keep pistols out of the hands of such persons as Graham, who was both a convicted criminal and a fugitive from justice. It certainly cannot be said that his use of the gun in such a way as to injure others was not foreseeable. Of course, it is not required that the precise sequence of events leading to the injury be foreseeable.[2]

Following the Supreme Court's decision, the case was remanded to the circuit court of Washington County for a jury trial. The case was then settled and a recovery made for widow and children of Gene Franco for his wrongful death.

"Each year, 639,000 Americans are confronted by criminals armed with handguns. More than 24,000 are murdered or wounded in these encounters."[3]

One essential deterrent to this mass slaughter by lethal weapons is to require that the supplier be held liable for damages foreseeably caused by the wrongful transfer of guns to murderers, fugitives, and dope dealers. This cause of action is frequently overlooked by lawyers in cases involving violent crimes. In such cases, the first fact question to be answered is: "How did the assailant get the gun that set in motion the tragic occurrence?"

The lethal weapon used in this case to kill two young men, two of them college students, and to cause severe and permanent injuries to another, was sold to a fugitive, a felon, in violation of the gun control law.

The purpose and intent of the gun control regulations are to prevent deadly weapons from being passed into the hands of felons, fugitives, dope addicts, and the insane who foreseeably will use these weapons to maim and murder innocent people.

---

2. *Franco vs. Bunyard et al.*, 261 Ark. 144, 547 S.W.2d 791.

3. Associated with me in *Franco* was Sen. John Lile of Springdale, Arkansas. John Curtin Jr., "Gun Control: The Time Is Now," *American Bar Association Journal* (July 1991).

APPENDIX VI ↪ ADVERTISEMENTS THAT PREY: NEGLIGENT INDUCEMENT

On September 22, 1978, at 1:00 A.M., Jo Ann Fitzsimmons was a young, beautiful, vivacious teenager, a high school graduate, with all the hopes, aspirations, and dreams with which young womanhood is naturally endowed. At 1:20 A.M., Jo Ann's life of promise had turned to ashes. She was a quadriplegic.

> Advertised Products—1978 Pontiac Firebird Trans Am—Death of two youngsters and quadriplegic injuries to another when Trans Am went out of control at 100 m.p.h.—Plaintiffs achieve successful settlement invoking concept of "invited misuse" by the manufacturer. Plaintiffs' employment of psychodynamics of subliminal advertising—plaintiffs' theory: Encouraged misuse is no defense . . . [1]

Andrew (Andy) Wright, age eighteen, with some of his friends, had seen a movie entitled *Smokey and the Bandit* starring Burt Reynolds. In the movie, Reynolds was a point man for an illicit eighteen-wheeler load of alcoholic beverages being illegally transported across several southern states. In a Pontiac Trans Am automobile, he decoyed and lured inquisitive state troopers, high sheriffs and their deputies, on a wild goose chase over country roads and detours. Stunt men stood in for Burt Reynolds and performed the maneuvers. They did the 180° donuts, jumped across a river where the bridge was out, and led the pursuing state troopers, high sheriffs and their deputies on a merry chase. Thus, the Trans Am automobile was a co-star in *Smokey and the Bandit*. A General Motors scriptwriter with a veteran's advertising eye wrote a letter approving the *Smokey* script. In the letter he stated:

---

1. For a penetrating analysis of the case of *Fitzsimmons vs. General Motors*, and poignant comments on negligent inducement, see Tom Lambert, "Tom on Torts," *ATLA Reporter* 24 (1978): 198. Lead counsel for Jo Ann Fitzsimmons, plaintiff, was Sandy S. McMath, McMath Law Firm, P.A., Little Rock, Arkansas.

·

This special edition of Trans Am is a standout—a hero in every scene. The end result should be an exciting motion picture-length commercial for our Pontiac.[2]

Pontiac's advertising manager testified in a deposition that:

Trans Am buyers are 80% males, younger buyers than for any other car in the United States; only 697 Trans Ams were sold in 1969, the car's first season. Ten years later, after the "Smokey and the Bandit" series, the sales climbed to 187,285 vehicles.[3]

Andy Wright and his friends had seen *Smokey and the Bandit* several times. The Trans Am was a star performer. When Andy went to the local car dealer, they had an advertising clip from *Smokey and the Bandit*; his desire for a Trans Am was keenly whetted. He simply had to have one. He pleaded with his mother until on August 23, 1978, she bought one for him.

On September 22, 1978, the month after Andy Wright's mother bought his Trans Am, he attended several parties following the high school football games. Accompanying him on his round of parties in his "iridescent blue Trans Am" were his high school buddies, Allen Wright, age eighteen (no relation to Andrew), and Scott Cox, age seventeen. They had some drinks and passed around some marijuana joints. The hour was late, and they offered to drive Jo Ann Fitzsimmons home. Andy decided that the time was right to "test the Trans Am" and experience the soaring speed of the Firebird. As it ripped down the state road, Arkansas Highway 88, at a speed in excess of one hundred miles an hour, the Trans Am "piloted" by Andy Wright hit a railroad crossing and took to the air. The car flew across the double tracks, flipping out of control for 535 feet. It grazed one culvert, caught the second one more squarely and was converted "into a huge airborne top," spinning across a ditch as it shed the two glass panels in its T-top roof. As it spun along a stand of trees, one tree caved in the rear roof of the Trans Am, crushing Jo Ann Fitzsimmon's spine and leaving her a quadriplegic. The result: Andy Wright, dead; Scott Cox, dead; Allen Wright, injured; Jo Ann Fitzsimmons, brain damaged and paralyzed.

---

2. See record transcript, *Fitzsimmons vs. General Motors.*
3. *Fitzsimmons vs. General Motors.*

The plaintiffs brought action against General Motors Corporation to recover for the wrongful death of Scott Cox and for the injuries and brain damage suffered by Jo Ann Fitzsimmons. The action was based upon negligent inducement and strict product liability. The negligence claims alleged:

1. GM designed and manufactured and marketed a vehicle, a street racer, with a speed performance capability in excess of 130 m.p.h. on public highways when it had reason to know that vehicles so designed could not be safely operated at such speeds . . .

5. The dangerous speed at which the ill-fated car was driven at the time of the fatal crash was a foreseeable response of a youthful driver to the stimulus of GM's promotional advertising of the Trans Am, designed to encourage high speed driving by risk-prone and inexperienced youthful drivers.

The plaintiffs were able to prove that General Motors' Pontiac Division followed a planned, systematic course of action to identify target customers that would be most attracted to the Trans Am Firebird, a sporty, street-racing car. A psychological profile was compiled by the marketing division of General Motors. Robert Bierley, director of market studies, General Motors Corp., testified by deposition:

Q: Do you have any social scientists on your staff? . . . sociologists, psychiatrists, psychologists?

A: The answer to that is yes . . .

Q: Would you name for me an individual in your department with a psychology degree?

A: Myself.

Q: . . . have you caused to be compiled a psychological profile of the purchasers of a given product?

A: It depends. What do you mean by psychological profile?

Q: But you do, do you not, seek to identify from a psychological standpoint the demographic type of individual who would more likely than not purchase, say . . . a Firebird?

A: No, we don't try to determine it. We just measure it . . .

Q: And then this information is fed into the computer from these questionnaires?

A: Right . . .

Q: So then the demographic data that we are talking about is retrieved by the individual division, such as in this case, Pontiac, whenever they need it?

A: Yes, they can retrieve it, we can retrieve it or anybody else can retrieve it who has access to the system . . .

Q: A major user of the information compiled by your department are the advertising departments of these various Merchandising Divisions, are they not?

A: Yeah, I'd say some of the information is used by the ad agencies.

The psychological profile prepared by the marketing division was turned over to the Pontiac advertising department for evaluation. The advertising manager, Christine Meyers Adamski, testified to the information obtained:

Q: Do you recall any of the demographic information on the Trans Am?

A: Yes . . . it was skewed heavily towards males, you know, maybe 75, 80, maybe more, 80 percent males, young, and not particularly up-scale.

Q: [The] purpose of soliciting this information, this demographic information, is so that the advertisements can be tailored to the group of persons in the general public who are expected to buy the car?

A: Right.

Harold D. Bay, president, D'Arcy, McManus and Masius, the agency that handled Pontiac Motor Division's advertising, testified:

Q: I will read to you a portion of the paragraph on p. 13 of [Firebird TransAm, a report by Ms. Jill Rogers, Supervisor, Public Relations, Pontiac Motor Division, General Motors Corp.]: 'According to Pontiac Motor Division's General Sales Manager, the key to the growing popularity of the Trans Am in 1977 was its appeal to the youth market. The average age of its buyers was slightly over 28, which was the youngest age for any car buyer sold in the United States, foreign or domestic markets.

Would you say that was a reasonably accurate statement?

A: Yes.

General Motors proceeded to collaborate with the film company in making *Smokey and the Bandit*. J. R. Graham, director of merchandising for Pontiac, wrote in a letter to J. G. Vorhes, August 2, 1976:

> I have read the revised script [*Smokey and the Bandit*] which was furnished to me by Universal under date of July 29. The screenplay is filled with exciting chase sequences. The Special Edition Trans Am is a *stand out hero* in every scene; the end result should be a full length motion picture which will be an exciting motion picture length commercial for Pontiac. In my opinion, this is an excellent exposure and an extremely worthwhile investment. (Emphasis added.)

General Motors spliced *Smokey and the Bandit* into a commercial film and distributed it to its Pontiac dealers where it was shown to prospective youthful customers. *Smokey and the Bandit* was shown at theaters in Benton, Arkansas. The commercial film shown by the automobile dealers, tailored by General Motors to display the speed and maneuverability of the Trans Am Firebird, was a continuous attraction to youngsters in the Benton community. Andy Wright saw both films.

Johnny Roberts, sales manager, Paul Jones Pontiac, Benton, Arkansas, testified:

> Q: In connection with the sales of the Firebirds at the dealership in Benton, a videotape commercial film narrated by Mr. Hal Needham was shown to prospective purchasers, was it not?
>
> A: Yes, it was.
>
> Q: This film was shown to Mr. Andrew Wright, was it not?
>
> A: Yes. It was shown by me to Andy Wright.
>
> Q: In fact, it was customary there for many of the young people in town to come by the agency and ask to see the film.
>
> A: Yes, because of the publicity that the film clips of the movies that were circulating at the time . . . we had film clips of those movies, and it was something to watch there.
>
> Q: I believe in a previous conversation with me you stated that

"Even the little bitty kids knew we had it and would come down and want to see it."

A: Right.

Q: The film "Smokey and the Bandit" attracted quite a few customers right there in Benton, did it not?

A: Yes, it was quite a turnout there.

Q: In your statement of February 9, 1979, you stated, "Oh yeah, shoot! There was people lined up for a block down there. It sold a lot of Trans Ams."

A: Yes, it did.

Needham, a veteran stunt driver, narrated the General Motors advertising film. In the film, during one of the more hair-raising gyrations of the vehicle, accompanied by hairpin turns and squealing brakes, he narrates:

> You know, one of the things about being a stunt man is to get behind the wheel of a car that responds. Now, this don't mean that I recommend you go out and do stunts, but I do recommend that you test drive a 1979 Firebird, and I'll tell you why. If you don't test it, you will never know what I am talking about when I speak of handling and maneuverability—try one!

Needham did not explain to the viewer of the GM Trans Am film the dangers of emulating the daredevil driving depicted in the movie—that safety equipment such as roll bars or roll cages were installed in the cars used for stunts, that each stunt was carefully planned and prepared before it was filmed. Nor did he warn prospective youthful customers, as he did when he gave his deposition in the Fitzsimmons case: "They are flirting with the undertaker if they go out and try and emulate a jump or any of these stunts. They are most likely going to kill their fool selves."

General Motors' defense against the allegations of the plaintiffs was that Andy Wright's misuse of the Firebird was not foreseeable. In other words, they adopted the automobile industry's traditional defense approach in crash-worthiness cases and "tried the kids."

The plaintiffs contended that GM made a Trans Am movie of its own, spliced together from *Smokey and the Bandit* and *Hooper,* purportedly to be used for the information and education of the Pontiac dealers, but in fact, intended to be used primarily to induce and ensnare young drivers.

Dr. Milton Rokeach, professor of psychology, Washington State University, and dean of psychologists in the United States, having reviewed the films *Smokey and the Bandit* and *Hooper* and the commercial film tailored by General Motors for their Pontiac dealers, and having read the depositions in *Fitzsimmons vs. General Motors,* testified by deposition:

Q: Dr. Rokeach, were you able (after reviewing the depositions, the films, and making the tests you described) to reach certain conclusions?

A: Yes, I was.

Q: And would you, please, tell us what those conclusions were?

A: Well, I think the best way to answer you is to once again refer to my six points. And, in that context, respond to each of these six questions.

Q: All right, sir, if you would.

A: I concluded, first of all, that a very sophisticated psychological strategy was being employed in the promotional materials for the Trans Am automobile. No question about it in my mind that the people who were doing this knew what they were doing and that they were doing it in what would surely be called a professional manner.

Secondly, the psychological strategy I identified as being one in which there was a focus on the beliefs, attitudes, and values of targeted groups and individuals. An analysis of what these beliefs, attitudes, and values were and then the tailoring of promotional material—whether or not they were advertisements, I don't know in the technical sense. I'm calling them promotional material. The tailoring of all this promotional material to—to gratify, to be compatible with, to be congruent with the beliefs, attitudes and values of target audiences.

Fourth—thirdly. Thirdly, I concluded that a particular subset of the American population, indeed, had been targeted. And I identified this subset or segment as being a group of post adolescent males with a—a macho orientation. And, moreover, I concluded that the particular personality syndrome of this post adolescent segment would be characterized as one that has psychopathic predispositions.

Fourthly, I concluded, moreover, that this particular subset or segment of the American consumer population was being induced by the Trans Am promotional material that I reviewed. It was induced to use the product in a lethal, unsafe, and dangerous manner.

Fifthly, I concluded that the strategies, the techniques that were being employed were not in accord with ethical professional standards and could not conceivably be in accord with such standards.

And, finally I concluded that it was, indeed, possible to verify whether or not the opinions and conclusions that I have just described can, indeed, be independently verified by scientific and objective means. And, by the way, I might point out that, as a scientist, I always worry about whether my opinions can be verified or whether they're just nothing more than opinions. So I always look for ways of independently checking myself out.

It was this film of *Smokey and the Bandit,* endorsed and supported by General Motors, and the tailored version of the film that the sales agent showed to Andy Wright, that induced this young man, in the exuberance of a victory celebrating round of parties, to "test" the Trans Am and demonstrate to his friends and to Jo Ann Fitzsimmons what this inherently dangerous instrumentality of the road could do.

Some product manufacturers, in a highly competitive business, hire market researchers and advertising agents, as well as psychologists and epidemiological experts, to target prospective customers: young people, females, minorities, blacks. The object is to entice the prospective customers into the belief that fame, fortune, success, and sexual conquest are dependent upon the use of their special brand or product. This technique is not new. Most Americans living today, those who have not died of lung cancer, can recall the early tobacco ads—"Reach for a Lucky instead of a sweet"; "not a cough in a carload"; the successful ball player, the idol of the youth of America, extolling Red Rooster snuff, Red Man tobacco, or Granger Twist.

Gin, vodka, whiskey, and beer dealers construct their ads around high romance, adventure, and success with the opposite sex. One brewery exceeded all ethical advertising standards. Targeting young black males, it adopted the brand name "Power Master" for a high alcoholic content malt liquor.

Some companies select euphemistic brand names to entice the customer. If the name of the company is "The Golden Rule Insurance Company," one might check the fine print in the policy. If the company sells tampons under the brand name "Security," one might check the records for the occurrence of toxic shock related to the use of the product in young women.

All of this is looked upon as part of the free enterprise system. At one time, drummers and salesmen, with their samples and satchel, traveled the railroads, through the towns and villages of America. Now, the ads are piped into the living rooms and into the schools via television advertising. Companies have an inherent right to sell their products. Advertising and salesmanship make the economy go. However, there are bounds beyond which manufacturers and vendors of products should not be permitted to pass without being accountable in tort (personal injury), in a court of law, for the damages which proximately ensue. As in the tragic case of Jo Ann Fitzsimmons, paralyzed and imprisoned for life by her injuries, "dangerous driving should be no defense for an auto manufacturer whose promotional advertising has encouraged or invited such expectable misuse by youthful drivers, who, as enthusiasts of daring driving, were special targets of defendant's aggressive advertising."[4] During the course of the trial, Jo Ann Fitzsimmons's case was settled in her behalf. Funds were obtained to provide for her care for life.

This concept of negligent inducement established in the Jo Ann Fitzsimmons case became a precedent, which ultimately was used in suits against the tobacco companies who had laced their products with increasing amounts of nicotine and targeted young people in their advertising campaign.

Sandy McMath, lead counsel in Fitzsimmons, advocated this theory of liability as a means of recovering from tobacco companies funds expended by the states in the medical treatment of tobacco victims. The

---

4. Tom Lambert, "Tom on Torts," *ATLA Reporter* 24 (1978): 198.

results in the Fitzsimmons case and its applicability to suits against the tobacco companies was submitted to the attorney general of Arkansas, July 17, 1991, in a letter in which McMath stated:

> The enormous profits of the tobacco companies, who leave addicts in their wake, to be cared for by the taxpayers, make a compelling contrast to the relative penury of a poor State like Arkansas.
>
> In a way, it could be said that the Arkansas taxpayer has become a vassal of the tobacco companies who forced our citizens to yield an annual tribute in payment of medical bills for diseased addicts, while the companies themselves gross ever-increasing billions of dollars in profit.
>
> The cost to the taxpayers for the treatment of lung cancer alone, according to the estimates of the University of Arkansas Medical Science, Department of Pharmacology is 25 million dollars per year.

Other states were urged to take action against the tobacco companies. Writing in *Health Span,* McMath wrote:

> *Tobacco companies should be vigorously and relentlessly pursued for the 25–30% of indigent care costs resulting from the use of their inherently hazardous products.* (Emphasis added.)[5]

States have brought suit against the tobacco companies and made recoveries. The attorney general for the state of Minnesota, in May of 1998, settled the state's claim against the tobacco companies for *6.6 billion dollars.*

Arkansas filed suit against the tobacco companies in 1998. The case is now settled. Hopefully, Arkansas will be similarly reimbursed.

---

5. Sid McMath, *Health Span* 10, 7 (August 1993).

APPENDIX VII ⟋ JUSTICE WEEPS: A PETITION FOR REDRESS

It is as much the duty of the government to render prompt justice against itself in favor of citizens, as it is to administer the same between private individuals . . .

—ABRAHAM LINCOLN

Lance McNeely was a quadriplegic from injuries he received when he dove into the water to rescue a drowning comrade at a designated recreational area owned by the government and operated by the United States Corps of Engineers. Three other young men had received similar injuries when they dove into the water at the same place.

McNeely filed a claim against the government under the provisions of the Federal Tort Claims Act passed by Congress in 1948.

The United States district judge, after an extensive hearing and having visited the scene where the young men's injuries had occurred, rendered a judgment for McNeely.

The trial judge found that the Corps of Engineers was guilty of "conscious indifference to consequences from which malice must be implied."

The government appealed. The United States Eighth Circuit Court of Appeals reversed the trial judge's judgment, stating that McNeely's injuries were caused by floods and flood waters and hence barred by the Flood Control Act of 1928.

The United States Circuit Courts in the Fifth and Ninth Districts had ruled in similar cases that the Flood Control Act of 1928 did not bar recovery, that these cases should be heard under the provisions of the Federal Tort Claims Act of 1948.

Customarily and desirably when there is a division in the United States circuit courts on a significant issue of law, the United States Supreme Court should resolve and clarify the law.

McNeely petitioned the United States Supreme Court to review his case and determine the intent of Congress on this vital issue.

The United States Supreme Court declined to review McNeely's case.

Having exhausted his remedies of law, McNeely petitioned the Congress through his representative whose district included the recreational area where McNeely and the other three young men had been injured.

The Honorable Bill Alexander
House of Representatives
233 Cannon House Office Building
Washington, D.C. 20515

Re: William Lance McNeely

Dear Congressman:

You are a very busy man. Many demands are being made for your time and attention. The coming session of Congress will be engrossed with the prospects of war, the budget, the inflation, recession, aid to the emerging democracies in Europe, and food for the Russian people. However, we never become too busy to right a wrong, redress a grievance, or to see that justice is done.

Yours sincerely,
Sidney S. McMath

In this spirit, and in order that the government might be just, as well as sovereign, the Congress of the United States in 1948, passed the Federal Tort Claims Act (Title 28, U.S.C. §2674), providing that:

The United States shall be liable, respecting the provisions of this title relating to tort claims, in the same manner and to the same extent as a private individual under like circumstances, but shall not be liable for interest prior to judgment or for punitive damages . . .

The United States Corps of Engineers, in addition to the navigational and flood control projects promulgated by Congress, has assumed an additional obligation of providing recreational activities in conjunction with its mandated mission.

"Rules and Regulations Governing Public Use of Corps of Engineers Water Resources Development Projects," Section 327.1, provides:

> *Policy.* It is the policy of the Secretary of the Army, acting through the Chief of Engineers, to manage the natural, cultural and developed resources of each project in the public interest, providing the public with safe and healthful recreational opportunities while protecting and enhancing these resources.

In pursuit of its recreational policy, the Corps of Engineers, Little Rock District, appointed a recreational officer to supervise recreational facilities under the jurisdiction of the Corps of Engineers in the Little Rock District. In the pursuit of carrying out its policies for providing recreational activities, the Corps of Engineers built Merrisach Lake Park, and, as an inducement to citizens to come and use the park, they constructed a swimming area at the Merrisach Lake Park in Arkansas County.

Four young men, using the designated swimming area at Merrisach Lake and diving from the retaining wall, received severe spinal cord injuries. Three are paraplegics.

William Lance McNeely, aged nineteen years, in an attempt to rescue a friend, dove from the retaining wall and fractured his cervical spine. He is a paraplegic. McNeely filed a claim against the government under the Federal Tort Claims Act. The case was heard by the Honorable Bruce Van Sickle, United States district judge, who was assigned to the case. After hearing the evidence and visiting the scene of the accident, Judge Van Sickle found that

> ... there is substantial evidence of "conscious indifference to consequences from which malice" must "be inferred." The United States, acting through the Corps of Engineers, in its layout, construction and administration of the swimming area paid little or no attention to any of the most elemental safety standards.

In finding for Lance McNeely, the court stated:

> There is no real issue as to the causal relationship between the conditions and the injury.

Following the findings of the court, the Corps of Engineers placed

"Danger" warning signs at the swimming area, fenced it off, and closed this hazardous recreational facility, which, according to the experts, should never have been built.

The United States appealed Judge Van Sickle's opinion to the Eighth Circuit Court of Appeals, and the judgment against the government was dismissed on the grounds that McNeely's claim was barred by the Flood Control Act, which provides as follows:

> No liability of any kind shall attach to or rest upon the United States for any damage from or by floods or flood waters at any place . . .[1]

In the case of *Denham vs. United States,* 646 F.Supp. 1021 (W.D.Tex. 1986), the District Court in the Fifth Circuit held that:

> Injuries sustained by swimmer were not caused by Government's operation of dam as flood control project, but rather, were result of dam's operation as recreational facility and, therefore, immunity provision of Flood Control Act did not bar suit against Government.

In the case of *Boyd vs. United States,* U.S. Court of Appeals, Tenth Circuit, August 2, 1989, suit was filed against the U.S. Government under the Federal Tort Claims Act for injuries sustained by a swimmer at a Corps of Engineers' recreational facility. A judgment was for the plaintiff. The government appealed, alleging the Flood Control Act as a bar to the action. The government's flood control defense was rejected, and the Tenth Circuit Court of Appeals held:

> We believe Congress' concern was to shield the Government from liability associated with flood control operations, not liability associated with operating a recreational facility . . .

The Eighth Circuit Court of Appeals, in reversing the McNeely judgment, relied upon the case of *United States vs. James,* 106 S.Ct. 3116 (1986). In *James* the petitioners were injured when they were swept over the dam, while the Corps of Engineers was releasing flood waters through the flood gates at Millwood Dam in Arkansas. The

---

1. Title 33 U.S.C. §702c; *DeWitt Bank & Trust Company, Conservator of the Estate of William Lance McNeely vs. United States of America,* 878 F.2d 246 (8th Cir. 1989).

Supreme Court held that this was a flood control operation; hence, a Federal Tort Claim was barred. Three of the Supreme Court judges dissented. Be it noted that the Flood Control Act was passed in 1928. The Federal Tort Claims Act was passed in 1948. The three dissenting judges in *James* stated:

> It would be regrettable but obligatory for this Court to construe the immunity provision to bar personal injury claims if such was the intent of Congress. But when a critical term in the statute suggests a more limited construction, and when the congressional debates are not only consistent with this construction, but nowhere reveal a recognition, let alone an intention, that the immunity provision would deprive those injured by governmental negligence of any remedy, a narrower interpretation is more faithful to the objective of Congress. It defies belief—and ascribes to the Members of Congress a perverse, even barbaric, intent—to think that they spent days debating the measure of extraconstitutional compensation they would provide riparian landowners but intended—without a single word of dissent—to condemn the widows, orphans, and injured victims of negligent operation of flood control projects to an irrational exclusion from the protection of the subsequently enacted Tort Claims Act.

The Eighth Circuit Court, in Lance McNeely's case, goes far beyond the Supreme Court decision in *James vs. United States.* In *James* the injured parties were swept over the dam in a flood control operation. McNeely was injured in an effort to save a life when he dove into the water at a designated swimming area.

There is a conflict between the Eighth and the Fifth and Tenth Circuit Courts of Appeals as to whether or not the Flood Control Act bars a claim under the Federal Tort Claims Act when the petitioner is injured at a designated recreational facility. Customarily, the United States Supreme Court would resolve this conflict on a petition for a writ of certiorari. The Supreme Court has declined to do this. Therefore, we must turn to Congress to determine its intent.

Was it the intent of Congress, in passing the Federal Flood Control Act in 1928, declining to award damages to property owners damaged by floods, to bar claims under the Federal Tort Claims Act passed twenty years later (1948) for injuries sustained at a designated recreational facility, constructed and supervised by the Corps of Engineers? It is inconceivable that this intent of Congress could be so interpreted. In *Denham vs. United States,* 914 F.2d 518, 521, the United States Court of Appeals, Fifth Circuit, 1987, held:

> We do not believe that Congress intended one who as injured because of a danger negligently created by the Corps within a designated swimming area to have no legal remedy.

Congress was deaf to Lance McNeely and the cause he represented and personified—

Justice wept while Congress provided for its own.

APPENDIX VIII ⟶ A SCREAM
IN THE NIGHT

During my forty plus years practicing law, I heard many tragic stories from people seeking my help. Each and every one sought answers. Each case was interesting in its own right and told its own story of loss. Each was a different story.

Then one day in 1971 a family came into my office and related to me the details of their daughter's behavior directly after receiving a DPT vaccine. They told how, following the shot, their daughter had prolonged screaming episodes and seizures that progressed into permanent brain damage and neurological dysfunction. From that day forward their daughter changed from a normal, healthy, and happy baby to an individual who would never be able to function independently in our society.

As I sat there in my office watching that loving family and listening to the nightmare their lives had become, I was humbled that they had come to me for answers and I was challenged to find those answers. Little did I know that day that finding answers would turn into a twenty-four-year crusade.

Before continuing with my case, let me provide some background. By the 1970s the whole cell pertussis, delivered in the DPT vaccine, provided protection against whooping cough for approximately 70 percent of the children under age five. However, the vaccination came at devastating costs to an untold number of children. This problem was first noticed in the early 1970s, and in 1976, Dr. Charles Manclark, a scientist in charge of bacteriology, at the Bureau of Biologics, wrote:

> We know the pertussis vaccine [although] passing the required toxicity and safety tests can cause adverse reactions in children—systemic reactions are less common, but include fever, collapse, seizures, persistent screaming and rarely, paralysis and death. Adverse reaction rates are not accurately reported, but more adverse reactions are probably experienced with the use of pertussis vaccine than the other biologicals.[1]

---

1. Dr. Charles R. Manclark, "The Current Status of Pertussis Vaccine: An Overview," *Advances in Applied Microbiology* 20 (1976).

Following Dr. Manclark's research,[2] the U.S. Department of Health and Human Services drafted and published a proposed regulation regarding biological products adverse reaction experiences. If adopted, manufacturers would be required to include a package insert in their pertussis vaccine. The insert was a request that doctors and/or users report any adverse reactions or product defects to the manufacturer. The regulations further stated that procedures for reporting such incidents include clear instructions on how to report such incidents.[3]

In response to the FDA's proposed regulations, the Pharmaceutical Manufacturers Association (PMA) mounted active opposition to this modest monitoring proposal. The PMA had a membership of 140 companies and was headquartered in Washington, D.C. The association's Biological Subcommittee met with the director of the Bureau of Biologics to protest the proposed regulation. Following the meeting, PMA issued a written statement to the proposal. In their words, "The proposed changes are unnecessary or unworkable requirements." In short order, the FDA withdrew the proposed guidelines without a public hearing.

But there was more to the story. In addition to Dr. Manclark's research and efforts by the Department of Health and Human Services, I learned that a cellular vaccine was being used in Japan with fewer and far less severe reactions. The vaccine had been developed by Dr. Y. Sato, a Japanese scientist. He had filed an application for a patent with the Patent Office in Tokyo in 1979. The Sato patent application demonstrated the feasibility of:

1. removing 99% of the endotoxin;
2. toxoiding or purifying the pertussis toxin; and
3. mixing the toxoided pertussis components with the Diphtheria and tetanus, making a purified DPT vaccine.[4]

---

2. Dr. Charles R. Manclark, "The Current Status of Pertussis Vaccine: An Overview," *Advances in Applied Microbiology* 20 (1976).

3. Draft of FDA's proposed regulations regarding Adverse Reactions and Product Experiences, published on April 24, 1979, requiring that manufacturers request, in their package insert, that doctors keep lot numbers and to report adverse reactions and maintain records of reactions and report them to the Bureau of Biologics.

4. Japanese Patent Publication No. 57-5203.

Most surprising of all, I learned that Dr. Sato came to the United States in the late 1970s and studied at the National Institute of Health (NIH) at Bethesda, Maryland. There he obtained information about the vaccine, then returned to Japan, and made a purified DPT vaccine. He conducted clinical trials on his cellular vaccine and *in one million immunizations, only one child experienced a convulsion.*[5]

The information to which Dr. Sato had access at NIH was public information; *it was available to the pharmaceutical companies engaged in manufacturing pertussis vaccine.* In addition to the information available at NIH, patents and learned treatises dating back over fifty years demonstrated the feasibility of producing a vaccine equally protective and significantly less reactive than the whole cell vaccine.[6] However, American drug companies had a guaranteed market on the whole cell vaccine, and it was the only vaccine available. Children were required to take it.

I did not know about Dr. Manclark's publications or the work of Dr. Sato when the family first visited me. However, in 1978 while doing research to help my client, I read about a seminar being offered in New York. The topic was on the DPT vaccine. I attended that meeting and met a number of lawyers from other states. We were all concerned with the mounting evidence of a relationship between the whole cell pertussis vaccine and brain damage in some children.

We exchanged information that we had gathered from our own research and through consultation with experts. By the end of the meeting, we were convinced that there was substantial evidence of shortcomings in testing and manufacturing the vaccine and that the

---

5. New Pertussis Vaccines Laboratory and Clinical Evaluation, Vol. 1, from DHHS, February 11, 1982.

6. Patent Specification 512, 196, October 15, 1939, Lederle Laboratories, Inc.: Method of Preparing Pertussis Toxin and Toxoid. Certified Copy of U.S. Patent No. 2,240,969, Patented May 6, 1961, Pertussis Toxin and Toxoid, Edwin Voigt and Sara Phillips, assignors to Lederle Laboratories, Inc. Studies on the Fractionation of Hemophilus Pertussis Extracts, Pennell and Thiele, September 29, 1950. U.S. Patent No. 2,701,226, Patented February 1, 1955, Prophylactic Agent Effective Against Hemophilus Pertussis Infections (Whooping Cough) and Method of Producing Same. Louis Piliemer, assignor to Western Reserve University, Cleveland, Ohio. U.S. Patent No. 2,837,460, June 3, 1958, Pertussis Vaccine Preparation, assignee: Eli Lilly and Company. U.S. Patent No. 3,141,824, July 21, 1964, Pertussis Antigen, by Robert V. Dahlstrom, assignor, to Eli Lilly and Company.

pertussis component was the culprit. It caused unnecessary reactions in many children and death or permanent brain damage in some. We were also convinced that Dr. Sato had demonstrated that it was feasible to make a safer vaccine. To that end, we organized, called ourselves "Advocates for a Safe Vaccine," and prepared to represent children negatively affected by the vaccine.

A few months after returning from the conference, I filed the first pertussis vaccination suit in Arkansas. The year was 1979. We processed this case successfully for this child, placing the funds in a trust for her future care and welfare.

In April 1982, a Washington, D.C., television station broke a story about the pertussis vaccine. The report stated that the drug companies had known about the risks for many years. Many physicians were also suspect of the vaccination. The reporter went on to say that while the DPT vaccine did provide protection to a majority of children, it caused reactions in most, and though rare, some children were severely and/or permanently injured.

The television story likened taking the vaccine to Russian roulette. The cat was out of the bag. I settled my suit in September after the story broke.

Over the years many families came to me seeking help with finding those same answers. The story they told was one that I had heard so many times before. All the cases were tragic examples of the injuries that could occur from the toxic effects of the whole cell pertussis vaccine.

These children had all been in good health, making a normal progress. They were disabled by *an old bacterial vaccine with old problems, substantially the same as it was fifty years ago, and not belonging in the last quarter of this century.*[7] The McMath Law Firm represented a number of these children. After legal proceedings spanning a number of years, we were able to recover awards for these children. The funds recovered were placed in trust and are still being expended under the supervision of the courts for the welfare of the children.

---

7. Drs. Cherry and Mortimer, "An Old Bacterial Vaccine with New Problems: Pertussis Vaccine—Recent Experience," Pediatric Immunization Today: A Symposium, held in Toronto, Canada, in 1979, in conjunction with the American Academy of Pediatrics and Spring Meeting and sponsored by Connaught Laboratories.

The story of whole cell vaccine and the countless children injured in its wake is a shocking reminder of what can happen when health policies are unduly influenced by pharmaceutical companies. It further emphasizes the need for the heads of regulatory agencies and their employees to pay particular attention to the public's health during their tenure in office. Moreover, the pertussis cases demonstrate that the general welfare suffers when treating physicians and parents are not adequately informed of the contraindications of a prescribed medication or medical procedure.

We had no way of knowing how many children had neurological damage from the pertussis vaccine in this country. No one had a monitoring policy in place. Doctors were not directed or requested to:

1. Keep a record of severe adverse reactions in a child;
2. Record the lot number and the name of the manufacturer of the vaccine used; and
3. Make a report of severe reactions to the manufacturer or Center for Disease Control.

Until 1982, many pediatricians and general practitioners did not recognize the relationship between neurological reactions and the pertussis vaccine. Even when recognized, many doctors felt that they did not have time to become involved in the paperwork for reporting such incidents. Some doctors were reluctant to tell parents that the vaccine which they gave, or had been given by a colleague, may have caused brain damage to their child. Dr. Manclark, in the report mentioned earlier, noted:

> Severe brain damage is so rare that most doctors will not have seen such a complication and may not associate it with the vaccine. Also, one is unlikely to associate a complication with a procedure which he has recommended and may have persuaded a mother to accept for her baby.[8]

The extent and severity of the reactions were not generally known because the manufacturers had a very passive monitoring program. PMA members responded to complaints and supplied copies of the

---

8. Prof. George Dick, "Convulsive Disorders in Young Children," *Proceedings of Royal Society of Medicine* 20 (1976).

report of the Bureau of Biologics, but they made no effort to survey the medical field, nor did they invite doctors to report adverse reactions observed when their product was used. Following the explosion of information by the television broadcast in April 1982, pharmaceutical companies battened down the hatches, went on the defensive, and prepared for the coming storm of litigation.

Over the years, after I filed that first case, I reviewed a mountain of documents produced by the drug companies. From my layman perspective, it appeared to me that the whole cell pertussis vaccine being used in the United States had biologically active toxins, endotoxins, and dead cells of the pertussis bacteria. However, I knew that it was possible to make a cellular vaccine that had the pertussis bacteria removed—our own research labs had demonstrated that it could be done, and the Japanese had done it. This cellular vaccine had most of the endotoxins removed or deactivated and underwent additional steps to further purify the vaccine and reduce its toxicity.

After the news story, parents with children injured by the vaccine began to organize. Calling themselves "Distressed Parents Together" (DPT), they formed the National Vaccine Information Center and contacted thousands of concerned parents across the country. The pharmaceutical companies also began tentative steps toward making a safer cellular vaccine. Sen. Paula Hawkins from Florida got involved and took a lead in pushing for a National Vaccine Compensation Act. A few other attorneys and I, involved in the push for a safer vaccine for our children, were asked to appear in Washington, D.C., before a congressional committee and to testify regarding the information that we had obtained over the years about the need for a Vaccine Compensation Act.

In 1986 Congress passed the bill. However, the program was not funded until October 1, 1988. The legislation provided for compensation to children injured not only by the DPT vaccine, but also the measles, mumps, rubella, and polio vaccines. In addition, the fund provided for further research into vaccines and a system for reporting and monitoring vaccine-related injuries.

Ironically, the monitoring system required by the Vaccine Compensation Act is substantially the same as proposed by Dr. Manclark and first published April 24, 1979. *That was the proposal opposed and defeated by the combined action of the pharmaceutical companies.*[9]

Less than a year after Congress passed the Vaccine Compensation Act, August 28, 1989, Connaught Laboratories, a member of the PMA, filed an application to produce and market a cellular (safer) vaccine. The company received a license to manufacture the vaccine in October 1992.

Over the years, my partner and son, Bruce McMath, my associate, Sandra Sanders, and I worked on many DPT cases. I witnessed their enthusiasm and commitment to help the children. In 1995, I settled the last DPT case that I had started years before. I then became "of counsel," turned the reins over to the next generation, and now serve in an advisory capacity.

In February 1997, the Arkansas Health Department received the first DPT vaccine with the cellular pertussis component, and since that time has continued with the use of only cellular vaccine. The Arkansas Vaccine Information Handout Sheet that is given to all parents of children receiving the DPT vaccine states:

> DPT is a safer version of an older vaccine called whole cell DPT.
> The whole cell vaccine is no longer used in the United States.[10]

When I think of all the changes that have occurred in our vaccine program since that first meeting of our committee of concerned lawyers calling ourselves Advocates for a Safe Vaccine, I know, no mater what the cost, the time, or effort it took, it has all been worth it. Our children are our gift to the future, and their welfare is everyone's responsibility.

---

9. Joseph Stetler, president of PMA, to Food and Drug Administration, June 18, 1979.

10. Arkansas Information Handout Sheet, Arkansas Department of Health, July 30, 2001.

APPENDIX IX✎ DEATH TAKES
A HOLIDAY

*John Burney, thirty-six years of age, happily married with a wife
and two children, disappeared on June 11, 1976. His truck was found
on the Arkansas-Mississippi River Bridge. Handprints were found on
the bridge rail, and it appeared as if "someone had just drug them off."*

*Burney's body was not found. A man's body with a wound in
his head was seen by two fishermen floating down the river. The body
was lost in a whirlpool and not recovered.*

John Burney was declared dead. Funeral services were held.

John Burney had two substantial life insurance policies.

The Arkansas State Police, county authorities, the FBI, and a private
investigator made an extensive search for John Burney. No trace could
be found. The life insurance company published an offer of a $25,000
reward for any information leading to the whereabouts of John
Burney in newspapers throughout the southwestern United States. It
continued to send premium statements on the insurance policies.
These were paid by Mrs. Burney.

At the time of Burney's disappearance, he was manager of the
Helena Arkansas Rice Dryer, which was in financial difficulties.
Burney had played the futures market, lost heavily, and sold farmers'
soybeans stored in the rice dryer at a substantial loss. The farmers
were furious. Threats had been made on Burney's life.

The family, convinced that John Burney was dead, held appropriate funeral services. His seven-year-old daughter, who was very
close to her father, participated in the services by reading a chapter
from Psalms. A grave marker was placed in the cemetery.

John Burney's wife made a demand on the insurance company
for payment of benefits under the provisions of the policies. The company refused. Mrs. Burney retained me to file suit against the insurance company on March 17, 1977. The life insurance company denied
liability on the ground that the "plaintiff has not submitted proof of

death of the insured, John Fuller Burney, and defendant denies that said insured is dead." Extensive discovery was taken, and the suit was set down for trial in the United States District Court, Eastern Division of Arkansas, on April 19, 1982.

On the date of the scheduled trial, Burney had not been heard from for six years. Arkansas has a five-year presumption of death statute. Under the statute, John Burney, by the time of trial, would be presumed dead. The Arkansas statute provides for a 12 percent penalty and attorneys' fees in cases where loss occurs and other expenses if the insurance company fails to pay.

The life insurance company, calculating its chances and the possibility of having a judgment rendered against it for the face value of the policies plus attorneys' fees, penalties, and prejudgment interest, decided that its best policy lay in settling the case. Accordingly, on January 26, 1982, the parties entered into a compromise settlement:

> It is understood and agreed that this is the compromise settlement of doubtful and disputed claims; that the payments shall not be construed as an admission of liability on the part of the parties released by whom liability is denied; that payment is made and received in full and complete satisfaction of the aforesaid actions, causes of action, claims and demands; that the release contains the entire agreement between the parties; that the terms of this release are contractual and not a mere recital.

The dispute having been settled, the U.S. District Court entered an order of dismissal with prejudice on January 26, 1982. The court order stated:

> Upon motion of the parties, it appears that the consolidated causes have been amicably settled and should be dismissed with prejudice.

Eleven months later, on December 1, 1982, John Burney's father received a telephone call. The caller announced, "Dad, this is John." Thus, after more than six years absence, thought to be dead by his wife, children, parents, and relatives, presumed to be dead under the law, John Burney "came in out of the cold," and rejoined the living, and the story of his deception was told.

On June 11, 1976, the date of his disappearance, Burney had abandoned his truck on the Arkansas-Mississippi River Bridge after colliding with the bridge rail. He slipped out of the cab of his truck, climbed over the bridge railing and down a pier to the river, and swam downstream for a distance, emerging on the east bank of the Mississippi. He walked into the state of Mississippi, caught a bus, and went to Louisiana where he obtained a job as a farm laborer. He changed his name to John "Bruce" and drifted down to Key Largo, Florida.

He told no one his identity for over six years. He ignored his legal and moral obligations, including his legal duty to support his wife and family and his responsibilities concerning the Helena Arkansas Rice Dryer. He caused great anxiety by not notifying his wife, children and his own parents that he was, in fact, alive. For over six years, John Burney concealed his identity and misrepresented facts about his background. He even falsified and filed an application for a marriage license indicating that he had never been married. He did not resurface until the Arkansas five-year presumption of death statute had run.

On December 1, 1982, John Burney returned to Arkansas to visit his father. He had been injured in an industrial accident and had filed suit against the manufacturer of the machine he was operating at the time of his injury. His "common law" wife joined in his suit and claimed loss of consortium.

During Burney's deposition of his claim against the manufacturer, he was questioned about his employment background and whether he had been previously married. Burney, thereupon, asked for a recess and told his attorney his story. His attorney advised him to go back to Arkansas and get his house in order.

After being informed that John Burney was alive, I, as attorney for Mrs. Burney and her children, notified the insurance company and the Social Security Administration that John Burney was not dead. The life insurance company filed suit against Mrs. Burney, seeking to recover the insurance benefits paid.[1] The insurance company, in its complaint, alleged fraud and mutual mistake of a material fact as grounds for setting aside the settlement agreement and recovering benefits paid to Mrs. Burney. After an extensive trial, the court found: (1) there was no fraud on the part of Mrs. Burney; (2) there was no mutual mistake of a material fact. On the issue of a mutual mistake of fact, the court held:

The settlement agreement in this case was a compromise of a "disputed and controverted claim." A claim was filed against the insurance company. To avoid a trial and the possibility of the beneficiary obtaining a judgment, the life insurance company settled the case. The settlement agreement in this case was a compromise of a "disputed and controverted claim." Both sides were represented by counsel. They had basically the same facts. They considered their own basic interests and entered into a binding contract. Accordingly, plaintiff's claim against Mrs. Burney is dismissed.

All insurance benefits were placed in an irrevocable trust for the education and welfare of the Burney children.

Mrs. Burney, following her husband's disappearance, had filed an application for Social Security benefits on August 6, 1976. The application for her and her children was denied on the basis that the facts and evidence did not support a finding that the claimant was dead. However, Mrs. Burney filed a request for reconsideration and the claim was subsequently reopened after extensive documentation was provided supporting the contention that Burney was deceased. Mrs. Burney and her children were subsequently awarded mother's and surviving children's Social Security benefits, which were paid commencing in January 1980 and continued through November 1982, when the secretary of health and human services was notified that John Burney was alive. The Social Security Administration discontinued benefits, notified Mrs. Burney that the benefits which had been received constituted an overpayment, and demanded reimbursement.

An administrative law judge found that the social security benefits paid to Mrs. Burney and the children represented overpayment. This decision was affirmed by the Social Security Appeals Council. The secretary of the Department of Health and Human Services ordered reimbursement. I filed suit in her behalf in the United States District Court asking for a review of the secretary's findings and order.

---

1. *Southern Farm Bureau Life Insurance vs. John Fuller Burney, a.k.a. John Bruce, Bonnie Burney et al.*, LR-C-83-589, U.S. District Court, Eastern District of Arkansas.

2. See learned opinion of Judge Elsijane Trimble Roy, *State Farm Bureau Life Insurance Co. vs. John Fuller Burney et al.*, U.S. District Court, Eastern District of Arkansas, Docket No. LR-C-83-589.

The case was set for trial before Judge G. Thomas Eisele, U.S. district judge, Eastern District of Arkansas. The case was to be considered by the judge, based upon the record and the findings of the administrative law judge at the hearing held on June 5, 1984. However, the transcript of the hearing had been lost by the government. The district judge remanded the case for another hearing.

A supplemental hearing was held on November 26, 1985, after which the administrative law judge issued a recommended decision finding the plaintiff (Mrs. Burney and her children) without fault for causing the overpayment and waiving recovery of benefits paid. The Appeals Council refused to accept the administrative law judge's recommendation that payment be waived and found that requiring Mrs. Burney to repay the overpayment would not defeat the purpose of the Act or be against equity and good conscience. The case again came before Judge Eisele. This time, the transcript of the record was intact. Having reviewed the record, Judge Eisele holding for Mrs. Burney and her children stated:

> The uncontroverted evidence reveals that the social security benefits received by the plaintiff were used for the daily living expenses of herself and her children. Additionally, the social security benefits were not placed in "trust," as evidence indicates that the funds in the "trust" resulted from the proceeds of insurance settlements and were the object of a separate lawsuit, which resulted in a judgment against John Burney. The evidence of record clearly shows that the benefits paid to the plaintiff and her children were used in the exact manner for which they were intended, and to refuse to waive recovery of the overpayment of these funds is certainly contrary to the purpose of Title II, as well as against equity and good conscience, in view of the particular circumstances of this case.

On June 11, 1976, John Burney climbed over the bridge rail and down the bridge piling and swam to the eastern bank of the river, walked into Mississippi, and then caught a bus south. He left his family penniless and believing that he was dead. Mrs. Burney obtained a teacher's certificate, went to work, and she and her children survived. They finally began receiving Social Security benefits in January 1980. The trials and troubles of Mrs. Burney and her children brought them closer together. Their family unity was bonded. They grieved together at the death of the husband and father. Their sorrow was compounded when they learned the truth that John Burney was not dead but that he had deserted and abandoned them.

Trial lawyers learn that the most heroic battles waged in our society are not in the political arena or the industrial sector, but in the homes of families wrung by a twist of fate, struggling to maintain family unity, integrity, and economic survival. We also learn that overcoming adversity and suffering may have compensations:

> I walked a mile with Pleasure
> She chattered all the way,
> But left me none the wiser
> For all she had to say.
>
> I walked a mile with Sorrow
> And ne'er a word said she;
> But, oh, the things I learned from her
> When Sorrow walked with me!
>
> —ROBERT BROWNING HAMILTON

APPENDIX X POISONING A NEIGHBOR'S WELL

A. CASE BACKGROUND

After suffering for over a decade the pollution of their wells, stock ponds, and streams, citizens residing east of Green Forest in the Ozark Mountains of Arkansas "took up arms against a sea of troubles."

After making every effort to solve problems with all government agencies concerned on a local and federal level, and failing to obtain relief, these abused citizens, having exhausted every reasonable recourse, asserted their rights as American citizens and took their case to court.

Green Forest is a small town in north Arkansas. Most citizens who live east of Green Forest operate small farms, orchards, and craft shops. It was here, in the late 1950s that a poultry processing plant was opened. As this business grew, so did the amount of pollution generated from the plant to the fragile mountain ecosystem.

This area of the state is characterized by karst topography, barren limestone featuring thin soils and fissures. This topography allows surface and ground waters to easily interact. In fact, anything that is discharged on the surface is likely to find its way underground rapidly.

These rural families relied on the purity of the ground water for themselves and for their stock. They had no choice. Over the years, these country people learned to protect these resources, and as the chicken plant grew, the threat to the integrity of their clean water supply—their lifeline—increased proportionately. Pollution flowed through a creek (known as Dry Creek) into the area where the concerned citizens lived.

The situation became even more complicated in the 1960s when a poultry processing plant, Franz Foods, began discharging its chicken waste into Green Forest's sewage treatment plant. In 1968, Tyson, Inc., bought Franz Foods. Tyson is an Arkansas-based corporation, often described as one of the largest poultry processing companies in the world. The company immediately increased its production, thereby increasing proportionately the chicken sludge which was already being discharged into the city's sewage treatment system.

Residents affected by the pollution of their water brought suit against Franz Foods, Tyson's subsidiary, for maintaining a public nuisance. The suit was settled in 1976. In the settlement agreement, Tyson pledged not to discharge waste material into the city's sewage treatment plant that would in any way alter the condition of Dry Creek, either visually or chemically. Tyson further promised that it would refrain from violating any city ordinance or county, state, or federal regulations or laws relating to the safety and purification of the water supply.

By the 1980s the city's sewage treatment plant was discharging waste stronger than domestic raw sewage. In May 1983, a sinkhole opened in Dry Creek and the creek's entire flow ran directly into the ground. At this time the wastewater disposal system of the city had a volume in excess of one million gallons per day.

When the sinkhole first opened, the implications were not readily apparent to residents residing east of the city. The first noticeable impact was that Shipman Springs, a shallow aquifer on one of the plaintiff's property, went septic. A Pollution Control and Ecology field representative recounted that when he first visited Shipman Springs after the sinkhole opened, "It frightened me." As a result of the contamination in their spring, the spring-fed pond, stocked with trout, had to be bulldozed.

As time passed, other wells and aquifers in close proximity to Shipman Springs and the sinkhole began to show signs of contamination. Ultimately, the state health department was called in to investigate. The city attempted to cap the sinkhole by filling it with concrete, but the sinkhole reopened nearby within a short time.

In the December 17, 1984, issue of the *Harrison Times* (a north Arkansas daily newspaper), a headline read: "Tyson Dumps Sludge at Farm." According to the article,

> Two truckloads of what was described as pre-treated sludge from the Tyson food plant at Berryville was dropped on a hillside of a farm south of here Friday.
>
> The sludge which contained grease, flowed down a hillside into a pond, and then into a wet weather creek which ultimately would have wound up in Dry Creek. It disappeared underground except during high water.[1]

---

1. *Harrison Times,* December 17, 1984.

On July 10 of the following year, the *Berryville Times* published:

"Overflowing Sewage Remains a Problem for Green Forest Area"

Sights—sounds—smells. These have each long been associated with the classic celebration of the Fourth of July. Usually, however, we tend to think of the sights as exploding fireworks, the sounds as the echoing bang of impending firecrackers, and the smell as a prevailing aroma of burnt black powder.

Such was not the case last Thursday for several residents of the South Springfield Street area of Green Forest. Rather, their morning hours became such as to treat them to the spectacle of raw, domestic sewage flowing down the street. Like the sounds of rushing water. The smell quickly became those of a stench that can only be associated with sewage.[2]

The following month, this appeared:

"Effluent Swirls down Sinkhole"

A new sinkhole that apparently consumes more than 600 gallons of liquid a minute has developed in Dry Creek about three feet away from a larger sinkhole in the creek capped by the city a year ago.[3]

Such streams as Dry Creek have an intimate contact with the ground-water system through sinkholes. The effluent (industrial sewage) from the Green Forest Sewage Treatment Plant was discharging into Dry Creek, above the sinkhole. With its limestone formation easily dissolved by water, surface water in the stream regularly permeates to shallow aquifers and the water frequently submerges and reemerges downstream.

For many years, the city of Green Forest had been knowingly polluting the ground-water supplies of area residents east of the city by the operation of its wastewater treatment plant. The plant had been in almost constant violation of Environment Protection Agency permit requirements over the years.

The principal industry in Green Forest, Tyson Foods, was also the principal polluter.

---

2. *Berryville Times,* July 10, 1985.
3. *Berryville Times,* August 1985.

Sewage was known to have shown up in the wells for a period of approximately twelve years before the committee chaired by Steve Work began taking appropriate corrective action. The water became so contaminated in the area that property owners had to haul city water to their homes and farms at considerable personal expense and difficulty. Their quality of life deteriorated and the value of their property depreciated.

Dry Creek is not a creek at all. It is a geological structure that serves as a drain over a rather large surface area during heavy rains. Otherwise, the only flowing water in the "Dry Creek" was the effluent from the Green Forest sewage plant, 1.3 million gallons per day by the city's estimates. A large sinkhole developed in the bed of Dry Creek about one-half mile below the city's effluent discharge point. Thereafter, all the sewage drained into this hole.

The stream bed was completely dry downstream from the sinkhole. No attempt was made to plug the hole until fish began to die in the springs two or three miles below. Prior to the sinkhole and since the sinkhole had been plugged, all of the effluent disappeared into the underground within two and one-half miles of the sewage plant.

Dye tests conducted by the Arkansas Health Department, engineering division, proved that the city's sewage was contaminating the area ground water. Further tests proved that other wells and fish ponds were likewise contaminated in this area east of Green Forest, below the discharge point for the sewage disposal plant.

Over the years the Environmental Protection Agency and the Arkansas Department of Pollution Control and Ecology (ADPC&E) appeared to be paper tigers in that they assumed threatening postures, but never did anything about the violations.

Green Forest ordinance, Article III, Section V, provided that, "Inappropriate discharge produced in violation of the above referenced sections or which otherwise constitute a hazard to life or a public nuisance could be rejected by the sewer superintendent, or the discharger could be required to pretreat to an acceptable condition for discharge to the public sewers."

The Clean Water Act passed by Congress in 1972 created a comprehensive program, "to restore and maintain the chemical, biological integrity of the nation's water." The EPA was created to supervise and carry out the Clean Water Act provisions.

Until a sinkhole opened in Dry Creek and the Arkansas Health Department declared an imminent health threat zone east of the city in 1984, the city never used this ordinance or any other ordinance to constrain Tyson's overflowing of the city's wastewater treatment plant.

The 1972 Act provides that the Environmental Protection Agency shall issue permits authorizing effluent discharge in strict compliance with the conditions specified in the permit. The EPA was empowered to take necessary steps, including court actions, to enforce the provisions of the Clean Water Act.

B. EPA WARNINGS AND ORDERS

The EPA's Clarence Edmondson inspected the city's sewage treatment plant in April 1979 and reported:

> . . . The City needs an administrative order to force compliance with the permit's general condition 1-d. This could prevent an increased flow into an already overloaded plant. Tyson . . . is planning to increase production over 67%. The increase is scheduled to be handled by adding an old floatation device (unused at another Tyson plant) which is intended to aid in solids removal. However, the BOD is too high for adequate waste treatment.
>
> The wastewater plant at present does not meet the permitted BOD[4] limits. Therefore, any increase in production would put the plant further out of compliance. The treatment plant as operating could easily meet a 20-20 criteria for BOD and TSS[5] if the poultry plant waste was not allowed in this system. Also, the company is obtaining an unfair advantage over other poultry processors by not having to treat their waste. The City will not force the industry to comply with industrial pre-treatment regulations as they fear financial and political reprisal. Therefore, an administrative order is the minimum effort which should be considered.

Replying to this report, the mayor of Green Forest reported to the EPA that Edmondson was mistaken about the prospects of greater loads from Tyson and that Tyson was taking steps to improve its effluent so that in spite of the increased production, no greater loading would be placed on the plant.

---

4. Biochemical Oxygen Demand (BOD).
5. Total Suspended Solid (TSS).

Reports indicated, however, that the effluent at Tyson did not improve, even deteriorating after Edmondson's inspection.

When Jewell Wise, wastewater superintendent at the Green Forest plant, was asked why he had not exercised his authority under city ordinance and cut Tyson off to avoid violating the City's permit, he responded: "You know what would have happened to me if I'd went and done it, don't you?"

On August 4, 1980, almost eighteen months after Edmondson's inspection, the EPA notified the mayor of Green Forest that the limitations of the city's permit were not met during the period from January through June of 1980. The notification continued:

> Those violations are subject to enforcement action as provided by the Clean Water Act. You must take action to eliminate or prevent the recurrence of the violations noted above.
>
> We will place a report of these violations in your file and will use this information to determine the appropriate action to take in the event of future violations. . . . We are especially concerned about the massive increase in BOD-5 over the last year.

The EPA dispatched Robert Reeves, a senior environmental engineer, to inspect the city's sewage treatment plant and to ascertain the reason for its inability to meet treatment criteria. In his report filed September 12, 1984, Reeves concluded:

> The city's plant was being overloaded, both hydraulically and from a BOD treatment standpoint; it was designed to handle an effluent of not more than 400 BOD-30TSS; Tyson's waste greatly exceeded these limits; the plant was designed to handle no more than 4,170 pounds of BOD per day and that if Tyson's waste was appropriately pretreated, the plant could achieve secondary standards of treatment; Tyson's waste flow represented 82.5% of the total loading on the plant and ranged from 500 to in excess of 1,000 MG-LBOD in concentration, with average monthly loading up to 12,760 pounds per day or roughly three times the design capacity of the plant; and peak loading could top 17,000 pounds per day.

In addition to overloading the city's sewage treatment plant, Tyson continued to dump waste in the land area east of Green Forest by pumping sludge into tanker trucks. The trucks would then spray distilled, liquefied materials on the ground. Some of this sludge dumping was being done in close proximity to the city's water supply (Henderson Springs) which, by that time, had also become the water supply for some of the plaintiffs and the hoped-for water source for all citizens who had lost their ground water east of the city. In addition, Tyson was also dumping in areas which had been designated by the state health department as an imminent health threat zone, thereby provoking even more serious damage.

C. THE CITIZENS' PETITION FOR RELIEF

In 1970, Tyson processed approximately 300,000 pounds of chickens per day. Wastewater treatment plant violations continued. Then in 1984, Tyson's production changed from a "cut up operation" to a "deboning" procedure. Approximately 700,000 pounds of chicken per day were processed. Waste water contamination increased proportionately.

In the same year, the Arkansas Department of Health informed the city that wells in the vicinity of the sinkhole were being affected and that these affected areas should be provided with city water.

Tyson continued to overload the system without any pretreatment, and the city continued to receive periodic warnings from the environmental agencies regarding permit violations. Thus, because Tyson never pretreated its waste to produce an effluent compatible with the wastewater treatment plant's design, the plant never achieved a quality effluent that would meet minimum safety and health requirements.

Louis Williams, Tyson's environmental engineer, observed that during this period:

1. he was aware of the prohibition against interfering with and overloading the wastewater treatment plant;
2. he was aware the City was having difficulty meeting its permit limits;
3. the technology to pretreat waste from such a facility existed in 1974 when the city's plant was built;
4. he had calculated the overload on the city's plant;
5. he had calculated the cost of pretreating Tyson's waste before loading it into the city's plant.

Tyson Foods, Inc., had full knowledge that the ponds, wells, streams, the fresh mountain water indigenous to the area was being polluted—rendered septic by Tyson's overloading the city sewage plant and by failing to pretreat the waste from the chicken processing operations.

Tyson also knew that technology had existed for over a decade to right this wrong being inflicted upon the area's people. Yet Tyson's excessive loading on the wastewater treatment plant continued to increase.

Pat Magner, a licensed wastewater treatment plant operator and city employee, became so concerned that he went over the head of Jewell Wise, the superintendent, and complained directly to the mayor and the city council.

There was no doubt that the families living in this area east of Green Forest, some 134, were having their rights violated, and so they petitioned state and federal agencies for relief. They petitioned and appeared repeatedly before the city council of Green Forest. Responsible federal and state regulatory agencies made inspections, wrote letters, and sounded alarm, but nothing effective was done to bring relief to these citizens, nor to compensate them for the depreciation and loss of the use of their property. They were having to haul water. Their quality of life was infringed upon. The right to their homes and land was being violated.

D. THE CITIZENS USE THE KEY TO THE COURTHOUSE

When all of their efforts to correct the situation came to naught, they finally questioned:

> "Can we find a remedy in law?"
>
> "Can we find a David to fight Goliath?"
>
> "Can we find a lawyer who will tackle the powerful and influential Tyson Foods, Inc.?"
>
> "If we find a lawyer, will he (or she) be willing to take up our cause on a contingency fee, that is, agree that if we do not make a recovery, they will not be paid?"

Lawyers were found to take the citizens' cause to court. They came from three separate firms: James Bruce and Phillip H. McMath, from the McMath Law Firm, P.A., Little Rock, Arkansas; James G. Lingle, Lingle & Lingle, Rogers, Arkansas; and Samuel E. Ledbetter, now with the McMath Law Firm, Little Rock.

After extensive study and preparation, the attorneys on behalf of the aggrieved citizens filed a suit on March 3, 1987, against Tyson and the City of Green Forest under the Clean Water Act (33 U.S.C. §1365(a) et seq.; 28 U.S.C. §1331, 2201) and their rights under common law.

Belatedly, some six months later, on September 28, 1987, the EPA that had been making inspections and filing reports over the years, filed suit against Green Forest. The citizens moved to have the cases consolidated or that they be permitted to intervene in the EPA suit. This motion was denied. Then, on the eve of trial in the citizens' action, the EPA's suit against the city was settled for a small fraction of the penalty that could have been assessed.

Prior to the EPA's action, on May 19, 1987, James Blair, Tyson's general counsel, wrote Dr. Ben Salzman, director of the Arkansas Department of Health, who had expressed concerns over the land application of sludge in the vicinity of Henderson Springs, the city's drinking water source. In that letter, Mr. Blair evidenced Tyson's corporate mindset and political power when he stated:

> It seems to me that it is time to have a major meeting in the Governor's office with the Governor's staff and get the turf problems ironed out so that the delays that cause us so much trouble now can be eliminated. I am, by copy of this letter, advising the Governor's Chief of Staff that we would be more than happy to attend a peace settlement between the agencies—my understanding is that we are going to, at this point, transfer some of the Green Forest work load to our Texas and Alabama plants so that we can voluntarily quit spreading on the Chaney Farm to show our good faith, even though we have a legal permit to do that, and even though we cannot find any authority that your Department has to request us not to do it.

The citizens' suit filed on March 3, 1987, apparently gave Tyson second thoughts about its land application of sludge in the Carroll

County area. This was the first tangible sign that Tyson was feeling a need to alter its mode of operations in north Arkansas.

The citizens' trial against Tyson and the city began April 4, 1989, and lasted just over a month, concluding on May 12, 1989.[7] A verdict was returned by the jury against Tyson for money damages and Tyson was found guilty of forty-three (43) Clean Water Act violations. The city was not found liable.

Both parties, Tyson and the citizens, appealed to the United States Eighth Circuit Court of Appeals. The judgment on behalf of the citizens for money damages against Tyson was affirmed.[8]

The citizens in their complaint had asked for punitive damages against Tyson. The trial judge granted a summary judgment on behalf of Tyson on the punitive damage issue. The trial judge based his opinion and judgment on the belief that Tyson had not intended to injure the citizens. On appeal, the Eighth Circuit Court reversed the trial judge. On the issue of punitive damages, the Eighth Circuit Court of Appeals stated:

> In this case, the fact that Tyson may not have intended to "punish" the citizens is not dispositive of the punitive damages issue. There was evidence from which the jury could have inferred that Tyson knew the risk involved in drinking water because of the chicken operations, and yet, *Tyson acted for years with indifference to that risk.* (Emphasis added.)

It is significant that the citizens brought suit against Tyson and the city under the Clean Water Act and the common law. It is significant because there is a movement to eliminate the common law of the respective states and have the common law of the state preempted by federal legislation, rules, or regulations and to eliminate the right of trial by jury in civil cases.

The right to bring suit for an injury under the common law and the right of trial by jury are one of the oldest remedies provided by English and American law. Common law has long been the vehicle

---

7. The citizens were left only with a claim against the city based on "inverse condemnation." In other words, the citizens claimed that the city's pollution amounted to the unlawful taking of their property without just compensation as required under the Constitution.

8. *E.P.A. vs. City of Green Forest, Ark.,* 921 F.2d 1394 (8th Cir. 1990).

for the protection of ordinary landholders against the more economically powerful, who operate their land to the detriment of their adjoining neighbors.

In a previous case, the court entered an injunction against a pulp mill employing hundreds of persons and representing a substantial $1 million investment, which was polluting the waters of a downstream neighbor. The actual damages the jury calculated at $312 per year. The court of appeals rejected the defendant's claim that the actual injury was small. It stated:

> Although the damage to the plaintiff may be slight as compared with the defendant's expense of abating the condition, that is not a good reason for refusing an injunction. Neither courts of equity nor law can be guided by such a rule, for if followed to its logical conclusion it *would deprive the poor litigant of his little property while giving it to those already rich.* (Emphasis added.)[8]

It has, historically, been the function of the common law to reconcile the differences between public interests and private rights. In the Tyson case, the wastewater plant was owned and operated by Green Forest, but the principal polluter using the facility was Tyson. The fact that the property was not owned by Tyson would not deter, under the common law, relief being granted to the injured landowners.

In *New York vs. Schenectady Chemicals, Inc.*, a case tried in 1983, the court approved the application of a public nuisance doctrine against the generator of waste, even though the defendant did not own the premises constituting the nuisance. The court in Schenectady held:

> The common law is not static. Society has repeatedly been confronted with new inventions . . . that have imposed foreseen and unforeseen dangers upon society.[9]

E. CONCLUSION

What we have seen in the case of *Citizens vs. Tyson* is a further dramatic illustration of the function of our justice system. These citizens spent over ten years in an effort to rectify the situation and to

---

8. *Whalen vs. Union Bag and Paper Company,* 101 N.E. 805 (1913).
9. *New York vs. Schenectady Chemicals, Inc.,* 459 N.Y.S.2d 971 (1983).

get relief. They sought help from the state and federal agencies. No help was forthcoming. These citizens, having been deprived of the use of their property and having their way of life disturbed and disrupted finally went to court and presented their case to a jury. They challenged Tyson, Inc. by bringing suit in court, and this malady was corrected and Tyson was restrained from further damaging the lives and property of these people—*justice was done.*

There is no judicial system in the world that matches America's in providing an opportunity for redressing grievances and righting wrongs in our society. Our country grants to every wronged citizen with a meritorious claim the right to the pursuit of justice.

APPENDIX XI ⇒ WILLFUL, WANTON, RECKLESS DISREGARD FOR SAFETY— A POLICY DECISION

In this life there are not many certainties. In the complex society in which we live events beyond our control may occur suddenly, unexpectedly, sometimes violently. These events alter our lives and the lives of those whom we love.

Some of life's tragedies are the result of others acting negligently, carelessly, or with malice.

The more grievous injuries are those caused by another whose actions or whose failure to act responsibly are willful, wanton, or malicious; behavior demonstrating a reckless disregard for the rights of others; consciously pursued as a reckless, predetermined course of conduct. This latter was the cause of the death of Mark Brown, seventeen years of age, son of Herman and Barbara Brown.

Mark, on July 22, 1979, was driving his father's truck on an assigned mission when he entered the intersection of the railroad tracks and Laurel Street in Prescott, Arkansas. The first opportunity, because of visibility obstruction, that Mark would have had to see the oncoming train was 2.5 seconds before the crash. The train would have been 180 feet from the intersection, traveling at forty-five miles per hour, moving across this abnormally dangerous intersection before it could be seen.

Mark Brown lingered three weeks in the hospital before his death.

This fatal collision which took Mark Brown's life was not the first fatality that had occurred at the intersection of the Missouri Pacific Railroad and Laurel Street in Prescott, Arkansas.

Barbara Brown, as administratrix of the estate of Robert Mark Brown, brought suit against the Missouri Pacific Railroad asking for compensatory and punitive damages on behalf of the estate and the parents and siblings of the deceased. The case was tried to a jury in

April 1982 in the Texarkana Division of the Western District of Arkansas. Judge Franklin Waters was the presiding judge.[1]

In the trial of *Brown vs. Missouri Pacific,* the following issues were addressed and resolved:

> 1. Was the Laurel Street–Railroad intersection abnormally dangerous?

Tom Bryant, Missouri Pacific's grade crossing signal engineer, participated as the railroad company's representative in a diagnostic team survey of the four unprotected crossings in Prescott, Arkansas, in 1976. This survey included the Laurel Street intersection. The members of the survey team found, and Mr. Bryant concurred in the findings, that the four intersections, including the intersection in question, were dangerous and recommended that they all either be protected or closed.

Mike Selig, a civil engineer with the Arkansas Highway Department, in charge of the traffic safety division which is concerned with grade crossing protection, testified that this particular crossing's hazard rating, where Robert Mark Brown was killed, was in the top 10 percent of all crossings in the state of Arkansas in terms of its likelihood of grade crossing collisions. In his opinion the crossing was dangerous and should have been closed or protected. He further testified that the crossing's hazard rating was 20.12, which is twice that which the state considered would justify flashing lights.

Dr. Heathington, a civil engineer and director of the Transportation Center of the University of Tennessee and former associate administrator for the Traffic Safety Program of the National Highway Transportation Administration, U.S. Department of Transportation, testified at length about the hazards and difficulties of safely negotiating this crossing where an excess of thirty of the railroad company's trains pass each day at speeds up to and in excess of forty-five miles per hour.

> 2. Did the Missouri Pacific Railroad have a duty to install active warning signals at the Laurel Street crossing?

---

1. *Barbara Brown, Administratrix of the Estate of Robert Mark Brown, deceased, et al. vs. Missouri Pacific Railroad,* (W.D. Ark.) Civil No. 80-4020. Lawyers for the Brown Family were James Bruce and Phillip McMath, McMath Law Firm, P.A.

Under Arkansas law, a railroad has a duty to provide active warning devices at "abnormally dangerous crossings."[2]

It was practically uncontradicted that the Laurel Street crossing was an abnormally dangerous intersection. The hazard rating system established by the Arkansas Highway Department was a valid method of assessing the relative risks of grade crossings in the state. This index is computed and maintained on computer read-outs for all the crossings in the state and is based on five elements:

a. the number of vehicles that cross the crossing;
b. the number of trains;
c. the number of tracks that are present;
d. the accident history; and
e. the particular local conditions

The Missouri Pacific Railroad Company had knowledge that the Laurel Street crossing was abnormally dangerous and operated its trains over the crossings up to and exceeding forty-five miles per hour through the town of Prescott, over a period of years.

The Missouri Pacific Railroad had knowledge that the fatality rate in Prescott was higher per capita compared with all the rest of the Missouri Pacific systems between Little Rock and Texarkana combined, a territory which includes four hundred miles of track.

Mike Gorman, assistant train master for the railroad in this area, testified that Prescott's fatality rate was alarming.

The railroad had been asked repeatedly (since the end of the Second World War) to install warning devices at all four of these unprotected crossings in Prescott.

Thus, not only was it clear from the evidence that the crossing in question was dangerous, but it was just as clear that Missouri-Pacific knew of this fact. There existed a hazardous condition, giving rise to a duty, on the part of the railroad, which was not discharged.

Not only did the railroad company have knowledge that this Laurel Street crossing was abnormally dangerous, but it had knowledge that the installation of active warning systems, signals, lights,

---

2. *St. Louis Southwestern Railroad Company vs. Jackson*, 242 Ark. 858, 416 S.W.2d 273 (1967).

and gates, would reduce the certainty of injuries over a period of time given the number of trains, the speed they were traveling, and the number of vehicles daily crossing the intersection.

Dr. Heathington testified that studies conducted by the National Cooperative Highway Research Program, sponsored by the American Association of State Highway and Transportation Administrators, determined that flashing lights reduced the likelihood of crossing accidents, by a factor of five, over crossings which only had crossbucks. This was obviously a dramatic assertion that the installation of lights can reduce accidents by one-fifth of the otherwise expected level.

Tom Bryant, the railroad's chief grade crossing signal engineer, also testified that these warning devices in fact do decrease accidents. Moreover, he testified that the federal program promoting the installation of signal devices had in fact already reduced accidents by 40 percent.

> 3. The Missouri Pacific Railroad made a policy decision not to install active warning signals:

Having knowledge that the Laurel Street crossing was abnormally dangerous, of the fatalities that had occurred at the crossing, that it should be closed or have active signal devices installed, what action did the railroad take? Why did the railroad not respond to numerous requests over the years to fulfill its obligation to the traveling public by providing protection at this and the other dangerous crossings in the city of Prescott?

Again, Tom Bryant, the railroad's chief crossing signal engineer, testified that the railroad had not installed any significant number of active warning devices at its own expense since the early fifties. He testified, in effect, that the railroad would not install active warning devices at a crossing system, even if the railroad agrees that it is dangerous and deserves protection, unless public funds pay for it.

Mike Gorman, a railroad company representative, at a Kiwanis meeting in Prescott was asked why the railroad did not install active warning devices at grade crossings such as those in the city of Prescott. His response was that it was cheaper for the railroad to pay the personal injury claims than to install and maintain the devices.

4. Would a claim for punitive damages lie in this action for wrongful death?

What are the moral and legal justifications for punitive damages in a civil action?

> Perhaps the most respected among moral and political values in this nation is freedom. This includes the individual's right to be free of unwarranted interference from both the state and other citizens. The Bill of Rights protects the former type of freedom (liberty). While the private law, including the law of torts, protects the latter. Freedom is the most fundamental right of the individual human being. Each person is a morally special autonomous creature who has the ability and right to control his own destiny and a duty to do so in a manner respectful of the similar right of others. Each person, therefore, is entitled to be treated as an end in himself who should not be used to his detriment merely as a means to accomplish someone else's ends. The individual's dignity derives from his membership in the human family.[3]

The Missouri Pacific Railroad, having knowledge that the Laurel Street intersection was abnormally dangerous, that the visibility of an approaching driver was limited, and that appropriate warning devices would substantially reduce the hazard to the traveling public, continued to operate their trains through the intersection and through the town of Prescott at speeds up to and exceeding forty-five miles per hour.

The need for reduced speed and adequate warning devices were crucial to safety at Prescott's crossings. Mr. John Peterson, train engineer, testified:

> There is a helpless feeling that an engineer, or anyone in the cab of a locomotive, has. You can't deviate from your direction. You are committed. You are on a set of rails. You can't turn the locomotive. Once you apply the brakes in emergency position, that's all you can do, there is nothing left.

---

3. David G. Owen, "The Moral Foundations of Punitive Damages," Symposium on Punitive Damages, *Alabama Law Review* 40 (spring 1989).

In this situation and in this environment the railroad did not install gates or adequate warning devices because it was cheaper to have the lawsuits than to put up the gates and warning devices.

The railroad company failed to carry out its moral and legal duty to reduce the hazard to the traveling public because it was cheaper to fight the lawsuits. The railroad's failure to take corrective measures was not a violation of the criminal law. The railroad could not be indicted or prosecuted for this willful and reckless and persistent disregard for public safety. The only recourse would be for a jury, representing the conscience of the community, and acting under the instructions of the court:

1. To compensate those injured as nearly as they could be compensated;
2. To punish the wrongdoer for his willful misconduct; and
3. By its verdict to set an example to the named defendant and to others that this kind of reckless and willful disregard of the rights of others would not be tolerated in a free society.

Mark Brown, seventeen years old, lost his life. He survived for three weeks following the crash. His estate incurred funeral and medical expenses. Mark's parents lost a devoted son. Brothers and sisters lost their younger brother. This close family relationship was severed.

The jury having considered the evidence awarded compensatory damages totaling $80,000 to the family of Mark Brown and his estate and awarded $62,000 to his estate for punitive damages. The award of punitive damages was approximately that which it would cost the railroad to have substantially reduced the risk of this fatality.

The amount of this award to the family and estate of Mark Brown flies in the face of and contradicts the "scare" tactics of those who would abolish, supposedly through "tort reform," our civil jury system and the right to recover for punitive damages for willful, wanton, and flagrant disregard of the safety of others.

Some advocates of "tort reform" are inundating the commercial media and the Internet with stories about excessive verdicts and runaway juries that are destroying the competitive edge of our free enterprise system.

Very few punitive damage awards are returned by juries. Juries generally reflect the common sense, decency, and sense of fair play dominant in American society. Even when punitive awards are returned by juries, they are reviewed by the trial judge and by appellate judges. Witness the case of Nellie Mitchell.[4]

The right of a citizen to recover punitive damages for injuries inflicted maliciously, intentionally, or by a reckless disregard for his safety, elevates the jury to a position where it can serve as an instrument for the pursuit of equal justice for all in our free society.

Our experience in over fifty years of trial practice tells us that punitive damages, where justified by the facts, serves substantially a legal and moral purpose.

The Brown case was a significant precedent for the right of an administrator to sue for punitive damages in a wrongful death case. Phillip and Bruce McMath were the attorneys for the Brown estate.

---

4. See Part 4, Appendix XII, "Insult and Outrage—Defamation—Projecting an Innocent Person in a False Light."

APPENDIX XII INSULT AND OUTRAGE— DEFAMATION— PROJECTING AN INNOCENT PERSON IN A FALSE LIGHT

"Pregnancy Forces Granny to Quit Work at Age 101"

Nellie Mitchell was ninety-five years old when she saw this headline next to her picture on the front page of the October 2, 1990, issue of the *Sun* publication. Mother of six children, a pillar in the community of Mountain Home, Arkansas, she was mortified, shocked, humiliated, and bewildered.

Turning to the inside story she again saw her picture. This time under the heading:

"Special Delivery"
**"World's Oldest Newspaper Carrier, 101, Quits
Because She Is Pregnant!"**
"I Guess Walking All Those Miles Kept Me Young"

The *Sun* (a tabloid) is owned by Globe International, Inc., a Canadian publishing company and is nationally distributed in grocery stores and news outlets throughout the United States. Though the article referred to her as Audrey Wiles, the photograph was that of Nellie Mitchell, and the story was based on Nellie's long career as a newspaper carrier.

We were retained by People's Bank and Trust Company of Mountain Home, conservator of the estate of Nellie Mitchell, an aged person, to sue Globe International Inc., doing business as "SUN." The attorneys for Nellie Mitchell were Sandy McMath, Phillip McMath, and Roy Danhuser. A federal jury in Harrison, Boone County, Arkansas, returned a verdict on her behalf for the sum of $1.5 million.

Globe International promptly filed a petition with the United States Court for a judgment, notwithstanding the jury verdict. Judge Franklin Waters, United States district judge, having presided at the trial, stood firm supporting the jury's verdict and held that the tabloid must pay for printing "sewage." Sustaining the jury award in a clear, concise, and moving description, he stated:

> Mrs. Mitchell is a 96-year-old resident of Mountain Home, Arkansas. She has operated a newsstand on the town square since 1963. Prior to that she delivered newspapers on a paper route, and according to the evidence, still makes deliveries to certain "downtown" business establishments and select customers.
>
> It appears that Nellie, as she is known to almost everyone in this small Ozark Mountain town, is a town "landmark" or "treasure." She has cared for herself and raised a family as a single parent for all of these years on what must have been the meager earnings of a "paper gal." According to the evidence, the newspaper stand which she operates was once a short, dead end alley between two commercial buildings on the town square. She apparently gained permission to put a roof over the alley and this became her newsstand and sole source of livelihood, apparently providing life's necessities for her and her family to this day. When one of the lawyers asked Nellie during the course of her testimony whether she lived with her adult daughter, Betty, she quickly replied, "No, Betty lives with me."[1]

One defense of Globe International was that *Sun* published only fiction and that no one would believe the story about Nellie Mitchell. Other headlines on the front page of the issue showing Nellie's picture were:

"Husband & Wife Live Together Without
Speaking for 56 Yrs."

"Woman claims: I'm mom of Jim Bakker's satanic love child"

"Brother & Sister Marriage Shocker—After 30 yrs of
forbidden love, they would rather go to jail than divorce"

"Miracle Hormone May Save Girl, 6, Dying of Old Age"

---

1. *Peoples Bank Trust Company of Mountain Home vs. Globe International, Inc.*, 786 F.Supp. 791 (W.D.Ark. 1992), at 792.

"Paralyzed woman walks after being hit by lightning"
"World's most honest cop arrests his own mother"

In the midst of these black letter headlines designed to arouse the curiosity of the reader, thereby inducing a sale, was the headline about Nellie. It was bordered in red, printed in large letters—with an arrow pointing to her picture.

Significantly, there was no disclaimer or any explanation or indication that these stories were fiction. In fact, editors of the *Sun* in their testimony disagreed among themselves as to which stories were fact and which were fiction and as to what parts of the respective stories were true or fantasy.

Attorneys for Globe International in the pursuit of their contention that the article on Nellie Mitchell was fiction, aggressively cross-examined Paul Greenberg,[2] appearing by deposition as a witness for Nellie:

> Q: If the author testified that he made up a story, isn't that fiction?
>
> A: Sir, it's false. All things that are false are not necessarily fiction.
>
> Q: Tell me the difference between false and fiction.
>
> A: I can give you an illustration. William Faulkner wrote fiction. Pravda published falsehoods.

According to the story, Audrey Wiles (of Australia) had been delivering morning newspapers for ninety-four years. However, Audrey Wiles was nonexistent, and the photographs used were those of Nellie Mitchell, apparently lifted from a story run in 1980 by another publication owned by the defendant, the *Examiner*. The picture used in the article were the identical pictures used in the *Examiner* story.

Defendant contended that the *Sun* usually used photographs of people who are nonresidents of the United States, thereby avoiding defamation suits in this country. It used the photograph of Nellie Mitchell in this case because "they believed that she was dead."

---

2. Paul Greenberg, editorial page editor for the *Arkansas Democrat-Gazette*, Little Rock, Arkansas.

The nonexistent Audrey Wiles from Australia (in the article carrying a photograph of Nellie Mitchell with an accurate description of her as a newspaper "gal") is quoted as saying, "When I made my weekly collections to get paid, Will always invited me in for a bite to eat and gave me a big tip. We became friends and before we knew it, we had fallen in love with each other."—"Will and I should get married soon so we can raise our child in the right way."

Other inside pages of the *Sun* issue in question contained what appeared to be news stories. Among these were:

"Highway to Hell"—Wicked witch casts her deadly curse on intersection mangling 21—accompanied by graphic photographs of mangled automobiles sitting at an intersection where the "witch" had caused a serious accident.

"Drug Dealers' Devil Dogs Replace Pit Bulls"

"Boy, 12, Gets Own Lawyer to Divorce Dad in Custody Fight"

Revealed for first time: "Churchill's Close Encounters with UFO Aliens"—the articles disclose that, although Winston Churchill implored them to do so, they declined to help the world defeat Hitler.

Mothers describe night of terror during . . . "20-Mile Ride with a Headless Ghost"

"'Dead Man' Revives As Docs Take Organs"

"Road Kill Cannibal"—He eats accident victims—a news story, accompanied by a photograph of a black man whom, the story says, had applied to the government of the "African country of Swaziland" to be allowed to pick up from along roadsides and eat bodies of persons killed on the roadway. He describes the taste of human flesh, saying that he prefers adult meat because it is "firm, succulent and salty and doesn't require seasonings," while, on the other hand, "children's meat is revolting because it tastes sweet and sticks to the teeth."

"Farmer Becomes Millionaire Making Whips for Wife Beaters"—the story which at least one of the defendant's "authors" thought to be true.

"Hell School" . . . Where students are chained to learn and whipped if they don't read properly.

"Students Kill Teacher with Voodoo Doll"

"Farmer Kills Self by Breathing Cow Gas"—He dies with his beloved animals[3]

Defendant, Globe International, in support of its motion for a judgment notwithstanding the verdict, argued that there was no evidence of an obvious injury to Nellie Mitchell, that she consulted no doctor, incurred no medical expenses, had no apparent injury resulting from the *Sun* article. In response to this argument, Judge Waters in his opinion denying Globe's motion stated:

> It may be, as defendant in essence argues, that Mrs. Mitchell does not show a great deal of obvious injury, but a reasonable juror might conclude, after hearing the evidence and viewing the Sun article in question, that Nellie Mitchell's experience could be likened to that of a person who had been dragged slowly through a pile of untreated sewage. After that person had showered and a few weeks have passed, there would be little remaining visible evidence of the ordeal which the person had endured and the resulting damages incurred, but few would doubt that substantial damage had been inflicted by the one doing the dragging. This court is certainly in no better position to determine what that is "worth" than 8 jurors picked from the citizenry of the Harrison Division of the Western District of Arkansas to hear and decide this case. The court concludes that reasonable jurors could find that it is "worth" a great deal to suddenly find your likeness buried in the slime of which this publication was made, directly in front of an article describing the relative tastiness of adult human flesh compared to that of children.[4]

Sandy McMath, co-counsel for Nellie, in his closing arguments had recommended one dollar for each copy of the *Sun* which was sold with Mrs. Mitchell's picture—almost 370,000—$1,000 per day for each day from the time the photo ran until an apology and retraction was printed November 12, 1991—406 days—plus $1 million for pain

---

3. *Peoples Bank Trust Company of Mountain Home vs. Globe International, Inc.*, 786 F.Supp. 791 (W.D.Ark. 1992), at 796.

4. *Peoples Bank Trust Company of Mountain Home vs. Globe International, Inc.*, 786 F.Supp. 791 (W.D.Ark. 1992), at 796.

and anguish. The total award brought in by the jury was $1.7 million substantially as had been recommended by the plaintiff's attorney.[5]

An attorney for Globe International in the defense of *Sun*'s action in publishing the photograph and story about Nellie Mitchell in closing argument called the article, "A simple love story. A sweet love story about two elderly people. What is defamatory about that?" He asked the jurors. Phillip McMath, co-counsel for Nellie, in his rebuttal, in response to defense counsel's statement that all it had done was to tell a little love story, argued, "To say this is a love story, a sweet little love story, is about as outrageous as the story itself—the truth is not in this—falsehood is their stock in trade, lies are what they sell."

The jury having been instructed by the court after deliberating almost four hours, returned a finding that the *Sun* had invaded Mrs. Mitchell's privacy by showing her in a false light and that it was liable for insult and outrageous conduct.

Globe appealed the case to the Eighth Circuit Court of Appeals which, after reviewing the facts, the transcript, and the opinion of Judge Waters, affirmed the judgment for punitive damages in the sum of $850,000 and reduced the compensatory award to $150,000, affirming a total award on behalf of People's Bank & Trust Company, conservator for the estate of Nellie Mitchell, in the sum of $1 million. The final award to Nellie, including interest and costs was $1.1 million.[6]

So Nellie Mitchell, having carried a paper route and operated a newsstand for over thirty years, supporting and rearing her six children as a single parent, obtained justice in a court of law. This judgment and award demonstrated dramatically that the common law and the right of trial by jury are still the citizen's main line of defense against corporate abuse.

This was not a victory only for Nellie Mitchell, her family, and news carriers who will benefit from the Nellie Mitchell Trust Fund, but is a victory for the right of privacy. It sends a message to the tabloids that they cannot create sensational falsehood about private citizens without being held responsible in a court of law.

---

5. Attorneys for Nellie Mitchell were Sandy McMath, Phillip McMath, and Roy Danhuser.

6. Globe International petitioned the Supreme Court of the United States for a writ to review the case. The petition was denied.

The jury verdict and the award rendered in the case of Nellie Mitchell again goes to the heart of what America is all about. It demonstrates the indispensability of our civil justice system in making it possible for our complex society to function. It demonstrates again that a jury drawn from different backgrounds with different minds and hearts and life experiences can come together and, representing the public conscience, hold wrongdoers accountable.

The American jury, the "twelve good men and true," is the people's main line of defense against corporate abuse; libel and slander; invasion of privacy; pollution of the environment; introducing into the stream of commerce defective products; and willful, wanton, malicious injury.

The right of trial by jury reflects America's devotion to justice, fair play, and the worth and dignity of the individual.

In the case of Nellie Mitchell justice was done; a wrong righted; and notice given to the tabloid press that they too have a responsibility, that there still exists in our society bounds of fairness and decency beyond which they cannot transgress with impunity.

Nellie Mitchell, a contented ninety-seven-year-old lady, remained a "treasure" and a pillar of strength in her community of Mountain Home, Arkansas. The only apparent change in her life was that she gave up her newsstand and no longer made deliveries on her paper route.

Nellie Mitchell died December 30, 1998, at the age of 103. Nellie died peacefully at home surrounded by her family and loving and caring neighbors. The local newspaper carried a half-page story on her life and death and included a color photograph of this remarkable woman.

Nellie was a good citizen, a provider for her family. She had worked all of her adult life. She began carrying a paper route when her husband left her in 1943. She had six children to support and she continued to carry her paper route until 1991—half a century.

Nellie was a small woman, but she possessed a physical and inner strength that tolerated no obstacle. Not deterred by cold weather, rain, sleet, or snow, her customers received their newspapers. In discussing her work, Nellie once said, "If you like what you are doing, it is not hard work."

A neighbor had this to say about Nellie, "Not only did she carry the newspapers, she could discuss intelligently anything that was in them."

After Nellie collected her judgment from the tabloid, her style of life remained unchanged. She continued her life as a caring mother, a grandmother, a good neighbor, and a model citizen of Mountain Home, Arkansas. Had Nellie Mitchell lived two more years, she would have had the rare experience of living in three centuries (she lived from 1895 until 1998).

Eulogizing Nellie Mitchell, Sandy McMath, her friend and co-counsel in her lawsuit, described her as "a heroine of freedom of the press and the right of the citizen to be left alone."

APPENDIX XIII ↝ GEE, DAD, THAT'S A LOT OF TOMATOES

Pesticides: Federal Jury in Arkansas Awards $10.65 Million, Including $3 Million in Punitive Damages to Twenty-three Tomato Farmers Who Suffered Crop Losses Caused by DuPont Fungicide Benlate 50 DF

A. CASE BACKGROUND

Where twenty-three tomato growers from south Arkansas suffered devastating crop losses caused by DuPont's fungicide Benlate 50 DF. The farmers sued DuPont and established a sordid course of corporate malfeasance in the development and marketing of the product.

Federal trial court and jury awarded $10.65 million, including $3 million in punitive damages against DuPont for flagrant corporate misconduct.[1] This judgment against DuPont on behalf of the South Arkansas farmers was rendered September 3, 1993. Counsel for the tomato farmers were James Bruce McMath and Evans Benton, both of Little Rock, Arkansas.

In the Harrod complaint, plaintiffs charged that the Benlate, allegedly contaminated with foreign and deleterious ingredients including Atrazine, a herbicide harmful to crops, was inherently dangerous for its intended purpose. The complaint further alleged that the Benlate which had laid waste and brought ruin to the crops of some twenty-three tomato growers was improperly labeled, contaminated with herbicides, that DuPont had knowledge that the product was deleterious to tomato crops and refused to recall the product until after the damage was done and the Environmental Protection Agency took corrective action against DuPont for its distribution of this product.

---

1. *Harrod vs. E. I. DuPont de Nemours and Company,* United States District Court, Western Division, Arkansas No. 90-1127. See also Tom Lambert, "Tom on Torts," *ATLA Reporter* 36, 10 (December 1993).

During the trial of the *Harrod* case in Arkansas, DuPont had settled a Benlate damage claim with farmers in Georgia. The Georgia farmers were paid $4.25 million, only a fraction of the $430 million in actual and punitive damages that the farmers had sued for.

After the settlement with the Georgia farmers, the DuPont chairman was quoted as stating with exultation that they had paid the Georgia farmers, "far less than one percent of the plaintiffs' claims, thereby avoiding costly and time-consuming post-trial motions and appeals by the farmers."

The DuPont chairman is quoted as also stating in the post-settlement of the Georgia farmers' case that "the company [DuPont] looks forward to defending its products in other trials." The next trial on DuPont's docket was the *Harrod* case in Arkansas which resulted in the award of $10.65 million, including $3 million in punitive damages against DuPont for flagrant corporate misconduct.

We see the result of the farmers' suit against this corporate leviathan, but how did it happen? What brought about this judgment, righting a wrong and holding DuPont responsible for its corporate misconduct?

DuPont has the means to hire batteries of lawyers and scores of experts and has resources and facilities to conduct numberless tests under the direction and supervision of its own experts who use these test results to support their testimony at the trial. As one DuPont expert stated, "we can pick apart a claim of any farmer."

Under our judicial system in America, any citizen with a meritorious claim can take it to court.

The contingency fee system in place within the plaintiff's bar makes legal counsel available to claimants who do not have the resources to hire lawyers. Under the contingency fee system, if the lawyer does not win the case, the lawyer does not get paid.

The contingency fee system permits the citizen with a meritorious claim to exercise his right to go to court and to have his case tried before a jury. A jury composed of disinterested citizens who know nothing about the facts in the case; who are seeking nothing for themselves; who are not running for office or soliciting campaign contributions, looking for a job, or seeking personal enrichment. The jury decides the case under the instructions of the court based upon the facts presented at the trial, brings in their verdict and returns to their respective places in society, hopefully feeling that as an instrument of our judicial system, they have done their best to act justly, correct a wrong, and fulfill their civic responsibility.

So the tomato farmers hired a lawyer, Evans Benton of Little Rock, who associated Bruce McMath of the McMath Law Firm. The lawyers agreed to represent the farmers on a contingency. If no recovery was made, the lawyers would earn no fee, thus making it possible for these farmers, unable to pay a lawyer up front, to have their cause heard in a court of law.

The tomato farmers' law suit against DuPont was predictably a contest between two lonesome lawyers and a corporate giant, reminiscent of the biblical battle between David and Goliath. Comparatively, the lawyers for the Bradley County farmers were armed with a sling and a stone, "but their strength was the strength of ten because their cause was just."

B. STATEMENT

The *Harrod* case began in April 1990, when tomato farmers in Bradley County, Arkansas, noticed something unusual about their tomato plants in the greenhouses. The plants were not growing properly and manifested a yellow cast. The farmers had, for many years, used DuPont's Benlate fungicide, principally as a prophylactic measure for control of fungi in their greenhouses. The warm, damp interior of a greenhouse is a favorable breeding ground for these pests. In April 1990 one farmer received a flier in the mail from DuPont stating that some of the Benlate 50 DF production had been contaminated with the herbicide Atrazine.

Atrazine is a herbicide, the use of which on tomato plants would be akin to consumption of cyanide by a human. The farmer took the flier to the farm supplier from whom he had purchased his Benlate. The farm supplier contacted his distributor, who in turn contacted DuPont. A representative from DuPont appeared a few days later, confirming that all of the Benlate which had been sold in the 1990 crop season by the farm supplier had indeed been contaminated with Atrazine. The farm supplier immediately contacted his customers to whom Benlate had been sold and recovered the contaminated products.

DuPont dispatched its representative and plant analysis experts from A&L Southern Agricultural Laboratories in Pompano Beach, Florida. The A&L representatives visited the farms in April 1990 that had used the contaminated chemical, confirming that damage had in fact occurred. This was further confirmed in letters on each farm by the A&L representative and was addressed to Mr. Clyde Roberts of the DuPont company. Each letter cited the symptoms observed on the tomato plants on each of the affected farms and expressed the opinion that the damage in question was caused by Atrazine contaminated Benlate.

DuPont's representatives told the farmers they would be compensated for their damage. Time passed. With no payments forthcoming the farmers had to make out the best they could with their damaged crops.

Having heard nothing further from DuPont, the farmers concluded that they needed legal assistance.

The owner of the farm supply which had sold the Benlate to the farmers, Charles Roy Harrod, himself a farmer who had used the contaminated Benlate, retained Evans Benton, who had been his lawyer for many years. Benton immediately retained an expert on horticulture and tomato production, Dr. Berl Thomas, from Bradenton, Florida. (At the trial, Dr. Thomas would be the sole expert witness for the farmers, pitted against a galaxy of experts called by DuPont.)

DuPont was allowed to dispatch additional experts to inspect the farmers' crops. The farmers wanted to give DuPont every opportunity to observe the crop injury first hand.

Before permitting DuPont to send additional inspectors to the affected farms, Evans Benton, an experienced trial lawyer, made a far-reaching decision which would ultimately influence the conduct and the outcome of the trial.

As a condition for sending additional inspectors, DuPont was required to agree:

1. to share with the farmers their findings, video tapes, and results of analyses of plants and soil;
2. to provide to Benton copies of the letter reports to DuPont made by A&L Laboratories in April 1990, at the time A&L had inspected the farmers' damaged crops.

These reports were to prove vitally important given the damaging admissions these letters contained. DuPont subsequently strove without success to bar the use of these letters at the trial.

All the farmers involved in the lawsuit against DuPont harvested some tomatoes, but the damage from the use of the contaminated Benlate had cut each farmer's harvest to a marked degree. For example, one farmer whose historical production average was 1,700 twenty-pound boxes of tomatoes per acre, produced only 700 boxes of tomatoes in 1990.

A settlement of a lawsuit is highly desirable. This is particularly true where the plaintiffs are in dire financial circumstances, as is the case most of the time.

Preparation and trial of lawsuits can be terribly expensive. There are two sides of every lawsuit that goes to court. Anything can happen. If the venue is in federal court, a unanimous jury verdict is required. In most state courts at least nine out of twelve jurors must agree on a verdict of liability and damages before judgment can be entered.

The farmers' continued efforts to settle their claim came to naught. Suit was filed October 30, 1990.

C. DISCOVERY: THE SEARCH FOR THE TRUTH

Evans Benton learned that suit had been filed in Wisconsin against DuPont by Greiling Farms, a large ornamental plant nursery, which had sustained a devastating blow, losing 20 million pansies from a single spraying of Benlate contaminated with Atrazine in early August 1989. Benton contacted the attorneys for Greiling and was able to obtain valuable information in the form of documents provided by DuPont in that litigation.

DuPont had altered the formulation of Benlate. There was a change in method and mixture of ingredients rendering the product harmful to plants.

An internal DuPont memo revealed that in May 1989, DuPont knew Benlate contaminated with Atrazine was causing damage to plants. Despite knowledge of damage being inflicted upon growers, the decision was made by DuPont not to recall the product. The memo contained such language as, "downside of recalling" and "concerned about long-term reputation to product," stating further, "we think prudent risk to do nothing and knowing though that there is some risk that not recalling could result in more claims."

Approximately 80 percent of the Benlate produced in 1988 and 1989 was contaminated with Atrazine and Prowl, both contaminants and harmful to plants.

In 1988 DuPont began the manufacture and distribution of Benlate 50 DF as a fungicide. On September 1, 1989, the EPA placed a stop order on the sale, use, and distribution of Benlate. In its order to DuPont, EPA stated, "EPA has reason to believe that you have been selling this pesticide in an adulterated condition which constitutes an unlawful act under FIFRA (Federal Insecticide Fungicide Rodent Act) . . . Analytical results showed numerous batches of Benlate and Tersan to be significantly contaminated with Atrazine."

The Atrazine contamination referred to by EPA occurred in 1988 and 1989 when the Benlate was being manufactured by a DuPont contract manufacturer, Terra International, Inc. Prior to producing Benlate, Terra had produced a herbicide called Prozine, which is composed of Atrazine and Prowl. Terra attempted to clean out the traces of Atrazine and Prowl from its plant equipment by flushing it with starch and sugar. The contaminated starch and sugar was then used during Benlate production as inert matter, or a filler. An attempt was made by DuPont to measure the contaminated levels of Benlate so that there would be no greater than 20 parts per million. DuPont was not only aware of this process at Terra, but "ordered it."

The contamination of the Terra plant with Atrazine and Prowl, the cleaning out of the contaminants with starch and sugar, and the use of this contaminated "sludge" as inert material or filler in the packaged Benlate distributed to the farmers for use on their crops and the failure to advise the farmers of the presence of this contaminated and adulterated material, formed the basis of the jury's verdict in this case.

Hear the testimony of William Lea, formerly production manager at Terra's plant in Blytheville, Arkansas, when the Benlate was being formulated:

Q: What had been run previously before the production of Benlate began?

A: We had run a Terra product fungicide by the name of Bravo.

Q: And prior to that, what had been run in the facility?

A: It was a product by the name of Prozine for American Cyanamid.

Q: And Prozine is a combination of Prowl and Atrazine?

A: Yes.

The testimony of Mr. Lea continued:

Q: Now after you ceased producing Bravo, did you start producing Benlate immediately?

A: Basically. We flushed the system. That's when we started flushing the system with the starch and sugar and we did that for about two weeks, maybe two and a half weeks, before we ever put any Benomyl Tech into the system and tried to produce the Benlate finished product.

Q: What do you mean by Benomyl Tech?

A: There were some of the first material that was put through that was relatively high. I don't recall the exact amounts, but several thousand, maybe as high as 20,000. I just don't remember.

Q: Is that 20,000 parts per million?

A: Right.

Q: Would that apply to Atrazine?

A: Yes.

Q: All right. Now, what was ultimately done with this starch and sugar that you just described?

A: It was put back into the finished product at a rate such that we could maintain 20 parts per million or less of the contaminated materials that we felt—had remained in the—that had been measured to be in the material, and we were trying to maintain the level of contamination in the finished product at 20 parts per million or less.

DuPont's authority over the process was further emphasized by Mr. Lea:

Q: Was there a DuPont contract administrator with whom you worked?

A: Yes.

Q: What was his name?

A: Ken Krupa.

Q: What was his function?

A: To oversee the run.

Q: Well, what kind of authority did he have?

A: I would say total authority. If he didn't like what was going on, he could shut it down.

DuPont had not tested Benlate containing Atrazine to determine its effect upon plants. However, DuPont set a trace contaminant action limit or "TCAL," for a permissible amount of Atrazine in Benlate. Notwithstanding overwhelming proof, DuPont continued to deny that it had allowed Atrazine to be in Benlate.

Dr. Hamlen and other DuPont representatives went to a meeting with the EPA in Philadelphia on September 8, 1989, in an attempt to persuade the EPA to allow DuPont to sell Benlate 50 DF containing 100 parts per million of Atrazine as attested to in Dr. Hamlen's deposition. This effort was unsuccessful as DuPont eventually recalled all Benlate 50 DF contaminated with 2 parts per million of Atrazine, the limit of analytical detection at that time.

The only action DuPont took from May to August 1989 was to attempt to recover the unsold quantities of Benlate containing the extremely high levels of Atrazine which was still in DuPont's warehouses. DuPont made no effort to remove or recall the contaminated Benlate from the marketplace.

In the first week of August 1990, DuPont learned of the Greiling Farms catastrophe. Greiling had called in the Wisconsin Department of Agriculture, and its personnel determined that Benlate was contaminated with Atrazine. The Wisconsin Department of Agriculture then notified the EPA which dispatched investigators who traced the contamination to Platte Chemical Company at Freemont, Nebraska, a producer of Benlate for DuPont. The Atrazine-contaminated Benlate 50 DF was produced under contract for DuPont at Terra, a chemical company plant in Blytheville, Arkansas. The Benlate was then shipped to the Platte factory for repackaging. This was ordered by DuPont. During this process the Terra-produced Benlate was mixed with Platte-produced Benlate, thereby contaminating the Platte facility with Atrazine.

On August 7, 1989, an EPA investigator visited the Platte plant. A DuPont employee on site at the Platte facility notified DuPont, warning of the EPA investigation. This prompted a telephone call from DuPont to the EPA on August 9, 1989, to advise the EPA of the contamination problem. This was the first contact by DuPont with the EPA on this subject.

The EPA directed DuPont to recall all Benlate 50 DF with levels of Atrazine at 2 ppm or greater, which was the lowest level at which it could be detected. DuPont's recall was limited to its distributors and not communicated to farmers in the field who were using the product. It was not until April 1990 that the farmers in Arkansas learned of the contamination problems. They had all sprayed their tomato plants at least once, some having sprayed several times with DuPont Benlate.

On March 22, 1991, DuPont announced a recall of all Benlate 50 DF, pulling it entirely off the market. By this time farmers over the country, but mostly centered in Florida, began to report widespread plant and crop damage from the use of DuPont Benlate.

In May 1991, Evans Benton and four other lawyers representing growers in claims against DuPont met in Philadelphia with EPA personnel concerning the Benlate controversy. The EPA still did not know how the Atrazine had come to be in the Benlate sold by DuPont. At this meeting, EPA employees referred to a "study" on Atrazine that DuPont had presented to them in September 1989 advising the lawyers that this DuPont information indicated that Atrazine-contaminated Benlate would not have injured their client's crops.

DuPont continued to claim it had no idea how the Atrazine had been introduced into the Benlate 50 DF. From internal DuPont documents, it was learned that two employees of the Terra DuPont plant in Blytheville, Arkansas, the production manager and the lab supervisor, had been fired. The whereabouts of these former employees was not known.

After the May meeting with the EPA, Benton hired a private investigator who located the lab supervisor, Mark Meyer in Ohio. Benton contacted the former lab supervisor and was informed by him that "DuPont had not only known of the introduction of Atrazine into Benlate, but had ordered it."

At the time the Arkansas tomato farmers, Harrod, et al., filed suit, there were a number of cases by farmers pending against DuPont. Lawyers for the respective farmer claimants were endeavoring to obtain DuPont's interoffice memos and documents revealing that DuPont was aware of the harmful effect Benlate was having on plants. The lawyers for each farmer claimant were endeavoring to obtain these incriminating documents by request for production or mandatory court orders.

D. DUPONT SEEKS PROTECTIVE ORDER

DuPont set up what is referred to as the Benlate Depository near Wilmington, Delaware, DuPont's home base. Millions of documents were housed in this depository, mostly pertaining to Benlate and other chemicals. The depository originally contained about 80,000 documents, but the number of documents increased to approximately 4 million. Many of the documents were duplicates, confounding and confusing the lawyers who were seeking these documents in the preparation for trials in their respective cases.

DuPont stamped most of the documents in the depository as "Confidential/Proprietary," claiming that the documents could not be given to any lawyer outside the specific case for which the documents were requested on the basis of trade secrets and confidential information. DuPont was endeavoring to wall off the separate farmers' lawyers to isolate them from each other so that they could not share the information that they were gathering. DuPont sought the enforcement of this policy in the *Harrod* case by seeking a protective order from the court prohibiting Benton and McMath from discussing or having any of the documents that had been obtained from the depository by lawyers representing other farmers. A magistrate judge initially entered DuPont's requested order. McMath and Benton appealed to the district judge, convincing him to modify the protective order to allow them to communicate with other lawyers representing farmers whose crops had been damaged by DuPont's product. This was an incalculable benefit. Within a week of getting this modification, McMath and Benton were on a plane to Orlando, Florida. They met with attorney Chris Skambis, who was representing several damaged growers in Florida. Chris had some 500,000 DuPont documents which he had obtained from the depository. He assisted McMath and Benton greatly in winnowing the information.

Other plaintiffs' lawyers with whom McMath and Benton collaborated were Ernest Sellers and Jimmy Prevatt of Live Oak, Florida; Dave Connor of Tampa, Florida; and Stan Roehrig, Andy Wilson, Chris Laguire, and Allen Williams in Hawaii.

DuPont's tactic in responding to discovery was to simply refer the lawyers to the several million documents in the depository in Wilmington, along with a cursory index consisting of a few pages. It was almost an impossible task to narrow the search and find the relevant documents. Only through the joint efforts of the above-mentioned lawyers did a nearly impossible task become manageable. One state court in Hawaii referred to DuPont's tactics as "dump truck discovery," by which a lawyer representing a grower was subjected to a paper shower in discovery. Thousands of pages of documents would be reviewed, supposedly responsive to a particular subject matter, only to find that little or nothing contained in this material, ordered at considerable costs, was relevant to the topic or responsive to the lawyer's request or the court's order for production.

McMath and Benton set up a ready room in Benton's office in Little Rock where they accumulated over 150,000 DuPont documents. Additionally, they obtained over 30,000 pages of depositions in other cases filed against DuPont. Computers were utilized for each document requiring individual review.

E. DUPONT'S REQUEST FOR SANCTIONS

The proof was overwhelming that the Benlate purchased from DuPont and used on the farmers' crops had caused damage. Nevertheless, DuPont contended that the farmers' claims were "frivolous" and that sanctions should be applied by the court.

Under Rule 11 of the Federal Rules of Civil Procedure, sanctions may be applied by the court covering costs of the litigation and the award of attorney's fees in the event the court determines that the lawsuit is frivolous. The intended purpose of Rule 11 is to discourage the filing of lawsuits having no merit; to save defendants from defending lawsuits that are groundless and have no support by the law or the facts; and to spare the courts from having to hear groundless claims when the docket is already loaded with meritorious cases crying to be heard.

Rule 11's laudable intent is frequently used by corporate defendants to intimidate and discourage claimants with moderate means from going to court.

Not only was the proof overwhelming that the Benlate obtained from DuPont was the culprit in causing the farmers' damage, but DuPont's representatives inspecting the scene of damage had told the farmers that they would be compensated.

DuPont's threat to have the farmers saddled with DuPont's costs and attorney's fees did not deter the farmers from their course.

F. DUPONT POLICY—DIVIDE AND CONQUER

DuPont filed a motion with the court to sever the plaintiffs' claims, that is, to have each farmer's claim tried separately, requiring a separate trial for each farmer.

Obviously, the plaintiffs could not have afforded a multitude of trials. Additionally, the core of the plaintiffs' case proving that DuPont's Benlate had caused the damage to the farmers' crops was to show that each of the twenty-three farmers had used the fungicide obtained from DuPont, had applied it in a similar manner, and suffered similar damages to their tomato crops.

Granting DuPont's petition for severance would have required the court and the jury to try each of the twenty-three cases separately, to go through the laborious process of resolving each farmer's case in a separate trial on the issue of both liability and damages.

The trial judge overruled DuPont's motion for severance. DuPont attempted to appeal the ruling to the United States Circuit Court of Appeals by a petition for a writ of mandamus. Neither McMath nor Benton had ever been confronted with a mandamus petition before, but they learned fast and successfully defeated DuPont's tactical maneuver to try the farmers one case at a time.

G. DUPONT INVESTIGATES THE FARMERS

Waiting for trial, the farmers were trying to survive financially. All had suffered heavy losses back in 1989 and 1990. Two of the farmers died before the trial. Each of the farmers had to sit for two separate depositions. One farmer was deposed up until 10:30 at night. DuPont requested every farmer's tax return, accounting ledgers, records of supplies, bank statements, and other information for the past several years. Every business in south Arkansas with whom the farmers did business was subpoenaed to produce any records of business transactions. This included banks, accountants, supply houses, Farmers Home Administration, and other government agencies. DuPont's demands extended to such subjects as the quantities of string and stakes purchased in each year which are used in tomato production. Airplanes flew over the farmer's properties taking aerial photographs. Satellite photographs were obtained by DuPont. DuPont's agents came to Bradley County many times to investigate each farmer, going through courthouse records, asking questions of neighbors, all in an attempt to dig up some incriminating evidence to defeat the farmers' claims.

H. PREEMPTION

The federal law of preemption applies if Congress has passed sufficiently comprehensive legislation governing a given subject or product, such as a pesticide in this case. In that event, federal law will govern and the law of the state is preempted.

One of the objectives of the advocates of "tort reform" is to have the common law of the states superseded or preempted by federal law.

Federal courts have ruled in pesticide cases that the state law is preempted and federal law will govern on the issue of warnings by the chemical manufacturer. There are exceptions. Under FIFRA (Federal Insecticide Fungicide Rodenticide Act) no pesticide may be sold in the United States unless registered with the EPA. A manufacturer wishing to market its product must first petition the EPA for registration. The manufacturer is responsible for filing with its application information and data regarding the product. The required elements of this information to be supplied are set forth in great detail in the Act. If the information provided by the manufacturer is not accurate or if important information is withheld, then the pesticide is misbranded.

In such case the manufacturer of the pesticide is not entitled to the sanctuary of preemption and the state law on warnings will apply.

In *Harrod vs. DuPont,* DuPont's motion for preemption was not timely filed, hence not considered by the court.

The issue of preemption was subsequently raised by DuPont in another case in which McMath and Benton were the lawyers. Their response to DuPont's motion for preemption was that DuPont should not find sanctuary under a law which it had violated.

DuPont's motion for preemption in that case was denied on that basis.

I. TRIAL—BATTLE OF EXPERTS

Cross-examination of witnesses is important in the outcome of any lawsuit. It is crucial in a case where the verdict is dependent upon the testimony of expert witnesses. The secret of successful cross-examination is preparation, preparation, and still more preparation.

The farmers' lawyers were prepared. They had spent a great part of three years in discovery, taking depositions of witnesses, and obtaining crucial DuPont interoffice memos and other documents.

These documents and memoranda were studied, analyzed, categorized, and filed so as to be immediately available in court.

The tomato farmers could not compete with DuPont in the number of experts on the playing field, but they could compete in the competence and credibility of their expert testimony.

Plaintiffs had the burden of proof. They had to prove their allegations against DuPont by a preponderance of the evidence. The scales of justice had to tilt in their favor. They had the burden of proving:

1. DuPont Benlate had been used on their tomato crops;
2. that the Benlate was defective;
3. that the Benlate was the proximate cause of the damage to their tomato crops;
4. that DuPont had knowledge or should have known that its product was damaging to plants;
5. that the Benlate was improperly labeled and that the farmers did not receive notice of the potential of damage to their plants; and
6. that the conduct of DuPont in manufacturing and marketing its defective Benlate was willful, and consciously pursued

with a reckless disregard for the potential damage to the farmers' crops.

Evans Benton, when first retained by the farmers, had the wisdom to enlist the aid of one of the foremost tomato experts in the United States. Dr. Berl Thomas has extensive experience in the area of tomato production, having consulted throughout the United States and in Mexico with tomato growers. Dr. Thomas, based upon his experience, his observation of the damaged crops, and his having reviewed the pertinent documents, testified unequivocally that Atrazine-contaminated Benlate had damaged the farmers' crops. Dr. Thomas was unmoved, his testimony unshaken by DuPont's attorneys' vigorous cross-examination.

The farmers proved that Atrazine was present in the Benlate by DuPont's own test data and by DuPont's interoffice memos of their own scientists and by the testimony of the farmers in the case.

Dr. Ron Hamlen, a DuPont scientist who had been heavily involved for years in the setting of permissible limits, in a deposition taken testified, "My understanding about permissible limits—would be that if it was Atrazine it would be 10 ppm to be in the box that would be sold to the customers. That was my understanding, permissible limits."

Dr. Ron Hamlen, DuPont's liaison with EPA, expressed his feeling about setting limits without testing as follows:

> The following has the smell of my frustration around the whole benomyl contamination issue . . . we jump from Atrazine to flusilazole to "what is next." . . . We do not test the magnitude of crops or ornamentals to allow a reasonable level of confidence that no problems will occur from trace impurities. However, we still establish permissible level limits and, I feel, it is a little like playing Russian Roulette.

The two discharged employees, the production manager and the lab supervisor, at the Terra plant in Blytheville, Arkansas, were located and deposed and their depositions read into evidence at the trial. They testified that DuPont not only knew about the presence of Atrazine in its Benlate, but DuPont ordered it. EPA called a halt to the sale of Benlate containing Atrazine on September 1, 1989.

Under pressure from the EPA, DuPont in September 1989 undertook a limited recall through its distributors, but did not alert farmers and growers of the danger from use of the contaminated product.

On March 22, 1991, DuPont withdrew all of the Benlate 50 DF, pulling it entirely off the market.

It was shown that DuPont never tested the Benlate contaminated with Atrazine to determine its effect on plants in the field.

The lead-off witness for DuPont was the top executive of the Agricultural Products Division, William Kirk. He was an articulate witness and had been carefully prepared to "pick apart the farmers' claims." However, Bruce McMath on cross-examination of Kirk meticulously went back through all the incriminating DuPont documents which the plaintiffs had introduced in the case. This had the effect of reinforcing and driving home the farmers' case in the minds of the jurors. It was demonstrated that Kirk did not even know about some of the damaging internal memos which the farmers' lawyers had obtained from DuPont and placed into evidence.

Plaintiffs, at trial, took issue with DuPont's claimed result of its 1992 tests in Florida which was supposed to show that Benlate did not cause damage to plants. A DuPont scientist came into court with a slide and video show to demonstrate to the jury the results of the Florida test. The scientist fast forwarded the portion of the video of some of the tests which showed damaged tomato plants. Apparently, neither the scientist testifying or DuPont's lawyers were aware that the farmers' lawyers had possession of some photos of half-dead tomato plants which the witness had omitted showing in his testimony. On cross-examination, the witness admitted that these damaged plants were from the 1992 Florida tests.

Another DuPont expert witness testified to a test he undertook with Benlate, supposedly demonstrating the lack of any damage. It was left to the plaintiffs, however, to show video tapes demonstrating that some of these plants had in fact died and others appeared withered and half-dead.

The jury was told that DuPont experts had analyzed the farmers' supply purchases and would testify that the farmers had misrepresented their acreage. There was no further proof on the farmers' alleged acreage exaggeration.

DuPont had argued in its motion for severance of the parties, in order to try each farmer's case individually, that there was a potential for confusion on the part of the jury, there being twenty-three separate farmer's claims to be decided. The solution by Benton and McMath was to prepare a booklet on each farmer, detailing information about his farm, his damages, and supporting documentation. On the cover of each book was a picture of the farmer, so that the jury could better relate the information in the booklet with the individual farmer, each of whom personally testified in the case. The last thing the plaintiffs wanted was confusion.

The plaintiffs called a Mr. Elton Passmore to corroborate the testimony of the farmers that the Benlate had caused damages to plants. Mr. Passmore was a greenhouse owner in north-central Arkansas. He came to the trial to give his testimony on the effect on petunia plants. Mr. Passmore testified that in his thirty-five years of nursery experience, he had never seen anything like the effect on plants of DuPont's Benlate. DuPont's lawyers strove mightily to exclude the testimony of Mr. Passmore, contending that his situation was not sufficiently similar to that of the plaintiffs for his testimony to be relevant. The court overruled DuPont's objections to Mr. Passmore's testimony.

DuPont had contended that the farmers' loss was due to the fact that they were poor farmers. DuPont's own representative from south Arkansas testified that these farmers were some of the best tomato growers in the United States.

J. SUMMARY

Judge Hendren instructed the jury on the law of the case. The jury retired to consider the evidence and reach a verdict.

The jury had been out only two hours. The lawyers received notice from the court to return to the courtroom.

This notice was ominous to the plaintiffs. It would be highly improbable for a jury, with all the claims that they had to consider, and the evidence they had to weigh, to reach a verdict for the farmers in two hours.

As the farmers' lawyers walked over to the courthouse, apprehensive as to what would unfold, Benton suggested optimistically that the jury might want a calculator.

A calculator was the precise request from the jury. Receiving the calculator, the jury returned to its deliberations, spent two days considering all the evidence and returned a verdict of $10.6 million for the farmers, including $3 million in punitive damages.

The Environmental Protection Agency barred the sale of any Benlate containing Atrazine.

DuPont settled with other farmers who had pending cases, paying out several hundred million dollars in claims.

A small band of Arkansas farmers who had refused to be intimidated by the threats of a giant corporate entity had gone to court, presented their case to a jury, and obtained a landmark judgment for themselves and indirectly for other farmers who had sustained similar losses.

The right of trial by jury and the contingent fee system again served as a check and balance on corporate dereliction.

The lawyers had spent three years in discovering the facts and researching the law, and then four weeks away from home trying this case. When Bruce McMath went home on the second weekend of the trial, he was welcomed by his wife and three sons.

Bruce's youngest son, then six years of age, wanted to know why his dad was gone so long from home. Bruce told him they were trying to recover some money for the loss of the farmers' tomatoes, and the inquisitive six-year-old immediately asked what had happened. Bruce informed his son that the jury had returned a verdict of $10.6 million for the farmers. The child exclaimed, "Gee, Dad, that was a lot of tomatoes."

APPENDIX XIV ⮞ THE WRONG
ROAD TAKEN

I. STATEMENT

The body of Ed Walden, an employee of the United Steel Workers of America, was found dead in an abandoned, flooded bauxite pit on February 29, 1958, at 4:25 A.M.

Walden's automobile was found partially submerged in water on a private road that led downhill into the flooded bauxite pit. The hood of the car was covered in water and the rear wheels were underwater up to the hubcaps. The gearshift was in reverse and the emergency brake was set. All car doors were closed and the windows were up, except the window on the driver's side of the car. It was rolled down.

The Walden car had come to a stop with the left front wheel resting on a steep ledge. Ed's body was found in fifteen feet of water, approximately one hundred feet from the automobile.

The bauxite pit in which Walden's body was found had been excavated and owned by the Aluminum Company of America (ALCOA).

Ed Walden was married and had three children. At the time of his death, he had for several years been an employee of the United Steel Workers of America. His responsibility was the handling of grievance matters for about twenty-five hundred workers in the aluminum industry. Many of the employees worked at night, and most of Walden's work was done after 7:00 P.M. On occasion, he would work all night, contacting union members in the Sardis, Bauxite, and Mount Olive communities.

The car keys were found in Walden's pocket. The autopsy showed Walden had met death by drowning. There was no evidence or suggestion that he had committed suicide.

ALCOA, since 1941, the beginning of World War II, had been extensively engaged in mining operations in the Bauxite area of Saline County, Arkansas. In support of its mining operations, ALCOA had constructed a network of roads leading into the pits and from the pits to processing and shipping terminals. These roads were built by ALCOA to carry heavy loads: tractors, steam shovels, cranes, and eukes loaded with bauxite ore. ALCOA's private roads were designed and constructed on a comparable level to the county public roads serving the Bauxite community, and were similar in appearance.

Customarily, when the ore in a bauxite pit had been excavated and exhausted, the pit was abandoned to the elements. In the course of time, the pit would become flooded and remain filled with water.

Herbert Jarrett was labor relations director for Reynolds Metals Company, where many of the steel worker union members were employed. On the evening of February 28, 1958, Mr. Walden, Mr. Jarrett, and Mr. Guy Bass, a labor union officer, met in Little Rock to discuss business matters. The meeting lasted until about 1:00 A.M. of February 29. At this meeting, Walden agreed to a change in the date of another meeting, previously arranged for the following Friday. This change placed a burden on Walden to immediately notify other members of the union about the change in date of the next meeting. After the Little Rock meeting between Walden, Jarrett, and Bass ended, Walden drove Bass to Benton, where they continued to discuss union matters until about 4:00 in the morning. At that time Walden drove away in his car. He was not seen again.

Ed Walden's body and car were found in ALCOA's flooded and abandoned bauxite Pit No. 14.

Pit No. 14 was approximately four miles east of Bauxite. A motorist driving east from Bauxite on the county road moving along the route BFAD would be led to the Mount Olive community.

The county road leading to the Mount Olive community intersects at Point A (14) with the ALCOA private road leading down to Pit No. 14; the Mount Olive Road continues generally east. The private ALCOA road leading to Pit No. 14, from its intersection with the Bauxite-Mount Olive public road, at intersection A, has the same width, appearance, and construction as the county road leading to Mount Olive. The only warning sign at this intersection is a "private road" sign on the left side of the bauxite pit road.

According to the evidence, a motorist turning from the Mount Olive road to the left, heading down to the bauxite Pit No. 14 at night, would not see the "private road" sign. It would not be visible at night. There was no other warning sign, danger sign, or any barricade to alert a traveler that he was heading into an open, abandoned, flooded bauxite pit.

Ed Walden left surviving him a widow and three children. The facts outlined above gave rise to the following questions:

1. Was the Aluminum Company of America at fault; if so, was ALCOA's fault a proximate cause of Ed Walden's death?

2. Was Ed Walden's death caused "while driving or riding within an automobile" so as to entitle Walden's widow to the benefits of a life insurance policy carried with the Automobile Owner's Safety Insurance Company?

3. Did Ed Walden's death occur while he was "acting within the course and scope of his employment" so as to entitle Walden's widow and children to benefits under Arkansas Workmen's Compensation Law?

A. WAS ALCOA AT FAULT?

If so, was this fault a proximate cause of the death of Ed Walden, so as to entitle Walden's family to recover damages in a wrongful death action?

ALCOA had been for over a half a century a major company engaged in the mining of bauxite ore. Bauxite ore was required to produce the aluminum required for manufacturing airplanes for the war.

ALCOA and the people of Bauxite and Saline County produced the bauxite needed for the production of aluminum to make the planes which supported the troops during World War II.

ALCOA, after the war, cut back its bauxite mining to prewar levels. But the land in the Bauxite area had been ravaged, pitted with abandoned, flooded bauxite mines. The land looked like the surface of the moon.

ALCOA had built a web of service roads to the bauxite quarries and pits and connecting with the county roads in the Bauxite area. One of the ALCOA bauxite pits left abandoned was Pit No. 14 with a private road intersecting with the county road leading to the Mount Olive community from Bauxite.

Ed Walden was an employee of ALCOA from 1935 until March 1946 in the capacity of an oiler foreman. As such, it was his duty to visit the mines in order to oil the mining equipment. From 1946 to 1948, Walden worked for Reynolds Metals Company as an operator in one of their chemical plants. In that capacity he made frequent trips in the general area of ALCOA's operations. Walden then went to work for the United Steel Workers of America as an international staff representative and served in that capacity until his death.

Was Walden aware that the road he took down to Pit No. 14 was a private road?

Was he aware that the road led into an abandoned, flooded pit?

Was there a sign or warning visible at night that would have warned him of this danger?

Was Walden a trespasser on ALCOA's private road? If so, the only duty that ALCOA owed to Walden was not to cause injury to him after his presence on ALCOA's property was discovered.

Did the private road to Pit No. 14 at its intersection with the Bauxite-Mount Olive road have the appearance of a public road? In that event, he would be considered an invitee and ALCOA would be under a duty to exercise reasonable care to protect him from injury.

Ed Walden's widow and children brought a wrongful death suit against ALCOA, which was tried and submitted to the jury. A verdict was returned for the family. A motion was filed by ALCOA requesting the court to set aside the verdict on the ground that there was no substantial evidence to support the jury's findings for the family. The trial judge entered a judgment based upon the jury's verdict, and ALCOA's motion to set aside the verdict was declined. ALCOA appealed to the Supreme Court of Arkansas.

We frequently hear of verdicts returned by a jury where it is contended by the losing party that the verdict was based upon purely circumstantial evidence, that there was no direct proof supporting the verdict. What is meant by circumstantial evidence? Circumstantial evidence may be illustrated by the following:

You go to bed at night; the sky is clear; the stars are out; there is no precipitation. In the morning when you get up, you walk out the door and you see snow covering the ground. You observe a rabbit's tracks crossing your yard. You did not see it snow. You did not see a rabbit. However, it is reasonable to infer from what you do observe that during the night it did snow and after the snow fell, a rabbit hopped across your yard.

Dealing with a contention by ALCOA that there was no direct proof supporting the jury's verdict, that it was based upon circumstantial evidence, the Supreme Court found:

> Viewing the evidence presented to the jury, we hold that there was sufficient proof for the jury to find:
>
> (a) Walden drove over the private road at night;
> (b) that he was not under the influence of liquor;
> (c) that he was misled into believing that he was on the public road;
> (d) that he did not assume the risk by reason of any familiarity with the private road; and
> (e) that his death was the result of ALCOA's negligence.

ALCOA, in its brief argument to the Supreme Court, in its efforts to reverse the verdict of the jury and the trial court's judgment, argued that to sustain the judgment it was necessary to base it on a pyramid of inferences, that there was no positive proof that:

1. Walden entered the private road and the water pit during the nighttime;
2. that he was traveling from the direction of Bauxite when he entered the private road;
3. that he died at the time his watch stopped;
4. that he did not commit suicide.

In dealing with this argument advanced by ALCOA, the Supreme Court stated, "*The answer to this argument is that it is within the province of the jury to draw certain inferences from facts and circumstances as we have frequently held.*"

It was, therefore, the opinion of the Supreme Court that the judgment of the trial court on behalf of the widow and children of Ed Walden be affirmed.

Thus, we see in the Walden case, another dramatic example where our system of law opens its doors to the humblest of citizens. We see how a great company, serving the country in time of war and contributing substantially to the economy of the community where it carried on its mining operations, is held accountable under the law by a jury drawn from the community where they all lived.

B. THE LIFE INSURANCE

> Was Ed Walden's death caused "while driving or riding within an automobile" so as to entitle Walden's widow to the benefits of a life insurance policy carried with the Automobile Owner's Safety Insurance Company?

Ed Walden lost his life by drowning in an abandoned, flooded bauxite pit.

The bauxite pit was owned and had been mined by ALCOA.

A private road leading to the flooded pit was built by ALCOA and connected to a Saline County road. The composition and structure of the private road leading to the bauxite pit was similar in appearance, width, and structure to the county road leading to the Mount Olive community, where some members of the steel workers union lived.

There were no signs warning of danger, nor barricades or obstructions on the private road. When Walden drove down the private road to his death in the flooded bauxite pit, he was an implied invitee. ALCOA owed Walden and the traveling public a duty of exercising reasonable care to avoid death or injury to a motorist, mistakenly taking the wrong road and driving into the flooded pit.

Walden left surviving him a widow and three children. Action was brought by the survivors against ALCOA for negligence in causing Ed Walden's death. The case was tried in Saline County before a jury selected from the Saline County community. The jury returned a verdict in favor of the Walden family and judgment was so entered by the trial judge. ALCOA appealed to the Supreme Court of Arkansas and the judgment was affirmed.

Ed Walden had a life insurance policy on which his widow was the named beneficiary. She filed suit against the insurance company under the provisions of the policy after her claim was denied by the insurance company on the grounds that Ed Walden was not killed "while driving or riding in an automobile."

The widow's insurance claim was tried before the circuit judge in Saline County, who ruled in favor of the insurance company and against Mrs. Walden. Mrs. Walden appealed. On the question of whether Walden met death while driving or riding in an automobile, the Supreme Court found that the accident occurred when Walden drove his automobile into the open pit. In an effort to reach safety, he was drowned. In holding for the widow, the court found that this accident was the proximate cause of his death and was covered under the provisions of the policy.

C. WORKMEN'S COMPENSATION BENEFITS

Did Ed Walden's death occur while he was "acting within the course and scope of his employment" so as to entitle Walden's widow and children to benefits under Arkansas Workmen's Compensation Law?

Ed Walden was working for the United Steel Workers of America which had workmen's compensation coverage on their employees. The family of Walden brought suit against the workmen's compensation insurance carrier after the company declined to pay the claim, contending that Walden was not within the scope of his employment at the time of his death.

The workmen's compensation claim was filed with the Workmen's Compensation Commission; the claim was granted and affirmed on appeal to the Supreme Court of Arkansas.

D. SUMMARY

Each of these three cases, on behalf of the Walden family, was opposed by ALCOA. Each was reviewed and judgment entered by the Arkansas Supreme Court for the Waldens. The Walden cases are another example of the workings of our judicial system and how the most humble citizens can secure justice under the law.

Ed Walden's youngest child at the time of his death was a daughter. I recently received a letter from her. She was prompted to write after having read a good article about me in the newspaper. She expressed her best wishes and thanks for what was done for her and her family nearly fifty years ago. A lawyer's greatest reward is a gratified client.

E. ADDENDUM

In the lawsuit of *Walden vs. The Aluminum Company of America,* we have described a view of approximately thirty-five hundred acres of land containing numerous abandoned bauxite pits. Then the pits fill with water; the water becomes contaminated from the acid-permeated soil; the run-off poisons the streams and rivers in the area, creating a severe environmental problem.

What were the circumstances causing the land to be devastated, the bauxite pits abandoned and subsequently flooded, creating a safety and environmental hazard in our state? I feel that a consideration of the background leading up to ALCOA's blighted land and open pits is in order.

In 1896, over one hundred years ago, Col. J. R. Gibbons came to Arkansas from Rome, Georgia. His quest was to check out reports of the existence of bauxite ore in Saline County. The reports of rich bauxite ore deposits were confirmed. Colonel Gibbons and his son began acquiring land and began modest mining operations, using labor, scoops, and mule teams.

By 1912, Colonel Gibbons had acquired 15,000 acres of land, built the largest bauxite mining company in the world, and built a community in the process. (He called this enterprise the Aluminum Company of America, later known as ALCOA.)

A short time before the beginning of World War II, ALCOA began to improve its mining methods by using more mechanical and hydraulic equipment. It was still a modest operation. ALCOA's mining policy was conservative, designed to husband its bauxite ore for the future. The attack on Pearl Harbor disrupted ALCOA's well-laid future mining plans.

Pres. Franklin Roosevelt, immediately after the Japanese attack on Pearl Harbor and the declaration of war, announced that America would build 100,000 airplanes to support our troops. The experts didn't believe it could be done. Hitler did not believe it. The bauxite needed to produce the aluminum to make the airplanes had been coming from South America. This supply was cut off by marauding German submarines which sunk the cargo ships loaded with tons of bauxite ore bound for the United States.

The German U-boats, virtually unchallenged, dominated the sea lanes from South America.

Roosevelt, in making his bold and optimistic announcement, had knowledge that the experts did not have and that Hitler did not have. The president was aware of the bauxite deposits in Bauxite, Arkansas.

He knew the company and the character of the people who would be called upon to dig out the ore.

ALCOA, in order to meet the demands of the government and the needs of war, accelerated its mining operations. The federal government furnished sophisticated mining equipment; labor and management merged; ALCOA and the people of Saline County went all out, working around the clock on twelve-hour shifts to get the job done. All the families in the community joined in support of this project with patriotic fervor.

The challenge was met. The ore was dug from the soil, aluminum was produced; planes were built; battles were fought; victories won.

Our armed forces were victorious. Their victory was shared by American industry and labor—by ALCOA, the people of Bauxite and Saline County, Arkansas.

Victory won: what about the land, the devastated land?

What about the environmental hazard, the pollution of water in the rivers and streams?

"The changes in the operation of the mines during the War, were instituted by the government over the strong objections of ALCOA management. Unfortunately, they resulted in significant environmental damages. Today, we can look back at decisions made by the government over fifty years ago, to provide the supplies it needed, as proof of the environmental problems of this State."[1]

Curing the despoiled land was undertaken tardily and tentatively. In the mid-1970s state regulations were put in place requiring reclamation of the lands disturbed by mining since 1971. The regulations further required the treatment of *all acid mine drainage, regardless of origin. All mine-damaged water must meet discharge quality limits.*

ALCOA's mining site contains 9,000 acres. Thirty-three hundred acres of this land has been mined, of which 1,830 acres were mined during the war. "The run-off from this acreage contains elevated levels of metals, [and] does not comply with Arkansas water quality criteria."[2]

---

1. ALCOA's Arkansas Operations Bauxite Mine Reclamation Program, January 25, 1999.

2. ALCOA's Arkansas Operations Bauxite Mine Reclamation Program, January 25, 1999.

In 1990 ALCOA launched a comprehensive rehabilitation program designed to restore the quality of this despoiled land to meet state mining and water quality standards. Approximately one thousand acres have been restored to date. The water quality of the runoff has been significantly improved in this reclaimed area. ALCOA is moving toward the objective of reclaiming all the lands, disturbed by the wartime conditions, to its natural state.

"To date, since 1990 over $25 million have been spent to reclaim mined-over lands and the disposal area created by the refining of the bauxite."[3]

ALCOA, working with concerned state agencies and conservation groups, expects to complete its rehabilitation plans by the year 2005. This area of reclaimed land will become a wildlife habitat and sanctuary. The bauxite pits will be "clear lakes." Vegetative cover, foliage, and flowers, once abundant, will again flourish.

This reclamation of ravaged land, this partnership between a great company, state agencies, and the local community is a model, an epic in the history of rehabilitation and conservation. It is a dramatic example of how a private company, state agencies, and local citizens can rehabilitate ravaged land and restore a poisoned water resource. It is a precedent to show how citizens on a community level can protect the environment for future generations. It is hoped that this combined action plan to restore this ravaged bauxite area will be completed.

---

3. ALCOA's Arkansas Operations Bauxite Mine Reclamation Program, January 25, 1999.

APPENDIX XV ⟿ SEEK JUSTICE, PLEAD FOR THE WIDOW, CHAMPION THE FATHERLESS, RELIEVE THE OPPRESSED—AND PUT THE MONEY IN TRUST

A missile silo cradling a Titan intercontinental ballistic missile caught fire and exploded, killing fifty-three workmen.

The fire and the explosion knocked out the electrical and communication systems. The elevators would not work. The workmen were trapped and could not escape from the existing exit. They perished from suffocation due to the lack of oxygen.

The missile silo was located between Searcy and Heber Springs. It was one of sixteen silos containing Intercontinental Ballistic Missiles ringing central Arkansas. The atomic missile seated in the silo was not damaged.

The silo was being modernized under contract with the United States Government by Peters Klewit and Company from Omaha and Newberry Electric Company of Los Angeles. Klewit was the prime contractor.

The workmen in the silo were mostly from around Searcy, Arkansas. Two of the workmen who were on top of the silo escaped injury.

The U.S. Air Force reported that the explosion and resulting fire occurred when a welder's electric arc welding rod pierced a steel grated hose containing flammable hydraulic oil.

Claims were filed by the families of the deceased workmen against the contractors and the United States Government. The McMath Law Firm was retained by twenty-five of the surviving families. Hence, the McMath firm was designated to investigate and prepare the case for trial and possible settlement.

After exhaustive research into the facts and the law and after extensive trial preparation, on the eve of trial the cases were settled. United States district judge Smith Henley approved the settlement. Funds received were paid to the widows and minor children of the deceased workmen. Funds allocated to the minor children of the workmen were put in a trust fund for the care and education of each of the minor children.

Subsequently, over the years, it was an exceedingly pleasurable moment when we would receive a graduation announcement or wedding invitation from the children of the workmen who had been provided for under the settlement and trust provisions.

Based upon our experience of fifty years of representing people in need of legal counsel, we have learned that the recovery of compensation for a client does not necessarily resolve the client's economic woes.

Sometimes an adequate award arduously won does not always prove to be a blessing, but may bring on additional concerns to the injured client. A substantial award may bring to the surface relatives heretofore unknown or remotely related. A widow is particularly vulnerable to con men, charlatans, and sometimes relatives who seek to advise her as to how she should "invest" her estate.

The *American Bar Association Journal,* July 1980, reported that 90 percent of all settlements are dissipated within five years. The *Journal* stated:

> In death cases, large sums frequently have disappeared leaving children uneducated and disadvantaged and the surviving widow virtually destitute.
>
> Large-sum settlements may attract mercenary friends and relatives, unscrupulous advisors, or such funds disappear through poor investment and well-intentioned, bad advice.

Often families do not understand that the settlement for a disabled family member or the wrongful death of the breadwinner may not be for the benefit of all family members. Our society places great value on the integrity of the family unit. This may lead to misunderstanding when the recovery is not available to meet the financial needs of all members that were not beneficiaries in the recovery.

In a wrongful death action, for example, the widow may recover her loss of consortium, that is the loss of her husband's society, companionship, and marriage relationship; for the loss of contributions which he would reasonably have made to her during his lifetime; and for mental anguish arising out of her husband's death.

The minor children in a wrongful death case may recover for mental anguish arising out of their father's death; for the loss of his parental control and guidance up to their majority.

An adult child, however, might be limited to a claim for mental anguish—a claim always difficult for a jury to assess. So frequently, the adult children may not receive benefits from an award or settlement.

Damages arising out of wrongful death or negligent injury are governed by state statute.

Most cases having been adequately prepared and ready for trial are settled. Settlement of a case where the client is being reasonably compensated is highly desirable. A trial is very expensive, especially when expert witnesses are required in order to establish liability or the nature and extent of the damage. Additionally, in state court, nine out of twelve jurors have to agree on the question of fault and also the extent of damages sustained. In federal court a unanimous verdict is required.

Assuming a reasonable offer of settlement has been made (reasonableness having been determined by the facts, the law, the venue, and the composition of the jury panel), and the client has been fully advised and is in accord, the case should be settled. If minors are claimants, the settlement is required to be approved by the court.

A lawyer having obtained compensation for the client, his legal responsibilities to the client may be concluded. What responsibility, if any, does a lawyer have toward advising the client as to how the money should be distributed, invested, or used?

The lawyer's responsibility is to secure compensation for the client's injuries. The lawyer does not, cannot, must not, handle the client's money or advise the client as to how the money should be spent.

However, the lawyer based upon his knowledge and experience in similar cases and circumstances should advise his client to seek counsel from a recognized expert in financial management and investments. An established bank with a recognized trust department with long experience in handling trust funds is a desirable expert in the field.

Usually the bank trustee is called upon to meet with the client at the time the lawsuit is settled or an award made and funds are available for use or disbursement. The trust officer of the bank meets with the client and family members to discuss how the funds will be invested and the amount of income that could be expected to be available for their needs.

Management of funds by the bank is under the supervision of the courts.

Reports to the court by the trust officer are periodically made. Distribution of funds are submitted to the court for approval.

Should the client at any time desire to change the trustee, a petition to the court may be made. When the trust is concluded, a full report to the court as to the distribution of funds is required.

A bank with an established and recognized trust department operates a number of income and equity funds that qualify under the Arkansas statutes as proper for court supervised accounts.

The trust administrator helps determine if there are any special needs to be considered and helps in setting up a budget that can be met from the funds available to be expended.

Some of the special needs that are provided for the client are transportation, housing, ongoing doctor or medical expenses, and educational needs for the children.

An annual report with the probate court that covers all activities, such as investments and distributions on behalf of the client, is made. The trust officer will meet with the clients and if the clients desire, with family members, to discuss the reports and answer questions they may have regarding the management of the funds.

The designated attorney for the client has an ongoing responsibility to assist the trust company with preparing and filing petitions with the court in matters that require court supervision and approval. The attorney's fee for this service is set by the court and is customary and nominal for the services rendered.

A lawyer, having obtained a just award for the client and observing that the funds will be used to meet family needs, may over the years receive a Christmas card, a graduation or wedding announcement, or some other communication indicating that all is well with the family he had the privilege to serve.

My life, Dear Reader, has been truly blessed: to be an advocate for justice in a court of law, to be a voice for justice in the political arena, to battle for justice as a solider; there is no higher calling, no greater reward.

INDEX

Bible, family, 51
Bierley, Robert, 375–76
Biffle, Les, 271
Billy (pet goat), 68–70
birthdate, 5
black citizens, 194–98, 233–34
"Black Widow" night fighters, 117–18, 120
Blair, James, 411
Blease, Cole, 24
boar, wild, 29–30, 57–58
Bohler, Queenie Esther, 213
Bonds, A. B., 205
"Bonus March," 40
Bougainville, Solomon Islands, 119, 127–54
Bowen, William H., 291
Bowser, Al, 147, 152
Boydston, Joe, 189
Boyd v. United States, 386
Boyington, Gregory "Pappy," 84
Boy Scouts, 70–71
Bradley County, Arkansas, 433
Bravo (fungicide), 436–37
Brewer, Sy, 322
bribery allegations, 283–84, 288, 290
Brinegar, Pat, 349–56
*Brinegar v. San Ore Construction
    Company, Inc.*, 349–56
Brody, Steve, 131
Broughton, Cecil, 91
Broughton, Elaine. *See* McMath, Elaine
    "Speck" Broughton
Broughton, Garnet, 75
Broughton, Verna, 91
Broughton, Willie, 75, 76, 97
Brown, Barbara, 415
Brown, Clyde, 93–94, 169, 172, 175
Brown, Herman, 415
Brown, I. G., 175
Brown, John K., 283, 289–90
Brown, Robert Mark, 415–21
Brown, Rosalee, 93–94, 175
Brown v. Missouri Pacific Railroad, 415–21
Brown v. Topeka Board of Education, 302
Bruce, James, 411
Bryant, Tom, 416, 418
Bueter, Patricia Anne McMath, 222, 223,
    322–23, 325
Bueter, Randy, 323
Bulga, 53, 54

Bull Shoals Dam, 256, 261
Bumpers, Dale, 320
Bunyard, Marion, 370–71
Bunyard Supply Company, Inc., 370
Bureau of Biologics, 389–90, 394
Burke, Arleigh, 133
Burnett, Russell, 78
Burney, John Fuller, 397–402
Burney, Mrs. John Fuller, 397, 399–401
Bussey, Arkansas, 7, 41–45, 331
Byrd, Harry, 196
Byrnes, James, 248

C

Caldwell, Oscar R. "Speed": American
    Samoa, 105; Bougainville campaign,
    134, 142–43, 147, 153; commander of
    Third Marine Regiment, 95, 97; gover-
    nor's inauguration, 212; Marine
    Replacement Training Command,
    156–57
Calhoun County, Mississippi, 162
Call, C. K., 235
Camden, Arkansas, 18
Camp, Virginia "Jenny." *See* Sanders,
    Virginia "Jenny" Camp
campaigns: bribery allegations, 283–84;
    campaign issues, 194, 332; campaign
    literature, 201–2; finances, 192, 194,
    200, 239, 283–85; governor of
    Arkansas, 187, 191–200, 236–37, 243–44,
    285–87, 305; prosecuting attorney,
    Eighteenth Judicial District, 173, 178;
    United States Senate, 297–99, 301–2
Camp Beauregard, Louisiana, 39–40
Campbell, J. O., 176–77
Camp Pendleton, California, 156, 159
Cape Torokina, 129, 132
Cap (horse), 63
Capone, Al, 168
Caraway, Hattie, 295–96
Caraway, Thaddeus, 295
Cardozo, Benjamin, 341
carrier pigeons, 67–68
Carter, Jimmy, 320
Cate, Horace, 211
Chambers, Carl, 219
Chapin, John C., 133, 153
Chenal, Dr., 208

NATO. *See* North Atlantic Treaty
Organization (NATO)
Needham, Hal, 377, 378
Nell (horse), 187
Nelson, Nancy, 159–60
Newberry Electric Company, 459
New Georgia, Solomon Islands, 119–26
New Mexico Military Academy, 181
newspaper delivery route, 66, 75
Newton County, Arkansas, 275, 292
New York v. Schenectady Chemicals, Inc.,
413
New Zealand, 109–11, 307, 317
Nicaragua, 83
Nicholson, Hayden C., 246
nicknames: "Cowboy," 49; "Horsefly," 14,
60
Nimitz, Chester, 115
Nixon, Richard, 302, 304, 306
Nixon, Vic, 325
North Atlantic Treaty Organization
(NATO), 308, 317
Numa Numa Trail, 138–47

O

Oaklawn School, 67
Oil Compact Commission, 262
Old Judd, 29–32
"Old Mamie," 56
Old Red, 220
O'Neal, John "Irish," 103, 125, 139–40,
149–50, 153
101 First Airborne Division, 302–6,
335–36
organized labor, 234–36
Oswald, Harry, 271, 275–78, 280, 320
Ouachita Baptist College, 79, 95
Owen, Robert A., 131

P

Pace, Frank, 271
Pacific Theater of Operations, World War
II, 100
Page, Will, 177
Pago Pago, Samoa, 99, 101, 107
Pap. *See* McMath, Hal Pierce
Passmore, Elton, 447
Peoples Bank Trust Company of Mountain

Home v. Globe International, Inc.,
423–30
Perkins, Rex, 76
Perkins, Sidney, 67
pertussis vaccine, 389–95
Peters Klewit and Company, 459
Peterson, John, 419
Pether, Laura, 126
pets, 41–42, 68–70, 186–87. *See also* dogs;
horses
pharmaceutical companies, 390–95
Pharmaceutical Manufacturers
Association (PMA), 390
Philadelphia, Neshoba County,
Mississippi, 162
Phillips, Dorris, 161
Phillips, James Fair, 161, 162
Phillips, Jimmie Vance, 161–62
Phillips, Sarah Anne. *See* McMath, Sarah
Anne Phillips
"Pig Trail," 301
Pike County, Georgia, 9, 10, 11
Piva Forks, 138–39
Piva Trail, 138–39
Platte Chemical Company, 438–39
poem on a United States Marine, 316
poem on farm life, 58–59
political rumors, 288–89
politics: Eighteenth Judicial District,
169–74, 178; election fraud, 167, 171,
175–77; GI ticket, 169–79; Hot Springs,
Arkansas, 167–79; student govern-
ment, 76–79
poll tax, 171, 173–77, 187, 194, 233, 333, 358
pollution, 403–10
Pontiac Firebird Trans Am, 373–79
Popham, Johnny, 305
poultry processing plants, 403–10, 412
power monopolies, 268
preemption, 443–44
Prescott, Arkansas, 415–19
Prevatt, Jimmy, 441
prisoners as slaves, 23–24
prosecuting attorney, Eighteenth Judicial
District: campaign for governor, 187;
criminal cases, 181–85; election campaign, 173, 178
Prowl (herbicide), 436–37
Prozine (herbicide), 436–37

trust funds, 461–62
Turnage, Hal, 83, 84, 134, 138–39, 155–56
Turnbull, "Bones," 149, 151, 153
Tutuila, Samoa, 99
Twenty-sixth Arkansas Infantry,
  Company G, 18
Tyson, Inc., 403–5, 407–14

U

Uncle Spooks. *See* McMath, Ray "Uncle
  Spooks"
Union County, Arkansas, 5, 33
United States Army, 119, 122–25, 144
United States compared to the Soviet
  Union, 263–64, 316–17
United States Corps of Engineers, 383–88
United States Marine Corps: American
  Samoa, 99–107; Basic School, 81–84;
  battlefield awards, 131, 154; Battle of
  Koromokina River, 134–35; Battle of
  Piva Forks, 140–54; Bougainville cam-
  paign, 127–54; Camp Lejeune, New
  River, North Carolina, 95–97; child-
  hood interest, 71; Civil Action
  Program, 312–13; combat casualties,
  155; commission, 79; Company F,
  Second Battalion, Fifth Marine
  Brigade, Fleet Marine Force, 81;
  Company L, Third Battalion, 148–51;
  First Battalion Third Marines, 131,
  134–35; First Battalion Twenty-first
  Marines, 135, 144; First Marine
  Battalion, 145, 151; First Marine
  Division, 113, 115, 307; Guadalcanal,
  Solomon Islands, 113–19; Harry S.
  Truman, 229; Japanese air attack, 132;
  Jungle Warfare School, 101–3; landing
  at Empress Augusta Bay, Bougainville,
  127–32; Marine Corps Headquarters,
  159–60; Marine Corps Reserves, 239;
  Marine Replacement Training
  Command, 156, 159; New Georgia,
  Solomon Islands, 119–26; New
  Zealand, 109; operations duties,
  137–38, 143–44, 151–52; poem on a
  United States Marine, 316; reconnais-
  sance patrols, 118, 122, 124–25; Reserve
  Officers' Training Corps (ROTC), 73;
  Second Marine Battalion, 135, 145–47,

150; Second Raider Battalion, 138–39,
  144; Sixth Rifle Company, 239–40;
  Solomon Islands, 113–19; Third
  Battalion Ninth Marines, 134, 144;
  Third Marine Amphibious Corps,
  309–10; Third Marine Battalion,
  134–35, 139–43, 144–51, 313; Third
  Marine Division, 115–16, 156; Third
  Marine Regiment, 95–107, 109, 115–19,
  126–37, 143, 153–56, 310, 313; Third
  Reserve Officers Training Corps, 91;
  training exercises, 96–97, 101–6;
  Vietnam, 309–18
University of Arkansas, Fayetteville, 76, 95
University of Arkansas Medical School,
  245–46, 332
Upshaw, William D., 72
Upton, Patricia P., 292
USS *George Climber*, 153
USS *Maddox*, 308–9
USS *Matsonia*, 98
USS *President Jackson*, 127, 132

V

vaccinations, 335, 389–95
Vance, Zebulon Baird, 161
Vandergrift, Alexander A., 115
Van Orden, George "Beast," 116, 119, 122,
  124–26
Van Sickle, Bruce, 385–86
Vehik, Mart, 321
Vella Lavella, Solomon Islands, 119
veterans, Confederate, 21–22
Viet Cong, 310–11
Vietnam, 307–18
Vorhes, J. G., 377

W

Walden, Ed, 449–55
Walden, Mrs. Ed, 454
*Walden v. The Aluminum Company of
  America*, 449–55
Walker, Bob, 143, 148
Wallace, Henry, 198
Walt, Lewis, 84, 310–12
Warner, Gordon, 96
Washington, George, 3
Washington University, 326